LIFELINES

LIFELINES

THE TRAFFIC OF TRAUMA

HARRIS SOLOMON

DUKE UNIVERSITY PRESS

DURHAM AND LONDON

2022

Printed in the United States of America on acid-free paper ∞
Designed by Matthew Tauch
Typeset in Garamond Premier Pro by Westchester Publishing Services

Library of Congress Cataloging-in-Publication Data
Names: Solomon, Harris, [date] author.
Title: Lifelines : the traffic of trauma / Harris Solomon.
Description: Durham : Duke University Press, 2022. | Includes
bibliographical references and index.
Identifiers: LCCN 2021057118 (print)
LCCN 2021057119 (ebook)
ISBN 9781478016212 (hardback)
ISBN 9781478018858 (paperback)
ISBN 9781478023487 (ebook)
ISBN 9781478092728 (ebook other)
Subjects: LCSH: Traffic accident victims—India—Mumbai. | Traffic accident
victims—Family relationships—India—Mumbai. | Hospitals—Emergency
services—India—Mumbai. | Emergency medical services—India—Mumbai. |
BISAC: SOCIAL SCIENCE / Anthropology / Cultural & Social | HISTORY / Asia /
India & South Asia
Classification: LCC RA772.T7 S65 2022 (print) | LCC RA772.T7 (ebook) |
DDC 363.12/5650954792—dc23/eng/20220225
LC record available at https://lccn.loc.gov/2021057118
LC ebook record available at https://lccn.loc.gov/2021057119

Cover art: Illustration by Harris Solomon.

Publication of this open monograph was the result of Duke University's participation in TOME (Toward an Open Monograph Ecosystem),
a collaboration of the Association of American Universities, the
Association of University Presses, and the Association of Research
Libraries. TOME aims to expand the reach of long-form humanities
and social science scholarship including digital scholarship. Addition-
ally, the program looks to ensure the sustainability of university press
monograph publishing by supporting the highest quality scholarship
and promoting a new ecology of scholarly publishing in which authors'
institutions bear the publication costs. Funding from Duke University
Libraries made it possible to open this publication to the world.

For Gabriel

CONTENTS

NOTE ON ILLUSTRATIONS

For the images that begin this book's chapters, I layer textures on traces I make from photographs to think about the gestures of trauma care that redirect and transform its traffic. I was encouraged to draw by one of the trauma ward's resident physicians. I noticed how they would sometimes sketch out a problem or issue at hand when we spoke because they felt pictures could explicate details better than words. They suggested I try it too. I gained inspiration from accounts of ethnographic drawing, including Czerwiec (2017), Hamdy and Nye (2017), Jain (2019), Povinelli (2021), and Taussig (2011). I learned how to shape ethnographic inquiry through drawing from Andrew Causey (2017) and how to stay with lines and transits from Renee Gladman (2010, 2016, 2017). I was also fortunate to take drawing lessons. My teacher, Zoe Schein, challenged me to see how lines of action and marks of stillness and shadow could scale up a feeling or an idea. I continue to learn about what lines can do from the artist Ranjit Kandalgaonkar.

I took the base-layer photographs, with two exceptions: the drawing that begins the introduction is a traced adaptation of a photo by Steve Evans (2008), and the drawing that begins chapter 1 is a traced adaptation of a photo in Ansari (2018). All the drawings include adaptations, rearrangements, sketched-in components, and textures that are not in the original photo. There are both additive and protective dimensions to this imaginative overlay. Inside hospitals, I never photographed patients (nor was I allowed to). I took very few photos, in fact, and most were of banal objects and architectural details: notebooks, machines, filing cabinets, washbasins, hallways, lockers, bins of medicines, paper piles, and storage corners.

Tracing these photos into a different medium—a line drawing—conjures memories and stories. It is an act that demands I remember who and what constitutes a given scene. It also compels me to sit with what I do and do not know. This involves filling in, erasing, or recasting things the base-layer image might suggest.

Holding a pen continuously for a stretch, and then braking, and then veering elsewhere are actions that shaped how I conceptualized, wrote, revised, and rethought prose. Tracing is a tactile enactment of intermittent gestures. It tracks constellations of discontinuities. This generates a sense of movement that words may strain to address, or the other way around. Approaching research material from both lines and words foregrounds uneven pathways as a critical ethnographic motif. It is a practice that catalyzes questions: How does a specific line come into being? What forces facilitate, constrain, and sustain one line's convergences with another's? What kinds of restraint are necessary in depicting scenes of extremes? What happens when lines run parallel, intersect, or diverge, even provisionally? Is there something important about that provisional relationship? What does it mean to gain proximity to a crossing—say, a critical decision—and to push forward? Or to see it ahead but remain stuck in place?

Tracing renders fluctuations in density, curvature, edge, and trajectory. Similarly, this book grapples with lines of life in flux.

ACKNOWLEDGMENTS

I thank the patients, families, doctors, nurses, and staff at the hospitals and emergency medical services who comprise the scenes of this book.

My research was made possible by the support of Drs. Vineet Kumar, Monty Khajanchi, Nitin Borle, Satish Dharap, Sanjay Nagral, Nobhojit Roy, Kalpana Swaminathan, Ishrat Syed, and Meena Kumar. Siddarth David, Jyoti Kamble, and Anna Aroke shared presence, analysis, and insight through spectacular research assistance. The Thursday Truth Seekers research working group at the Tata Institute of Social Sciences listened to in-progress versions of the research, offered feedback, and provided an intellectual home base each week. Ansul Madhvani always shares a home away from home, and in this case a home away from the hospital.

My fieldwork and writing were supported by a National Science Foundation Cultural Anthropology Program CAREER Award (Award Number 145433). Thank you to Jeffrey Mantz and Deborah Winslow, who made this possible every step of the way. Funds from Duke University and the Duke Global Health Institute also supported research.

As the material simmered, many people moved it in new directions. My gratitude goes to audiences at the University of North Carolina, Chapel Hill; Princeton University; the University of Chicago; Tufts University; Ohio State University; the University of Amsterdam; King's College London; the University of Toronto; the University of Chicago's New Delhi Centre; the University of Pittsburgh; Northwestern University; Keio University Tokyo; the Indian Institute of Technology, Hyderabad; McGill University; the University of Pennsylvania; and the University of California, Berkeley. A wonderful group of scholars from the University of Virginia's Department of Anthropology energized a writing group about care and offered generative feedback.

A visiting fellowship at the University of Amsterdam enabled me to revise and complete this manuscript. I am deeply grateful to Anita Hardon for the invitation and for enduring scholarly care. Annemarie Mol, Emily Yates-Doerr, Robert Pool, and Hayley Murray shared ideas and walks to think outside the box. Niko Besnier shared a space to watch the water and wonder. In the United States, Joseph Fischel and Igor Souza offered serenity and hilarity at a seaside haven where I was able to revise, again.

In the early weeks of pandemic disarray, the Franklin Humanities Institute at Duke stayed the course with a book manuscript workshop that sharpened and opened up this text. Thank you, Ranjana Khanna, for your vision, guidance, and engagement with the text at the scales of both the line and the aggregate. I thank the participants: Anne Allison, Nima Bassiri, Mara Buchbinder, Jocelyn Lim Chua, Louise Meintjes, Townsend Middleton, Diane Nelson, Charlie Piot, Sumathi Ramaswamy, Barry Saunders, and Orin Starn. And to the discussants, William Mazzarella and Sarah Pinto, and to my editor Ken Wissoker, thank you for making the time to read and for creating space to think, especially amid so much uncertainty. Thanks also go to the institute's staff, who pivoted things online, seamlessly: Christina Chia, Sylvia Miller, and Sarah Rogers.

My colleagues in the Department of Cultural Anthropology give vital energy to ideas and ethnographic possibility. As I detail in "Seeing," they also kept me afloat when things were not looking good, and for that I am grateful. Thanks to Charlie Piot, Lee Baker, and Louise Meintjes for all your support, along with Pat Bodager, Bernice Patterson, Pam Terterian, and Jamie Mills. At Duke, I also thank Elizabeth Ault, Nicole Barnes, Nima Bassiri, Courtney Berger, Rich Freeman, Ranjana Khanna, Eli Meyerhoff, Jessica Namakkal, Mark Olson, Sumathi Ramaswamy, Priscilla Wald, and Ara Wilson. Thanks also go to my colleagues at the Duke Global Health Institute. Diane Nelson's friendship and imagination are treasures that live on.

Different orbits of writing groups have been honest, creative, and patient. Mara Buchbinder, Jocelyn Lim Chua, Nadia El-Shaarawi, Dörte Bemme, and Saiba Varma keep things moving each month. Maura Finkelstein and Megan Crowley-Matoka stay with storylines, arguments, and voice and make writing come alive.

Along the way, during walks and chats and exchanges of ideas, I have been fortunate to learn from Sareeta Amrute, Nikhil Anand, Anjali Arondekar, Dwaipayan Banerjee, Tarini Bedi, Kavi Bhalla, João Biehl, Alex Blanchette, Charles Briggs, Carlo Caduff, Julie Chu, Veena Das, Naisargi Dave, Lisa Davis, Robert Desjarlais, Angela Garcia, Rakhi Ghoshal, Radhika Govindrajan, Jeremy Greene, Shubhra Gururani, Deborah Heath, Sarah Hodges, Lochlann Jain, Annu Jalais, Sharon Kaufman, Naveeda Khan, Alok Khandekar, Junko Kitanaka, Hannah Landecker, Marianne Lien,

Julie Livingston, Ken MacLeish, Anindita Majumdar, Tomas Matza, Ramah McKay, Amy Moran-Thomas, Sameena Mulla, Haripriya Narasimhan, Vinh-Kim Nguyen, Kevin Lewis O'Neill, Stefania Pandolfo, Juno Salazar Parreñas, Sujata Patel, Heather Paxson, Adriana Petryna, Anne Rademacher, Laurence Ralph, Lucinda Ramberg, Peter Redfield, Elizabeth Roberts, Rashmi Sadana, Barry Saunders, Bhrigupati Singh, Kalyanakrishnan Sivaramakrishnan, Lisa Stevenson, Kaushik Sunder Rajan, Noah Tamarkin, Sharika Thiranagama, Saiba Varma, Megan Vaughan, Bharat Venkat, Kath Weston, and Zoë Wool.

Previous components of material in this book appeared in *Medical Anthropology Quarterly*, and I am very grateful to Vincanne Adams for her guidance and insight.

During the late stages of this project, three brilliant physicians entered my life to become collaborators and co-ethnographers on a project about COVID-19: Drs. Peter Kussin, Neelima Navuluri, and Bill Hargett. In studying the social life of intensive care unit (ICU) care in the United States together, I have learned so much from them about critical care and what really matters in medicine.

My students at Duke continue to keep me on my toes. Several current and former students have left a lasting impression on my thinking, and my thanks go to Christopher Webb, Kelly Alexander, Kayla Corredera-Wells, Yidong Gong, Jeremy Gottlieb, Jay Hammond, Alyssa Miller, Jieun Cho, and Sophia Goodfriend. Thanks to students in Medical Anthropology for reading and commenting on in-progress versions of the book, to students in two graduate seminars (Between Life and Death and Science, Medicine, Body), and to Anne Allison for being a wonderful teaching companion.

Lawrence Cohen continues to expand the possibilities of having a thought when fueled by an ethics of kindness. Sarah Pinto is a marvelous friend and mentor, a guide on how to write fearlessly, and a constant source of new ideas, frames, and possibilities. Lauren Berlant shaped this book profoundly and taught me how to think with situations.

A heartfelt (and additional) thank you to Anne Allison, Megan Crowley-Matoka, Maura Finkelstein, Sarah Pinto, and William Mazzarella, who read the entire manuscript, step by step, draft by draft, line by line, idea by idea.

Thanks to Ranjit Kandalgaonkar for his expansive imagination of bodies.

Ken Wissoker has connected encouragement to feedback with patience and precision over many years. Thank you, Ken, for the time you've invested in making this project happen, and thank you, Joshua Gutterman Tranen, for supporting it along the way. The manuscript's two anonymous readers debated it, guided it, stretched it, and strengthened it; thank you. I wish to thank Lisl Hampton, Kim Miller, Christopher Robinson, Matthew Tauch, and the production team at Duke University Press, and thank you to Matthew John Phillips for the index and Drew Keener for the map.

Nobhojit Roy, Kalpana Swaminathan, Ishrat Syed, and Sanjay Nagral guide my understanding of what is truly at stake in a life-and-death moment in medicine. They answer late-night phone calls and texts, cook meals, and offer an anchor when I become unmoored. They feel the inseparability of medicine and Mumbai in their bones, and they generate new ways to think and speak about it. They also remind me what ethnography has to offer medicine.

My mother, Dale Solomon, is an ethnographer at heart, always curious about the backstories of the everyday. She sent love and encouragement from afar and never flinched when hearing me relay difficult moments from the hospital; instead, she responded, "And what did you learn?" I've tried to stay with that question.

This book is dedicated to Gabriel Rosenberg. He has kept me alive and moving in ways neither of us imagined would ever be necessary. His brilliance, patience, and clear seeing charge me and my words with momentum. There is something gravitational to his love; it draws me home.

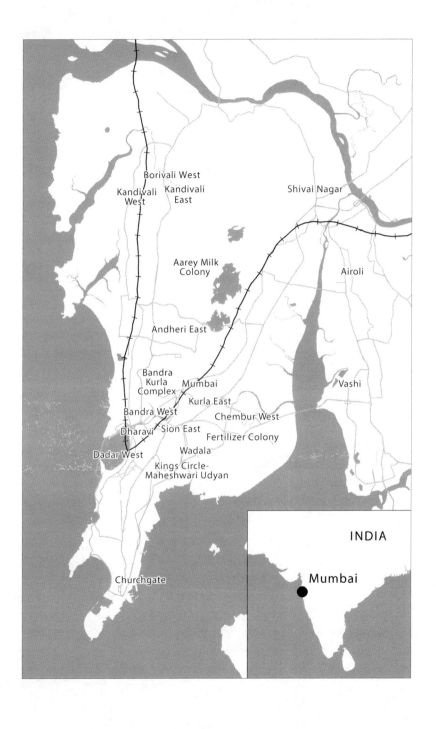

Borivali West
Kandivali West
Kandivali East
Shivai Nagar
Aarey Milk Colony
Airoli
Andheri East
Bandra Kurla Complex
Mumbai
Vashi
Bandra West
Kurla East
Chembur West
Dharavi
Sion East
Fertilizer Colony
Dadar West
Wadala
Kings Circle-Maheshwari Udyan
Churchgate

INDIA

Mumbai

Introduction

THE TRAFFIC OF TRAUMA

I reckon the siren like thunder: threat, distance, relation.

The sound is high-pitched, continuous, and mechanical, and I do not recognize it at first. The siren does not warble; its pitch is constant. Suspended in traffic, the ambulance proceeds fitfully next to a Shiva temple and does not move fast enough for me to perceive the wave changes of the Doppler effect. Cars and rickshaws and motorcycles edge around the accident scene, which is less a full stop and more a diversion. The siren joins the sonic fold of Mumbai's traffic alongside horns offering "you go" or replying "my turn" as cars dance. From a distance, the road looks frozen. Up close, things are stop-and-go as injury and repair churn.

I reach my destination an hour later and never learn about that ambulance, but the siren stays with me. It broadcasts traffic's milieu, mobility's tectonics, and the challenges of moving injury in Mumbai. Who was inside that ambulance? How did it get to the hospital, and once there, what ensued? How does injury move after the accident? And what of traffic: How do people clear paths through the traffic of trauma?

A Crossing

A year passes. I am researching the social trajectories of traumatic injuries from traffic accidents as they move into, through, and out of Mumbai's largest public hospital trauma ward, at a hospital I call Central Hospital. Hearing of my work, a friend tells me to meet Kalvin, because Kalvin's friend Raghu died in a train accident. Kalvin tells me the story as we navigate Mumbai's streetscape on foot.

Raghu left work one evening and headed home on the local train with two friends. He stepped toward the train's always-open door to take a phone call, and to give him privacy, his friends moved further into the compartment. People began yelling that someone had fallen out of the train. The friends could not find Raghu. Later a witness told the police, "He just fell, gone" (gira, ho gaya). The train continued on, moving everyone else who needed it. The friends got off at the next station and circled back to search the tracks.

Kalvin reflects on the moment when the friends phoned him. He knew what had happened from a lifetime of riding the train through the city's construction zones. "You know the iron rods that go in concrete? He fell off the train and onto those rods."

Kalvin sees an opening in the congestion, and we dash into the street as he continues.

The police joined the two friends and walked along the tracks with flashlights. They called an ambulance when they saw Raghu lying unconscious. Rush hour delayed the ambulance, so one of the friends attempted rescue. He gathered Raghu's body in his arms, carried him back to the station, lugged him onto the next train, and disembarked at the next station closer to a hospital. Police there flagged down an autorickshaw and forced the driver to head toward the hospital, where doctors declared Raghu dead on arrival.

Kalvin wards off oncoming vehicles with his outstretched palm, so we can live to finish the story.

So much hope was invested in moving and being moved. But Raghu never moved *through* the hospital trauma ward. The orderlies would not wheel Raghu down the hall from the emergency room into the trauma ward's resuscitation area. The nurses would not twist open IV drips to address his pain and raise his blood pressure. He would not be pushed into the operating theater for surgery to stop internal bleeding, lying flat. He would not exchange breath with a ventilator in the intensive care unit (ICU). His movement stopped at the hospital's entrance, so medicine could not attempt to make him live through its rhythms and tempos. Raghu navigated a lifeline en route to his home. After the accident, his friends navigated him along a lifeline to the hospital. But trauma medicine would not be able to shift things further.

Kalvin rode the local train to view Raghu's body at the hospital, and he rode it home afterward. It was the journey's enduring embodiment he remembers. "It made me shiver, the iron on the train. The sound is terrifying. It's like we are traveling in death ... a vehicle of death."

Traffic transforms in the street. A clearing expands, and we cross to the other side.

Lifelines

In Mumbai, like in many places, living demands movement through traffic to survive. Traffic is mobility's vital forces at work: a flux of discontinuities. As in my crossing with Kalvin, living with traffic is a matter of being in punctuated transit. Even if one moves alone, both constituting and navigating traffic, this is often done for someone else: commuting to work, shopping for vegetables, taking the children to school, driving for a customer. Yet after a traffic accident occurs, uneven movements do not cease. How might traffic continue in order to shape someone's potential survival? How does trauma move after the accident? And how does medicine move us?

Lifelines addresses these questions through an ethnography of mobility and mortality in Mumbai. It traces traumatic injuries from traffic accidents through differences in motion. It is a book about social life in situations of life-threatening imbalance. It is about trauma in its surgical sense—wounds that are immediately life-threatening—and about the intimacies of trauma's treatment in a hospital. It describes the transitional qualities of relations among medical crisis, medical care, and social life. Scenes of life at the edge of death in a public hospital trauma ward demonstrate the increasing ordinariness of traumatic injury in India and the Global South. They exemplify how movement shapes contemporary health crises globally, how irregular stoppages and flows constitute clinical forms and social relations, how injuries inflect moral and technological dilemmas, and how medical anthropology might address these matters in new and necessary frames.

My research tracked trauma through its different contact points with medicine, from an ambulance's arrival to a patient's surgery, and from family visitation to recovery back home. Throughout, in-motion embodiments would take on new urgencies after a collision. This suggests that the collision is not always an ending. It can be a beginning for medicine to make injured bodies matter through volatile activities of different forms and scales.[1] Those activities may be openings and closings, the staving off of bleeding or the shifting of beds in the ward. They could be efforts to hold someone still or to shock them into activity. They may be transfers out of the ward or regulations on access inside.

Trauma care exemplifies this clinical kinetics. People in the wake of trauma's forces discern changes in movement as central to survival. Patients and their families constantly ask what the hospital's next move will be. A change in motion causes injury; injury demands medicine; and medicine constitutes new and vital possible holds and shifts. In this light, medicine is ultimately a problem of how to move, as much as it is a problem of what to know. Medicine, then, is a process of traffic.

The movements of locomotion endanger bodies in terms of risk or exposure. Assessing such risks is crucial for understanding the uneven distribution of traumatic injuries from traffic accidents. This frame of thinking asserts the trauma of traffic: how malfunctioning, overburdened, or degrading transport structures and infrastructures are injury's causal conditions. By working from this perspective, large-scale quantitative and epidemiological studies emphasize trauma's conclusion in injury or in death in order to compel policy change.

Studying the trauma of traffic is certainly necessary. Everyone working in Central's trauma ward agrees that transit structures can disable and that movements and countermovements on the city's roads and commuter trains shape the likelihood of a patient's arrival at the hospital ward: a motorbike skids on uneven pavement, tumbling riders onto the road; a car dashes a rickshaw; a truck plows down a woman crossing the road; a luxury vehicle runs over pavement dwellers; a man falls out of a railway carriage. Traffic as injury's cause is not a matter up for dispute. The trauma of traffic delivers bodies to them to work on, every day.

That is the arrival story. But what's next, in terms of trauma's continuities?

What follows is an argument about how traffic can constitute a social field, an embodied process, and a clinical infrastructure beyond the accident scene. The argument is this: bodies may appear to leave traffic, but traffic does not necessarily leave bodies. This argument hinges on the idea that movements aimed at keeping someone alive continue after the collision, and that such movements constitute traffic too. In contrast to the trauma of traffic, this book describes injury's relational kinetics after the accident. That is, it describes the traffic of trauma.

Lifelines affirms moving and being moved as core powers of embodiment, medicine, and social life. It describes the intimate, irregular, syncopated, and negotiated activities resulting from the occurrence of traumatic injuries. Casting these activities as traffic, the book takes injury, injury experience, and injury care to be matters of differential motion. One of its aims is to unsettle the fixity of injury, of wounded bodies, and of sociality. I show how injury and movement connect people, even as a given wound lodges in an individual's body. This means that trauma, embodiment, and care exist in terms different than those premised on a singular wounded body at rest. By contrast, I argue, they come to matter through patterned and relational movements that might remedy life-and-death situations. I call these movement patterns *lifelines*.

Lifelines are relational survival projects. They involve ideas and actions chained together to transition a body through time and space. They materialize through real and imagined differences in movement and have the potential to shape the outcome of trauma. Their potential has a doubled kinetic quality. Vital movements may become injurious, and dangerous moves may aid treatment. Consider how Raghu went onto the train, then off the train, first for his commute and then in his fall. Then his friend brought Raghu's body back onto the very same conveyance by which he had thrived moments before. Carrying the body rather than waiting for an ambulance to stabilize it may have worsened Raghu's injuries, perhaps, but the friends decided that there was no choice: his survival was on the line. So Raghu went back onto the train and toward the hospital. In this example, commuting and carrying mark out provisional lifelines: they shift embodiment by shifting movement. Because these changes may have life-and-death consequences, lifelines are projects of kinetic, clinical, and vital differentiation. The lifelines in this book span the arc of trauma care, from the accident scene to the hospital, through triage, treatment, surgery, intensive care, death, and discharge. The chapters show how the particularities of traumatic injury shape different lifelines. Together, these lifelines create terms of relation for trauma's traffic.

My perspective on traffic's connections between moving and living derives from the local description of Mumbai's local train system, which is known colloquially as the city's *lifeline*—an English word used across vernacular languages. Mumbai's local train moves life. The lifeline in Mumbai is a material metaphor for the shaky differences among the bodies of the riders, the traffic of the city, and the politics of their relations. It signals movement's necessity in the face of traffic's obstacles, because the train makes transit faster amid heavy road congestion in an island city with a population density of nearly thirty thousand people per square kilometer. It marks the train's politics as multiscalar, folding Mumbai's bodies into

India's broader history of colonial and postcolonial development through the railways (Aguiar 2011; Bear 2007; Hurd and Kerr 2012; Kerr 2003; Prasad 2016) and connecting somatic movements to crowds (Canetti 1962; Low 2000; Mazzarella 2010, 2017; V. Rao 2007b; Tambiah 1996; R. Varma 2004).[2]

This connection is at once vital and lethal. Mumbai's local train moves life at considerable bodily risk, killing nearly ten people each day and injuring many more. To accommodate the rush hour density of fifteen people per square meter, the carriage doors remain open while the train moves.[3] The city's residents observe that Mumbai's lifeline, in Hindi called *Mumbai ki lifeline*, is simultaneously Mumbai's deathline, *Mumbai ki deathline*. The train is a lifeline because it is a traffic infrastructure whose relation to survival is provisional. It is a dangerous savior, always containing the possibility to effect both livelihood and death through its moves.

The varied movements that assemble a lifeline might also be productively figured as the casting out of a life preserver to a drowning person. In this instance, throwing the life preserver is a provisional move. But it is a two-way situation, one that brings the person who is throwing and the person who is drowning into relation. The person who throws the preserver pulls on the rope so that the drowning person might live. Otherwise, the drowning person might not be able to navigate the sea's undertow. Yet the drowning person can be moved in another direction by the sea's waves if forces on the body add up differently. Agencies of pulling may momentarily change. Any attempt to shift a threat to life is always subject to such differences in surrounding turbulence and interpersonal action.

A broader question of this book is how thinking about such differences in movement can enable thinking about what lies at the heart of medicine. Medicine unequally navigates bodies through obstacles toward treatment, always with the potential for both healing and damage. Even at rest, or stuck waiting, patients in the grip of trauma care eventually get shifted (willingly or not, alive or not). Strict categories of moving versus not moving may strain to describe the power formations at stake in any given scene of medical care. Just as I am calling for a conceptual shift from the body static to the body kinetic, I pay attention to bodies as they move unevenly through medicine. To describe lifelines in this context is to develop a vocabulary for survival projects, and to specify medicine's stutters of both fixity and flow.

In the case of Mumbai, medicine and urbanism must be thought together through such moving terms. The "urban" of the hospital certainly refers to its location geographically in a city, but it also entails the internalization of the city's unequal somatic pressures. Trauma medicine operates on the urban environment's fleshy incursions and focuses on injuries that open the body's interior to its lived milieu. By invoking the "traffic of trauma" to think about embodied velocities, I do not remove *traffic* from the street and neatly apply it idiomatically to traffic in the ward, such that the ward mirrors or magnifies the street. To do so would be to separate bodies from infrastructures and to keep bodies in aggregate, an approach often found in the sciences of urban planning and engineering. It is in many ways a useful approach: traffic engineers and scientists optimize that aggregate through complex and varied calculations of how drivers, pedestrians, and cyclists move. They suggest how behavior may be modified through changes in roadway design, signage, speed limits, and redirections of flow (Wolshon and Pande 2016). This approach can reveal breakdowns (a traffic light blinks out) and deviations (as a police officer diverts cars). Yet bodies are not always "users" of transit infrastructures who can move through infrastructure untouched. Traffic's complexities stem in part from its qualities of both particle and wave. Road traffic produces wounded bodies, and trauma medicine picks up the task of moving them through its own traffic forms. Ethnography in this context involves rethinking the yoking of bodies to traffic, through an anatomy and physiology of traffic from the ground up.

Trauma

The biopolitics of trauma is a politics of moving and being moved. Traumatic injury results from shearing or puncturing forces; movement is its very condition of possibility. Clinically, *traumatic injury* (and its more abbreviated form, *trauma*) refers to a blunt or penetrating wound that is immediately life-threatening, as well as the body's response to that wound. Objects at rest cannot cause trauma and accidents. Only moving forces can. Because trauma has a kinetics, it can cause a disturbance: concrete is on the road; now it is in your head; now the surgical instruments in the hands of the neurosurgeon are in your brain. Disparate materials of the world collide, damaging tissue in the skull. Organs and circulatory vessels tear, and blood flows into spaces of the chest where it does not belong. Medicine intervenes and makes prior circulations possible again.

In the trauma ward at Central Hospital, the English-based clinical term *trauma* is used in local languages to classify such wounds. The ward treats major trauma from two categories of traffic accidents: road traffic accidents and railway accidents. It also treats falls and wounds from physical assault, but it tends to refer sexual assault cases to the hospital's gynecological and obstetrics department. This has consequences for the gendering of trauma in the trauma ward and is not a categorical quibble; it is a reminder of how violence achieves unequal forms of clinical legibility (Mulla 2014).

In speech, injury's circumstances may become known as an *accident*. This is glossed as *hadsa* in Hindi, *apghat* in Marathi, and *aksident* in Mumbai's colloquial Hindi dialect. Both the Hindi term *chot* (meaning "wound") and the English-derived term *injury* are used in conversation to refer to an accident's outcomes.[4] There is much to be said about whether accidents are really accidental—that is, about how intentionality and structural violence bear on events that are hardly matters of chance (Figlio 1983; Fortun 2001, 2012; Jain 2013; Lamont 2012; Perrow 2011; Petryna 2002). Public health scholars tend to use the term *injury* to assert that there are really no accidents because all events have underlying causes. I am mindful of this distinction, and it is indeed important. However, I will stay with local linguistic forms, and so my use of *accident*, *injury*, and *wound* reflect translations of the terms that ground the work of the ward.

The ward's work tells a broader and troubling story about the extensive burden of road and railway traffic accidents in contemporary India and in the Global South. For example, taking into account the variation of rural areas less defined by traffic congestion, nearly four hundred people die each day in India as a result of road traffic injuries. This makes India the source of over 20 percent of global road traffic deaths (World Health Organization 2014). Each year, nearly one million people in India die from trauma (India State-Level Disease Burden Initiative Road Injury Collaborators 2020), and many more are hospitalized; road injuries have been the primary cause of death among men age fifteen to thirty-nine in India in several studies (India State-Level Disease Burden Initiative Road Injury Collaborators 2020; N. Roy et al. 2010, 2011). Traumatic injury and death shift gendered and socially classed household wage-earning structures and broader care economies.

Living with and being in relation to traumatic injury sets the central narrative condition and case study for this book. Being subject to lifeline projects in a hospital is a selective affordance. In India half of the people who experience major trauma die at the accident scene or during the journey to the hospital; they are more like Raghu than not. And of those who make it to the hospital, studies estimate that between 12 percent and 20 percent die within thirty days of admission, although clinical researchers believe that more than half of in-hospital trauma deaths are preventable with early resuscitative treatment and close monitoring of physiological signs such as systolic blood pressure that can predict mortality (Bhandarkar et al. 2021; Gerdin et al. 2014, 2016; V. Kumar et al. 2012; N. Roy et al. 2016; N. Roy 2017).[5] The costs associated with treatment and death or rehabilitation can easily exceed a household's limits, sending already-poor families into catastrophic expenditures, poverty, and debt in a country that spends 1 percent of its gross domestic product (GDP) on health and where families pay for at least 70 percent of most health-care costs out of pocket.[6] The implication is that I am telling stories about a representative sample of people situated between walking away with minor injuries and dying on the spot. But not everyone gets to be in the middle, and not everyone follows a linear path through treatment.

The violence of trauma's causes is selective and, like its consequences, defies easy alignment with accusations of absolute speed or certain immobility. Vehicular traffic in Mumbai can keep many roads in a trickling gridlock, but the intervals between speedup and slowdown make accidents between cars, pedestrians, motorcycles, and trucks very high.[7] Those who can afford to be in the protective cage of a car or in less crowded, more expensive train compartments experience exposure to risk and the pleasures of mobility differently from pedestrians or commuters in more crowded, less expensive train compartments. While traumatic injury may be attributed to chance or misfortune, it is also the case that bodies do not move at random. Rather, they are invested with unequal propulsions, inertias, and repulsions that derive from gender, caste, class, age, family position, and community of origin (to name just a few of the many interlocking forms of social stratification in India). These investments shape the aftermath of injury too, in movements toward a public hospital instead of a private facility. Trauma produces, and is produced by, these forms of structured inequality and inflects the lifelines forged in response.

Senior surgeons in Central's trauma ward describe these inequalities partly through changes in injury patterns over time. For instance, head injuries increasingly define the clinical profiles of patients. A surgeon named Dr. D runs complex epidemiological studies in the trauma ward and is attempting to create India's first trauma registry. He attributes the change to transformations in local and national political economies. During the 1980s and 1990s, which he describes as the heyday of Mumbai's gang violence and communal rioting, he would have to separate young men in the trauma ward according to their different gang affiliations. Limb and chest

wounds dominated the cases. But in sync with India's economic liberalization in the 1990s, the world adjustment that brought in Toyota compact
cars and Honda Hero motorbikes, social class dynamics shifted transit patterns. More people moved through the city in owned, rented, or borrowed
vehicles. Economic precarity amplified the number of passengers on the
local trains, particularly in the less expensive and more crowded second-
class compartments. Everyone negotiated spatial displacement as skyrock-
eting rents made living in the city's center unaffordable and as work became
synonymous with extensive commutes.[8] Scooters became ubiquitous, and
helmet laws were only intermittently enforced. The underworld invested
in lucrative real estate and construction projects, diminishing gang fights
but intensifying the ways that everyday urban mobility entailed navigating
an obstacle course of concrete and potholes.

As Tarini Bedi notes, Mumbai's "progressive registers of infrastructural
modernization have a dual face—of building and making and of destruc-
tion, demolition, and phasing-out" (2016, 388). When Kalvin asked me,
"You know the iron rods that go in concrete?" he was not only asking
about the thing that killed Raghu. He was also asking that I recognize an
ever-present feature of Mumbai's landscape: the intrusions of *salli* (iron
rods) sticking up out of the ground in construction sites or fast approaching a car's windshield when the *salli*-ferrying truck in front of it comes to a
sudden halt. In theory, one may take something like a pothole and cast it
as the exceptional sign of injury causation. Yet something else is at work
here: the absolute ordinariness of iron rods, potholes, dug-up pipes, and
stray bricks and the ways that people shift around and through spaces
of injurious obstacles as they navigate those same spaces for everyday
needs.

The ordinary unevenness of motion suffuses clinical spaces. Trauma
surgeons deal in a currency of morbid jokes, in casual conversation or at
work. These jokes, which trauma surgeons fully recognize as modes of coping,
can distribute from doctor to patient. For instance, Dr. D, the surgeon, re-
called operating on a patient who had been run over by the train, a seeming
collision and deceleration. Beyond the trauma of the injury, the patient
was also intoxicated. He was missing both lower legs, and they were going
to have to do an above-the-knee amputation—"one of the worst kinds of
procedures," Dr. D said. When the patient woke up, he looked at Dr. D
and posed a very reasonable question: "Where are my legs?" (mazha pay
kuṭe ahe?). Dr. D offered what he thought was an equally reasonable reply:
"They're coming on the next train" (agli gaḍi se aa jaege).

The image of dismembered legs riding the train is jarring enough. But just as striking is Dr. D's droll certainty that a different train, right behind the index of the event, will deliver the feet back to an injured person lying in the hospital. It is a dark reminder that inequality's kinetics continue after the wounding, that there are multiple and terrifying ways that bodies can become part of the city's traffic, and that the city can become part of the body's traffic. This insistence on moving embodiment as the link between the city and the clinic also appears in the lifeline Kalvin's friends forged to bring Raghu's body back onto the next train that arrived at the station, certain that it would arrive and take them onward, to the hospital. Not every person working in the trauma ward may share Dr. D's telling of the changes in trauma cases. But it is indisputable to those in the ward that what it works on, what its epidemiology estimates, and what my own ethnography tracks is kinetic violence in a space that is *of* the city, even as it is *in* the city.[9]

The City and the City Hospital

When I see injuries in the trauma ward, I am seeing the city at work. Systems of roads, railways, and hospitals are interfacing, each of them producing and produced by structural conditions such as class and caste.[10] A lifeline in this context is a transitional infrastructure, something that provides the lifeworld of structure (Berlant 2022). I am an ethnographer, and for me, methods and concepts are descriptive. Yet an enduring challenge to describing infrastructures—even provisional ones—is the problem of overcoming their determinism (Anand 2017, 172) and attending to their episodic qualities (Berlant 2016, 2022). Closed-ended deterministic frames about injury's cause (e.g., automobility will always injure, or, the railway system embeds its own killing force) may not in fact structure how people find themselves in a given scene of injury. Conditions of cause and consequence do not always match.

Therefore, with emergent motion as its focus, this book develops a social theory that is somatic and situational. It acknowledges infrastructural wounding but does not assume that trauma resides only in infrastructure's failures. That framing is inadequate for the task of addressing how conditional movements generate inequalities (Farmer 2004). What is necessary is to develop a framework that foregrounds how people live out infrastructural disruption and infrastructural repair; I trace lifelines to do so (Anand 2017; Anjaria and McFarlane 2011; Baviskar 2003; Chu 2016; Coleman

2017; De Boeck and Baloji 2016; De León 2015; Finkelstein 2019; Jusionyte 2018; Melly 2017; A. Roy 2009).[11]

History imbues these connections. The powerful polysemy of railway accidents in urban India is a historical feature inseparable from colonial power. Laura Bear explains that accidents on trains in colonial India marked the "uncontrollable nature of commodities and markets" while also confirming British colonial fears "that Indians could not be trusted with the supervision of industrial machinery" (2007, 65). Railway accidents are historical forms that evidenced the otherness of Indians to colonial bureaucrats and exemplified "hierarchies of Indian society that emerged from nationalist responses to the coloniality of its spaces" (62; also see Goswami 2004; Thiranagama 2012). I would add to these insights that contemporary road and railway injuries are inseparable from the politics of the contemporary hospital, whether or not the injured make it that far.

The railway is more than just its accidents. Marian Aguiar argues that the railway is the infrastructure that, for British colonial powers, promised to make colonial India "a more manageable state" (2011, xiv). Bombay, later Mumbai, has often been at the center of this mythical and material project (Prakash 2010a). This occurred through the nineteenth-century urban planning efforts that transformed the city's fishing docks into ports of colonial, global trade (Dossal 1997); the industrial booms of the city's iconic textile mills that circulated cotton, textiles, and wealth for family-firm investors (Finkelstein 2019); the clearing of those mills and the attendant real estate speculation that made way for pharmaceutical industry centers in the twentieth century (K. Sunder Rajan 2006); 250 years of circulating capital through the Bombay Stock Exchange of Dalal Street (Kulkarni 1997); the dominance of Hindi-language mass mediation through the film industry (Ganti 2012); the circulation of commodity promises through product advertising (Mazzarella 2003); and the ongoing dispossession of the city's poorest inhabitants from their homes (Appadurai 2000b). In other words, transit infrastructures must be understood as historical nodes of possibility for capital flows and their attendant affects and practices of global cosmopolitanism and modernity. Traffic is not just a decontextualized "problem," then. It is the site where Mumbai's deep layers of urban planning transform into embodied realities, through a politics of uneven motion that connects the city's people to capital and labor through local, regional, national, and global frames.

I foreground the hospital in those shifting frames. The site at the book's center, a large municipal public hospital I call Central Hospital, has been connected to traffic accidents since its opening in the mid-twentieth century. Central sits in the heart of the city, and the city pumps through it. It began as a military hospital in 1944 for the Indian naval forces involved in World War II and was built at a central railway node to handle the transport of the sick and injured. After Indian independence in 1948, the hospital's governance shifted over to the municipality of Mumbai. Its trauma ward is the city's busiest Level 1 trauma center and one of the few such dedicated centers in India. The trauma ward is a point of pride for the hospital's administration. This fact is often a talking point for visitors, the other being the hospital's proximity to one of the country's largest slum neighborhoods, which the hospital serves intimately.

Sarah Hodges notes that hospitals in nineteenth-century India materialized state power and "provide distinct templates for our understanding of the colonial state's crisis-driven extension of public welfare" (2005, 398). I would suggest that Central Hospital's trauma ward offers a contemporary resonating case. Its rhythms are modes of postcolonial governmentality and reflect the challenges of providing public medicine as public works (Adams 2002; Amrith 2006, 2007; Arnold 1993, 2004; Baru 2003; S. Patel and Thorner 1995; Qadeer 2000, 2013; Sivaramakrishnan 2019).[12] This too constitutes the cityness of the city hospital. In this light, I offer a contrast to important works about the politics of injury that begin after the injury has settled into either tort law (Jain 2006) or traffic policy (Barker 1993, 1999). The cases I describe in this book are still in motion and set the public hospital into counterpoint with other movement crises.

The hospital's cityness often gains legibility in scenes of somatic disruption. Perhaps it is not surprising that scholars of urban South Asia turn to the gruesome injuries that occur on transport systems to theorize sociality, a conceptual approach that I extend from the street to the hospital. For example, cultural theorist Ravi Sundaram (2009) details how the bodily and psychic shock of the modern and the urban in India now forms as road accidents. Centering his analysis on Delhi in the 1990s, when spectacular car accidents proliferated as private car ownership did too, Sundaram argues that contemporary India is suffused with what he terms *wound culture*. He critiques contemporary, Eurocentric urban planning logics that uncritically map cities metaphorically as pure flows. In such Enlightenment-inflected models, the intersections of the city are like agile connective joints, and expressways are like unobstructed blood vessels. Unobstructed movement gains centrality among such ideas.[13]

Wound culture, by contrast, is a framework open to the ways that urban public culture may operate in terms different than flow. Through an analysis of Delhi's widespread traffic accidents, Sundaram argues that in India there is a public cultural sense of being overwhelmed by trauma on the road, such that "divisions between private trauma and public tragedy blurred, suggesting a traumatic collapse between inner worlds and the shock of public encounters" (2009, 170–71). A focus on wound culture highlights the interruptions of moving between flesh and space and shows that wounds can emerge from *both* stasis and flow (Edensor 2013; see also Hansen and Verkaaik 2009; and Gidwani 2008).

Sundaram writes of Delhi, but his insights can certainly be considered in Mumbai, Lagos, Jakarta, Mexico City, or many other settings where traffic is "absolute" and seemingly intractable (Lee 2015). He develops a way of thinking urban entropy differently than scholars who take the generalized, unwounded body as the city's metonym (Sennett 1994). He challenges models in which the crash and the wound are destined to be aberrations because of erroneous assumptions about circulatory flow and equilibrium. In regimes of wound culture, injurious traffic *is* the city, and cities must move with crashes. Processes of moving and processes of wounding must be thought together.[14]

Movement

Raghu did not move through the trauma ward at Central Hospital, but Subhash does. It's a few years after Kalvin and I talked. An orderly wheels Subhash in on a gurney; his leg is crushed, and a friend accompanying him explains how kinetic actions turned deadly. Subhash leaned out of the local train's open door, and as a second train passed by in a different direction, a man on the passing train grabbed Subhash and pulled him out of the compartment. He fell underneath one of the moving trains. Someone must have pulled the emergency chain to alert the driver to stop the train, and once it halted, a group of men extricated him from under the train and carried him to a taxi. The doctors attend to the most visible wound—Subhash's leg—and begin assessing him for signs of chest and head trauma. Subhash's brother arrives soon after; walking into the ward, he takes in the scene, halts, and falls to his knees. He gathers himself, wipes his tears, and positions himself by the gurney, in Subhash's field of vision, and tells him that things will be okay and he will move again.

Trauma frustrates but may not always exceed singularity. There are often many unknowns that suffuse moments when the injured person may be unable to speak and/or should not be queried so that they can recover. For the surgeons, Subhash's injury has a precise location. Subhash's brother sees this too. At the same time, for Subhash's brother (and for the surgeons too), trauma extends beyond the bounds of the subject in a not-injured person's commitment to stand by the one whose life is in danger.[15] This means that trauma is relational and social but also that these terms require greater specificity to address the intimacies between bodies on unequal terms of activity.[16]

To specify these terms requires an expansive sense of the metacategory of movement involved in the trauma care context. Movements may take shape as speedups and slowdowns. Sometimes they involve a change in place but sometimes they take form as a desire to shift out of being stuck in one spot. A binary framework that opposes absolute flow to absolute stuckness is inadequate for the task of describing movement and traffic in this context. In such a binary framework, important but intermediate movement relations might get muted in the service of affirming extremes of stoppage, attrition, schism, and loss accompanied by surplus signification (Caruth 2016; Leys 2010). There are consequences to depicting movement in extremes. A focus on interruptive freeze and amplified signs tends to fix trauma in an individual's struggle against the immobilizing grip of a collision event or to pin trauma to particular historical trajectories (Fassin and Rechtman 2009). Stuck in the crash and a stop-go frame, it can also be difficult to ascertain the ongoingness of the injured present (Berlant 2011, 81) and the moving after-ness of injury (Wool 2015).

Recall Kalvin's invocation of the local train as a "vehicle of death" as he heard the sound of its rustling metal components, a sound of motion. He heard these sounds as he continued to ride the train, a habit he did not cease. Intermediate, reverberating, habitual, and emergent shifts may shape how beyond clinical technicalities, traumatic injury becomes traumatic. A halting collision may not be the only place to find trauma's signs. I am suggesting that to understand the impacts of mass injury and death, intimate episodes of transition deserve close attention. To people caught in these episodes, they may feel different than aggregate extremes. Being subject to trauma's movements may not be the same thing as being broken by trauma.

Nor must "movement" mean a large-scale change in location. Consider the ways Robert Desjarlais (1997) discusses movement in his ethnography of a homeless shelter in Boston. Desjarlais describes how residents of the shelter pace, come and go according to scheduled routines (or not), how they shift from one spot to another. Homelessness, he suggests, may not neatly align with "a metaphysics of presence, dwelling, and stasis" and instead entails dislocation and movement (103). Dislocation can mean the difference from standing in one corner of the shelter compared to another. Movement involves transition, desired and/or actualized, but often does so in ways that are different than a grand journey.

Thinking about movement in terms of small but vital displacements can address a tendency in some trauma studies scholarship to frame trauma as knowledge that the individual or collective should or should not face. While important, this stance may make it harder to grapple with trauma's terms that may operate beyond reconciled knowing. For instance, debility and disability can simultaneously mark bodily difference and the unequal ability to make claims on that difference (Addlakha 2018; V. Das and Addlakha 2001; Friedner 2015, 2022; Jain 2006; Kohrman 2005; Livingston 2005; Wool 2015). Furthermore, trauma and the medicalization of trauma are not the same thing (Ralph 2020). The medicalization of injury and disability may in fact have depoliticizing effects (Dewachi 2015, 2017; Jain 2006; Kafer 2013; Ralph 2014, 2020). As Lochlann Jain (2005) explains, injury and its reverberations in medicine and law should be understood as more than a sum of individual harms. Injury is materially and socially generative precisely because it is structural, relational, and unequally distributed. These scholars point toward the need for the ethnography of injury to situate itself somewhere between individuals and collectives.

Differences in bodily movement are a powerful site to do so, because movements can be ambivalent, powerful, elusive, and transformative. In Subhash's case, this could mean considering trauma's disturbance in family ties and also in Subhash's leg. It also could mean understanding Subhash's injury as a disturbance to a specific space—a public hospital ward—where there is no guarantee that individuals are afforded the space and time to encounter their calamity alone. And it could mean considering how medicine, the family, the state, and the law can disturb Subhash, as each domain struggles to authorize a connection between itself and his wound.

My emphasis on describing bodily movement patterns, assembling them as lifelines, and aggregating them as traffic is a way of thinking about relationality. Relationality can mean how persons and structures intersect. For example, in *Rhythmanalysis*, Henri Lefebvre writes of bodily rhythms that he calls "becoming irregular" (*dérèglement*)—rhythms that are "symptomatic of a disruption that is generally profound, lesional and no longer functional" and that occur "by passing through a crisis" (2004, 44). For Lefebvre, irregular bodily rhythms and movements mark an impasse between how authoritative institutions demand that bodies move and how bodies may not comply.

Relationality can also mean how people interact with each other in a crisis situation. Focused more on crisis as an ordinary form than Lefebvre, Lauren Berlant takes the glitchy rhythms of everyday life as a site for "inventing new rhythms for living, rhythms that could, at any time, congeal into norms, forms, and institutions" (2011, 9; see also Berlant 2022). Berlant calls these rhythms *disturbances* and highlights how movement can be something that brings people into relation (2011, 6).[17] Infrastructure, agency, and embodiment can change terms through a small gesture, and a disturbance's potential lies in its power to shift situations. Movement is what makes relationality; it's not just what signifies it. Movement is "the activation of a new field of relation," Erin Manning argues. It is "always cueing in the complexity of the speeds and slownesses around you" (2016, 18, 120). Always containing the potential for both habit and novelty, movement blurs a singular body and the situation in which it is emplaced. Movement can also underlie therapeutic relations: the demand for subjects "to realign themselves with the timings and shared truths of others" (Desjarlais 1997, 175).

Social infrastructures emerge through relational movements (Elyachar 2011, 96). Relational movements also constitute subjects: "Bodies do not map easily onto subjects," Lawrence Cohen observes, and subjects emerge "as relations among and between bodies and their presumptive parts" (2011, 50). Ethnography attentive to such moves can deepen analyses of medicine, certainly, but also forms of vulnerability more broadly (De Boeck and Baloji 2016). It can shift the frame from injury to injury's sociality, and from the wound to the attempts to reckon with and repair the wound. This is because movements are provisional and therefore political. They bridge bodies and environments. They seed crisis, crisis response, and crisis theory. If sociality can be located in "a provisional moment," as Lauren Berlant and Kathleen Stewart (2018, 21) argue, the sociality of trauma might be located in provisional movements, through subtle gestures that amplify structural intensities: A scalpel's incision. A limb's jolt. Pushing a hospital trolley into the operating theater. Queueing to see the doctor, shuffling forward. Fingers dialing a phone number to notify a family that their child is in critical condition. Easing someone into a hospital bed. A test run of walking with crutches. A palm's muscular compression on an open wound.

Any analysis of the movements of medicine in contemporary India must begin from the social fact that differences in flow and stuckness concretize home, work, kinship, classes, and castes, determining who facilitates which critical transitions (Narayan 1992; Raheja and Gold 1994). Movement can render life transitions into metaphor, allegory, and poesis. This occurs as marriage, aging, and death are spoken of as shifts in time and place (Cohen 2000; Desjarlais 2016; Parry 1994; Pinto 2008b). Movement is a site of social and personal valuation in South Asia, a way of describing both ordinary life and life's crises, and movement constitutes the dependencies that make social relations legible (Bedi 2018; Sadana 2010, 2018). Urban settings organize these phenomena, from the "train friends" of daily commutes to threats of sexual violence in transit systems (Amrute 2015; Phadke, Khan, and Ranade 2011). Lifelines entail such differential shifts and affirm Central's trauma ward as a South Asian lifeworld because of motion's continuities and breaches.

Medicine

Each of the book's chapters examines how different lifelines shape trauma's traffic. This includes *carrying* the injured, done by emergency responders and ambulances, which forms lifelines of transfer (chapter 1); *shifting* patients and evidence awaiting care in casualty wards, which constitutes lifelines of triage (chapter 2); *visiting*, as patients' kin visit the ward and the ward visits its workers, moves that constitute lifelines of home (chapter 3); *tracing* the identities of the high number of unconscious, unidentified patients with traumatic brain injuries, done by medical workers and the police to constitute lifelines of identification (chapter 4); *seeing* an operation, in the context of both my fieldwork and my own personal surgical crisis, to grapple with lifelines of surgery (an interlude titled "Seeing"); *breathing* through mechanical ventilation for chest trauma and the bioethical dilemmas of life support, which makes up lifelines of ventilation (chapter 5); *dissecting* corpses in the hospital's morgue, which forges lifelines of forensics (chapter 6); and *recovering* with disability back home, which forms lifelines of discharge (chapter 7).

As a book structure, these chapters may seem to suggest that trauma's traffic has a linear shape. However, the path I follow from transfer to treatment to discharge is an ideal type and only one model. At any point, things can branch in different directions. I do not claim that it is the only shape or that it is the path that everyone follows. But linearity and seriality, real or imagined, often guide confrontations of trauma as patients, their kin, and clinical providers contemplate what happens next, and how. Even in the stickiest traffic, people reach a destination, eventually.

Together, these patterns tell a story about the power of movement into, through, and out of the clinic, one that joins accounts of the clinical and political potentials of movement by medical anthropologists. In an inpatient psychiatric hospital in North India, for instance, Sarah Pinto (2013, 2014, 2015) examines the "choreography" of patients as they wander, itinerant both physically in the ward but also in narratives that shift genres among personal accounts, dreams, films, and clinical notes. Ethnographies of postcombat wounded soldiers in the United States describe how care involves movements of limbs and of labile diagnostic categories such as post-traumatic stress disorder (PTSD) (MacLeish 2013; Messinger 2010; Wool 2015; Wool and Messinger 2012). In Sharon Kaufman's (2005) work on dying in American hospitals, movement structures medicine's ethical textures, a matter also described by Scott Stonington (2020). I share with these scholars an interest in how movements constitute the lived dilemmas of medicine and how that which moves around and through an unresolved wound can easily flicker between the concrete and the illusory.

Trauma medicine is a particular site of uneven motion because it is multiply institutional. The story of trauma in the United States is often the story of large public hospitals in major metropolitan areas. Traumatic injury in India demands an especially *public* sort of medicine, a government-funded health-care apparatus that is in constant relation to the casualization of labor in the health-care sector and the privatization of health care more broadly (Baru 2003). Most large hospitals have an emergency department, especially newer, private and corporate-run hospitals. Most smaller public hospital emergency departments are staffed with general practitioners, but they are not necessarily staffed with the surgeons and ready-to-go operating theaters that are necessary to address life-threatening major trauma.

Trauma surgery is primarily practiced in public, government hospitals and is crisscrossed by ambulances and also by the private hospitals that patients often arrive at first, only to be refused care on the grounds of inability to pay, which shifts them to public facilities as a consequence (see Bhalla et al. 2016, 2019; Sriram, Gururaj, and Hyder 2017; and Sriram, Hyder, and Bennett 2018).[18] The exceptions are higher-end private hospitals that draw the very few specialists in emergency medicine in India, a field that few physicians will specialize in because of limited residency spots (Sriram, Baru, and Bennett 2018; Sriram, Hyder, and Bennett 2018). The setting of Central Hospital's trauma ward is thus unequivocally biomedical. While people in urban India seek out varied health-care providers and medical modalities for sicknesses from colds to tuberculosis, and while medical expertise mingles forms of "traditional" and "modern" medicine (Naraindas 2006), everyone knows that a major accident requires biomedical attention, and it is unthinkable to go anywhere but a hospital.

Based in the trauma ward, I explore a return to the hospital to craft an ethnography of medicine and science. Hospital ethnography is often regarded as an institutional study by medical sociology, and like similar institutional studies, sustained research "inside" the site can yield insight into social life "outside." And yet there are also calls to move hospital ethnography out of this edifice complex and to describe it neither as a mirror of its presumptive outside nor an exceptional space. What, then, can a hospital be?

In foregrounding differences in motion, I hope to reveal the instability of what counts as "the field" in the rapidly shifting scenes of a hospital. This is not just about getting out of the edifice complex; this is about finding analytic terrain to address how the hospital is both institutional and transitional. The hospital can indeed be a space of reification (Taussig 1980), and bodies in clinics are a canvas for power over life, formations of self, and sovereignty (V. Das 2003). But this does not mean that the hospital is a fully insulated institution. It cannot be, because it is selectively open to shifts in people and situations. In my previous work (Solomon 2015, 2016), this idea guided my approach to questions of how the clinic inflects lifeworlds inside homes, in markets for drugs and therapies, and in public spaces. Moving back into the hospital, I am guided by ethnographies and histories that track social inequality as a clinical intensity and that depict how social class, kinship, religion, ethnicity, and community histories infuse clinical spaces (Banerjee 2020; Livingston 2012; McKay 2017; Pandolfo 2018; Pinto 2014; Rosenberg 1987; Street 2014; Van der Geest and Finkler 2004; Van Hollen 2003; S. Varma 2020; Venkat 2021; Winant 2021; Zaman 2004, 2005). If the hospital is understood less as epiphenomenal and more as a process of embodying motion, the social worlds of the hospital can be better understood as emergent and in transition.

Annemarie Mol has written at length about the doing of medicine, that is, the ways that medicine must be approached as a matter of practices

(Mol 2002; Berg and Mol 1998). This framing moves away from medicine as a problem of knowing. Mol suggests that we understand medicine through its praxiographic terms. This entails tracing particular medical practices and reflecting on what these practices do rather than limiting the ethnography of medicine to what medicine knows. For Mol, differences in medicine are differences in doing medicine.

For me, differences in medicine are differences in moving medicine. Trauma medicine produces shifts in sociality and technics and relocates the consequences of unplanned convergences from the street to the clinic. It closes open wounds and manages spaces that have been breached. It shifts bodies into different shapes and shuttles them through different specialties. Pain medications stream through IV drips, and air courses through a ventilator's breathing tubes. Care also trudges through paperwork and multiple consults. In medicine, differences in moving are the differences in doing at stake.

Methods and Writing

What sorts of methods are adequate for researching and narrating trauma's traffic? As people move through situations of injury (and *people* here includes the ethnographer), the lifelines of trauma are wrought from within the domain of movement, not outside its bounds. Lifelines create possibilities and problems for ethnography, because narrating lifelines means narrating how people are in the middle of injurious transitions that may be generative even as they are exhaustive.[19] How might ethnographic writing account for such scenes?

Methods are part of the answer. I began this project in 2014, struck by the significant number of injuries and deaths from traffic accidents that kept appearing in the Mumbai neighborhood I had lived and conducted research in for many years. My sense was that traffic was deeply embodied. I wondered if conversations about infrastructure in anthropology and beyond might look different if infrastructure and flesh were not so easily separated. I questioned why scholarship on cities had mostly overlooked medicine as a critical site of the urban. Perhaps because of reasons of access, medical anthropology had to date not addressed injury from within clinical spaces.

I met with epidemiologists in Mumbai who study traumatic injury. The social dimensions of trauma were not yet part of their mostly quantitative research, and they were interested in a qualitative study of the contexts, causes, and consequences of trauma. I proposed fieldwork in two clinical settings: in the casualty ward of a smaller hospital I call Maitri Hospital (detailed in chapter 2) and in the trauma ward of the larger hospital I call Central Hospital (detailed from chapter 2 onward). Two municipal hospital surgeons I knew introduced me to the staff and faculty at Maitri and Central and facilitated discussions and the formal institutional permissions from hospital deans and municipal health authorities that enabled me to conduct fieldwork. My research was governed by three institutional review board approvals. One approval came from my home institution in the United States, and two approvals were secured in India: at each hospital the research was governed by an independent ethics committee protocol review process. In the day-to-day activities of research, I was supervised by senior faculty, attending physicians, and charge nurses. I presented deidentified research results at various stages of the project to hospital staff, and to a study group of Indian physicians, public health workers, social researchers, and students.

The trauma ward at Central was the site of my most intensive periods of fieldwork over eighteen months between 2014 and 2020. I observed cases from arrival through treatment, as they progressed through different way-stations of care and endured the choreography of trauma's different clinical practices: general surgery, anesthesiology, neurosurgery, orthopedic surgery, and nursing. At Central, like at many public hospitals, the team of providers who make the thing called *trauma medicine* happen approach a single case by integrating these different domains of medicine, each with its own epistemological orientations and habits of practice. This is because there are few seats for postgraduate training in trauma surgery and for specialized trauma nursing in India. The trauma team includes other workers who add another layer of specialization, a labor of care that I try to spotlight through accounts of technicians, orderlies, sweepers, paramedics, police, and mortuary workers, who each connect differently to a traumatic injury, to a patient, and to patients' kin. Their connections could be dismissed as informal clinical labor in contrast to the work of doctors, but I have chosen to treat them as central because they shape lifelines too. My purposeful inclusion of them in the book emphasizes the diverse ecology of a public hospital, upholds the power of clinical labor, and reveals how the social in social medicine coheres beyond doctor-patient relationships.

I conducted observations during different hospital shifts (morning, afternoon, and overnight) to understand different rhythms of the ward as well as to ensure repeated, representative interactions with the ward's staff. Individual interviews with staff were conducted at a time of the worker's choosing, secured through a formal informed consent process, and recorded when possible or allowed by the interlocutor. Semistructured interviews elicited data on a staff member's own educational and work experiences, memories of the first day in the ward, notable/memorable cases, and opinions on the ward's functions and on the social aspects of trauma care. Interviews were conducted by me along with an independent research assistant who was not a hospital worker and who was a Mumbai local able to converse fluently in the respondent's preferred language. Interviews were transcribed and translated by me and by the research assistant and were analyzed for emergent concepts and connective themes. My understanding of the broader contexts governing the municipal hospital system and traffic accidents came from analyzing city newspaper coverage of health care, transit and traffic politics, and specific accidents. This was done using database software set to search Marathi, Hindi, and English sources.

In each chapter I reflect on different methodological modes and the resulting differences in narrative conditions. In stretches of more accelerated storytelling, I do not wish to attribute a sense of chaos to those working in the ward and by extension to attribute blame to providers. In trying to capture intervals of downtime, I do not wish to paint a one-dimensional portrait of bureaucracy's gumminess. Rather, I develop an emergent ethnographic method to contend with ethically complex situations. This method is grounded in questions of what the ethnographer can and should follow and what they should leave unmoved. The difference between *can* and *should* matters, especially when one accounts for patients and families. I did not pursue an interview with a patient until they were deemed stable, or they requested that we speak. At that point, informed consent would be solicited for an extended, recorded interview. While the circumstances of injury events sometimes surfaced in those interviews, I did not ask about them. Inquiry can be disturbing in this context, and disturbance is not what I want someone with traumatic injury to experience. I want them to rest, en route to discharge. I do not want the people who make my study possible to continue to make my study possible. I want them to exit the ethnography alive. So there are limits to my understanding, and there are time delays. I see this as a research ethic of measured refrain.

I also came to understand the necessity of being careful in research and writing regarding eventedness. I did not assume I knew what "the event" of trauma was for anyone else. The ethnographer may enter a scene after its "original" event—in my case, I enter the scene of the hospital after an accident that I do not see—but people may still be processing the event. Furthermore, "the event" as such is often unstable and plural. Ambulance workers might compare dangerous intersections. Triage doctors inquire what is happening in the patient's body, right now, and remix the responses with perceptions of a wound's backstory. Visiting family members and police sometimes ask questions about "the event." Sometimes the events of the accident are withheld from the critically injured, especially those who cannot speak when on ventilator support. The hospital morgue attempts to derive causes of death from the postmortem. Patients who achieve discharge may revisit the accident once home, in reflection, in accusation, and in appeals for compensation. Simply being a patient in a hospital involves its own qualities of eventedness. Consequently, the chapters pay close attention to what elements of trauma get to become an event, for whom, and on what terms.

It is inaccurate for me to assume that when I see someone in the hospital, I am definitely seeing the bottoming out of their world.[20] This can be a difficult ethnographic commitment to uphold, given the severity of injuries one observes in trauma and the intensity of care that providers are making happen to ensure someone will survive. But there is also the risk of assuming the injury and its care completely define someone's life in the present and for the foreseeable future. The injury and the hospital are parts of someone's world but not the only parts. For the person who has been injured, what matters to them may not plot out on a grid with clear-cut coordinates. The psychic resonances of trauma do not necessarily operate through ready-made scripts. Experiences of street, train, office, ambulance, hospital, and home often mingle. One cannot assume that the clinic must be the de facto narrative anchor for clinical stories, especially at the hinge between living and dying. Trauma—like any medical calamity—is multivocal, and those voices can be out of sync and out of place (Briggs and Mantini-Briggs 2016). It is also critical to remember that many of the patients in Central's ward *do* survive.

A person in a hospital bed in pain can do many things besides feel pain in a hospital bed. They can put themselves together and reflect on life's circumstances. They can reaffirm assertions of the self that may not be allowable or hearable elsewhere. They may resist lifelines: changes in movement deemed helpful by others may in fact be experienced by patients as violent or unnecessary, because medicine's potentials can be damaging even as they are therapeutic. Patients devise their own lifelines too, presenting themselves to hospital staff in ways they think the institution desires, because they believe this may secure their release. The ethnographer, the patient, and the doctor may be in the trauma ward together, but that does not mean trauma moves them all equally. Traffic is always open to novel micromaneuvers, even if not much appears to have moved from a distance.

Where does that leave the ethnographer? For my own part, I regard my position as one principally defined by a freedom of mobility that grants the privilege to observe, listen, ask, and write on terms of my choosing. I could always calibrate my own proximity to scenes and could always leave the hospital. I had the ability to exit, to *not* have to be in situ in the ways patients, families, and health-care workers must be. My engagements with this project also stem from relations to Indian physicians and researchers who authorized my presence and guided the work. To the degree that ethnography operates as a lifeline for me, the traffic it produces connects to my own gendered, racialized, nationalized, and professional mobilities.

Narratively, I employ different forms of pacing to contend with visceral scenes that may shift quickly or may get bogged down. Care may sound clamorous or register as laggy; wounds appear as gross and extraordinary even as they get normalized. One might address this as a matter of content: What does the reader need to know? However, I work from a different question: How does a scene need to move? This is a question about different aspirations and actions of transition and one sparked by the drawings that begin each chapter. Wondering how people come to inhabit movement's language and action, I looked to photos of transition. I then traced the lines of the photos in drawings, because tracing lines compelled me to stay with the constitutive elements of a given situation. This is more than a question of representation. It is also a matter of action. Implementing this book's findings to improve trauma outcomes requires focused attention on the different ways medicine moves people. I aim to model that process by tracing trauma's shifts.

In traffic, so much moves while slowing. So much drags while quickening. Lines through traffic may not guarantee resolution, yet they create potentials for transition. Where will these lifelines lead?

I Carrying

THE LIFELINES OF TRANSFER

Next station, King's Circle. The hospital gate is blocks away. Steam rises; something's cooking. Laundry machines are boiling scrubs, which will hang on courtyard walls to air-dry like deflated doctors.

"I know you are writing a book about the accidents," Dipen says when he first contacts me. Someone shares my name with a disability social group, and Dipen reaches out. He wants to describe his accident on the train several years ago, and we meet near his flat. It's close to Central Hospital; signs for the casualty ward background him through the window. I see the orderlies joking with each other, heading in from the highway underpass, where people trace love messages in the dusty windshields of impounded rickshaws.

Dipen's voice carries in the empty coffee shop. "I was standing inside the train. On that day, you could call it my destiny, there was a man standing inside the train's open doorframe. His hand got caught." Dipen moved to grab him. Acting on someone else's risk can send both people tumbling out; gestures of kindness can turn deadly.[1] His balance faltered, and he fell past the man, out of the train, onto the tracks:

> You must have seen the local trains, how people rush into the train, how people stand outside the door. I lost my balance, and then I was outside the train, and the train ran over my feet, and I also lost two fingers. Within ten minutes, a man came. He looked like he was on his way to a job interview. With his handkerchief, he tied a knot on my knee to stop the bleeding. He told me, "Wait, I'll come back." He went to the station and came back with the stationmaster, a stretcher, and a water bottle. He called many other people. He took me in his lap. He told me to sleep on the stretcher, which

was on the tracks. But many people are needed to carry a stretcher. Other people had gathered, but at that time our law did not encourage people to help with trauma. The man told the other people, "You have to come forward" and "Show some humanity" [*kuch toh insaniyaat rukho*].

They did come forward, even as no ambulance came. The ethic of being accountable to a body took shape through movements.

Dipen speaks through remembered images. There was the accident scene ("My father and sister and mother had come to the railway station, but the police wouldn't allow them to touch me") and the hospital ("I ended up in the trauma ward. They started cutting my clothes, my flesh. I remember looking up at the ceiling lights"). He cannot recall the face of the man who assisted him, mobilized the crowd, and appealed to their humanity (*insaniyaat*) to get them to stop watching and to do something. It was an image element of the story that remained hazy despite his insistence on its centrality: "We were in such trauma. We couldn't recollect his face. After that day, I've never seen him, nor [have] my mom or dad. They offered him money, but he would not accept it. I remember that he wore a pink-and-white-striped shirt, his hair was parted in the middle, and he had a black folder that he told me was for his job interview. You want me to describe him? I can do it in one line: he was an angel for me." After a long stay in the hospital, different pools of resources, and many subsequent surgeries, he received a prosthetic leg. He is working in the small family business again and is training to run a race. He received a small amount of compensation from the railways for his injury years after the accident and donated some of it to the hospital.

The cascade of coordinated, dependent movements seems almost unbelievable to Dipen, but it enabled him to survive. One man, an angel with a face he cannot recall, transforms a dangerous situation of flow and freeze. The man opens up the accident's impasse. He walks along the train tracks (itself a risky venture), locates the stationmaster at the next station, brings the stationmaster back to the accident scene, puts the stretcher on the tracks in a moment of overlaying rescue with risk, enjoins the crowd to move Dipen, and leads the group in putting Dipen on a stretcher and into the police van that transports him to the hospital. The angel attempts to restore the vitalizing potential of motion, cleaves the crowd into carriers and the carried, and reshapes traffic's embodiment by shifting its terms of transport. The angel *carries* Dipen. Carrying becomes the site to enact lifelines of transfer, transforming the lethality of urban transit into the vitality of conveyance.

———————

In the immediate aftermath of injury, before a case reaches the trauma ward, trauma and emergency transport relate through interpersonal and bodily dependencies. Focused on the transport of injuries in ambulances, I develop the contrast that Dipen poses between mobility (being able to move) and conveyance (carrying another). Amid high rates of traumatic injury over the past decade, health-care policymakers in India implemented both statewide and citywide ambulance services and introduced the problem of how to mobilize forms of trauma medicine outward from the hospital to the street and back to the hospital again. This intensified conveyance as a vital form of traumatic injury care. With attention to the traffic of trauma as a peopled form, I analyze conveyance as a lifeline, and carrying as its key gesture.

Carrying shapes lifelines of transfer at the interfaces of health-care reform, urban public culture, and caste. Consequently, heightened social differentiation occurs in the space-time after the accident. Such differences emerge as ambulance-focused systems of trauma care work with street-level forms of conveyance. From the figures of the angel and the hero to the figures of the inert, unhelpful crowd of bystanders, conveyance entails embodied, intersocial dependencies between the injured and their carriers.

In one sense, conveyance defines the lifeline and deathline dyad of Mumbai's transit systems, because carrying underlies the very purpose of public transport. Roads, highways, and railways carry commuters through the city to achieve the daily needs and aims of life, and traffic accidents can be understood as ruptures in the social body. Yet, at the scale of mass transit, it can be difficult to see specific and meaningfully different movements that unfold after the accident. It can also be a challenge at the macrotransit scale to see vital dependencies in action. In the time and space en route to the hospital, survival depends on highly intersubjective bodily norms, expectations, and practices concerning who mobilizes whom. Relations between carriers and the carried occur through embodied patterns of mutual speedup and slowdown.

Traffic thus continues to shape chances for survival as bodies move from public transport systems to prehospital transfer systems. Yet, global public health research about prehospital trauma care often frames traffic as the obstacle to better clinical outcomes. That is, traffic operates in health systems research as the literal roadblock to the idealized flow of transfer between the accident scene and the hospital. But what might become known if traffic is understood to work in ways beyond uniform blockage?

Public health scholars in India argue that there is no way to get around the social fact that traffic is rooted in intersubjective urban public cultures of mobility. As a result, "traffic" in trauma research should be framed as social from the ground up. For instance, an important epidemiological study of prehospital care in Mumbai notes that "in the absence of a formal EMS system, victims in Mumbai are rescued, given first aid, and transported by a series of informal agencies and networks." Prehospital care is best understood as "a citizen responsibility using societal networks" (N. Roy et al. 2010, 148). While an ambulance-based EMS (emergency medical services) system may be a net public health good, the article recommends that policymakers address networks of unrelated bystanders, police, or relatives of the injured who transport injured persons from accident scenes to hospitals.[2] Put differently, public health scholars in India suggest that prehospital care is as interpersonal as it is infrastructural. They argue that the stakes of surviving traumatic injury may depend as much on *who* is doing the carrying as on *what* is doing the carrying. The terms of conveyance among people must cohere before any vehicle may move. Traffic depends on human carriers and therefore works through human relations.

Working with this social concept of traffic allows researchers to consider different remedies for the problem of the "second delay" in trauma care. The second delay is the time frame related to arriving at the appropriate facility to treat traumatic injury. It is a window of time that occurs after the "first delay," which is the time frame between the injury's occurrence and the decision to seek care (N. Roy et al. 2016). The second delay in trauma cases is defined by shock—and specifically hypovolemic shock caused by sustained blood loss from internal or external injuries. For both ambulances and hospitals, traffic on roads is clinically crucial during the second delay time frame.[3] The traffic that hinders trauma care during this time involves bystanders and the aggregate form of the urban public. It also disaggregates into carriers ranging from railway porters to ambulance drivers. The shock of the urban, realized through traumatic injury, must be understood as corporeal and interdependent in this light (see Geroulanos and Meyers 2018, 49).

Conveyance also can be a fruitful site to reframe conversations about the fault lines of urban mobility. In their work on automobile politics in the United States, anthropologist Lochlann Jain (2006) develops the notion of "kinetic subjectivity" to detail how American automobile industries and legal cultures endow cars with a sense of independence. Naturalizing this independence, Jain suggests, makes it difficult to stake claims on how relationally lethal cars can be when they injure others. In a similar vein, I wish to denaturalize the assumed automated capacity of mobility, which may gloss over the relational stakes of carrying. I hope to bring to the critical mobilities and infrastructure literature a clearer sense of who enables movement, in contrast to the tendency to focus on what enables movement (Thrift 2004). In other words, I am interested in how mobility emerges through relational kinetic subjectivities and how carrying shapes what Mimi Sheller (2004) terms "mobile publics" and what Arjun Appadurai (2000a) calls "mobile civil forms."[4] I wish to better understand who and what in the city make the city the ambulance service's best client.

Consider Dipen's case: a bystander ceases his own mobility—and perhaps his chance at a job by skipping the interview—in order to move an injured person ejected from a train toward a hospital. The man appeals to the humanity of the onlookers, foregrounding the problem of mobilizing an injured person for a seemingly static crowd. Such scenes may be fleeting, but they reveal the shifting political economies of carriage whose valuation may not easily fall into set oppositions between stop and go or between jam and flow.

The costs of ambulances depend on their actions. Private ambulances may transport patients from the scene of the accident to the hospital, or they may transport patients from one hospital to another. The public ambulance service—a venture that is a public-private partnership known as the 108 service based on the phone number one must dial to summon it—is a crucial public health development because it is free of cost. Crucial, that is, to the poor clients who are least likely to be able to bear the cost of private ambulances. It is also crucial to the service's investors, who see in emergency services the combination of unmet need coupled with high mortality and thus a significant and sustainable supply for a public-private partnership service that has only a few select conglomerate bidders for tenders, which guarantees a high success rate of winning bids.

This attractiveness owing to high volume may be limited to urban centers, where most calls originate. The free 108 service does not do interfacility transfers. Families who need transfers, whether for treatment or for diagnostics like a CT (computed tomography) scan, must hire a private ambulance, which can cost several thousand rupees. It was the norm, not the exception, that the patients in Central's trauma ward were moved from the site of injury to one hospital by the 108 service and then transferred to the trauma ward at Central in a private ambulance. On paper it might look as if the two forms of conveyance are the same—two ambulances—but their cost is absolutely different. Paying out of pocket for an ambulance sets up cascades of care decisions later on. Conveyance can quickly eat away a family's emergency reserves and affects how they confront costs down the line.

The 108 service began in 2005 in Andhra Pradesh, after which it was expanded to many other states. It launched in Maharashtra in 2014. Its primary role is to take clients to the nearest government hospital in relation to the location of the call—an especially important feature for trauma cases from traffic accidents, given the tight time frame in which resuscitation must occur. The 108 service has a multilayered structure and varies across India. Its first implementation in Andhra Pradesh was managed by the Emergency Management and Research Institute (EMRI), a private body funded through a registered society linked to Satyam Technologies Inc. (Chakraborty, Nair, and Dhawan 2009). As the service expanded after 2005, EMRI shifted into a public-private partnership model and received contributions from the government of Andhra Pradesh to fund more ambulances, wider coverage, and operations. In other states such as Gujarat, EMRI's operations began as, rather than developed into, a public-private partnership. This model, albeit with different players, is the model for Maharashtra, in which the state government Department of Health and Family Welfare initially provided the governing structure for the free 108 number, under the mandate of the National Rural Health Mission via the Union Ministry of Health and Family Welfare.

Unlike in several other states whose private partner is EMRI, Maharashtra's financial implementing partner—the party that controls the operation, coordination, and maintenance of the ambulances as well as the Pune-based call center—is the cleaning-service corporation BVG India Ltd. The UK-based Specialist Ambulance Service Ltd. works with BVG to contribute technical training and education. As the ambulance service has grown, BVG has also taken on training responsibilities, and ambulance clients will see BVG stitched onto a medic's shirt, suggesting a totalizing operation. Since 2017 the state has taken on the full responsibility for the public element of the public-private partnership. The state gradually increased its contributions as the central government's contributions decreased (PTI 2017). The labor arrangements for the 108 service fall under the Essential Services Maintenance Act, 1980, although, as Subramania Rajasulochana and Daya Maurya point out, "violation of contractual labour norms, denial of benefits and pay as mentioned in the contract have led to conflicts between the employees and the contracting company across various states . . . [which] . . . may increase the risk of medical errors and consequent loss of clinical quality of EMS" (2018, 2).[5]

Ambulances share qualities with other forms of clinical and public health shifts, such as the ways corporatized health-care structures in contemporary India put limits on responsibility and may "evacuate the political" (K. Sunder Rajan 2017). As Kaushik Sunder Rajan argues, this is because forms like corporate social responsibility ventures and public-private partnerships work on health through logics of win-win, naturalizing their interventions. They can withdraw their support and responsibility at will and can evade public accountability (238). Sunder Rajan suggests this is a problem of limits on democracy as much as it is a problem of health policy, because the features of corporatized health-care structures make it difficult to imagine or implement a relationship to a state. The challenge he poses is to imagine politics and democracy with the state still present alongside nonstate actors, even in spite of its frailties.

I want to take seriously this call to grapple with neoliberal forms of capital's displacement, limitation, and evacuation in health. To do so involves paying attention to qualities of movement and to the way the politics of these qualities reflect the status of ambulances in India's broader landscapes of health-care transition. Privately owned ambulances are common in Mumbai; they are owned and operated by local entities ranging from nongovernmental organizations (NGOs) to private companies to local political parties, the latter often adorned with pictures of the state minister, prime minister, or other political figures on their sides. Many large public hospitals and most private hospitals have their own ambulances as well, maybe one or two, but most public hospitals rely on other ambulance services to transport patients. With the 108 system, emergency is differentially distributed across public-private relations at the macro scale and across forms of gestural value more locally.

This occurs in part through spatial distribution. The 108 ambulances operate as vehicles of anticipation as much as vehicles of response. Many cluster around the train stations of the city's Central Line, one of three main railway lines (some do roam but always near to key train stations).[6] I begin at the railway station closest to the hospital. A routine emerges: I sit in the back of a parked ambulance and begin interviews with the driver. If the doctor is available, we chat. I ride a few times in the front of the ambulance, squished in, taking in the movements and nonmovements of traffic in response to the ambulance. This only occurs when there is not an active call. I do not ride when the ambulance must carry an injured person. This is purposeful. It is cramped inside the van, and every bit of space is necessary to perform resuscitation. I believe my presence could be a burden, specifically one that could drag processes that require less and not more obstruction. Frequently, at the scene of an accident, there can be uncertainty, confusion, and questions. Onlookers, colleagues, or family may wish to ride in the ambulance in the event of an emergency. It is simply inappropriate to observe and this means different ethnographic moves are necessary.[7]

I take the trauma ward as a comparison point in making this decision. In the trauma ward, I quickly learn how to get out of the way while doing something potentially useful. Often that something is communicative; I hold mobile phones to doctors' ears to call consults, my body serving as the conduit outside the sterile field. Ethnographic methods for me are often methods with getting out of the way as their baseline ethic. Getting out of the way seems impossible to navigate in a moving ambulance on an active call. There is nothing of value I think I can convey during an active call. So I sit in unmoving and empty ambulances, their back resuscitation areas transformed into scenes of reflection and anticipation. Before injury reaches the hospital, and across the stations of the city, lifelines of conveyance generate the social of social medicine, the public of public health, and the pre- of prehospital care.

––––––

Next station, Dadar. Dadar Station in the midafternoon is brisk, and trains spit people out onto the platform. Spring has started to escort out winter's remnants, and soon it will be premonsoon, with heat and humidity but no rain. I watch the stop and go: a train arrives from Uttar Pradesh, in the north; another one departs for Kerala, in the south. Teens gather around a mobile phone and catch up in sign language with someone via video chat. People ask each other questions: Where is the stationmaster's office? The bathroom? Platform 3? A voice speaks muffled announcements of arrivals and departures. A chalkboard of the railway worker trade union (Central Railway Mazdoor Sangh) displays the union's most recent discontents with the government. Overhead, CCTV cameras watch. The activity subdues in the minutes after the trains depart; it's as if the station is bleeding out.

Vivek, the driver or "pilot" of the ambulance, is shaded by the sari fabric against the windows that gives patients a modicum of privacy. He calls for chai and recalls his first day on the job. "I was there for the launch. These people from outside Mumbai came. That's when I started." The launch he mentions was the formal beginning of the public-private partnership ambulance service in Maharashtra. On March 1, 2014, the Maharashtra chief minister launched 161 ambulances down Marine Drive in central Mumbai. This began the work of a thousand ambulances supported by the state government that would provide emergency medical services to residents of Mumbai and its surrounding areas. "With the launch of EMS ambulances, we will save lives in the crucial golden hour," noted state health minister Suresh Shetty at the launch (see *Indian Express* 2014). Shetty, like many policymakers, framed the ambulance as a technology of accelerated conveyance. These ambulances could shorten delays in caring for trauma, especially during the first sixty minutes following injury, called the *golden hour* for its presumed influence on an injured person's survival.

Even the best of intentions and interventions is up against the temporality of traumatic injury, especially falling blood pressure from internal or external bleeding. Some forms of bleeding are more urgent than others in terms of their systemic effects (internal bleeding from trauma to the gut can be far more serious than bleeding from an amputated limb, for example, and takes longer to identify and address). The conditions for vulnerability depend on differences in the delay before treatment, not on absolute differences in injury. Yet these important differences in delay can be effaced in appeals to the golden hour and policies structured with it at their center.

Emergency medicine physicians often point out that the golden hour is at once a highly cited and often-unrealistic policy stance. It is also the butt of jokes by many of the doctors in Central's trauma ward. Sometimes the ward would be informed of a traumatic injury case that was on its way—this was the exception rather than the norm, but advanced notice did happen occasionally. Estimated times of arrival were fluid, owing to traffic. "Golden day! Golden year!" one trauma surgeon would joke when treatment delays kept extending. The golden hour seemed like a fantasy derived from medicine's desire for protocols and obedient substrates, as if the city could be ignored, as if the ambulances could fly.[8]

This recent ambulance system intensifies a shift toward public-private partnerships as a mode of health-care provision in Mumbai. By 2018 the state of Maharashtra's ambulance service had grown quickly, and so ambulance response time quickened for those injured in Mumbai. Frequently, stories circulate about waiting for an ambulance because it was stuck in traffic. A private ambulance service may charge thousands of rupees to move a person, while putting them in a taxi or rickshaw costs far less, and transport by the police (fraught as this is) is ostensibly free.

Since the time of its founding, Central Hospital's trauma ward has received patients arriving in ambulances. However, during my fieldwork the trauma ward began coordinating with the 108 ambulance service.[9] I begin to see the 108 ambulance service coordinator, Prasad, in Central's trauma ward; the trauma team hopes that regular meetings with him will smooth out the logistics involved in patient transport. Prasad and I often walk around the hospital campus and take in the ambulances coming, going, and parking. I ask if I could spend more time in off-duty ambulances, alongside my regular fieldwork in the trauma ward. Prasad arranges for this to happen.

Now I am in the back of the ambulance, and Vivek inhabits it like an office, one of its guises when patients are not present. He speaks briskly in between sips of tea.

> Before this work, I was a municipal garbage collector. During that job, four or five of us together thought about making a difference for the country, doing good work, because accidents kept happening, and the police were the first ones to come in that area. When there was an accident, the public didn't rise up [and help the injured] because at first it wasn't allowed, because of a High Court case. But we thought that helping the injured was a good thing. It would make a difference. With just a free phone call, I could take an injured person and help anyone. I'm not a Catholic, but I believe in Jesus. I visited the ashram [Mother Teresa's ashram, where his wife and mother volunteered]. I gained some knowledge, so I said to some friends, something good is going on there, it's making a difference for the poor, so I left the garbage-collecting work and started doing this work.

Like many of the ambulance drivers I spoke with, Vivek had expertise in driving large vehicles such as garbage trucks, school buses, tourist buses, and company carpool vans. If he could skillfully navigate Mumbai's traffic in a large vehicle, he could learn to drive an ambulance, convey medicine into the street, pick up the injured, and carry them to the hospital. His invocation of the word *public* to assert that "the public didn't rise up" to help at the accident scene draws on the English loanword used to mean a mass of people in conversational Hindi in Mumbai.[10] In the context of an accident scene, *public* refers to the spectating crowd that may also be witnesses. Witnessing the accident may be key for downstream legal action, but from Vivek's perspective, the immediate possibilities of movement constitute the politics of the public, because people may go from inert to irate in a moment. Witnessing can arc across knowing something, saying you know something, and taking action because you know something.

Vivek highlights the ways in which formalized ambulances must contend with the informalities of the street, a matter that also shapes how doctors in the hospital critique the work of the ambulance. Many contend that although ambulances succeed at connectivity, they are less assiduous when it comes to resuscitation. Private capital allows the vehicles to look good on the outside, but what is happening inside? This raises a key question for public health researchers of whether or not it is better (and faster) to simply have the police or a rickshaw or taxi take the injured to hospitals (Bhalla et al. 2019). The critique here is that if ambulances are only conveying patients but not doing resuscitation work, then they are no different from any other form of conveyance, and, in fact, their large size makes them a liability in traffic in comparison to motorcycles or rickshaws.

One doctor in Central's trauma ward would joke, "What's the difference between an ambulance and a hearse? The color!" He described a pair of photos, one of the back of an ambulance and one of the back of a hearse, both empty, a diptych of death on wheels. Even after regulations in Mumbai prohibited ambulances from transporting persons who are dead at the accident scene, I would still hear the joke in the hospital. Reaffirming color as the critical difference between the vehicles presumes that death moves through the city's transport infrastructures; the figurative body of the city is as much a carried corpse as it is a pedestrian. It is part of the currency of dark humor that sustains difficult work, and it also points out that carrying is not the same thing as caring.[11]

Another critique of ambulances among hospital staff centers on the perceived inability or unwillingness of ambulance medics to insert IV lines and perform airway interventions. The ambulances may be accelerating the passage through the city, but they are not decelerating the threat of death in the injured patient. The trauma ward doctors often argue that IV insertion is easy to learn and highly impactful, whereas airway interventions require much more training (Khajanchi et al. 2019). The body might move to the hospital, but as for life, that was uncertain.

Consequently, what gets counted as care inside the ambulance depends on staffing, training, and equipment. In Maharashtra an ambulance may have a doctor and a driver, or it may just be the driver alone. In the past decade, Indian cities and states have invested in basic and advanced life-support techniques, the professionalization of paramedics, standardized equipment in a networked ambulance service, and specialization of ambulance services in that network (such as cardiac ambulances or maternity-care ambulances). These developments refigure the historical legacy of ambulances in India as forms of mobile medical outreach and as planned extensions of primary care, just as much as they are forms of on-demand emergency response.[12]

A third critique of ambulances centers on the crowds that tend to surround the accident scene: the public. One ambulance doctor I speak with, Dr. R, does not like it when the public gets involved at an accident scene. She feels that many people in Mumbai would simply put an injured person in an autorickshaw or taxi, or, as is quite commonly the case, the police would take them. It is better, she thinks, to leave an injured person alone and have a properly trained medical professional, a paramedic or doctor, attend to the injury. Moving someone with fractures and spinal injuries specifically could do more harm than good. Immobility of the body, more than the temporality of shock, is the key in this framing.

Medical expertise is, of course, variegated. For every trauma surgeon at Central who would critique the resuscitation work of ambulances, there was another who would say that it didn't matter at all what happened in the ambulance. "Just get them here," one surgeon says. Let the crowds facilitate carrying the injured to the hospital and then let the specialists do their work. The risk of spinal injury is lower, in his estimation, than the risk of dying from the consequences of shock owing to delayed care. But enabling crowds to do carrying work requires convincing them. He worries about a commonly held public sentiment that getting involved in an accident will automatically ensnare an involved bystander in a police case, and potentially even a court case, a form of legal traffic that might continue for years. Tensions evolve between the figures of the Good Samaritan and the idle and indifferent public that imbue these ideas.[13] It's a matter of trade-offs, of carrying the injured so that the injury does not carry them.

Next station, Sion. "I didn't fear seeing the blood," Vivek says another afternoon. He's seen injured bodies for a long time. "I had experience. When I was a child, I saw people fall from the train onto the tracks, and the *hamaals* [railway porters] who took them. I saw these things. I had a neighbor who broke both his legs and one hand [in a train accident], I was around nine years old. I sat on the corner, and I saw it all. The 108 ambulance wasn't around then. Two *hamaals* took him. They put him in a wagon and carried him away." As a child, Vivek observed how moving the injured made their treatment possible. He watched railway porters carry bodies, and years later, he watches them do the work of carrying. Who were these luggers of luggage who now lugged bodies?

Railway porters, or railway *hamaals*, are regular features of the casualty and trauma wards of the hospital in cases of railway accidents.[14] They often accompany the police. *Hamaals* as a class of workers are carriers of goods, and *hamaals* who specifically move bodies enact mobility that is relational and somatic. Their work also elucidates structural shifts in public health-care services in urban India, particularly the ways that the casualization of care labor interfaces with privatization's demands (Baru 2017).

Most *hamaals* I speak with identify themselves using the term *hamaal*, or, as one man explained to me, a *railway accident hamaal*. It is men's work. I ask if there are women who work as *hamaals* and am told this does not happen. Some *hamaals* I meet have been working the job for decades, like Rama, who arrives at Central's casualty ward one evening with a dead-on-arrival case of a patient run over by the local train. As he waits for the casualty medical officer to stamp the death papers, Rama explains that he has carried injured bodies for forty years. Moving along the tracks to collect body parts makes the work very risky, he says ("bahut risk ka kaam hai"). But the police who pay him his fee of 400 rupees per body (around US$5.00) have a rule concerning his (informal yet quite structured) compensation: no full body, no money. He moves his hands against his legs in sawing motions to explain: "This [piece] is broken off, that [one] is broken off, and I collect them. They remind me of mutton pieces" (yeh tukḍa, yeh tukḍa, ikatha karo; mutton ka piece yaad aata hai). The deeply carnal dimension of this labor, and its possibilities for remuneration, unfolds through carrying, piece by piece.[15]

I begin paying attention to *hamaals* outside of the hospital. I go to railway stations, starting at Sion Station, at the bend of a main road that traces one of Mumbai's largest neighborhoods, Dharavi. I ask the staff in the ambulance parked behind the station whether they work with the station's *hamaal*, and they tell me to find Lalit, who sits in the station's breezeway.

I am momentarily confused, because the man they are pointing me to is the station's shoe cobbler.

Lalit sits with his wooden box in the patch of open space beside the automated ticket vending machines, the box neatly arranged with shoe polish, brushes, and extra laces. As a cobbler (*mochi*), he is a key figure of Mumbai's railways stations, shining shoes and patching up punctures and rips in the short minutes between trains. There are other constant figures of the station too, the men who wear red caps to signal their role as luggage porters, the men I might assume to be carriers of persons in addition to being carriers of suitcases. But bodily conveyance work distributes in complex ways; the *hamaal* who carries luggage may not necessarily be the *hamaal* who carries the injured. In Lalit's case, his work is twofold. He shines and repairs shoes as train passengers rush to and from work. He carries dead and injured bodies as accidents unfold and the stationmaster issues a call over the station's loudspeakers. He polishes shoes, and then when there is an accident, he is a first responder.

Usually, a railway station's speakers transmit prerecorded announcements of whether the approaching train is late or not, what its destination is, and whether it's a slow or fast train (stopping at all stations or just a few).[16] When there is an accident, the recorded voice stops, and the stationmaster speaks in real time, calling out for a *hamaal*, a railway police constable, and a stretcher. If an ambulance with a doctor and driver are present, they respond too. The call is Lalit's signal to shift from cobbling work to carrying work. He will take the injured person from the tracks and move them onto the stretcher. The stretcher goes into the ambulance, if one is present; otherwise, either the police take the injured person in their van, or someone hails a taxi or a rickshaw. Lalit will often stay with the injured person all the way to the hospital, where he will wait until the police paperwork reaches an acceptable level of completion. Then he can get paid. Conveyance entails accompaniment, with the rules for payment aligned in parallel. Lalit feels that tempo and rhythm are problems at the accident scene, too, before the hospital comes into the picture. Too often, bystanders do nothing when an accident occurs. "The public just stands watching," he says (public bas dekhti rehti). The urban public is constituted through both movement and stasis, not one or the other, and what matters is his position amid this complex dance. A public can be moved to response, but response is a dependent form.[17]

Lalit describes his position informally as a *hamaal* but formally as a *railway polish karamchari*, a railway (shoe) polish worker. He became a cobbler in 1965. A few years into the job, a railway police constable asked him to lift a body from the platform. It was an attempted suicide case, with multiple amputations, the man's arms and legs scattered in different places because of the train's impact. When he saw the body on the tracks, Lalit was scared, but the pressure to earn extra money for his family was enough to make him agree to do the lifting. He began doing it regularly soon after. He earned a hundred rupees for each body in the late 1960s, an amount that has increased to four hundred rupees today. He does bodily multiplication tables and estimates he has handled fifty thousand dead bodies since 1970.

At first he was unsure about the work, but soon enough, he became habituated to it ("adat lag gayi"). It is unremarkable now, Lalit says, and it earns him at least five thousand rupees per month, which he sends back in remittances to his family in rural Bihar. The job has transformed his family's home into a permanent brick (*pucca*) structure, paid for the education of all five of his children, and secured the marriages of his three daughters. He comes to the station when he pleases and leaves when he wants. It has been a pathway to the good life (*achchha zindagi*) for him and his family, he says. The ticket sales staff at the station want him to apply for higher posts in the railways, jobs like clerk and ticket collector that as permanent salaried government jobs can move someone toward class ascendance. He refuses; he likes the flexibility of his job.

However much Lalit found his work unremarkable, he also kept it secret. No one in his home village knew that he was a *hamaal*. But ten years ago, he was in Bihar visiting family. One day while they were working in the fields, he noticed a foul smell in the air and began walking around nearby homes to trace its origin. He arrived at the home of an elderly woman who lived by herself and was adamant that the neighbors break down the door, and they did, revealing the old woman lying dead inside, her body decomposing. Amid the questions that circulated around the cause of her death, someone questioned Lalit's hunch: How did he know to break open the door? How could Lalit smell death? He felt he had to open up to his family. He showed them photos on his mobile phone of the bodies he handled. He explained the smell of bodies from the train station back in Mumbai and explained how he worked with the police and the ambulance service. "They were surprised, but they praised my courage."

In both his discussion of the flexibility of his job in the city, and his revelation of the elderly woman's corpse in the village, there is a certain silence in Lalit's account on the matter of caste. Perhaps affirming the connections between the work of the *mochi* (historically connected to Dalit communities of leatherworkers) and the workings of the government emergency response service may blunt the stigmatization of caste-specific forms of labor (Gold 2017, 50). In certain ways, Lalit affirms that his work is no longer simply about contact with the dead and injured but rather is about contact with a governmental apparatus of emergency response. Caste can affirm the common sense that certain bodies should stay immobile, like the cobbler who sits and shines shoes for the male commuter who will hurry onto the train, or that some bodies deserve to be moved aside, such as women who may not have the protections of dominant caste, class, religion, and age status to assert their stability in and around the train (Phadke 2007; Phadke, Khan, and Ranade 2011). The caste work of carrying must be understood in relation to these forms of casteism that always inflect public transport, wherein bodies are invested with different terms of mobility.

Lalit sees this work in terms of a complicated relation to the formalized 108 ambulance service. Sometimes, he suggests, it would be easier to hand off an injured body to the police rather than to the 108 service, because if he joins an ambulance call, sometimes he must wait hours to give a statement to the hospital and the police. If the injured person has no clear identity and no family members are at the hospital, he might be kept even longer to shuttle paperwork back and forth. As Lalit found himself moving the injured into 108 ambulances more often, his carrying was part of the movements of health-sector reform, of medicalized mobility.

Next station, Kurla. One bank follows the next on the smooth roads of the Bandra Kurla Complex, a neighborhood of reclaimed land also known as the BKC. The BKC offers incomparable velocity on its flat, well-paved roads. It is primarily a commercial area; poor-quality roads simply won't suit the mobility needs of the global capital centers of banks and pharmaceutical companies. Kurla Station is one of the busiest hubs of the city's train system, supplying the offices, embassies, banks, and private hospitals with workers who cannot afford taxis, Ubers, or carpooling.

I sit upright on the gurney in the ambulance behind Kurla Station; my shoes touch the ground, and my notebook lies on my lap. I feel around in my mind for a sketch of the person who sat there before me. Someone was injured, lying flat, no ground to feel under their feet. They saw the ceiling of the van, not the sides and the windows. It was the same gurney, but it carried someone different, the vinyl rippling out from under the supine body, imprinting blood and story. The drivers would hose the van down eventually, but the imprints persist, as the ambulance carries the memories of cases past.

Dr. Y and the driver, Shiv, are finishing their shift. My arrival prompts them to reflect on a case we saw yesterday at Central—he and Shiv brought the patient into the trauma ward, where I was sitting at the main desk. It was an alleged attempted suicide, a man who jumped in front of a moving train, resulting in a bilateral lower-limb amputation. None of us in the trauma ward knew it was an attempted suicide; later, someone in the ward sent around a WhatsApp video clip about the event. A bystander had captured the event on their phone, and the WhatsApp clip alternated between this handheld footage from the bystander's camera and excerpts from CCTV footage from inside the station's control room. Dr. Y, Shiv, and I reflect on what the video showed and what it didn't show: the moment when the man's wife arrived at the trauma ward, and how, just before she walked in, the doctors covered him with a sheet from the chest down, in an attempt to dampen the blow of the scene.

Now, a day later, we sit in the ambulance and sip boxes of Mango Frooty. Dr. Y and Shiv debate attempted and realized suicides, attributing them to people with broken hearts, experiences of abuse, or too much family and work pressure to excel. Striving can no longer be contained, and someone seeks out what is possibly the most visible node of life in the city—the train station—to end things, a public sign of aspiration's limits (Chua 2014). Dr. Y reenacts yesterday's event on the bench of the stretcher, using his water bottle and his phone. The water bottle is the train, and the phone is the man, and the train hits the man and then reverses so that *hamaals* can pull him out. We're all sickened by it. Dr. Y is also angry. All the commuters saw the event happen, he says, but they did nothing. It was an inert public, unmoved, uncaring, more invested in spectatorship than assistance. It reminds him of the first case he ever saw as an ambulance doctor, another traumatic limb amputation, and he had to do the carrying alone because no one else would help, an event that nauseated him for days. He had served in the navy as a doctor and ran his own clinic for several years in Pune but had never been so struck by a case.

Shiv, the driver, also feels lingering effects of the cases. He was sleeping in the ambulance one night, early in his first year on the job. Before driving the ambulance, he had worked as a tourist driver; it wasn't the driving that was different, he says, it was the interactions connected to the driving. He was in Byculla, by a hospital, when he became a bit frightened by a ghost ("night ko main thoḍa dar gaya tha bhoot se"). There was a patient who had died the same day. "That day, an old person died on the way to the hospital. Later on, I felt that he would come into the ambulance, so I was frightened a bit." The scene stayed with him, like the image of the body of his cousin who had committed suicide years back.

"When did this fear stop?"

"Two years after [I began] working, it stopped."

His friends thought the ambulance had ghosts, at first. "My friends would say, 'You carry dead bodies, and you must be living with ghosts.'" His family at first thought he conveyed dead bodies too. "They feared the job initially, they would tell me to stop the work, and then I told them, 'I don't take dead bodies, we don't even look at dead bodies.'" He found the accusation of ferrying the dead understandable; even he had felt scared, before he started the job, whenever he would hear an ambulance siren. His family had mostly become habituated to his work, and some of his friends praised the work he did as good, because he worked and helped out in emergency situations. Amid the praise, though, there were still challenges. Shiv often speaks about the imprints of blood. "Bleeding is a problem. There are no safety precautions for us. The problem is cleaning the blood and also doing the driving work." He doesn't want to clean. He hates cleaning. He was always cleaning the ambulance of dust, trying to find new angles to park it that would accumulate the least sun (to temper the heat inside), the least dust, the least maintenance. Each disturbance from the world outside meant more cleaning. His shirt was clean. It was gray, with the 108 logo, "Humanity Ahead," stitched on the front.

The situation of injury can force one person to work with another to enable movement. I ask Shiv if he has formed any relationships with the *hamaals* as a result of working together. "We talk only when the patient comes," he says. "Otherwise we don't talk with them. Those *hamaals* aren't always very professional; they live like people living on the roadside. They don't talk much, and it's not necessary to be close to them." *It's not necessary to be close to them*: class and caste work themselves out through the proximity demands of moving an injured body. Shiv often expresses contempt for beggars (*beggar log*) and pavement dwellers (*sidewalli*), which in his taxonomy includes the *hamaals*. This strikes me as a notable and expansive sense of *sidewalli*, literally, "the people on the side" or "the people living on the roadside," a term that can refer to both pavement dwellers and beggars. Some of the ambulance staff I speak with paint pictures of cooperation between the paramedics and the *hamaals*, with stories of shared aims and smooth handoffs. Shiv paints a different picture: he doesn't care for the

hamaals because they are *sidewalli*, and their unpredictable habits of movement make emergency response unnecessarily complicated.

One reading of this dismay might be that Shiv articulates casteist sen-
timents. I would also suggest that his expression points to the ways caste
comes to matter through comparative mobilities. To Shiv, *sidewalli* include
people who are immobile on the roadside, mostly, but who may drift into
train stations as well. The work of the ambulance is largely premised on
moving toward a stationary injured body and then moving the body
into the ambulance for transport to the hospital. Who gets to move and
who must lie still are matters of clinical protocol. Simultaneously, these
are matters of caste. Drifting people and agitated masses complicate the
frame.

Yet Shiv also acknowledges that *hamaals, sidewalli*, and *beggar log*
maintain a fixed presence at train stations. Consequently, they can also be
available witnesses for the police. They see things. And even if they don't
see, precisely, they possess a certain authority over other bystanders, in
part because of their (perceived or real) entrenched presence and in part
because they are already involved with police and generally this relation is
one of being paid for body-part collection. Being paid to be an informant
can sit relatively easily in this relationship, much more comfortably than in
the kind of relation many commuters wish to have with police.[18] Conveyance, authority, and mobility can converge.

Just as Shiv does not like roadside people because they slow down
the ambulance's work, he also expresses a dislike of roadside patients. He
doesn't like the way the ambulance could be called to get rid of them from
a particular corner or storefront. In later conversations I learn that his
dislike extends toward the store owners or other presumably middle-class
persons attempting to rid public space of nuisances. Roadside patients
are dirty, he says, and they also are society's desired objects of disposal.
"Some people casually call the ambulance, but it's not an emergency case.
These roadside patients are dirty, and if we take them to the hospital, they
stay for two days and then go back to the same place. Their smell doesn't
leave the ambulance and is off-putting for good patients, and it becomes
unpleasant to us too, sitting in the ambulance."[19] The ebb and flow of bad
patients and good patients inflects the rhythms of life he has crafted at the
station through interactions with the man who brings chai, the man who
runs the canteen/snack shop, and regular commuters.

These moral qualities worked out through carrying—good service and
dirty service, good patients and bad patients—are foundational to the ways

that social class and caste get produced partly through an ambulance's trajectory. Decisions about where to take a patient are intimately tied to estimations of a patient's social position. The ambulance is not just conveying the injured, pushing saline, and stopping bleeding. As it carries the wounded, it conveys social inequality.

_____

Next station, Mumbai Central. All this time in ambulances at train stations makes me wonder about the trains.

Vinod wants to meet at the train station depot where the trains resupply. The railway tracks bifurcate the building, a warehouse split in two. He has retired from his work as a local train conductor (a "motorman"), and the depot has an office where he visits his former colleagues and where he is comfortable chatting.

Vinod studied physics and mechanical engineering and began driving the local train in 2001. He drove trains during the 2005 floods, the 2006 bomb blasts, and several other disasters in the city. He is not a doctor, and he is not an ambulance driver. But for decades, he drove the local train, and he knows much about conveyance in the context of injury.

New motormen on the local train apprentice under another driver for at least one year before they are allowed to drive alone. During his apprenticeship Vinod remembers his first accident experience:

> As I saw my first accident, I couldn't even bear to look. I mean, I was very scared and didn't go to look. It was evening, it happened around 8:30–9:00 p.m. It was some *hamaal*. The train dashed him. I didn't see and did not even go to see; I was so scared at that time. After that, just like that, [seeing accidents] became a habit. I learned that if it is your time on the line, then you have to go. Only if your time is up, then you meet with an accident.[20] A lot of people get saved. We save them. I mean, by sounding the horn or applying the brakes, and the train stops at the proper time. Such people get saved. It is like this, even with those who are unaccounted for, like drug addicts who have no one to ask about them. Even they get saved like this. We pull the brakes at the right time, and they move to the side.

In Vinod's account here, the line is at once existential and spatio-material. It is the line of life, this life, this incarnation: "your time on the line." And it is the space of the railway line too. At stake is what Vinod calls "line crossing": how persons both as passengers and as pedestrians come into relation with the train, through collision and through collision's aversion.

He recalls his first months sitting in the front of the train, his hand on the emergency switch (called the *dead man's control*), ready to stop the train in an instant. He navigated people and cattle crossing the tracks, especially at night (people, he says, who were mostly *beggar type* or *pagal aadmi* ["crazy people"]). Night is difficult for driving, because one's field of vision is not clear. One does not so much drive the train, he explains, as one sees the train through: the driver is supposed to look only at the track and the signals along the track. Anything that interrupts that field of vision amplifies the possibility of an accident on the driver's part. Accidents often happen when people fall out of the train, though, and these are not things he can see from up front. Instead, motormen rely on people pulling the emergency chain in the carriages or banging on the door of the driver's compartment. "The public makes noise: 'Someone has fallen! Someone has fallen!' They make a lot of noise" (awaaz kiya public: 'gir gaya! gir gaya!' itna awaaz). The public's noise is his signal to stop the train. This all occurs in compressed time frames. The train halts at most stations for only twenty seconds before the guard on the platform flags the motorman that the passengers have alighted and the train can move on.

The accidents continued once he began driving independently:

> My first accident happened at Elphinstone Road. An old man was crossing the tracks, and he fell down, and his legs were cut off. At first, I was a bit scared: Should I get down to see or not? But then I followed the procedure we have to follow and informed the guard. The guard informed the nearest railway station under whose jurisdiction the accident falls, through the control room. The stationmaster of that station came. Then I gathered the courage to go see. I saw that his legs were cut. Time was passing by, yet the ambulance had not arrived. It took some time. The people who were with him were panicking. They were asking us to put him in a vehicle.

Vinod was able to stop the train, get down, go to the injured man, and work with the others to untangle him from underneath the train. The mobility of the train stopped, so that the injured man could be carried.

The critical difference of the train, he says, is not the difference in the presence or absence of accidents, since accidents are normal. Rather, the difference at stake is sensorial, a sense forged between momentum and braking, and between speedup and slowdown. Vinod constantly would calculate the relationship between his desires and attempts to brake and their effects on the train. If someone crossed the tracks in a rush or a suicide attempt, should he brake suddenly? In the unlikely event that the train would slow down enough to avoid hitting the person on the track, what would the sudden braking do to all the people riding the train? Might it throw them out of the open doors? The critical differences between rush and slowdown reveal how the city's rhythms crystallizes comparative bodily risks. For Vinod, accidents and urban life are coterminous. His account draws attention to how the rupture of an accident changes the city's fabric through carrying. Train conductors are conveyors of the public but in an instant can be the conveyors of injured bodies.

I realize my questions to him are falling into the very trap that I set out to critique. He has so many stories of accidents and says he is utterly used to them, and I have difficulty finding words to form questions that don't begin with assumptions of exceptionality. My words struggle to talk about accidents as normal. I ask about "memorable" accidents and events that stand out in his mind. He corrects me. Accidents are part of life for a motorman, he says, and they are part of the city; they cannot be thought apart from it ("alag se nahin hai"). Bodies and infrastructures are both matters of relation. The train is the city, and so are the bodies involved in making life amid injury. These threads are inseparable, he says: "I am part of Mumbai's lifeline."

———

Next station, Wadala. Vivek is on duty, and the ambulance is parked outside Wadala Station. I never ask for it, but often the ambulance driver would switch on the air-conditioning when we sit in the back. Vivek doesn't. He likes to crack open the van's sliding windows. It is still a hotbox inside. After an hour, my notebook is sticky from sweat. He decides we need juice to deal with the heat. "Why do you think the accidents are increasing?" I ask. He squeezes his juice box down to the last bits. "Some people are going to work, some people wear headphones," he ventures. People don't pay attention to oncoming cars or the train. But it is difficult to pin down one cause. It is like the juice we drink, he says. "How can you separate the water from the fruit essence?" Fate, good or bad, mixed with the trappings of injurious infrastructure, is similarly difficult to piece apart.

One thing he is sure of, though, is that he does not like public hospitals. Regard about conveyance cuts both ways; even as I hear critiques about the 108 service from the trauma ward staff, I also hear certain disinclinations toward the public, government hospital from the 108 staff. This is especially around the more common but less-resourced neighborhood-level secondary hospitals that tend to be closer to the accident scenes, in contrast to better-resourced but fewer in number hospitals like Central with dedicated trauma units.

The ambulance's destination can also be a vortex, snagging ambulance staff in bureaucratic machinations and taking them away from their work of maintaining the ambulance to anticipate the next accident. Many ambulance drivers worry about scarcity of medical supplies in smaller hospitals. "Not a single government hospital is good in Mumbai," Vivek declares. "They make us roam around for around one to two hours, and only then will they take the patient on a bed. This is a very bad thing." He summarizes Mumbai's public hospitals as places of "dirty service" (ganda service), with few available clean stretchers.

Vivek's critique of hospitals connects to a broader sensibility about the relationship between movement and mass publics. He frequently talks about the problems of the public. With anyone connected to medicine, the word *public* can be an adjectival shorthand for a public hospital, as in a government hospital (*public hospital*; also *sarkari hospital*). The 108 ambulance service policy is that the ambulance will take an injured person to the nearest government hospital. This is for affordability reasons but also for the related problems of admission. Legally, a private hospital can refuse admission, but a public hospital cannot. In practice, however, a public hospital may not have the available resources—like a ventilator—to support a patient, and if the patient is stable, the hospital doctors will ask the ambulance to take the patient to another government facility. If the patient is not stable, they will be admitted and treated with the resources available. Public is the destination, and it marks uncertainty about stability, always containing within it the possibility for more movements and distractions and lethal delays.

Here the *pre-* in *prehospital care* is public not only as public health expertise but also in the ways the movements of the mass public and the ambulance come into relation to the hospital. Moving the injured may be a public good and a public responsibility: onlookers should take action and help in some ways. Yet the public can also get in the way or at minimum may pose another layer of interaction for paramedics to confront. The politics of urban public culture under conditions of pervasive injury materializes through habits of dependent and embodied movements and mobilizations.[21]

As traumatic injury transforms infrastructures through different orders of embodied mobility and immobility, conveyance reveals the instabilities of this transformation, because carrying both relies on and produces social differentiation. My aim in this chapter has been to emphasize embodied, interpersonal forms of carrying, to detail precisely who puts events in motion for someone who is critically injured, how that might happen, and to what ends. Urban mobility "is a complex of institutions that bear on the social and affective relations between individuals and notions of self, family, and caste," Rashmi Sadana notes (2018, 54; also see Amrute 2015; Bedi 2018; S. Benjamin and Bhuvaneswari 2001). Attention to conveyance sheds light on how individuals come into mobility relations around injury, through connections of carrying.

Conveyance is also a site to apprehend infrastructural vulnerability. Infrastructures "are made from within relation" (Berlant 2016, 393; Finkelstein 2019), and this chapter has demonstrated how conveyance materializes infrastructural transition. Relationships of conveyance constitute what Lawrence Cohen has termed *clinical mobility*, which he defines as "the extent to which institutionalized practices of therapeutics organize or interrupt the movement of persons or populations" (2013a, 213). Cohen sketches a historical shift between the 1950s and the 1980s, as transnational and state efforts extended the clinic out of the hospital to India's generalized poor masses through health camps and public health campaigns. Cohen tracks India's promise of a "health utopia"—the promise of health for all—and argues that the utopia can be achieved only by the clinic's movement, and consequently the politics of public health in India must be understood as mobility politics. In a related vein, I have considered prehospital care for trauma as a promise of mobility forged in the time-space after the accident and before arrival at the hospital. I have focused specifically on the intersubjective situations of carrying that make trauma's first stages of mobility cohere, across the spatial social forms of the city. These situations are as elemental to trauma medicine as to urban sociality.

In a sense, the ambulance in India constitutes a health utopia, in part because of its ability to move between the worlds inside and outside of the hospital. It draws technology and medicine closer to sites of injury outside of the hospital, and delivers the injured to hospital spaces. It mobilizes and demobilizes. The ambulance becomes the means of addressing the problem (getting someone to the hospital) and, potentially, the solution itself (maybe some saline in the ambulance will help). This is premised on forms outside the car, like vehicular traffic and human publics, that part, give way, and offer passage by treating the ambulance as something exceptional rather than as just another vehicle. Traffic, onlookers, cars, and other obstacles might make movement challenging, but the ambulance can cut through. It expands clinical space outward from the hospital into the city and then back to the hospital again. It offers a clinic on wheels. Ambulances promise connection with a difference, because ideally there is an attempt at resuscitation inside the van as it shifts the injury to a site of treatment.

No longer should a man have to forgo his commute or his job interview to stop and carry someone when they become injured. Instead, trained paramedics will arrive and mobilize the injured—carefully—toward the hospital, in a vehicle equipped with things that might save their life, like drugs and a siren. This is the promise of conveyance and this promise poses a double bind: one must move for life, but too many people attempting to move creates traffic, which impedes the movement of resuscitation. Traffic is baffling in this way; how can so much stuckness deliver one to the possibility of living? Carrying someone, dealing with traffic, getting to the hospital: it can require an angel to manage the city in order to make trauma's treatment possible and to save a life. Perhaps as a *hamaal* might, I find myself attempting to pick up the pieces of these stories but do not get to choose the order in which I find them, as the lifelines of conveyance scatter before converging at the hospital.

On every trauma ward admission sheet, there is a space for information marked as *b/b*—shorthand for *brought by*. For those who arrive of their own accord, the sheet will simply read "b/b self." Conveyance moves people into medicine; the doctor-patient relation is preceded by being brought by someone. How medicine knows the patient, marked in the history of the file, is tied up with how the patient moves into clinical space. Over the years I would look at the admission sheets, fixated on the "b/b": brought by self, brought by sister, brought by police, brought by a fellow commuter, brought by the ambulance. Moved by someone else.

2 Shifting

THE LIFELINES OF TRIAGE

"Accidents happen." Mr. Karve confronts his dilemma in a voice both distant and edgy. Two hours ago, a car collided with the autorickshaw carrying Mr. Karve's wife, their ten-year-old son, and the family's housemaid, a woman in her twenties named Usha. Usha is in the ICU. The wife and son are in the casualty ward at Maitri Hospital, and they are stable. Mrs. Karve knows that the car was white and that it emerged from nowhere at full speed. She and her son are injured but not grievously; they wait in the queue for treatment. Their bodies remained inside the rickshaw as it somersaulted across the road, a miracle of containment. "Complete tumble," she says.

The story is different for Usha, who tumbled incompletely out of the rickshaw and hit the pavement headfirst. The casualty medical officer suspects both head and blunt abdominal trauma and orders emergency intubation. That means a shift elsewhere in the hospital. An orderly and an intern roll her gurney across the hospital courtyard into the summer air, up a ramp, into an elevator, and down a corridor to the ICU. An hour later, Usha remains unconscious with poor vitals and as-yet-unknown neurological damage. She requires immediate imaging for the possible traumatic brain injury, but the hospital does not have a working CT machine at this time. A new machine has been on order for several years now. The ward's supervising doctor has engaged in a multiyear lobbying effort with local politicians to question why the municipality took the money for the equipment from the hospital's budget, yet no machine has arrived.

In the impasse around the necessary-but-not-available-here CT scan, the doctors instruct Mr. Karve that Usha's best option for a CT scan lies in a larger, tertiary-level hospital several kilometers away. That hospital has working facilities for CT and also for trauma care. *Shift her*, they say. *Shift karo.*[1] *Shift karo* is the English-inflected Hindi imperative command to move a person or a thing. It means "shift him, her, or it," and in a hospital, the body is often its object.

Shift here means that Usha's body would be reconfigured for transfer and moved. Nurses would disconnect her from monitors in the ICU and lay her arms by her side. A resident doctor would squeeze an Ambu bag over her mouth, to keep her oxygen saturation up. He'd keep an eye on her blood pressure too, as it has not been stable. Orderlies would lift her body from the ICU bed onto a steel gurney and then wheel her down the corridor, down the elevator, back outside, into an arranged ambulance, and into the stop-and-go of Mumbai's roads. Shifting Usha is medically important, and her shift might also open space in the casualty ward for someone else. The bodies moving between beds are always interrelated, and the spaces between them shrink and expand like paper-doll chains.

Doctors and nurses share varying guesstimates of the time required to reach the private hospital: *Thirty minutes. An hour. If the driver knows good shortcuts, maybe forty-five.*

Mr. Karve hears Usha's treatment rendered as spasms through tangled urban infrastructures, and that a driver's street smarts might determine her survival. He hears that after all the shifting just to get her to the hospital, Usha still should keep moving, a reminder that the story may not stop when the rickshaw halts or when people pass through the casualty ward's doors. And he hears the underside of shifts too: traffic is inescapable, and in order for medicine to make Usha live, it would return her to the traffic from whence she came.

He replies by invoking something that he believes will *not* budge: the obligations of patronage for families in India with domestic servants. "She is like a daughter to us," Mr. Karve says, gesturing in her direction with a hand wave that gathers her into the fold of domesticity that so often imprints the clinical worlds of India (V. Das 2015). "We know her [natal] family, and we've known her for a decade. We will do anything, whatever it costs." "Anything," however, encompassed the impossibilities of traffic, and only shifts could open up a space for survival.

If triage was like a flowchart, then things would look like this: propulsive forces create traumatic injuries. From the street, cases move to the public hospital casualty ward. The casualty ward sorts out the major trauma cases and sends them to the trauma ward, either at the same hospital or at a different facility, but only if the patient is stable enough to endure the delay. This is the shift's ideal form. Degrees of acuity are agreed upon, and treatment protocols follow. Downstream institutions (smaller neighborhood hospitals like Maitri) treat and transfer to upstream institutions (larger specialty hospitals like Central), and no one gets caught in the middle. In this ideal type, triage is frictionless flow: all trajectory and no traffic. But as Usha's situation foregrounds, jams are inescapable, both on the roads and in the hospital, and shifting constitutes the lifelines of triage.

As a public facility, the municipal hospital's casualty ward cannot refuse patients, and so shifts are the means and the ends of triage for trauma cases. I detail the gestural qualities of shifts through three forms of action that constitute lifelines of triage: transformations in queueing as medical staff displace attention from one patient to another in the casualty ward, changes in bodily evidence as the causes and contexts of the injury get codified as a case, and maneuvers of comportment as medical staff attune agitated patients' kinetics to the norms of clinical spaces. Throughout, I address how a body and a case move in and out of relations in the spaces of emergency medical triage.

Two ethnographic sites ground this chapter. I begin with an analysis of the casualty ward of a smaller neighborhood hospital I call Maitri Hospital, where major trauma must be sorted from less severe matters through movement. Smaller, secondary-level neighborhood hospitals like Maitri are typical first stops for traumatic injury in Mumbai and are an important node in the story of trauma's trajectories. Later in the chapter, I move the account from Maitri to a tertiary-level hospital I call Central Hospital, which is the hospital that anchors the remainder of this book. In the casualty ward at Central, and down the hall in its trauma ward, differences in bodily movements continue as both problems and correctives.[2] Across both hospitals, I describe cases of major and minor trauma, as well as cases that are not traumatic injuries at all, and this is purposeful. I wish to convey how trauma intersects with other acute problems that casualty wards regularly face. Doing so clarifies how shifts constitute lifelines, as bodily movements produce and reproduce social forms through translocation and gestural adjustment.

Shifts can signify the success of medicine when a case resolves, and shifts can also mark medicine's failures, as patients waiting in the casualty queue make claims around the failure to shift properly, seamlessly, and efficiently.[3] I examine these different registers of shifts for what they move and what they prevent from moving. This entails narrating registers of *both* movement and stasis. Such narration may read as sometimes speedy and occasionally sluggish. Fieldwork in a casualty ward poses an ethnographic narrative challenge because there is a cascade of cases and because medical staff in a high-case-volume setting may respond to urgency differently than patients do. Trauma's interrelated, comparative velocities shape these differences in idealized pace. During the first hours after injury occurs, death from hypovolemic shock is a serious threat if a case does not get immediate attention. But attention to one case is always in relation to another in a high-volume context. Shifting is a genre of structural change borne out in bodies, and its dynamics of space, time, and comportment implicate survival. This often happens relationally, and therefore unevenly. If one's aim is descriptive fidelity to a scene, then the unevenness of these relations will necessarily inflect the unevenness of narration.

Shifting bears costs to patients and their families on multiple fronts. Often people come to a government hospital after first trying treatment at a private hospital to no avail or at too great a cost, meaning that they have shifted themselves before arriving in the public hospital. People also make a comparative calculus *between* public hospitals, secondary and tertiary. There are also the complex calculations people make in deciding to go to a public facility rather than a private one where costs can be exorbitant (see J. Das and Hammer 2004).[4] Access and triage must be thought together as purposeful shifts that the injured and their kin often do, well before the authority of the public hospital does it to them.

Shifting also wedges bodies between institutions. Doctors in smaller hospitals like Maitri know that much of the major trauma they see in the casualty ward must be shifted to a more specialized facility like Central. They are well aware that trauma patients often die during transfer from the smaller, secondary neighborhood hospitals that mark the first site of care to the larger, specialized, tertiary hospitals where trauma medicine is institutionalized. The dilemmas they face at the first point of care are crucial turning points: Should the patients have stable blood pressure before transfer? Should they have an IV inserted with active fluid perfusion before transfer? And at what costs? For instance, if the smaller center knows that more diagnostics and imaging will happen at the larger center, should doctors at the smaller center still pursue these options and force the family and patient to wait and potentially wind up paying for the same thing twice? Imaging is one of the costliest out-of-pocket expenses in public hospital care, so if it will be repeated at the larger center, what kind of damage might be done if families must pay for the same procedure twice?[5] Will a family make different downstream decisions about surgeries or intensive care if simply arriving at those decisions has been too costly? What ultimately counts as stability in medicine, given these tensions between staying still, being in motion, and life's valuation?

Doctors in trauma wards at tertiary hospitals like Central feel strongly about these dilemmas. They often blame the doctors at secondary hospitals like Maitri for transferring patients their way without stabilization measures, or for sending them at all. Basic trauma triage procedures, they say, lie within a secondary hospital's scope of expertise and resources (Gerdin et al. 2014). They want the secondary hospitals to keep patients still, when it is clinically appropriate and the resources allow. For instance, Maitri has an operating theater where surgeons can perform exploratory laparotomies to assess and address bleeding from blunt abdominal trauma. Minor trauma care such as suturing and minor orthopedic care are within the secondary hospital's scope too. Neurosurgery is a different matter, because not all secondary hospitals have neurosurgeons on call, and this becomes increasingly true the farther one travels from urban centers. For doctors at tertiary trauma facilities, holding patients at the secondary facility rather than moving them on may decrease trauma's immanent life threats of shock. It has the added benefit of not overloading the already-strained specialty trauma centers.

However, doctors working at a secondary hospital like Maitri may have a different perspective. They face manifold issues in their casualty wards and feel that the best way to treat trauma's arrival in these smaller facilities is simply to get it out and onward, elsewhere, toward more expertise. These internal and interfacility differences in movement politics are critical and may get ironed out if triage remains underspecified. This is why I remain committed to describing triage through shifts ethnographically. To do so is to specify the conditions under which people get caught in emergency medicine's often-conflicting kinetics.

At the broadest scale, clinical studies of triage usually analyze it through the lens of the word's French derivation of "sorting out" or "marshaling" (Edwards 2009; Moskop and Iserson 2007; Moskop et al. 2009; O'Meara, Porter, and Greaves 2007). Clinical service evaluation research tends to approach problems of triage as problems of efficiency and throughput, assessing the optimal time to sort cases and measuring waiting times (Wiler et al. 2010). The flow of cases through treatment is the ideal value in this framework, although what precisely constitutes movement often remains unclear. What is quite clear, however, is that waiting is flow's presumed opposite and that delay constitutes a threat.

Global standards for trauma care that emerge from this clinical literature dictate that the highest priority for an emergency trauma case is to move the patient to a center of trauma expertise as soon as possible. Shifting is a clinical good in this light, but often a frictionless pathway of motion is assumed in these protocols, most forged in the Global North. Standards for transfer may acknowledge obstacles to mobility, in the form of road traffic or queues in the casualty ward, but traffic as such tends to be rendered more as glitches in movement rather than as the constitutive feature of movement itself. What might be gleaned about triage if *both* the mobilities and immobilities of bodies are taken into account, in relation? What might the ethnography of medicine learn from bodies caught in the interstices of moving and waiting? What if movements are the structure rather than the consequence of the structure?

Medical anthropology's engagements with triage offer some preliminary answers. While their conceptual goals differ from those of clinical studies, ethnographies of triage tend to share a focus on flow. Anthropologists often use the word *triage*'s semantic property of "sorting" to describe governing practices of processing enacted by states, NGOs, clinics, and families (Biehl 2007; Redfield 2013; Ticktin 2011). This makes triage a political technology, physician-anthropologist Vinh-Kim Nguyen (2010, 176) explains, and the politics of triage lie in decisions to provide care both within and beyond the clinic. In his ethnography of HIV treatment programs in West Africa, Nguyen defines triage as a practice of "selecting those who would receive the treatments and those who would not" (109). Nguyen uses this rubric of triage to describe treatment interactions in a clinic, to assess the relationship between a national health program and its subjects, and to understand how Africa figures into the unequal politics of resource allocation and expertise in global health.[6] This multiscalar approach to thinking triage is important: it reveals the selective flows of care provision and medical discrimination.

Yet I believe triage as it is understood by both clinicians and anthropologists may also be refined by approaching it as a tension *between* moving and halting. Waiting is, at once, an obstacle to care and the grounds of care's possibilities. One must pay attention to the differences that constitute a jam and to shifts into both motion and stillness. This offers analytic purchase beyond sovereign decisions to provide care, which, while important, may not reflect the entirety of triage's social and political trajectories.

Relations between bodies and state power are highly volatile, and because they are volatile, they can be intermittent. Usha's case makes clear that tensions between movement and stasis continue after treatment begins and after it is denied. Sorting and processing—which are flow projects—mark the beginning of the clinic's power. But the clinic's continuities also lie in shifting. Trauma medicine—and the politics of public medicine that encompasses it—involves practices of shifting and of relaying mixed messages: *The hospital needs you to move. The hospital needs you to stay still.*

———————

When people enter Maitri Hospital's casualty ward, they hear and see fractured motion as they take their place in the queue. A security guard hiccups by the line's start near the door, and another bangs his baton on the floor, a thwack of assertion that forces momentary quiet. The windows are open, and the ward's door closes just once a day at 2 a.m. for ten minutes, when the sweeper mops the floor and the staff break for chai. Sounds of road traffic filter in, and mobile phones ring with film soundtracks. Police constables question a man hit by a car and draw *X*s and circles in their notebooks to diagram the accident and its impact. Patients cough while lying on the three beds against the room's perimeter. Some ask the nurses to translate instructions from neighborhood chemists on scraps of paper. Sandals shuffle on the concrete floor, a staccato rustle-scrape that signals that the jam is transforming. The queue ends at a desk where the casualty medical officer (CMO) sits and decides what to do with patients: keep them here in casualty, send them to a specific ward in the hospital for admission, or send them to a different hospital entirely. The physiology of the injured shifts even if their limbs remain still. The queue may toggle between bustle and freeze, but human hemodynamics is, definitionally, always on the move in the living.

These are speedy intensities, and the queue introduces deceleration. Yet the queue also yields a decision and a direction of what and where next; its qualities are both "massified" and "interactional," to use the descriptors that Ajay Gandhi (2013) develops for queues in urban India. Sometimes the line is thick and hides the desk, so it looks as if there's no end and things will stay suspended. Closer to the desk, frustrations and nerves can erupt in laughter, like when the CMO asks a patient to stick out his tongue, which is bright red from chewing *paan* (betel nut), and this startles her, and he smiles big. At the desk, the phone rings. Staff circulate: male "ward boys" (orderlies) and "dressers" specializing in wound care are called *mama* (elder maternal uncle); female sweepers (janitors) are called *maushi* (maternal aunt); female nurses are called *sister*, and male nurses *brother* (a colonial holdover).[7] Or nurses can simply be called *staff*. Proper names are infrequently used. Often one's job role stands in for a name, depending on how well a given person knows the workers of the ward, which is a function of experience, age, and an edifice of caste-inflected labor. The mass, shifting body called *relatives* or *sagewale* by the doctors, nurses, and staff comprises the kin of patients.

Above the desk on the wall, there is a buzzer button that rings like a school bell: one buzz to call the orderly, two for the sweeper, three for a dresser (an orderly who does bandaging, suturing, and plaster cast work), and four for a "barber" (an orderly with expertise in shaving the skin with a straight razor, especially necessary in the case of head injuries). In the treatment area behind the desk, nurses hit glass ampoules of liquid medicines one, two, three times to break them open. The insectocutor on the wall glows blue and zaps mosquitoes.[8]

The principal duty of the CMO is to "direct traffic," a doctor tells me one evening about her work. Another reflects that managing the queue is akin to cricket batting: a case comes at you like a ball, and a good doctor is a good batsman who can hit the ball in just the right way to send it where it needs to go. Nursing staff half-jokingly, half-seriously, describe triage as the motion of a funnel (*nasraale*) that sluices patients through a crowd.[9] In moments of tension, the guard, the police, or the doctor may order everyone into a single line (*line lagao* or *eki line karo*). Sometimes the CMO will instruct the people in line that they should not cut in front of each other ("beech beech mein mat ke jao"). Further riffs entail commanding the crowd to go to the presumed opposite of the ward, "the outside" (*baahar/baaher*). This is done by asserting that only one relative per patient is allowed in line, and all others must go outside (*baki log baahar chelo*), or that *everyone* must go outside and leave the patient to the doctor's care (*sagle baaher taamba*).

I begin at Maitri Hospital because it is the government hospital nearest to where I have lived in Mumbai, on and off, since graduate school. I know the neighborhood well, and, by chance, a surgeon I had interviewed years before for a different project has joined the faculty at Maitri and helps facilitate my work. Maitri is *for me* very much a neighborhood hospital. Central is a neighborhood hospital too, of course; people living nearby gravitate toward it. However, at Maitri I often recognize people in the casualty ward. I see police constables zoom by on motorcycles down my street and then see them in the ward in the evening, accompanying unidentified patients. The woman who sells me eggs in the mornings appears at dusk with a rat bite, and the butcher shows up with a sliced finger. The casualty ward can be a space for familiars.

Being together in the ward can invite a partial sense of urban togetherness. Geographies of risk get localized through events: the exact locations of crashes and skids can lead to discussions about the qualities of the neighborhood's specific roads and intersections and histories of construction. And sometimes I see neighbors in dire straits roll in on trolleys, facing a moment that Julie Livingston captures as "the sinking *feeling* one has on looking up from one's task to see a friend unexpectedly walk into the clinic . . . even while one tries to ensure that feeling is not conveyed on one's face" (2012, 27). It isn't a small neighborhood, but it's small enough for people to see familiars in a space of nested nearness, meaning that the queue may reflect everyday proximities between people in homes, schools, temples, mosques, *gurdwaras*, community gatherings, and social services. Through shifting the queue, the casualty ward shifts a neighborhood.

The queue sets the political terms of clinical attention in this public hospital setting. Anthropologists have argued that queues affirm the power and proximity of the state and that political subjectivity gets organized around waiting (Bourdieu 2000; A. Gupta 2012; Hull 2012; Jeffrey 2010). For Ghassan Hage, waiting is an echo of governmentality, specifically "a conservative governmentality that aims at de-legitimising impatience and the desire to disrupt 'the queue' even in the face of disaster" (2009, 7). Yet the authority that queues can enforce—the power to make people wait— may still be in play even if the line resolves. As Akhil Gupta (2012, 25) argues in his study of poverty-reduction programs in India, the amelioration of structural violence does not happen automatically in the ramp-up of efficiency. Shifting the queue does not mean the end of the queue's powers. This suggests that a more expansive sense of queues as political technologies can emerge when both moving and waiting come into the frame, a frame that hospital queues are ideal sites to address (Gore 2019). A queue may seem like a static form, but in fact it is dynamic and may also constitute downstream jams as well.

———

The first question a CMO asks a patient is, "What happened?" (kya hua?) or "What's afflicting you?" (kya taklif hai aapko?).[10] As the answer unfolds, the doctor may take a pulse, measure blood pressure, and listen to the banalities and enormities of everyday life condensed into bullet points.[11] Bus drivers come in complaining of foot pain, the aches of long hours meting out acceleration and braking on the pedals, legs never resting in between. A woman who begs for alms at a street intersection gets dashed by an autorickshaw. An elderly aunty has rats in her house, and they bite. Small kids shove small toys in their mouths, ears, and noses. The CMO diagnoses the neighborhood through these maladies, usually as an aside relayed to me in my assigned chair at the corner of the table: "People in this locality tend to eat late at night, like you see in this case of acid reflux." An adult man yells at his mother, who brought him to the hospital, that he was not born of her womb and that she should leave. The doctor observes, "Life in this neighborhood can be difficult."[12] Two twenty-something women bring in a trembling elderly woman, whose shivers began in the ladies' compartment of the local train. She has diabetes and forgot her insulin and avers that she is alone, that no one from home will come to the hospital ("gharwale nahin hai, aanewale nahin"), and that these two young girls are all she's got. Social marginalization asserts itself in the queue, and strangers shift their own mobility to help bring someone to the hospital. The neighborhood can register with the hospital staff as kind, heroic, foolhardy, and tragic, often all at once.

It can register as violent as well. One evening the CMO examines an assault case, a man hit by a bamboo stick. Her hand travels up his arm, feeling for fractures, and she turns to me with an observation about the comparative materiality of wounding: "Everyone in *your* country has guns, right?" I excuse myself to the small suture room in the back and check the news on my phone. There has been a mass shooting in the United States, again. In five years I never once see a gunshot wound at Maitri or Central. Years later, when I begin informal observations in the Duke University Hospital Emergency Department, I see six in four days.

The hospital can wind up mediating prior medical failures of localized medicine. People see unqualified neighborhood doctors who give them bad medicines, one CMO says, and their problems aren't solved, so they shift themselves to the government hospital. "Everyone wants instant relief from their pain," he says. They want their case to be resolved definitively and swiftly. "They want it to be like a movie. The hero loves, the hero fights, the hero dies, all in three hours." Whatever the time it takes, Maitri's casualty ward winds up triaging the problems of efficacy (of bad and misprescribed drugs). He thinks this is particularly challenging in situations involving "local" doctors who practice traditional forms of medicine such as Ayurveda or Unani. The broad referent of "local" doctor can also include neighborhood allopathic doctors, whose expertise some hospital doctors call into question.[13] When their prescriptions don't work, people turn to the government hospital, as much for affordability as for expertise. Medicine can shift medicine in the neighborhood too.

The queue can be a technology of social class production and reproduction as it cleaves people into doctors, patients, and relatives.[14] Because Maitri is a government facility and its casualty ward orients around a queue, its clients comport themselves mostly in the ways one might do in other government facilities or in a bank, but this is not just any queue, after all, and a doctor does not belong to the same category of person as a bank teller. A government hospital is a space for lower-class and poor communities, and there are complex class and caste interactions between patients and doctors. Patients often presume these doctors to be of a higher class and caste position, even when this may not actually be so. A lower-caste person from rural Maharashtra who becomes a doctor, works in an urban center like Mumbai, and is the first person with medical authority encountered in a public hospital may be reckoned with the social positioning being a doctor can confer. Language use can change: the linguistic formalities of the government space (especially the use of more formal and less colloquial Marathi) color the ways that doctors speak to patients, whom they may presume to be less educated.

The shifts that originate in the casualty queue also produce social inequality's durational and kinetic effects. I learn that Mr. Karve decides against shifting Usha to a different hospital; he decides that staying at Maitri is best for her. It is unclear what her natal family thinks is best, nor what she wants. Nine days later she regains consciousness in the ICU. I join the attending surgeon to visit her. "Are you eating, Usha?" he asks. Her brother and mother are with her. She casts her eyes downward. "Yes," she says. "Dal." The surgeon encourages her to eat more than just dal, and her brother repeats this instruction. The surgeon takes me aside to reflect on the case. She likely has memory loss owing to the brain injury, he thinks. I revisit Mr. Karve's early words of "she is like a daughter to us." "That was just an exaggeration," the surgeon says. When life gets a specific rupee value, social positions such as employer and servant will dictate how far a shift might stretch.

I return to the casualty ward and see how certain forms of queue jumping upend any notion of triage based solely in the actions of the medical officer. The CMO is often assisted by the people in the line, without instruction. People in line will always give way to a pregnant woman, a child, or an elderly person. This is also the case for anyone presenting with breathlessness, or anyone brought unconscious. It may seem as if a uniform crowd of people is waiting to be shifted by a uniform medical authority. But most often, there is a group of people constantly reckoning with forms of difference and making their own shifts. This is why it is less precise to describe the ward through the lens of totalizing, top-down institutional adjudication than through scenes of unequally distributed relational shifts.

Experiential velocities of triage vary. "These government hospitals are so slow," says a man whose foot was hit by a bus as he waits for the orthopedic surgeon to read his X-ray. At Maitri, the feeling of resource inequity begins far before one gets in line. People are intensely aware of the hospital's shortcomings, but emergencies and economies bring them there nonetheless. The state can be assertively present through its absences and can make time sense-able through its evasive velocities. My neighbors would often critique Maitri in everyday conversations for its resource problems and cast it as a space of lethargy owing to bureaucracy yet also a space of rapidity because indifferent government doctors hasten treatment without reflection. Several of my neighbors also work at Maitri as clerks or lab assistants; some are social workers in NGOs that the hospital calls on for aid in cases of orphans or domestic violence. When I ask what they would do if they were in a road or railway accident, most say if they had to be taken to Maitri, they would draw on connections they had to the hospital to ensure faster and better treatment. This is the case at Central too: the nurses, orderlies, and sweepers all say that inside connections are essential to better care. In this sense, the absolute speed of a shift is important, but so too are the kinds of relational demands one can make upon it: *who* you know in the domain of the shift can be as meaningful as *what* the shift does, and these demands illustrate the complexities of social capital in public medicine.[15]

As day turns to evening, the casualty queue transforms. Caseloads during the daytime tend to be lighter because the outpatient department handles general coughs, colds, fevers, and stomachaches. When the outpatient ward closes in late afternoon, all these cases shift to casualty, turning it into a general clinic even though its mandate is to treat emergencies. When it gets crowded, hospital staff describe it as hot (*garam*), busy (*bizzy-wizzy*), or full (*pura*). "It's like VT" (aisa VT), one nurse says, comparing the busyness of the ward to Victoria Terminus, the former name of Chhatrapati Shivaji Terminus, one of the city's two main rail stations. Busy but not novel. A nurse tells me the work is tedious (*kantaḷavan*), a description I initially find surprising because my inexperienced eyes see movement as the sign of novelty, with apparent disarray signifying emergency medicine. I have watched too much *ER*. It is not disarray at all; it is a scene of exhaustion. It is also the system at work and the sign of a neighborhood's maladies, whose care labor can register as repetitive and draining. Patients may be frequent visitors (which I begin to see over time), and common diseases put certain treatment needs on repeat.

For instance, malaria and dengue strike hard in summer (winter is a relief on this front). Tuberculosis is a constant, as is asthma. The casualty ward is a dynamic ecosystem, and trauma appears amid cases of dizziness (*chakar*), nausea (*ulti ulti*), coughs (*khassi*), fever (*bukhar*), headache (*dokedukhi*), and all-over discomfort (*bodyache*). Nor is trauma wholly unpredictable, either. Some injuries have seasonal rhythms in accordance with festivals. Kite strings slice hands on Makar Sankranti, a kite festival; head traumas reign on Dahi Handi, when troupes all over the city compete in human-pyramid contests, some reaching forty feet high. On Holi, booze and bhang turn clumsiness into emergency. As the neighborhood lives, labors, and celebrates, the casualty ward must enact shifts in sync.

The pharmaceutical supply also shapes the neighborhood's relation to the queue. At 10 p.m., the hospital's emergency pharmacy shuts. The pharmacist is a kind man, and every evening at closing time, he brings in a tray of medicine and plunks it down on the CMO's table. The drug tray has syrupy paracetamol for pediatric doses and a bin of small triangular paper packets each holding one tab of ranitidine (an antacid), one tab of diclofenac (an anti-inflammatory for pain), and two tabs of paracetamol. Patients see the packets and simply state, "Doctor, give me medicine" (doctor, dawai do). The pharmacist prepacks some of the triangles before he leaves, and I am tasked with continuing the job. I try to keep up with the line, folding for the neighborhood again and again these druggy paper samosas.

Patients and families might initiate demands to shift, asking nurses how much longer the wait might be. "These people change the definition of casualty," a nurse named Sister Sita says. She moves aside so the orderly can light incense under the Ganesha icon overseeing the ward. She eyes the line of coughs and colds that is on hold as the CMO examines a construction worker who slipped off bamboo scaffolding and fell two stories to the ground. For Sister Sita and other nurses working in the ward, the casualty ward is designed for acute cases, with *acute* defined by people trained to spot acuity. This is as much about materiality and economy as it is about clinical expertise. The resources are limited in casualty, Sister Sita explains. She points out the notebooks she fills with entries recording the medicines in short supply or on backorder. The ward is already stretched thin in its infrastructure and labor, and what's available should be directed to acute emergencies, she says. She understands that patients and families want quick resolution, but she does not think they always understand how triage is relational.

At the heart of triage is the shifting of bodies. Focusing on how bodies move in and out of the queue relationally, rather than focusing on the queue as a static form, reveals that the people in line do not simply absorb the political subjectivity the queue demands. Attention to desires and frustrations around the line's moving and stopping illuminates the power of triage beyond sovereign decisions about care. Shifts can shortcut the authority of the queue, and transpositions can enact tactics. The longer I stay inside the casualty ward at Maitri, the more I realize how piecemeal my sense of traumatic injury's shifts is becoming. It is dynamic, but it does not yet address the bigger picture. The point of Maitri's casualty ward was to send trauma cases elsewhere, "elsewhere" being a different hospital with resources to treat trauma. I do not understand that elsewhere yet.

A large blue sign on the wall above the CMO's desk demands stillness and quiet (*shantataa*). "You can say it, but it doesn't matter," the CMO says. And so I shift, to Central.

In Central Hospital's casualty ward, a man walks with uneven steps toward the triage desk. He was riding his motorcycle down a one-way road, and a rickshaw barreled toward him going the wrong way, clipping his bike and his leg. He does not give details on the rickshaw driver in his statement to the doctor about how the injury happened. The driver stopped and helped him, he tells the CMO. And the rickshaw driver "is a poor man, a laborer," the motorbike driver says, and "blood won't go back in," meaning that the injury is already done, and chasing after an *autowala* for something minor won't make the injury heal any faster.

Not everyone is as ready to forgive, and reporting the injury at the doctor's desk can indeed be like reporting a crime, because it is. Blame circulates in and around the line. Time and space condition the scale and kind of blame. On one hand, the constancy of cases means little time and space for reflection or critique of deep structures. On the other hand, doctors, nurses, or the patients themselves might blame persons or communities for making bad choices, engaging in risky behavior, or courting danger.

Each trauma case that arrives at a government hospital is considered a medicolegal case, or MLC. Assaults, poisonings, attempted suicides, and falls also are recorded as MLCs, because this allows the police to investigate possible malfeasance. What looks like a fall down the steps could have been a push. What looks like an accidental ingestion of rat poison may have been attempted murder. This is the law. There is a ledger called "the MLC book" on the CMO's desk, and unlike the coughs and colds that get "regular" admission sheets, trauma cases get a sheet with "medicolegal case" stamped at the top and are copied into the MLC ledger. Each detail recorded regarding the injury is official state evidence. Most people are aware of its implications, and so the moments of recording can be moments when silence and speech matter.[16] There are shifts of bodies, but there are also shifts of information as an event moves from something experienced to something recorded. This occurs as the hospital moves bodies into cases, and as medicine and law come into amplified proximity.

One evening, patients watch carefully as the CMO of Central's casualty ward, Dr. Arun, writes down their accounts in the MLC book. "Write it properly" (thik se likh do), a patient says, and suggests that the report should contain as many incriminating details as possible. The details in the MLC book hold out the promise of one official record (from the hospital) wielding influence when or if the police or courts become involved.

Another patient wishes to ensure punishment for the person whom he believed caused his injury. He tells Dr. Arun to write the report in the MLC book in such a way that the perpetrator would receive the most severe punishment ("aisa report banao ki kadi se kadi saja mil jaaye").[17] One day a person accused of assault is brought in by the police along with the person he allegedly injured. He whispers a promise of a bribe to the injured person (*juice piloonga*) to entice him to downplay the severity of his condition and, presumably, any police action that might result. The ward's register of injury can be scripted and rescripted in these moments, depending on how the CMO, the police, the patient, and other related parties interact.

I look at the MLC book one evening at Central, counting on a random page roughly five cases recorded per hour, bodies brought in and checked for their appearance, smells, movements, and histories of truth claims, some of injuries by others, some of injuries inflicted by the police.

> **4:05 p.m.** Inf/bb [informed/brought by] self with relative with a/h/o [alleged history of] assault by hot tea. 5–7% burns.

> **4:07 p.m.** Assault by 15–20 persons by beer bottle 1.5 hours before. HI+ [evidence of head injury] with blunt abdomen trauma.

3:40 p.m. Inf/by pt and bb PC [police constable] for alcohol estimation. Pt gives h/o alcohol consumption at 12 p.m. today, one Kingfisher beer large. Smell+, Gait n [normal], Speech n. Pt gives h/o hitting by police.

3:30 p.m. b/b self b/b PC with a/h/o drunk driving. He admits to drinking Red Bull, but says he did not drink alcohol. Smell neg; Speech n.

Categorically, these claims are considered *complaints* in medicolegal terms. Akhil Gupta notes that complaints "are a highly important modality through which structural violence against poor people becomes visible" (2012, 167). In Jocelyn Chua's study of mental health clinics in Kerala, she finds that "the typology of 'complaint' and the dialogic interactions involved in its production marked a far wider catchment area for the grievances and morally weighted accusations that circulate among patient, kin, and clinicians" (2014, 222). Sameena Mulla (2014), in her study of forensic nursing in the United States, highlights the ways that clinical spaces selectively hear complaints and transform them into evidence. Similarly, the MLC book in the Mumbai public hospital casualty ward is a selective ledger of hurts. It archives the state's selective recognition of traumatic injury and, sometimes, of the contexts of violence behind it. Shifting a case into the ledger opens the case up to police inquiry and, potentially, matters of the court, where issues like damages and compensation might be worked out. The agents of violence matter: it is harder to know how medicolegal evidence of police violence, as in "Pt gives h/o hitting by police," may gain attention, because much depends on the CMO's decision to pursue further details. At the nexus of a writing hand and that which is written, jams condition justice.

However, blame is not always formally speakable. One evening a large group of shirtless teens, barefoot and drenched, bring in a young boy on a makeshift cloth stretcher. Dr. Arun gets up from the desk, directs them to a room in the back, and listens to the story. The boy fell into a deep pool of water that had collected at a construction site. The construction had been going on for five years. The teens were playing around the construction site, climbing and jumping. The boy fell into the water, which was filled with iron rods and concrete pylons. When he did not resurface, the others began looking for him. The water was so dirty they couldn't see beneath the surface. They called the fire brigade, who eventually found his body.

Dr. Arun says very little until after he confers with the nurse, who applies electrodes to the boy's body and reads the flatlined EKG (electrocardiogram) printout.

The announcement of the boy's death sends waves through the room. Security guards take turns bringing relatives in and out to see the body. The police arrive for questioning. There are discussions about legal action against the builder who let the construction site remain unfinished. I am sickened. I ask the CMO if he will write an agent of death in the MLC book: The iron rod? The standing water? The builder? The real estate developer? The city? Will the structure of structural violence find a way onto paper? And if so, will it be a static or dynamic thing? I am unsure to what extent anyone has the time, energy, or resources to track what architect Eyal Weizman (2017) has termed *forensic architecture*, the tracing of structural violence through built environments.

Dr. Arun tells me that the final decision on the agent of injury will be in the police report, just as a police report will declare a specific weapon used. Whether or not structural explanations will bring relief or compensation to the boy's family is unclear. In many cases, it will be up to local politicians and lawyers to sort things out. In the meantime, certain injuries raise the question of their cause, others do not, and others allow for the environment to enter but only in certain fetishized ways: a metal pipe, a train track, a pool of water. The time-space of triage often conditions what kinds of evidence might shift, and how.

Dr. Arun tells me that he is always concerned about the gravity of the words he writes in the MLC book and finds communicating and managing that gravity with relatives and the police to be essential and exhausting. Other CMOs feel similarly. One says that as tiring as the work can be, there is a residual "charge" of energy that weighs on the mind after leaving work ("yahan peh aane ke baad dimaag charge ho jata hai"). He can't sleep after a shift. Dr. Arun watches lots of films to unwind and tutors a medical school student. He has a keen interest in basic science, not general medical practice, but like many of the CMOs, he received funding from the state to attend medical school and is now repaying it through government service in the casualty ward. The job of the CMO is often the job of someone paying back an educational debt through public service. Theoretically, he could pay back the debt with cash, and some young doctors draw on family resources or moneylenders to do so, because they don't want to complete the government service as triage doctors in municipal hospitals. But Dr. Arun doesn't have those options. His family is not wealthy by any means. Regardless, he says, he likes the clinical experience of being a CMO. It makes him a better doctor, he thinks.

He also thinks there are specific ways shifts should be communicated. He speaks to patients only in formal Marathi and Hindi, always with the politest pronouns of address, and never draws on the city's local dialect of Bambaiyya Hindi. His questions are open-ended and aimed at eliciting narrative rather than fill-in-the-blank answers. It is the speech of a government official, with all of the power such speech may carry. Sometimes it registers with people as respectful speech. "He speaks properly," one patient says, less a compliment and more an assessment that while each person's injury may be unique, everyone deserves equal respect as they demand care from the state.

The CMO's speech, and their ability to listen to evidence, has shift effects. It accelerates the movement of cases, because there are always more to see. It decelerates information, fixes it in the ledger, and makes it authoritative. Still, though things may seem to slow down once written in the MLC book, velocities linger once treatment begins down the hallway, inside the trauma ward.

If a case of major trauma comes to Central's casualty ward, the CMO will direct an orderly to move the patient to the trauma ward. The patient will be wheeled down the hall, around the corner by the tea stall and waiting-area benches outside, into a cool corridor, and through the garlanded double doors that mark out this dedicated space. The patient will arrive in the trauma ward's resuscitation area, called *resus*, with enough space for three gurneys to fit side by side, a desk that faces the room's entrance, medical supplies, and a small area for X-ray technicians and medical supplies. A swinging door leads into the trauma ICU with fourteen beds. Across from resus is the space reserved for the orderlies and sweepers, a small office for the nurses, and a room for the resident doctors to sleep and eat. Around the corner is its emergency operating theater for trauma-specific surgeries, so patients need not be moved to other operating theaters in the hospital.

Once patients arrive at the trauma ward, demands for movement and stillness continue. Resus is for initial assessment and immediate resuscitation techniques such as oxygenation and intravenous fluid perfusion. A patient's body must be both moved and stilled throughout. The ward has two mobile X-rays and a mobile ultrasound machine, which are helpful in assessing orthopedic questions and determining possible bleeding in the abdomen. For further imaging and for CT necessary to assess head injuries, an orderly and usually a family member will push the gurney out of the ward and down a hallway to the hospital's radiology suite. Consults will be called; a resident (usually the person who first sees the patient upon ward entry) will phone up the ladder of medical authority, notifying a senior surgeon if necessary. Commands come back down the ladder. In the meantime, if surgery is necessary, the trauma operating theater is prepared, and the patient is kept in a holding pattern. Surgery can take hours. Then patients recover in the trauma ICU until doctors deem them ready for transfer elsewhere or discharge. All of these maneuvers add up, temporally, and resolution is hardly sudden.

That, in aggregate, is the line of trauma treatment: the flow of a case from arrival to discharge from the unit. But too much focus on this flow would overlook critical stretches of stillness and nonlinearity and elide the relational and reflexive gestures that constitute shifts from the ground up. Traumatic injuries can make the dyad of a doctor instructing a patient to move a limb and the patient complying rather irrelevant. There may be gross and apparent reasons for this, in the case of injuries such as amputations. Many patients arrive in states of hypovolemic shock. There may be subtle reasons too, as many have brain trauma. Put simply, one of the first acts of care that occurs in the trauma ward is that patients are moved in order to be treated.

This usually means putting patients into flat, unmoving positions. The orderlies of the trauma ward (*mamas*) mediate much of the mobility and immobility of patients. They are often called in to fix bodies into place. This might be done by force and sometimes through restraints, which are necessary according to some doctors owing to the threat of involuntary self-harm. Restraints are by no means the default; most patients do not express motions that seem harmful. Yet a patient might express a reflex move and attempt to take off their oxygen mask or pull out IVs or intercostal drains. This may be reflex alone, or it may be reflex in relation to delirium or agitation from the injury, medications, or both. Whatever the source of the moves, things like oxygen masks and IVs are the primary supports that are drawing patients away from the edges of shock. Furthermore, getting agitated can exacerbate a person's tachycardia and distress, potentially complicating plans for surgery or recovery. To stabilize the movements of blood and oxygen, other movements may need restriction.

This is one of the ways a person gets gestured into patienthood: by dampening their reflexes in a moment where a real sense of threat is felt by both the patient and those tasked with their care. (Once, a patient untied himself from the restraints and sat up, wriggled out of his hospital gown, and, naked, made a run for the back door, disappearing into the city.) If an anesthetist has given the patient a sedative, agitation may not be as evident, but sedatives may also depress respiration. Because many patients in the ward are perioperative, the benefits and risks of sedation are always weighed in relation to surgical fitness and recovery.[18] Through the overlaps of agitation, sedation, and palliation, and in relation to bodily reflexes, the ward can assert a kinetic moral economy.

One afternoon a young man, Piyush, arrives after a railway accident. He lies on a metal trolley at first but then exclaims that his pain is too much to bear and begins sitting up and banging his upper body back down on the trolley, a clanging boom that he repeats. The clips holding the trolley's hinges begin to buckle; if they come undone, he'll tumble to the floor. I am sitting with Sister Jaya, the charge nurse, and an intern at the desk. We rush to his side, stabilize the trolley, and try to encourage him to breathe through the pain. Piyush says he feels that his leg is going to burst open ("pair phaṭ jayega"). His femur is fractured. He exclaims that the pain is terrible, and we acknowledge this. He then says someone should kill him ("mujhe jaan se mar do"). The intern tsk-tsks at the kill-me comment and tries to soothe Piyush, saying, "The doctors are here to save you, not to kill you."

The charge nurse, Sister Jaya, is concerned about getting his analgesics right. She does not dismiss what Piyush says. She wants to give him more pain relief. As a senior nurse, she also knows all too well how traumatic injury scrambles the relationship between what someone says and how their body moves. She worries about him hurting himself and hurting his chances for survival, another good reason to alleviate his pain. She examines Piyush's file and confers with the anesthetist. Sister Jaya has given him two doses of tramadol and diclofenac already. She knows that the surgeons want to operate on him soon, and she knows she can't dampen his blood pressure too much, or the surgery will be delayed until his blood pressure is stable. There's a tightrope to walk between stillness now and movement toward a better outcome.

"Lie down quietly" (shanti se so jao), she urges Piyush. He complies with muffled protest. She pushes another dose of tramadol into his IV and monitors him, waiting to see if it addresses his pain. The anesthetist stands by her and reflects that she hates seeing how patients with orthopedic injuries must lie down. It forces them to endure pain while they also must look up at the ceiling's fluorescent lights, which are institutional and stressful. There are side effects to shifts, the restrictions of sight lines that take shape by enforcing a lying-down position.[19] And yet being supine is the body position that usually works best for the ward, because nurses and doctors need to be able to rush to the bedside at any moment and address airways and IVs for blood pressure. Flexing bodies will get shifted into certain shapes to contend with trauma's immediate effects and with its downstream threatening potentials.

———————

Mechanisms of injury and the body's responses to those mechanisms can cascade into categories of persons. The stilling of the body may conclude some scenes of agitation, but there is a deep history to agitation and its rebuke in South Asia, a history that continues to thread through the hospital ward. Some hospital staff deem agitation, especially in men's bodies, to mark when a patient "gets rowdy" (*patient rowdy zhala*). This is meant to be more than a description of action, because *rowdy* is a term that appears across India to refer to a figure—most often a man—who causes public disturbances.[20] Given the blur between purposive bodily actions and uncontrolled reflexes among injured patients, *rowdy* can be blurry too. Rowdiness conjoins masculinity with disorder and manifests in the ward as an agitated body that needs a shift toward stillness so that medicine may do its work. While rowdiness is a quality of public culture, in the trauma ward it also marks a site where the lifelines of triage come into focus. This is especially the case in terms of medicine's attempts to render the rowdy more static.

Doctors and staff tend to give film examples when I ask about who best defines a rowdy person or a rowdy movement. "It's a bully, an antisocial person, a hooligan, a *mawali* [rogue, loafer], a ruffian," one senior surgeon says.[21] These examples accord with South Asian studies scholars' arguments that the rowdy is a historical figure whose legacy partly lies in colonial police charge ledgers called *rowdy-sheets*. Its contemporary form is a person-body who "inhabits the dark zone of the city . . . always threatening to spread to the safer, cleaner habitat of the city," as political and cultural theorists Vivek Dhareshwar and Radhika Srivatsan point out (1996, 202).[22] For Dhareshwar and Srivatsan, writing in conversation with the Subaltern Studies Collective, the rowdy is a figure who embodies the lumpenproletariat in contemporary India. Although the authors are more concerned with what the rowdy means than how it is embodied, they do note that the politics at stake is the *disincorporation* of persons from polities. The rowdy is a middle-class nightmare precisely because he is the disordered double of the middle-class body.

In Central's trauma ward, this holds true: rowdiness can mark the publicness of the public hospital, a reminder that this institution must enforce shifts on bodies that would never be granted entry into the kinetic economies of a private facility. The staff in the ward, medical and otherwise, often remark that the cause of rowdiness tends to be brain injuries that can shift mood and behavior. But they also note that rowdiness signals problems beyond the brain, specifically in matters of gender, social class, and caste. Social and structural realities converge with physiological markers, as rowdiness asserts excessive masculinity, class status, and neurological impairment at once.

The rowdy is almost always a masculinized figure in the ward, even if a woman is at the center of attention. A security guard recalls a case of a young woman on a motorbike who was speeding and hit a pothole. She fell and hit the asphalt, and a car ran over her head and killed her instantly, but she was still brought to the hospital to confirm the death. He calls her "Activa Lady" repeatedly, naming her through the Activa line of Honda motor scooters. He points out her forms of rowdiness and bodily activation—driving a motorbike, rather than riding pillion, which is an assumed position for women—that mark her gender as threatening. Yet threats also can manifest through gender's disappearance, too, in the ways that women's lives, deaths, and injuries frequently get absented in the overattention to rowdy masculinity and the norming of rowdiness as a problem of and for men. This erases the range of effects that gender, sexuality, and intimacy have on mobility in South Asia (Amrute 2015; Brunson 2014; Sadana 2018), effects that absolutely stretch into clinical spaces. At the same time, gender alone does not fully encompass the attributions of rowdiness in the ward; kinship matters too, as some patients get cast as rowdier when their relatives are present, while kin may dampen expressions of agitation in other cases.

Head injuries pose particular sites for shifting rowdiness toward stillness. The police bring a young man named Emran who has been in a railway accident and who is agitated. The resident attempts to insert an IV, and Emran yells at her to stop what she's doing. He then apologizes profusely a moment later: "Sorry, sorry yaar, sorry!" The resident asks an orderly to help her, and the orderly proceeds to tie Emran's hands and feet to the bed. When CT scans arrive, and it is decided that he requires neurosurgery, Sister Jaya calls a senior orderly, Raju Mama, to shave his head. Emran thrashes. Raju Mama wields the straight razor expertly, somehow managing a clean shave. "Don't talk! Don't make drama! Don't shake!" Raju Mama warns him as he works (Bol mat kar! Natak mat kar! Hilo mat kar!). Raju Mama has worked this job for forty years, he says; you need to be "fast-fast" with the razor. The shave is complete, and Emran grows quiet. Later, when I speak with the relative of another injured man in the bed next to Emran, the relative complains that Emran has yelled at him to untie his binds, and the situation repeats. Agitation often can be like a finger trap. Every shift a patient makes with their own body can tighten the ward's care, a grip that can make shifting out ever more difficult to achieve.

An orthopedic surgeon must have left a reflex hammer on the bed by a patient named Kishor, who sits up from a supine position in his bed and proceeds to bang the hammer on the bed frame. Kishor's file indicates he was in a road accident. The CT scans indicate that he has an extradural hematoma. Just as important, Kishor is feeling unwell. He is struggling to sit still. This is common: many patients in the ward with traumatic brain injury become easily agitated. And the hospital beds are exceedingly uncomfortable, I learn from sleeping on the spare one in the back room, so I cannot imagine what it feels like for a person with injuries.

Kishor's arms and legs are stiff, and the nurses and doctors ask him to relax, but he cannot, and he yells frequently. Kishor's uncle stands by his side. A nurse sends the uncle away to take care of paperwork. Raju Mama is called in and ties Kishor's hands and feet to the trolley with gauze. This also doesn't go well; it rarely does. Anyone would be terrified and angered, in a highly agitating place like a hospital. Kishor squirms and struggles. "Stop, stop" (bas, bas), he says. He exclaims, "You tied me up, and now where are you taking me?" (kidder kidder band kiya tumne yaar?). He yells at Raju Mama to let go of his hand and announces, "These people will kill me" (mar denge yeh log mujhe). Raju Mama tells him, quietly, that no such thing will happen and that things will be okay. The nurses join in this chorus of asserting that things are all right and attempt to soothe him. I do not know how Kishor might be seeing it. But the scene opens up the possibility that the order the orderlies enforce is in fact the rowdiness at hand. It is worth pausing on the potential for Raju Mama to be the rowdy here, or the way he may be amplifying a situation of rowdiness from a different position of power. Maybe rowdiness in fact describes well how triage's gestures shift persons into patients.

―――――――

The early stages of trauma care move and halt bodies through queues, evidence, and gestures, and the ward produces tensions between motion and stillness in turn. There are broader implications of better attention to shifts, including some implications that may affirm stasis as a structural good. Several epidemiological studies of trauma outcomes in low- to middle-income countries suggest that when district-level, secondary hospitals (like Maitri) shift patients to level 1 specialized trauma centers (like Central), patient outcomes are no different or even worse than for patients who arrive directly at the trauma center (V. Kumar et al. 2013; Veetil et al. 2016).

In practice, this means that it may be unwarranted for policymakers to fund and build more level 1 specialty trauma centers—as has been done in Mumbai, where a brand-new trauma hospital was built in 2013. It may be unwarranted to create hospitals that invite the shifts of transfers. More patients may survive traumatic injury with investments in secondary-level hospitals that can enable safe surgical care. Instead of creating pressures on specialty trauma centers and condemning patients to the instability of shifts, staying in place—rather than moving up the ladder of medical specialty—may be most beneficial.[23]

And yet, if neither flow nor stasis can be an absolute goal in the lifelines of triage, what remains in question are how shifts become the basis for managing trauma and the site for triage's social force. Sometimes vital signs and the hospital's understanding of those signs are in alignment. Often they are not. Triage is a site to explore what Lauren Berlant calls a *glitch*, a temporal-political sense of "what it feels like to be in the middle of a shift." Through glitches, people may embody inexact replicas of institutional norms. This means that when "bodies figure glitches in the conditions of the reproduction of life," it is differences between bodily movements that "reproduce and reconfigure institutional logics" (2011, 198). Attention to these differences shows how trauma's pressures on the hospital tighten and loosen the seams of public health care. As people move each other and must adjust, and as medicine enacts its own moves, shifting constitutes lifelines of triage. Attention to shifting can address the granularities of the broad-scale movements in hospitals called *transfers*, the turning over of responsibility and action when the current situation either resolves or hits an impasse. Shifts entail waiting, which shapes attachments to the velocities of handoff and transfer. Shifts involve bodily gestures, both voluntary and involuntary, in moments of life-threatening injury. Across these scales of movement and stillness, shifting pulls people and problems through overlaps between here and there and between now and next.

Scholars have suggested that unlike most medical specialties, emergency medicine has no clear organ or system as its focus (Cooter 2003;

Cooter and Luckin 1997; Schlich 2006; Zink 2006, 2011). This means that the knowing of emergency medicine is based on knowing relative differences in injuries as the basis of triage. Focusing instead on the *effects* of this differentiation, and opening up movement as emergency medicine's proper object, I have approached triage based on what it moves and what it stills, often at once. The pain of the accident is borne out in movement, so there may be desires to stop shifting. Yet shifting is also desperately wanted, because a total stop means waiting, no treatment, or death.

Shifting enrolls multiple people at once. Even without kin to accompany them, injured persons may arrive in the ward in the care of another: the passerby who sees a man fall from a crowded bus as he attempted to alight; the rickshaw driver on a tea break at the corner who witnesses another rickshaw driver being rear-ended by a garbage truck and brings him in; the coworker riding pillion on the motorcycle driven by his friend, whose lower limb is split open after the bike hits a pothole. The statistical appraisal of trauma's incidence counts the singularities of cases, and the conclusion sections of research articles offer prescriptions for better triage based on handling the singularities. This makes sense in part but also overlooks how trauma's existence depends on trauma's movements. To better capture this distinction requires backing up from the question, "How do we move the line faster?" and pressing on a question of internal heterogeneity, "How and when are cases being moved and being stilled?" To ask this latter question is to pursue the pressures of movement on injury, on the subject of triage-oriented medical knowledge, on something that gets called *health-care access*, and on the possibility of survival. It is also to move toward a harder question: Who gets to move a situation, under what different conditions, and to what ends?

Dr. V, a CMO, arrives thirty minutes late to the casualty ward one evening, sweaty and hyperventilating: "Traffic," he huffs. He sets his backpack and motorcycle helmet down on a metal cot in the back room, where we would sit for chai break, sipping from tumblers of steaming tea, parceled out from a plastic bag that the orderly fetched. Dr. V sits down at the casualty desk, eyes the queue, takes out a blank triage record sheet, and faces the first case.

3 Visiting

THE LIFELINES OF HOME

DOCTOR CALLING A
PATIENT'S FAMILY
TO THE WARD ON
THE MICROPHONE.
DRAWING BY
AUTHOR.

Sister Jaya approaches the microphone on the shelf by the window, beneath scraps of paper with the phone numbers of doctors, other wards, and ventilator technicians. A calendar from the municipality is turned to last year, September. The theme is heritage architecture, and Chhatrapati Shivaji Terminus, the city's central railway station, glows at nighttime. The ward's official mortality register, called the Death Book, sits above. Sister Jaya flicks on the microphone and calls out the patient's first name, plus *sagewale* (relatives): "Saad ki sagewale, Saad." She calls again, "Saad's relatives, come inside" (Saad ki sagewale, andar aa jao). The microphone broadcasts to kin waiting hours, days, and nights outside the building, waiting to visit.

Farzan, Saad's father, enters through the doors. He stands by Saad's bedside and watches his son for signs of movement. Saad's motorcycle slipped on the road, but the relatively small size of the brain hemorrhage and Saad's low blood pressure led the neurosurgeons to decide to let the brain sort itself out. Neurosurgery right now might do more harm than good, they say. So the doctors "wait and watch," and Farzan does too, making the ward his temporary home. Farzan often pulls the doctors and nurses aside to point out Saad's subtle twitches, jerks, and blinks, wondering if they signal a change for the better. He watches the ward with similar intensity, attuned to its comings and goings of care.

Traumatic injury demands relations with families. Communication with families is a way of communicating the situation of injury, and so relatives like Farzan are summoned into the ward frequently, every visit purposeful. Once morning rounds are complete and each patient has been assessed, both faculty and their residents call in family members to offer updates. Some of these updates are plans of what will happen, like a surgery. Others may be updates on the results of surgery or a timetable for discharge. Still, patients are often in "serious" condition, unable to speak or judged to be too injured to reflect on necessary decisions about their care. Families may need to sign a waiver acknowledging that the patient's death is a real possibility and the hospital will not be held at fault.

What is home under conditions of traumatic injury? For patients, the traffic of their home worlds into the trauma ward is hardly one-way. Their kin come and go often, if they are allowed to, and these visits entail labor. A summons for an update may also be an instruction for relatives to stay for a while and do physiotherapy, thumping on chests that struggle to breathe or moving limbs in partial traction to encourage muscle redevelopment. Kin must purchase and deliver medicines the hospital cannot provide. They pass through a door stating in English, "Patient relatives are not allowed," and then a second door with a sign in Marathi warning, "PATIENT RELATIVES DO NOT HAVE ACCESS TO THE WARD" (RUGṆANCHYA NATEVAYKA WARDCHYA AAT PRAVESH NAHIN). Perhaps for balance, a stenciled message on the opposite wall cues the staff: "Remember that anxious patient relatives are waiting outside. Please talk to them." Visitation is vitalizing but also threatening and makes home a lifeline through trauma's traffic.

A hospital is hardly hospitable, notes surgeon and writer Dr. Kavery Nambisan. Nambisan describes the contemporary hospital, in India and elsewhere, as a "coldly professional, regimented form" where "cure has relegated care to the backseat" (2020, 123). For Nambisan, the care marked by the "hospice" in every hospital—that kernel of homelike support for the sick and dying—has "more or less bowed out" in the hospitals of today. This may be so, in aggregate. Nonetheless, domestic relations suffuse the trauma ward, especially when patients' kin visit. Homelike life coheres through the movements of everyday clinical labor, through scenes of pervasive violence, scenes that may not shake off easily for either regulars or visitors in this space. Differences in visitation's kinetics are a core feature of traffic in the ward. Beckoned by the microphone, the families that constitute home move into the ward, and, simultaneously, the ward's workers make home in the ward. Qualities of domesticity shift, and care emerges through lifelines of home. Questions about the power and politics of state medical institutions merit deeper engagement with matters of home, specifically home as a primary quality of the hospital.

Domesticity inflects the sociality of hospitals. Many accounts of public hospitals assert the unique interiority of the hospital, that is, framing it as *if* it were a home. This is a common framing in the medical humanities, often routed through appeals to William Osler and the beginnings of medical residency and through texts such as Samuel Shem's *The House of God* (2010). Some of this is resonant at Central, to be sure. The hospital retains many colonial forms of clinical labor, and among them are the ways that medical residents are termed *housemen* in their first years of residency and indeed do sleep in the wards, on seemingly endless shifts.

Yet there are also limits to the hospital-as-home isomorphism. Mapping one space onto another is too inert. One might glean useful spatial insights, but one can also become so focused on comparing hospital to home as to overlook how unstable the domestic qualities are that constitute clinical space. My approach instead is to track how those qualities emerge, sustain themselves, and devolve through differences in movements. When kin visit, home moves into the hospital, and the boundaries and passages between home and clinic can be rescripted. Shahaduz Zaman elaborates this point at length in his ethnography of an orthopedic hospital ward in Bangladesh. Zaman argues that "patients oscillate between biomedical authority and domestic authority," depending on what time of day it is or what specific situation is at hand (2013, 286). Visitation renders patients' family members as "silent saviors," as Zaman describes them, saviors who provide care labor in resource-strapped circumstances. But the heterotopic ambiguities of biomedical space and clinical space render the visits of kin as uncertain. And because visitation is uncertain, it is subject to shifts in movement.

The contingencies of visitation are fundamental to the traffic of trauma. As a lifeline, home makes its mark through what I call the *clinical domesticities* of visitation: the moving atmospheres of care labor through the time-space of the ward that visiting foregrounds. Clinical domesticities derive from the ways care labor is frequently shuffled around, sometimes in contradictory ways. Caring is often an act of interrupting something else. Thinking about the care labor of home through both its flows and its interruptions raises the questions of what restricts and allows that labor, when it is called for (literally, in the case of the microphone), when it is policed, when it is allowed to do its work, and why. Attention to its rhythms may enable the ethnographer to attend to the backstories of patients, families, and ward staff in ways that the time-delimited nature of emergency triage makes more difficult to ascertain.

There are narrative limits to this approach. Visitation's backstories cannot offer a sense of the ward's inhabitants separate from the hospital. This is an enduring problem of method and writing in hospital ethnography: of making claims on persons *as if* the hospital can be bracketed. Patienthood is one version of personhood, but it is not personhood's entirety. The same is true for families who visit the hospital. A person who visits is far more than a visitor, and a focus on differences in movement rather than fixed positionality can open up a more expansive sense of how so. Still, I do not dispense with backstories entirely, because they can surface questions about which features of the self and the home may be voiced in the hospital.

I also focus on visiting's echoes of home life because the street—that sacred rubric of both chronicles of city hospitals and urban anthropology—is not the only spatial form that holds sway over the cityness of the city hospital. Overattention to the street's impingement on the clinic risks glossing over how domesticities both flourish in and threaten the clinic. Overattention to the hospital as a consolidated home may miss the ways that *for the staff* it may be a makeshift work-home, but theirs is not the only home in the picture. Home, as a polyvalent problem and solution site, can mark the place patients and kin come from and the place they wish to return to.

This home cannot be presumed to stay still, because families do not stay fixed. To provide care, kin move in and out of the ward. Movement gains its charge of value and meaning from the home as much as from the hospital writ large, because these institutions are tightly intertwined. The daily workings of a public hospital space are inseparable from domesticities, the structuring of gender, kinship, and labor brought to bear on clinical spaces (Street 2014). Both patient kin and medical staff bring home to bear upon the ward through visitation. The lifelines of home both constitute and reshape the traffic of trauma through visitation's shifting labors of care.

I track clinical domesticities primarily through the accounts of kin, nurses, and service staff. Doctors certainly communicate with families, often in fraught moments, but the everyday management of visitation and some of the closest interactions between families and the ward emerge through interactions with nurses and service staff. Collectively, the staff may think that home is what patients have and what their relatives move into the ward. But staff also acknowledge that the ward is not a blank slate. Rather, the staff in the ward work in rhythms that differentiate work time and break time, often during teatime and at night when there may still be new admissions inside the ward but when families of patients are not visiting. These rhythms may blur images and textures of home and work for the staff, and the high caseloads of injury come to shape daily rhythms of work and retreat. Across visits by both staff and kin, trauma moves home from multiple directions through seriality and familiarity. Through reiteration and remembrance, past patients and their injuries connect to those in the ward at any given moment. Through familiarity and repetition, families encounter the movements of ward staff, staff encounter the movements of the families, and this traffic grounds the serial everydayness of the ward.

Just as it reveals how the clinic intertwines with the home, visitation also reveals that the event that scholars term the *clinical encounter* between patients and doctors is perhaps not so dyadic as it may seem. The clinical encounter often assumes a patient who faces medical authority and can suggest a one-off event. However, this framing may ignore the pivotal presence of kin and, more important, the multiple, overlapping interactions kin have with workers other than doctors in the ward.[1] Nurses and service staff often have the most frequent and extensive contact with families, which adds layers of encounter that may not be captured by framing medicine only as that which occurs between doctors and patients. Clinical scenes may be encounters, but differences in movement condition who is in the scene, when, and why.

The clinical specificity of trauma is one factor here. Like Saad and Farzan, patients and their relatives stay in the hospital for unpredictable lengths of time, according to the particularity of injury. Some traumatic brain injuries and abdominal injuries require surgery; others may not progress quickly, and so waiting ensues. Since bodies are never universals, doctors time treatment partly according to age and medical history. Hypotension is always a concern in trauma patients, especially those who require surgery. Fluids get pushed to raise blood pressures, to steel against the incursions of surgery. There is repeated imaging, consults from other specialties, surgery, postoperative step-down, and sometimes more surgeries. There are wound debridements and amputations, and the stretches of waiting for orthopedics to do these procedures. There is the lookout for improvement or worsening across specific time periods, which may predict survival and shape how doctors update families. Doctors, nurses, staff, and kin engage this work as they see what is happening around them, which is the work of making people live, often but not always successfully. Given the prevalence of traumatic injuries in Mumbai, one might assume that workers in the trauma ward are always busy during their shifts. Yet, as anyone who has worked in a hospital knows, clinical work does not distribute evenly. Cases cluster; time stretches; and formations of gender, caste, and class underscore these dynamics.

For this reason, attention to clinical domesticities may offer a closer account of the clinical encounter, an account in which both families and staff must navigate the ruptures and routines formed at the nexus of hospital and home. To claim that the hospital *has* domesticities is not to claim that the hospital replicates a household; instead, it is to pay attention to flows that constitute care labor with presumed spatial insides and outsides, to track this flow as a sign of the public-private dynamics of health care in contemporary India, and to grapple with the ways the intimacies of care gain a moral charge in scenes of visitation.

The specificity of India matters. Moving through boundaries of allowable and forbidden spaces in the household constitutes forms of ethical life in South Asia, particularly the affordances and threats of the household for women (Dickey 2000). The boundaries between the home writ large and other formal institutions are also meaningful. The public hospital in India is a key site where the state makes contact with poor and low-income families, and this contact zone is politically and ethically charged (V. Das 2015). Similarly, I am interested in signs of domestic life as they appear inside the hospital. I also wish to account for the ways that staff in the ward cast their workspace as a homespace in certain moments, and the ways people inhabit space when they are confined to a bed, a critical sign of the home's dynamic qualities and an enduring sign of colonial power over bodies (Ramphele 1993).

Medical anthropologists have considered complex ties between the family and the clinic as important grounds of care. For instance, Sharon Kaufman (2005) describes how "managing the family" is key to intensive care medicine in the United States. Kaufman demonstrates how confusion and tragedy deepen because communication among doctors, patients, and families may not sync with the actual physiology of patients' bodies. Nonetheless, doctors try, and through cooperation and conflict between hospitals and those they serve, doctors treat families while they treat patients. Margaret Lock (2002), in her work on organ transplants in Japan, observes that doctors who engage the families of near-death patients assert this work as integral to medicine, since family work is part of turning a person into an ancestor at the time of dying. Medicine and domesticity are tied tightly, and this tie gets worked out in medias res. Michael Nunley argues that the presence of kin by the bedside of patients in psychiatric units in North India has the potential to teach the West about different (and possibly better) means of patient care. For Nunley, the role of relatives is a form of power in the clinic: it lends a "counterweight . . . against the dominance of biomedical authority" (1998, 320).

Managing the family is intensely operative in Central's trauma ward too, but my own observations suggest something different from Nunley's conclusion. Perhaps it is the specificity of trauma medicine compared to psychiatry, but families in the trauma ward do not have a single role that can easily be leveraged as resistance to doctors, compared cross-culturally, or conceived of as a policy solution for better care. Kin do not have a role in the trauma ward so much as they have a moving presence during visitation, and visitation is inseparable from the ward's care labor. Owing to their mobility and immobility, their presence is deemed both a catalyst and an obstacle. Families concretize traffic; managing the family is managing that traffic. This is an uneven power relationship that emerges through visiting's different maneuvers.

Chottu holds the rope tight; he loosens his grip to let the door to the ward open and pulls it shut at will. The meter-long rope connects from his hand to the door handle. As a military commando who sits at the threshold to the trauma ward, his job is to move visitors in and out. Security guards are here for the security of patients, but they are also here because of several attacks on doctors in Central and in other hospitals throughout India by relatives who allege malpractice and neglect. The guards were initially private contractors: women and men, young and old, some in uniforms that were a perfect fit and others in belts that didn't cinch things quite right. The nurses address commandos and guards not by individual names but by their collective task: *Security*.

After a set of high-profile attacks against doctors by frustrated patient relatives, the hospital administration fired the private contractors and replaced them with state military commandos at the door. Assaults on doctors often cause residents to go on strike, and during one of these strikes, one of the chief residents working in the ward on a strike day (trauma must remain open) sympathizes with the relatives. "It's a vicious cycle," he says. The hospital requires relatives because of tight resources and dispatches them to do essential labor. It is understandable, he thinks, that they would turn against this system. Outside, a group of medical residents hold signs that read, "Doctors are not safe at Central Hospital."

These attacks span both private and public facilities but are especially pronounced in private hospitals. When high costs for care meet undesirable patient outcomes—especially a patient's death—families may deem formal channels of regulation and compensation like courts and consumer tribunals to be ineffective and may take action of their own accord.[2] Attacks against doctors happen occasionally at Central, and the turn toward privatized security to regulate visitation marks a broader attempt by the state to securitize public services (which can intensify further as the state then pivots to military forms of security). In this context, access to the affordances of an already-strained public health-care system becomes subject to further gatekeeping, this time not in price and quality but in the threat of force. This gatekeeping can be frustrating for patients' kin. It can also register with staff as a much-needed action by the municipality to insulate the hospital against the threats of "the public" and to more closely align the public hospital with the presumably less porous forms of spatialized access to care that expensive private hospitals exemplify.

Chottu notes that relatives are always asking him for directions. It is one of many turns in the maze of language that relatives face, as their requests are constantly passed along. "If you ask the orderly something, they say ask the nurse; if you ask the nurse, they say ask the doctors. Doctors don't say anything," he says (Mama ko pucho, toh nurse puchne ke liye bolenge, nurse ko pucho toh bolenge doctor se pucho. Doctor toh kuch nahin bolta hai). He feels that all of this bouncing around can mean that some relatives hear about the status of their family member only after the person is dead, and this confusion is the source of much of their dissatisfaction and anger. He wishes that families got clearer answers.

Doctors in the trauma ward say that the clinical specificity of traumatic injuries makes that clarity rather difficult to convey. Getting better and getting worse aren't always linear, and so much can get miscommunicated amid the ups and downs. Faculty instruct their residents to be mindful about communicating with families, especially around issues of prognosis. Trauma is fickle, and things can change rapidly. While the guards manage the movement of people at the scale of the ward, doctors manage the movement at the scale of the beds. They bear out the hospital administration's pressures to empty beds to ensure room for future patients, and good communication with families may facilitate this goal. The less formal work of updating, the kind of work that is most frequent, often falls to the nurses, orderlies, and guards, and families learn quickly that these staff have a more consistent presence in the ward and may offer reliable sources of information. Still, no amount of updating can change how mazelike the hospital can be and how the maze is one of both language and space. A ward staff member says that for the relatives, the hospital is a "labyrinth" (bhool bhoolaya). Counter 4 is not next to counter 5; sequential ward numbers may stretch across different buildings. Things don't line up. People are constantly asking each other for directions, because passages are puzzling.

In Saad's case, Farzan is the primary family member to stay in the ward. Sometimes he exchanges places with his brother. Weeks later, when Saad is transferred from the trauma ward to the general ward, I meet Saad's mother and siblings, who remain outside on the benches of the open-air waiting area. In his position as father, Farzan is the designated watchman inside. Gendered positions of authority often bear upon decisions about the primary visitor and who else may come in for shorter visits. Many families implement this way of doing rounds of their own. For relatives, the guard at the door can offer a constant person, a touchstone, who might remember a note, a name, or a quick trip out to get medicine or food. Guards are asked to remember details, faces, and situations in order to allow visitation. But this can come undone when the guard asserts institutional authority and tells relatives they are not allowed back in.

Unmet expectations of respectful speech in a government facility can stir up frustrations. A young man lies in the ward following a motorcycle crash; his uncle who waits outside the ward approaches Chottu, the guard, whose chair sits underneath a chalkboard listing today's admissions. Can someone go inside to visit? No, Chottu says, the young man already has two family members visiting, the limit. More visitors spread germs. The uncle peers through the crack in the door that Chottu tries to close. Chottu suggests they wait down the hall, outside, in the designated waiting area. They do not move, and Chottu repeats himself, voice rising. "Speak with mercy and care—why are you shouting?" (Daya aur pyaar se bolo na—itna chilla kyun rahe ho?), the uncle responds. Chottu says that he *did* speak quietly first. Another family member leads the uncle away, cooling off the moment.

A "good" guard, according to ward staff, knows who to keep out (relatives, unless they have been called on the microphone) and who to let in (resident doctors, faculty doctors, nurses, orderlies, ward boys, sweepers, X-ray techs, *hamaals*, ambulance staff, medical equipment repair techs, hospital administrators, tiffin delivery boys, pathology lab techs, organ donation teams, social workers, physiotherapists, medical students, pharmaceutical company representatives, the anthropologist). A different guard replaces Chottu a few hours later; it is his first day on the job, and he doesn't know anyone. He tries to block the entry of one of the ward's X-ray technicians, and the tech ignores him, laughs, and breezes in past the guard's outstretched arm. The real joke, the tech says, is how pathetic these attempts at order can be. "Security! It's your job!" (tuzha kaam ka hai), the charge nurse reminds the guard.

Farzan sits outside on the street curb one afternoon and shows his phone to Nilesh, the father of another young man in the ward soon to be declared brain-dead. Taxis and ambulances deliver emergencies to the entrance to the casualty ward a few steps away. The ward is full now, and the fathers' two sons are at opposite ends of the ICU, but Farzan and Nilesh connect despite the thirty feet of distance between their sons' beds. They share information, stories, and updates. When the nurses and orderlies flip their sons' bodies to wash and powder them to prevent bedsores, the fathers help. They exchange mobile phone numbers and work out a sleep schedule in shifts so that one of them is always in the ward. If something happens to the other's son, the person on watch sends a text message with whatever updates they hear and the name of the resident on duty. It is a watchful relationship, premised on managing the maze.

It is a relationship of clinical domesticities crossed with difference. Farzan works in an office as a lower-level administrator. Nilesh is a truck driver. Farzan is Muslim, and Nilesh is Hindu. They live in areas of the city that are far apart, and their daily worlds are not necessarily destined to overlap, but they share certain features. Neither Farzan nor Nilesh can afford a private facility; their sons are in the same ICU because the public hospital connects people across different gradations of economic precarity. That their sons are in critical condition for weeks also cements their connection. It's not equalizing, and the interactions are not compulsory, but the ward does offer potentials for relation amid existential and economic instabilities.[3]

Kin like Nilesh and Farzan face a double bind in terms of their proximity to patients during visitation. On one hand, their labor draws medicine closer, if for some reason it drifts away to another case. They push gurneys, help in resuscitation sometimes, advocate for their injured family members, and keep attention going. They protest if things don't seem attentive enough. They make care event-full. Farzan does this frequently with Saad. He sits by Saad's bed, focused on his son, but the moment a doctor or a nurse passes by, he stops them for something: a piece of gauze to dab Saad's sweaty forehead or a request for an update on when things with Saad might change. He does not hesitate to make use of clinical resources. Yet, on the other hand, kin multiply too quickly during visits, according to some ward staff, and can become too emotionally overwhelmed. So they are also kept at bay.

Sister Anju returns from puja in the hospital courtyard one afternoon; it is Maha Shivratri, and the peepal tree in the courtyard anchors the celebrations. Bells and *bhajans* (devotional songs) echo through the hospital's corridors. She sees that I'm interviewing one of the orderlies, Dilip

Mama, and stands by us, listening to him detail the first time he saw a dead body in the trauma ward. She offers some advice: if I truly want to learn "the tale of the ward" (wardcha goshta), I need to pay better attention to the turbulence the relatives introduce. "Tell him how relatives make a ruckus" (relatives hungama kartat), she instructs Dilip Mama. The ward may produce sounds, but the home produces noise (although she admits that hospitals are incredibly noisy). To her, patients with trauma need rest, not visitors, and require as sterile an environment as possible, with limited exposure to the commotion (*hungama*) of kin. In a place where achieving stability means the promise of discharge, "bad" families might exacerbate already-stretched infrastructures of care.[4] Michel Foucault (1975) may have described clinical work as the quieting of background sounds, but the presumed noise of relatives also localizes the clinic. The clinic is a space of disturbances.

Some of those disturbances come from workers in the ward who must update families on the status of patients. "Today I'm telling lots of people that their relatives are going to die," a surgery resident named Dr. F tells me. We're standing by the sink in the ward's resus area, underneath the silver-plated Ganesha altar. Raju Mama walks by and checks his mustache in the small plastic mirror on the wall. Dr. F is mostly fine dealing with her patient Gaurav, who was in a motorcycle crash. It is Gaurav's father whom she does not want to face. Gaurav's father waits by his son's bed. Visitation often involves such stretches of stasis. After some time, he asks me to put a small plastic-framed picture of their family's guru next to the vital sign monitor, an anchor for the family's prayers. I manage to balance it atop the machine, whose readout indicates that Gaurav's vitality is dissipating. Also, the father would like Dr. F to give him an update on Gaurav's condition.

I return to the desk in resus. "I don't want to talk to him," she says when I relay his request. She spent half an hour yesterday explaining to him that Gaurav, who is in high school, is not going to make it. *Nonsalvageable* is one of the ways she drives it home, invoking clinical language that marks the approach of this road's end. She dreads repeating this update. She cried yesterday after talking to the father. He cried too, but then the situation pivoted: he began to console her, and this provoked in her a little bit of wonder and a lot of shame. The man whose son is near death is consoling the surgeon? Gender, age, and futility create unexpected vectors of relating, even temporarily.

The other surgery resident on duty, Dr. N, has drafted permission papers for Gaurav's father to sign, a form called the "Poor Prognosis Consent" that attests that the father knows that his son's condition is critical and that the doctors will try everything they can but offer no guarantees. "Don't get emotional," Dr. N says to Dr. F, not looking up from his notes. Dr. F hears this sometimes from the other residents, who worry that she tends to grow too attached to patients. When patients don't have good outcomes, she gets too weighed down by the what-could-have-beens. She certainly should be sensitive to the loss facing families, her colleagues say: allowing patients' homes into the ward, and acknowledging the concerns of patients' kin, is the basis of good doctoring. A good doctor allows visits. Doctors know that families are facing the unthinkable: a sudden loss, unlinked to disease or any other precondition, that likely will reshape the economic livelihood of an entire household. It's the loss of the eldest son, in this case, and weighted with complex values.

Dr. F's peers respect her skill at something no surgery exam can test: her ability to stay in the scene of delivering bad news and to hear out a family's pleas to know *kya hoga* ("what will happen"). As residents spend more time in the ward, their hunches get refined; whether or not their predictions are correct, they learn when to trust their own clinical instincts, to feel in their hearts that a patient is simply not going to survive, and to still keep working. But her colleagues insist that Dr. F cannot be *too* sensitive to these feelings, lest they slow down her momentum. There is always more work ahead. Good doctoring means not letting the ward visit oneself so much that it destabilizes work. This is a challenge given the prevalence of trauma. Dr. F says Gaurav's situation reminds her of what she feels she keeps seeing in the ward: a young man's bike slips; someone brings him to the nearest hospital, which happens to be a private facility; the family can't foot the bill; and so he is shifted to Central. By the time he arrives, his condition has reached a critical point, and few options remain. Familiarity visits the ward; her patients seem to be lots of Gauravs lately.

During night shift, things get quieter. At night, relatives are not visiting, and senior faculty are not rounding. It's the residents and the nurses and the orderlies moving from bed to bed. Sister Anju checks IV drips. Raju Mama checks urine output, calling out the number of milliliters of liquid he sees, and another nurse jots this down in the file. The patients sleep. Night removes certain demands on the nursing staff to interact with visiting relatives, and the policing of proper versus improper forms of domesticity can soften. It's a shift in the balance of visitation's presence. Night dampens this presence and opens up space for the ward to visit its workers.

Sister Jaya picks up her needlepoint when she sits down for a short break. She has worked at Central for thirty years. We talk crafts. I admit I'm a lousy knitter, a round- or straight-project kind of person, hats or scarves, nothing fancy. She can get fancy, though. She shows me photos of past projects on her phone, elegant scenes of forests, tea parties, dancing Ganeshas, swans, and waterfalls.

She lands on a photo of a female patient with major crush injuries; the young woman's *dupatta* (scarf) got caught in the turning grinder cylinders of an electric sugarcane press, the kind that's on many of the city's street corners to make sugarcane juice. Her body got pulled in. Sister Jaya talked to the young woman at length while she was in the trauma ward and keeps the photo to remember. This kind of nursing, the kind that is about connection, is key. It is part of the reason she got into nursing, although she admits that as a child she also had what she calls a *uniformcha craze*, a craze over uniforms, a nostalgic delight in seeing nurses in white caps, white socks, and white shoes, all pride, an added spark to enter the profession. She likes the iterative contact with patients, joking with them, teasing them, helping them improve, an intensity of contact different from the more episodic interactions that senior physician faculty have on rounds. Nurses both uphold and defy the mixed messages about moving kin into the ward, and this may crystallize in favorite patients or always-remembered ones.

She asks me about my family, and I talk about my mother and about my father's illness and death, another time in my life spent in a hospital, one when medicine's dark passenger—treatment futility—grabbed the steering wheel. She talks about her daughters, their aspirations to study engineering, and the difficulty of making the cutoff in state exams to enter college to turn fantasy into reality. Like several of the nurses in the ward, she once took an exam to get certified to work abroad. But the next steps of preparation after the exam were too expensive, and who would look after her daughters? Sister Jaya has done her job for decades and doesn't fully trust the newer, younger nurses; the training has gone downhill, she says. These young nurses seem to have just book knowledge, a sign of bad schooling and a sign of the times, of a nation whose postcolonial condition in her youth was angled toward access to education, but now education is expensive and exams are corrupt. Put into action, this inadequate training denies nurses their potential, rendering them unable to predict and manage clinical problems in the ward. It can quickly add up to negligence (*negligency kartat*), where patients aspirate tracheostomy secretions or experience septic shock.

Sister Jaya's approach seems different from Sister Anju's. Sister Anju tends to lead with a steely grip, and her words can bounce between castigation and conciliation within one sentence. At work, Sister Anju self-presents as the picture of tough love. She excoriates the orderlies for delayed, incomplete, or improper work, and then by the end of the screed, they joke like old friends. Affective oscillations like this condition some of the intensities of ward life. There can be toasting, like when a senior nurse retires and a formal celebration is held in the corridor between the operating theater and the ICU; the nurses wear formal saris, and I am asked to deliver a speech about the virtues of nursing, and everyone chips in to order biryani from the hospital canteen, and the neurosurgeon's drills whir in the operating theater as we estimate that the *degchi* (vessel) containing the biryani is big enough to feed Dilip Mama's home village.

There also can be roasting. A nurse wears pancake foundation makeup in a shade far lighter than her skin and is taunted as "Sister Pancake." An orderly wears his uniform's standard white pants in a size way too large. The pant legs billow out dramatically like those of a Rajasthani prince, and people don't let that one go for days.

Roasting has its limits. Dilip Mama pushes the X-ray cart hard one afternoon; he just had a spat with the charge nurse, who tells him that he's not working hard enough. This *bakwas*, this nonsense, is insulting. He's worked here for decades. He was working in the ward during the terror attacks in 1993, 2003, and 2008, bodies stacked everywhere. He has worked his way up through the ranks: servant, ward boy, foreman (*mukadam*), and now technician. He has *experience*, he has seen this place through its darkest days, but sometimes his colleagues dismiss his work ethic and work history. Instead, the charge nurse just yells orders at him, "her words like bullets" (shabdaanchya goliyaan). In these tugs-of-war, certain forms of social reproduction happen between staff that lacquer onto forms of social attrition happening with patients and their families. Inequality isn't just something that people wear like a sociological name tag; it is actively reproduced and contested through assertions of authoritative differences in clinical labor.

Nevertheless, my identification of markers of clinical domesticities is partial. Sister Anju may be quite similar to Sister Jaya, in fact, or quite different in ways I cannot see or know. I find myself lulled into the serial familiarity of the ward, and I try to resist the lull, the apparent slowness at night that seems like succor from the day's speedy intensities, lest I fool myself into thinking that I am seeing the fullness of persons when no such thing is happening. These velocities are not oppositional, and they are also not the point, because in fact it is gender and caste that underwrite the pace of clinical labor and its domestic resonances. Gender does so through the continuation of colonial and postcolonial histories of nursing in India, histories that bring the patriarchal state into complex relationships with the feminization of care professions (Healey 2013). And caste does too, as a moving form that shapes attachments to inequality that both expands and constricts freedoms of passage between home and work.

Night shift, when things are especially quiet, is sometimes when nurses talk more freely about attachments to forms of caste difference among the ward's workers and about the importance of trust across those differences. During the day, when faculty are present, the doctors on rounds may uphold a discourse of equality, a pretense of everyone working together as a trauma care team, all on the same side. This is a refrain that certainly can bear out in practice.

Nonetheless, *saying* that everyone is equal is not the same as everyone *being* equal. Rather, these refrains of teamwork rely on trust across differences that must be earned. Senior doctors often have parents who are or were physicians, which may confer class stability although not necessarily wealth. The senior faculty tend to be from upper-caste backgrounds with professional education and come from communities across India. Those born or brought up in Mumbai or in Maharashtra speak Marathi to the nurses and service staff, even if they speak Hindi, English, or other languages at home. This habit is built from the recognition that Marathi can ground trustworthy familiarity. It's a gesture that moves trust along by crafting shared speech when visiting the ward for work.

The younger doctors—especially the residents—concretize a different history of state and national education policies around caste-based reservations for medical school admissions (Thomas, Srinivasan, and Jesani 2006). There are policies that emphasize recruiting students from outside Mumbai to the city's medical schools, to decenter the reproduction of knowledge capital away from elite centers. There are policies that reserve medical school seats for students from specific caste communities. This means in practice that in younger cohorts of surgery and anesthesia residents, there is more variation in caste and social standing in comparison to more senior cohorts. The nurses and service staff are highly attuned to these differences, as are the doctors from underrepresented caste communities.

Nighttime conversations reflect on the ways that people are not all the same. Sister Jaya worries about her daughters' school admissions, about seats held for scheduled castes, and about the complexities of merit (Subramanian 2019). She thinks through differences she encounters in caste communities and reflects these matters back onto what is possible for daughters, girls whose mother has a government job as a nurse and whose father works odd jobs now and then when he is around, which is not always. She is not as economically secure as the more senior nurses. She has more stability than the resident doctors on meager stipends, who subsist on instant noodles. They will eventually become licensed surgeons and earn a salary far greater than hers. She never directly compares the lives of the patients. Certain inequalities manifest as fact (the patients are poor, and that is why they are here and not in a private hospital), and others manifest as bias (you have seniority, but your colleague is getting better shift assignments than you, what's that about?).

Nighttime is also a time to take in the familiarities of the cases, as clinical domesticities accrue qualities of iteration. Sister Jaya explains that the longer a nurse works in the same ward, the more she may register the repetition of troubling scenes. Trauma's epidemiology means that it is mostly young male bodies who are in the ward. It's not that she can't tell them apart; it's that someone in front of her on a gurney can remind her of someone in a similar situation, days or months or years before. One case can have all-too-familiar reverberations of a previous patient. The case of a cop with both legs amputated after a suicide attempt on the local train is horrifying on its own but also because a nurse remembers someone just like him from five years back. A young woman riding pillion on a motorbike with severe head trauma is tragic on her own but also because this happened last week, and the orderly had to console the family, who had trouble absorbing the doctor's assertions of brain death. Night can be the canvas for memory.

Familiarity with the injured body comes about because of immobility, the ways that certain people in the ward stay there for months or years at a time and experience its repetitive visitations. Almost all the nurses and service staff recall their first day working in the trauma ward and relay accounts of being disturbed. Nirmala Maushi, a sweeper, remembers that on her first day years ago, she had to clean and remove tubes and bandages from a dead woman's body. Even today, she says, "I am scared to touch any lady patient's amputated body parts; otherwise, I don't feel any anxiety. But I find small kids with trauma scary; it reminds me of my brother's kids, and I get panicked." Tippu Mama, an orderly, remembers a case from his first day, a triple fracture in a woman's leg. He got dizzy (*chakar*) and lost his appetite. His family had drumstick vegetables (*shevga*) one night, and the sharp angles of the sticklike vegetables reminded him of the patient's body, and he would see flashes of her face in the curry.

Another nurse, Sister Poonam, has no such problems anymore: "Initially I felt bad, but once your vision is dead, then you have no more feelings about it."

Many of the staff anchor experiences with traumatic injury in relation to their own relatives. Sister Nidhi recalls how she had just given birth to her daughter when she learned that her cousin had fallen out of the local train onto metal rods and was brought to Central and died in the trauma ward. She has seen a lot in the ward; she joined in the early 1990s and witnessed the injuries and deaths of the 1993 bombings and the riots that followed. Sometimes, she says, you do what you can clinically, and that's all that's possible ("aaplya parine aapan karu shakto fakta evdech aahe"). Sister Nidhi's steadfastness conjures the image of the indefatigable nurse, the woman who moves everything without being too moved herself. But resilience and interruption can share the same space. Sister Nidhi is always shaken by pediatric cases. Children "have not seen the world," she says, and her own growing kids remind her of this every day.

Many of the staff live either in nearby slum neighborhoods within walking distance of the hospital or far enough away that they must take the train. They often see accidents and injuries on the road and find themselves scolding young men for doing stunts near the open doors of the moving train or for not paying attention when crossing the road. "I will see you in the hospital" is what Tippu Mama warns them, a preview of a visit wherein the city and the home will be reconfigured in the ward.

———————

It's Monday, and the pace is energetic, a shift from the more muted weekend. Mangala Maushi sweeps empty bandage packets into the middle of the ICU. Dilip Mama gathers soiled bedsheets to take them to the laundry. "Why do you spend so much time watching the doctors?" Raju Mama, one of the orderlies, asks me. "You'll learn more in here." *Here* is the area in the ward called the "servant room," though it is more like a passageway between the resuscitation area of the trauma ward and the nurses' office. The service staff use it as a home base when they are not cleaning, pushing trolleys, assisting doctors, restraining and freeing patients, collecting urine, ferrying blood to and from the blood bank, flipping patients over to prevent bedsores, fetching tea for the nurses, removing tubes from dead bodies, changing living patients' clothes, cleaning the ward, interacting with relatives, or performing any other of the many duties that fill out their roster of responsibilities. The servant room is also where they can sit, change clothes, eat, rest, and gossip. A picture of Ambedkar on the wall looks out over a sink and a bay of lockers, some personalized with names in fading marker.

Tonight, the monsoon lashes the roof. We are having a midnight picnic, an idea that Raju Mama cooks up and coordinates. The servant room has enough floor space to spread out flattened cardboard boxes that used to hold gauze rolls. The younger orderlies bring hot boiled eggs, the X-ray techs bring a curry of *bombil* (a small dried fish), a sweeper brings *bhakri* (a sorghum flatbread), and the senior orderly brings chicken curry from the hospital canteen. I bring drinks. It is night shift, quiet but for the ventilators beeping across the hall and the hum of our chat.

Some of the service staff claim Other Backward Caste or Scheduled Caste backgrounds. Some (but not all) say they got their jobs at the hospital through reservation schemes whereby certain government positions are earmarked for lower-caste groups. Others began their jobs through compensation claims. A sweeper's husband was a municipal government employee who was killed in a job-related accident, and part of the compensation package she eventually received as his widow was the offer of a municipal government job, and the position of municipal hospital sweeper was what was available, so here she is. Before working at the hospital, some of the service staff were sewage workers, some were construction workers, and some of the women had been domestic servants. There is a portrait photographer and a farmer. Some are Buddhist and Muslim; most are Hindu. Satish, an orderly, points around the room at the attendees to differentiate personhood by home districts in Maharashtra. Some belong to the black soil of villages near Nasik that grow grapes. Some people are born of the red soil of villages near Ratnagari that produce the treasured Konkan mangos. Some are from Mumbai, city soil, soil now constantly dug up to build apartment towers for hi-fi people.

The possibilities and perils of urban political economy and labor shape these expressions of caste and also shape the spaces in which they are uttered. In the hospital, caste shapes assignments *for* labor, and it emerges *through* labor, in the ways someone may critique a job as being below, on par with, or above their capabilities. It would be limiting to render the denizens of the ward only in terms of overlapping hierarchies, given the enduring challenges of an anthropology of caste that too readily takes hierarchy as its central analytic (Ramberg 2014). It is also limiting to presume that caste is always speakable when in fact it is often hidden, both strategically and by force. Accounts in Dalit literature, sociology, and memoir make this clear, as in the writer Baburao Bagul's Marathi short story "When I Hid My Caste" ("Jevha Mi Jaat Chorli") (Bagul 2018; Dutt 2019). When I am asked by colleagues and students in the United States how caste works in the trauma ward, I usually ask what the intent of the question is. Often it is an inquiry into the touchability of dead bodies and specifically the caste-specific labor of touch work. It can also be a question about how patients from certain caste groups might experience discriminatory treatment, akin to medical racism. There may be an intent to discern caste through symbolic practices and to wonder how ideology becomes concrete.

I find myself trying to answer these questions while also trying to question their premise, and I begin from the proposition that the fullness of caste may not and should not necessarily be made available for a visiting researcher to ascertain. In the trauma ward, lower-caste "servant" staff certainly handle dead bodies, especially in the hospital's mortuary, but upper-caste doctors touch the dead too. I could take the case of the picnic and point out potential markers of lower caste such as nonvegetarianism, sitting on the floor, the portrait of Ambedkar, and Marathi spoken in rural dialects different from forms used by upper-caste urbanites. That would not be sufficient, however. In brief, historian Anupama Rao (2020) explains, caste "is a millennial social order with an equally long history of conflict and transformation." The dynamism of caste, notes anthropologist Ajantha Subramanian, makes it "irreducible to a set of traits or a worldview," and therefore it is useful to think about caste as a processual form—that is, to reckon with its continuities (2019, 12; also see Pandian 2009).

These continuities may lie in the reproduction of labor forms outside of the usually invoked four-*varna* (social category) system, argues the scholar of caste Anand Teltumbde (2020). This means that caste can be materialist and not just ideological, but it may be so in ways that existing analytic frameworks may miss. Furthermore, caste identification has locational specificities. In Mumbai, scholars have understood caste as derived from late nineteenth- and early twentieth-century politics of urbanism and urban "improvement," in contrast to being derived from a generic and absolute metastructure of hierarchical positioning (Masselos 1982; Shaikh 2014).

Clinical spaces are part of, not separate from, these specific and urban resonances of caste. The hospital can be understood to add to what historian Shailaja Paik (2014) terms the "dilemmas" of how caste recognition inflects Dalit lives in Maharashtra. Caste as an unspecified, blanket social form may be rejected by those to whom it may be applied, because those individuals have widely differentiated political claims. This is especially the case for women, Paik argues, a point that anthropologist Sharika Thiranagama (2019) elaborates. Historian Sarah Hodges notes in her study of the politics of medical waste in Indian hospitals that the caste dimensions of handling that waste conjoin the materiality and sociality of caste relations. But, she asserts, "the direction of travel" between materiality and sociality in terms of caste "is difficult to disentangle" (2018, 190). These routes of cause and effect are complicated, and medicine inflects these complications of touchability, as anthropologist Lucinda Ramberg (2014) describes in her analysis of the incorporation of caste in South India.

To these diverse and important insights, I would add that one way to understand clinical domesticities in the urban hospital is to think about how situational mobilities make caste variably meaningful. Social and economic exploitation through caste can unfold in different ways in the hospital, from structuring who works which kind of job to determining which people comprise the students in the medical school and nursing school through admission policies. Caste underwrites sidebar conversations about the politics of those admissions. Caste shapes who can and must enter clinical space, and under what conditions. It also shapes attachments to ideas of deservingness and inequity that coalesce through the movements of persons in any given scene. Gender and caste make the ward a space for realized, constricted, and imagined social and professional mobilities.

There is also something else that makes caste resonant in the ward, and that something is the space and time for an event to flourish in the servant room: a picnic. It is less the specificity of the event and more the possibility of the event, the possibility to sit, eat, talk, listen, and take up social space, and to do so even as caste's logics of enclosure, forced endogamy, and threats to intercaste sociality still operate. It is the potential for twenty minutes to pass without interruption. That doesn't make the picnic uniform or redemptive. Some at the picnic might rather be home with their families if a meal is going to be formalized, and others may be really into it or find it just fine but nothing special. Maybe some are balancing *this* meal, where each person is responsible for providing something, against the labors and costs of being responsible for all the things: the work of shopping, cooking, cleaning, and childcare that the women of the service staff must do at home, both before they come to the hospital and after they get back. Break time spent with colleagues is break time not spent talking on the phone with children and spouses, who may also be working. There is the contemporary reproduction of professional positions of servitude too—sweeper, dresser, ward boy—that weaves histories of casted labor into biomedicine (Mukharji 2016).

The picnic does not resolve inequalities, but it does move with them—it *happens*—and similar situations are not guaranteed when people leave the servant room. The contours of caste may shift both inside and outside the room. The service staff in the trauma ward have friends who are orderlies and sweepers in other units, and these connections can develop over decades. But the space and time to activate and sustain those connections can be hard-won, they explain, because duty calls, particularly in the trauma ward, where the urgency of work can be asserted and felt. Forming alliances along caste lines is an act that sits in complex relation to caste-inflected clinical labor. Once service staff leave their break room and step into the "official" area of the trauma ward, they move into the midst of nurses, doctors, and patients and their families, and the multiple different ways in which gender, age, caste, geographic origin, primary languages, and education all stream differentiation. This occurs outside the hospital too: during the walk or ride home, in the neighborhood, in encounters with strangers and familiars, and inside the home, where questions of social aspirations and obstacles get debated.

The picnic is sensory and perceptual, and thus it is also social. The smell of the food relates to the smell of phenol. The sound of laughter relates to the sounds of ventilators and the nurses summoning the staff by name to do tasks. The sound of the rain relates to being sheltered from it because of one's job. The taste of home food relates to the chicken curry brought in from outside. Indeed, it is *because* of this relational differentiation that the picnic may constitute what Gopal Guru and Sundar Sarukkai (2019) term the *everyday social* of caste: the nexus of sensory immanence with historical, structural discrimination.

So when people ask me to explain how caste connects to trauma, I share the story of this picnic, not to assert recuperation but to question the traffic generated as caste and medicine visit each other.

———

As staff make themselves at home, domestic actions and images appear. Tea break happens several times a day—this is a government institution, after all. The nurses take turns buying biscuits for each other from vendors outside (and sometimes the residents to whom they are close or who are courting their favor buy the biscuits and vice versa). The nurses' break is the ward boy's work: he brings them the tea in a huge blackened kettle, scalding hot, and despite his dexterity I wonder if he'll drop it, sending himself and everyone else to the burns unit a few buildings away.

Yet sometimes the staff can seem *too much* at home in the ward, as if they are *not* visitors but anchored fixtures. Their fixity can get mapped onto the failure to carry out work responsibilities. One afternoon, Saad's father, Farzan, is frustrated (*niraash*), he tells me. He dabs Saad's forehead with a handkerchief. Farzan has been waiting several hours for someone to take Saad to his daily CT scan. Because Saad is a wait-and-watch patient and is being managed medically rather than surgically, the repeated CT scan is a critical feature of his diagnosis and his prognosis: Is the hemorrhage getting worse or clearing up? Should Farzan expect Saad to recover or to decline? Or maybe Saad will stay the same, in the bed, on the ventilator, offering bodily signs like wiggles and squirms that Farzan often takes as signs of hope, of Saad's mind and body evidencing the person before the accident.

Not all the staff are properly attentive, Farzan thinks. His frustration today centers on the orderlies. Where are they? They are supposed to take Saad to his next CT. What kind of place is this, where the people who are supposed to keep a space in order cannot or will not do their work? Would anyone behave like this in their own home? Farzan's critique of improper domesticity raises the question of how the ward can be a home for many different parties and can slow down proper care, forcing patients' kin to absorb all the labors that the hospital cannot or will not do. There are proper and improper forms of clinical domesticity. Drinking tea while patients are waiting for care is not proper. What nurses might see as an essential break from long labor, relatives might see as neglect.

Farzan is not alone in making accusations of absenteeism. He flags down a nurse, who calls out to the orderlies in the servant room and gets no reply. Perhaps they are following up on trauma's multiple pathways. Tasks related to imaging, microbiology, blood, drugs, orthopedics, social work, transfers, and discharges pull the orderlies from the trauma ward into other parts of the hospital. Perhaps they are not following up on anything because they are not in the hospital. The hospital requires staff to use digital timecards to register their work hours, and in the trauma ward, senior nurses track staff attendance in small notebooks. In my discussions with nurses, orderlies, and sweepers, there is a refrain of "my duty" (*mazha duty*), the things in one's job description that are often outpaced by various requests. Duty can be individuated (the *my* in *my duty*), but the sense of work here can also be relational, because nurses and other staff often help each other out. A nurse finishing her shift does a little extra to make the next one's shift easier. A sweeper can do an orderly a favor and run an order or grab some supplies. When the administration piles on more tasks, staff express varying degrees of willingness to stretch beyond *mazha duty*, and it often depends on what else is on their plates. At stake are how patients can get immobilized in the labor gaps and how these issues sometimes remain muted until something goes awry.

<hr />

During teatime, Mangala Maushi takes her break. Along with cleaning up the garbage of the ward, including biohazard material, one of Maushi's many jobs includes making tea for the nurses. As the chai bubbles in the pot, she sits next to me and takes out her mobile phone to share some photos. She flicks the screen, her finger moving across it to advance through the album, one picture replacing the next.

Flick. She is dressed in a formal sari in the hospital auditorium. A few weeks back, the hospital held an event to thank the service staff, and all the women sweepers received a sari as a token of appreciation, a nicer one than the regulation blue-and-white municipality-issued sari she must wear to work.

Flick. She is next to the buffet at the appreciation-day ceremony.

Flick. She is in a different sari, now at home, in front of her home altar, one dedicated to the Hindu goddess Laxmi, who presides over other household gods.

Flick. The screen fills with a man's face. It is taken from above, and the man is on a metal gurney. A quarter of his head is bashed in, his eyeballs squished.

Flick. She is in a sari again, back in front of her home altar. It is Laxmi Puja, and her home shrine holds fruit, coconuts, giant *laddoos*, and a broom to sweep things anew, a key part of worship on this auspicious day.

"Very nice" (khoop chhaan), I say, tentatively. I am unsure if I should say something about the bloody head.

She notices my apprehension. "Oh, that picture," she says, referring to the head injury. "Those boys might have taken it" (mulaani kaadla asel). "Those boys" are the ward boys, the orderlies. The man was a patient in the trauma ward a while back; he had been in a railway accident. They took her phone, apparently, and snapped a few shots of a patient. This is what she seems to suggest. She flicks to the next photo, a selfie in front of her home altar again.

There is a sense of invincibility that many working in the ward profess to have, but scenes of injury are nonetheless disturbing to them. But *how* they are disturbing, and *when*, emerges in specific situations. I focused intently on cases of trauma in my early months of observation in the ward, trying to uncover patterns in injury and circumstance. But over time, it seemed that the cases were episodes of interruption to clinical domesticities. I began to question how certain moments seemed to reinforce or contest tempos of familiarity.

In the servant room, people take stands on social issues, woes about corruption get worked through, and fake news and real news get discerned. Quips by gurus and pirs on WhatsApp and Facebook circulate religious and ethical ways of living. Political parties are ripe for debate at the municipal, state, and national scales. Some people think politicians are finally improving things, and some people think they're ruining things forever. And then there are the real estate developers; Tippu Mama says that they're running out of room to ruin the city with their skyscrapers for the super-rich. They are so shameless that soon they will build on the *kabrastans*, the city's cemeteries, the little open space that remains.

I see Raju Mama in the room and sit down to chat; I ask if his work in the ward affects him, and he shrugs. He begins sending me WhatsApp videos of gruesome car, motorcycle, and train accidents with amputated bodies in full view. I think he is trying to help me understand something, but to grasp it I must attune to the ethical acts of hospitality extended to me as a visitor. I realize I am asking only about effects, because I want to focus on what happens after the crash, but this rules out the ways that scenes of injury's causation permeate the ward, out of sync. Raju Mama cannot see the accidents that send *these* patients in; he is not a witness to those scenes, a bystander. Yet he visits injury scenes in the videos he watches and sends. Some appear doctored, I think, and my eyes scan the crash scenes, trying to discern the recursivity in terms of what's *filmi* and what's real.

Raju Mama sends the videos when he's not at work. The next time we're both in the ward, we watch them in the servant room, tea and a horror movie. He says they're good lessons about how to take care on a motorcycle. Another afternoon, Raju Mama is watching something with Shuki Maushi, one of the sweepers. I hear the video before I see it because it involves a chilling scream. It is a WhatsApp video of a man being butchered alive in a mob attack; the attacks against Muslims and Dalits are steadily increasing, they tell me. This, they say, sickens them. If one can see the horrors visited on men, just imagine what happens to women, Shuki Maushi says, and so she will not let her daughters out of her sight. Every break she gets at work, she sends a text to check in on them. In a clinical space where the effects of certain forms of violence are regularized, other forms also filter in, and they are absorbed in relation to valued life.

However, sometimes the domestic worlds of patients are at odds with the habituated rhythms of the ward, and gender can shift the tenor of clinical domesticities. One afternoon a young woman named Amrita arrives with her foot amputated and the stump wrapped in gauze. The ambulance doctor says that Amrita gripped her hand so tightly during the ambulance ride that she winced. Amrita says that she was collecting plastic bottles to sell for recycling and collected some on the train tracks. She did not hear the train coming and was run over. The ambulance doctor holds up a small brown glass bottle. It is *solution*—an inhalant, sometimes lighter fluid or cleaning solution, or something else with fumes that offers a quick high. Perhaps this is why Amrita didn't notice the train coming, a nurse suggests. The ambulance doctor claims that Amrita does not appear to have inhaled it; she probably drank it, and that's why she is able to withstand the pain of an amputated foot. The surgery resident immediately calls for toxicology and psychiatry referrals and consults with the orthopedic surgeons about scheduling the operating theater to address her foot. Amrita asks for water.

The psychiatrist arrives quickly and is careful and clear with her questions to Amrita. The psychiatrist finishes the conversation and returns to the desk where the nurses and I sit. According to the psychiatrist, Amrita says that actually, she wasn't on the train tracks to collect plastic bottles to sell. She was on the train tracks because she was angry, and she was angry because a neighbor deemed her unfit to take care of her son and took her son away from her. Amrita decided that she wanted to die; she says she wanted to be "under the train" (gaḍi ke niche). So she drank the solution and went onto the tracks and waited.

As her case proceeds through the care machinations of the ward, I wonder what sort of home Amrita will be returned to after the ward is done offering what it can. To the surgeons, one of the case's most pressing issues is her foot. They want to operate quickly, to stay ahead of infection and tissue decay and to maximize the chances of success for a prosthetic. A page in the file contains the psychiatrist's suggestions about how to handle an attempted suicide case, and there is a suggestion for social work. The nurses suspect this referral may stay buried, as the hospital's social workers are strained by their workload. The ward will repair the foot, and Amrita will get discharged back into the fabric of a domestic world that is inseparable from her appearance in the ward in the first place.

I also wonder how trauma when defined as a railway injury may operate as a cover for domestic violence and suicide, especially when women appear in the ward. Certain forms of home are absorbable in the ward, but if a home is thought to be violent, there is no guarantee of the degree to which the ward's forms of knowing will register this. Violence in a home, or "bad families," may get labeled as the social dimensions of a case and may be grounds for social worker and psychiatric consults. For the surgeons whose expertise dominates the ward, it is unclear whether knowing details about *this* "social"—a contested home world that visits the ward through bodies—is necessary for trauma medicine to proceed. Perhaps it is more a question of *if* and *when* and *how* the home can visit as a problem of movement, as the ward selectively attends to the social in tense situations.

———

The trauma ward wants and needs the kinetic care labor of kin to a degree but it cannot fully accommodate the disturbances—however palliative— their visitation concretizes. Nor does it fully absorb their imagined "real" home lives. Relatives of the injured are suddenly forced into a hospital ward with no preparation, and some may have never been inside a hospital before. What they are facing is manifold. They face pivotal, time-sensitive decisions of life-and-death gravity. They must sign consent forms and wait for long stretches of time in the presence and absence of their injured kin. There are times when they are granted the possibility to visit, and there are times when they must wait when a body disappears into the operating theater for surgery, a time when visiting the ward would reveal only an empty bed and reaffirm uncertainties about what the hospital might be doing. They are asked to make complex decisions that will restructure the life of a household. They must do so from within the hospital, a space that is supposed to shore up life's fractures but that will make no promises. Insofar as the street is asserting itself in the hospital, the home certainly asserts itself too.

Kin do not simply "bring the home" with them to the ward as they visit and work. Health-care workers cannot sustain an essentialized home on their own terms, either. Visiting is a matter of relational traffic. Precisely *whose* home life is getting asserted is what conditions lifelines of home. Kin must work with a constantly in-motion set of doctors, nurses, and orderlies who have been trained by school and experience to have a mask to witness pain but not absorb it. In this context, efforts to make home in a place that is not home become part of the ward's work. The home can also have multiple valences. The home may be the place where kin learn about the accident. Often neighbors, the police, or total strangers may be the ones to witness the accident, and news comes to families through mobile phone calls. Someone will go to the hospital and then inform other members of the family. These are clinical domesticities too, and they often take place just outside the doors to the ward so that someone can come inside if the patient's name is called. Visiting, as a critical gesture constituting the lifelines of home, can move in different forms and directions.

Visiting also bridges worlds that may have already been connected via news. Being watchful, and staying in place, takes work. Once kin are in the ward, this work of clinical domesticity continues. The hospital is usually the first place where a family will see the injured person. Onlookers may conflate this scene with a sense of the family's home life and possibly deem it too much for the patient or other patients to take, and so relatives must manage their comportment. They must don masks and emotional distance, even though the expansive meanings involved in the encounter with an injured family member do not conform to simply domestic matters. These are *human* matters. In these moments, visitation can be apprehended and leveraged to different ends.[5]

The ward allows certain impressions and practices of some domesticities but disallows others. All the while, makeshift or fictive kin relations can emerge. The doors to the ward with their mixed messages ultimately are a sign of the enclosure of clinical space that in practice can never be realized. The domestic world threatens the fiction of the hospital as an unshakable, sovereign space with orders and borders that can stand on their own, even as families are a vital resource of care labor that must be moved in to shore up what the hospital cannot always provide. Nurses can assert the rules to curb visitation, and they can bend the rules to catalyze visitation. For relatives, the ward interrupts life, their life, domestic and otherwise. It is an interruption because injuries are devastating and inconvenient: relatives must reshuffle jobs and rhythms and care work for others in order to be present in the hospital. In these situations they become attached to signs of change, a squirm or a twitch that could announce some movement toward one's more familiar home. Throughout, they must be knowledgeable but not too knowledgeable. Pushy but not too pushy. Obedient but not too obedient. Present but not too present. Movable to action in terms of their labor but not too moved by the terrible things they see.

Through these lifelines, marked by fraught movements, home for the patients with kin seems a relative certainty. But this is not always the case.

4 Tracing

THE LIFELINES OF IDENTIFICATION

DOCTOR PHONING
A PATIENT'S FAMILY
WITH A PAPER ON
HIS LAP. DRAWING
BY AUTHOR.

The man is not conscious, and his formal name is not known. So the ward names him "Unknown," and a nurse writes this on a file folder. Patients like him receive names in sequential order of their arrival at the trauma ward, designated by gender. This man is Unknown Male 3, which means two others have come before him.[1] Window curtains block the sunlight; inside, it's fluorescent. Shadows and highlights outline a twenty-something's taut face. His admission papers offer only a sketch of the circumstances that delivered him here: a second-class journey on the Western Line, headed south toward Churchgate Station, and a lean out of the train car's open doors.

Perhaps he was taking a phone call, since reception can dampen as the train sluices through town. Maybe he wanted fresh air. It can be stifling inside a crowded carriage. Like his name, the details are unknown. But the debris in his hair suggests that a rock hit his head, probably dusted up from a construction site. The vital sign monitor next to his bed blinks the words "Circuit Problem," a loop that won't close between body and inquiry, and his eyelids flutter.

A government railway police constable in a khaki uniform enters the ICU and approaches the Unknown patient's bed. A pin on his uniform declares his name, and he introduces himself; he is Arif. Arif explains that he received the call about the accident, oversaw the removal of Unknown 3 from the side of the railroad tracks into the police van, and drove him to the hospital. According to police procedure, Arif must take a statement from Unknown 3, meaning he must continue to visit the hospital until Unknown 3 regains consciousness, dies, or is transferred out of the hospital in some in-between state. A few papers found in the man's pants suggest that he may be from the northern state of Uttar Pradesh, which along with his age (he is in his early twenties) suggests to Arif that he may be a labor migrant and possibly may not have relatives in the city. Arif fills in a form that documents the effort to get a statement. He writes an X in the box next to the option "patient is unconscious" and marks today's attempt at identification as unsuccessful.[2]

"This is my patient" (hamaara patient hai), Arif says, gesturing to Unknown 3. "I am his parent" (hum usko maa baap hai), he continues, using the Hindi term *maa baap*, literally "mother father," which conventionally refers to parents or caretakers. Arif stands on one side of the bed, a surgeon on the other, and in the middle is Unknown Male 3, who is likely far from his natal family. He is a subject who is currently not speaking, now in the hands of postcolonial medicine and postcolonial policing. His unconsciousness, coupled with the consciousness of doctors, nurses, service staff, police, and the anthropologist engaging him, enables the care grip of medicine and law. This relation emerges through identification practices that draw bodies into domains of state power.

Questions of *who* a person is and *how* a person is constitute lifelines of identification and emerge through practices of tracing. Tracing is an act of directional speculation and entails presumptive differentiation of two things at once: the injured body's capacities to be both fixable and movable, and the way a person's identity may be learned rather than given. Tracing works through vectors: it can fix people in essentialized terms, yet also seeks clues that might move the injured toward family and out of the hospital. For both identity and injury status, what counts as fixed and what counts as dynamic may shift. These instabilities charge tracing with the potential to form lifelines.

Without a name for Unknown Male 3, Sister Jaya cannot call out a name on the microphone to the waiting area outside to summon his family, so other attempts at tracing unfold. Arif pulls out his mobile phone and photographs the man's face, arresting it as an image. As he snaps photos from different angles, Arif and Dr. K reflect on the lethality of the local trains. "If only the doors of the trains closed," Dr. K says, "at least 50 percent of injuries and deaths could be averted." "Easily," Arif replies. "You know," Arif reminds me, "ten people die every day on the railways."[3] I nod. The conversation halts with the weight of the statistics and the open question of whether Unknown Male 3 will become one. Dr. K signs the "too injured to give a statement" paper and hands it back to Arif. Law and medicine plot to handle this circuit problem.

––––––––

Efforts to trace the relationships between trauma and personhood often anchor scenes in the trauma ward, especially in cases of Unknown patients, the category of patients who arrive at the hospital ward unidentified and with compromised consciousness. While the previous chapter considered the movements of a known home in relation to trauma, this chapter details the problems (and nonproblems) that develop for injured patients who arrive *without* kin and who cannot name kin owing to loss of consciousness. These patients, who are living, share some features of persons Jonah Steinberg (2013, 2019) has described as "the kinless dead"—without kin by their side, their social mattering becomes an emergent social property. Trauma medicine can work without plumbing deep into an unconscious person's interiority. Surgeons certainly don't need a name to cut. But trauma medicine must monitor neurological status to predict improvement toward living or worsening toward death. Care can be predicated on consciousness, and not just for doctors. Because trauma cases are medicolegal cases, police must investigate who an Unknown patient is, in order to inform their family. The care of the law, too, connects relation to cognition.

Lifelines of identification are indeed lifelines because tracing the identity of a patient bears vital significance in trauma medicine. Epidemiological studies conducted in the ward do not track the known/unknown status of patients, but the researchers who carry out the studies—along with nearly all the doctors, nurses, and service staff in the ward—contend that the clinical outcomes of Unknown patients are often far worse than those of patients who are identified. Based on experience, they believe that Unknown patients are more likely to die than known patients with identical injuries and in the same ward. This is simple: patients with family members have people around to advocate for them, to inquire, to answer questions, and to demand that the hospital reckon with an individual's particular needs. Unknown patients do not have this affordance of care.

How does care unfold in this context? By tying medicine to law, and cognition to social belonging, tracing is identification's key gesture. Agents of both medicine and law do tracing. Their objects are persons with the instabilities of brain injury, who enable two questions that can be difficult to distinguish. One is the question, *Who is this subject?* The answer is as much a shifting clinical relation as it is a legal, juridical, and familial status. The second is the question, *What is wrong with this body?* The answer is a dynamic relation to law as much as it is a patient's cognition-dependent survival probability. The body depersonalized through traumatic injury can be a site for different agents of the state to imprint care, in moving terms. Detailing how reveals the ways that the public hospital and trauma itself are critical sites of state power, and the importance of describing rather than assuming how consciousness, identity, and bodies come into relation.

Unknown patients with brain injuries also reveal the limits of scholarly arguments that cast depersonalization as the sign of medicine's work. Consider Arif's two assertions as he faces Unknown Male 3: "This is my patient" and "I am his parent." The latter claim might be taken as a form of personalization routed through state law and order, one that renders the police constable an authority and the injured, comatose person the passive recipient of that authority. That may be so; I have no way of adjudicating this claim, for it is impossible to assess it from Unknown 3's point of view. One of my aims here is to assert that comatose states are precisely where ethnographic knowing and attempts at personalization falter. Still, in the face of such incompleteness, one may still assess Arif's first claim: "This is my patient." An officer of the law takes on a patient, a category of person usually reserved for medicine. What might this assertion suggest at the convergence of medicine and law?

Medical anthropology tends toward a strong critique of depersonalization and often draws on Irving Zola (1972), Ivan Illich (1976), and Peter Conrad (2007) as touchstones. This approach aims to show how people experience depersonalization amid the medicalization of contemporary societies (Becker 2007; Scheper-Hughes and Lock 1987). The ideas here are twofold. Medicine, as an institution of social control, turns persons into patients and consequently renders people into objects of knowledge. In turn, medical anthropology and allied forms of social scientific and humanistic inquiry insist on humanity and as a result, ethnography might *re*personalize what medicine has objectified. Vectors of depersonalization may shift, as feminist scholars have detailed in terms of the punitive, carceral, racist, and racializing forces applied to women's bodies (Bridges 2011; Davis 2019; Deomampo 2016; Rapp 2004; E. Roberts 2012). Depersonalization can also occur in different guises and agencies. Patients may face demands to depersonalize their own bodies, as the case of organ donation reveals (Cohen 1999; Crowley-Matoka 2016; Sharp 2006).

It is not only the ethnographer who registers a person without an apparent backstory as a problem to be solved. The work of Central's trauma ward also does the work of repersonalization, even as it does the work of depersonalization and objectification. This simultaneity is a key feature of medicine in cases of compromised consciousness, such that repersonalization is a fraught ethical and political effort. The task at hand is to examine who traces, what tracing generates, for whom, and to what end. As Unknown patients anchor demands for medicine and law to repersonalize bodies, doctors and police reinscribe social forms and stock characters of everyday South Asian social life onto bodies whose injuries have dislodged names from flesh. As tracing happens, trauma's medicolegal qualities are amplified.

In this light, tracing can be a site to understand how trauma puts law and medicine into relations of differential motion.[4] The clinical specificities of traumatic brain injury and attachments to personhood underscore these relations. In the trauma ward, the Unknown is not a matter of the unexpected but, rather, a category of person (Fruzzetti 1982). This is because the ward repersonalizes an unidentified person the moment they arrive. The Unknown label refers to the ways that the ward may not know a patient's name and family, yet the ward *does* know that the person's cognition is impaired. Framing the medicolegal through lifelines, I suggest, reveals how authoritative institutions move through and around bodies, sometimes in collusion and sometimes in passing, one decelerating or accelerating the possibilities for another to do its work at different turns.

Recall the case of Unknown Male 3: he presumably has a home, a job, and a name. He has a life and a life story. Then he falls out of the train. *To the ward*, he may be an Unknown person, but that is only one perspective, and it is inaccurate to assume it is the only one. I choose instead to detail a perspective built from describing efforts at tracing, some that belong to what gets called medicine, some to what gets called law, and some to what gets called ethnography, each differently configured through terms of individuation, relation, cognition, and embodiment. At stake is the effort to make someone live through balancing inquiries into *how* a patient is and *who* a patient is, through lifelines of identification.

These lifelines offer a window onto biopolitical subjectification. Subjectification, via much biopolitical theory, has often been analyzed as the ends and means for making death (Agamben 1999). The harsh conditions of rural-urban migrant labor may underscore the causes of Unknown Male 3's traumatic injury. My aim is to examine how these conditions do and do not inflect efforts to make someone live after the injurious event occurs and to offer a perspective on care defined through these efforts. Tracing is not always redemptive. It is better understood as a contested site where subjecthood, kinship, and survival may achieve relation (see S. Gupta et al. 2019). This occurs in terms of differentiated palliative and punitive movements, rather than in terms of unwavering stability.

The ward stretches to accommodate Unknown patients but also distributes the costs of such efforts. Focused on tracing's moves and consequences, the chapter's sections elaborate attempts to resync bodies and the narratives of differential motion accorded to them. Care for Unknown patients demonstrates readings of the body anchored in something different than the "What happened?" of the examination. Some of these lifelines are clinical, like the Glasgow Coma Scale, a neurological scoring system used to assess comatose states. Some are forensic, in the ways that constables like Arif trace clues on the body of the injured person to pursue identity through markers of community belonging. Patients enact lifelines of identification, too, as they attempt to speak through the fog of both brain injury and the surgeries and drugs used to treat it. Collectively, these lifelines show how traces of movement get drawn over injured bodies, dotted and interrupted by both traumatic injury's neurological effects and the absence of kin.

There is also a sense of unknowing that inflects my narration of these cases. This is not a matter to be resolved but rather one to be questioned. If medicine and law already are doing the work of repersonalization, what are ethnography's terms as a tracing practice? What moves is the ethnographer willing to make to pursue vital knowledge? And with what consequences? As I wonder about the circumstances of Unknown patients and about what their unconsciousness makes possible and impossible, my own queries trace care's proximities: not closure but closeness.

In the aftermath of traumatic injury, people float at the edges of consciousness. The trauma ICU is a room for intensive care, and it is a room for dreamlike states. Patients call out through the fog of anesthesia and brain injury, and residents calibrate sedation in a sleep-deprived haze. One patient repeatedly calls out, "Don't chase me!" with his eyes closed. One bed over, another man calls out, "Hema!," which a resident assumes is the name of his girlfriend or wife. Two beds away, Dr. U untangles headphones that have loosened from the ears of a patient who fell from the train. Dr. U believes in the healing power of music and often encourages the relatives of comatose patients to play looped audio files of prayers, devotional songs, and favorite tunes, anything calming. He sings as he checks vitals, a little louder when he gets to the refrain of "Zindigi Ban Gaye Ho Tum" (You've become my life), from the film *Kasoor*. His song envelops the patient, who arrived recently from the casualty ward, still with a bandage taped to his chest labeled "Unknown (M)."

Over time, I began to think of the ICU as a reverie room, where certain utterances get left alone as part of the effects of trauma or its treatment, while other utterances may be investigated for their referents in the uninjured world. In reverie, Gaston Bachelard sought to account for the solitude of imagination in waking dreams through poetry, a method he termed "reverie on reverie." Reverie entails moments "when we are so profoundly liberated that we no longer even think of the virtual rivalries" of the waking world (Bachelard 1971, 62). For Bachelard, reverie is the daydream of pure solitude and imaginative joy, unhinged from bodily attachments. Yet the trauma ward blurs the domains of sleeping and waking, of reverie and consciousness, and of body and psyche. What, then, is entailed in the shifts between reverie and identification?

The answer to this question relies heavily on the utterance of names. Names, like the callout to "Hema," may denote context or may leave context out. Names may mark a shift in neurological status and the revelation of certain angles of personhood, as patients assert themselves even as it may seem that they are lost in thought. To cast patients only as dreaming and dreamy, only as suppliers of reverie, as talking only *bakbak* (nonsense), would be to miss so much. Rather, names spotlight a feature of trauma's consciousness effects and a site for tracing to twist who and how a patient is (see S. Varma 2016, 51; Hunt 2015, 20).[5] Names, then, are traces of movement's completed, current, and conditional acts. One must listen for what names move, even as one listens for what they denote: this is how traces get inscribed.

Names can be fleeting things in the trauma ward, and this instability is connected to how names mark caste, class, religion, and community status in South Asia (V. Das and Copeman 2015; Hansen 2002; Paik 2014). The ward's staff generally remember the names of patients who stay more than a few days, but the rotation of cases can strain this effort. For some, it is more clinically meaningful that a person is named first by their injury, such that the damages of traumatic injury cement identification: Mohammed is "road accident with degloving," and Vikram is "subdural hematoma." The constraints of confinement can be markers, also, since patients may be identified by bed number. A nurse might call out to the service staff to shift the patient in bed 2 to CT (*do number-chi shift karetze*), and for the nurse, the bed matches the injury on her master list of cases in the ward at the moment. Another way staff know patients is by the nicknames they give them, both the Unknown and the known. They talk to comatose patients and greet them with good mornings and good evenings. It keeps a sense of work moving. It is a way to work when one's focus of care is unresponsive. Maintaining labor's momentum matters here, amid the frequent changeovers of patients that demand anew a memory match among bodies, names, problems, and locations.

Alongside this tension, the clinical profile of a person matters to ward staff. For instance, the proper name Rahul denotes little about treatment needs and urgency—that is, the relationship between this person's injury and the injuries of others in the ward. Rahul may denote Hindu and male but not brain injury or abdominal injury in need of a consult from neurosurgery or anesthesia. Nor does a name automatically align with the logic or work of triage. When neurosurgeons come down to the ward, they need to know which patient they must examine. The name, when it is called from the microphone to summon relatives from the waiting area outside, is the start of news about a clinical condition for people outside the ward, or the name's calling can be for purposes of gaining consent for a surgical procedure. For relatives, the name has meaningful importance. For physicians, this importance in terms of categorizing persons is germane, but a name isn't a grand reveal so much as an acknowledgment that the ward needs families for care labor, families that are not locatable for Unknown patients.

This reckoning of names and their differences in reception may have different ends. Scholars who track discriminatory practices in Indian public hospitals note that staff inquiry into patients' names can be a signal of caste discrimination and unequal care provision (Ghoshal 2015). As Rakhi Ghoshal points out, public hospitals in India can be Janus-faced when it comes to discerning caste in processes that are formal (e.g., patient admission) and informal (e.g., conversations between staff and patients). On one hand, the urban public hospital's claims to treatment equity regardless of ability to pay may offer rural-urban migrants a space of relief from explicit caste-based identification demands in more rural areas. When these persons become patients, there may be a reconfiguration of the ways caste matters in relation to care. It still matters but perhaps in different ways. On the other hand, Ghoshal argues, higher-caste staff and administrators in the hospital may justify assigning undesirable forms of labor based on the caste-inflected names of workers. They may also use the names of lower-caste patients to imagine their lifeworlds as inferior, which could potentially influence the care provided. Names of persons and of caste communities are always at work.

Things do not resolve automatically when Unknown patients are named by family members. Patients in the ward have varied reactions when they first see their kin. People can be relieved to see their families, and they also may not be so thrilled. While *relatives* is a generic term, its specificity matters because certain family members may induce tension and can register as threats from the patient's point of view. The context of accidents heightens this, as some members of the family may be more inclined to ask questions about blame and responsibility, questions that are especially amplified around cases of attempted suicide and may be strongly differentiated by gender and age.

Furthermore, a hospital is already a confusing-enough place, and medicine's practices and substances can crowd and cloud these encounters. Surgery, especially neurosurgery, involves a cascade of interventions and chemicals whose metabolism may take time. They can cause changes in perception and mood, from corticosteroids that may cause agitation to anesthesia that causes somnolence. The structural circumstances of the public hospital setting, and of medicine itself, complicate the connections between kin and patients' poorer outcomes. Yet with these complications in mind, it is still the general position of the ward's workers that even if a patient does not want their family around, and even if kin are not happy to be at the hospital, their labor and attention can still be a life-or-death matter.

The ward gleams under fluorescent lights. Patients and their families often find what is illuminated in the beds around them worrisome: identification not of personhood but of circumstance, the what-ifs of potential bad outcomes. By the time I finish fieldwork, the hospital has installed curtains around each bed for privacy. Before this, rolling cloth trifold screens were used to cut off lines of sight between one bed and the bed of someone who has died. But people still know things even if they can't fully see things. As for me, I'm always rubbing my eyes, a terrible idea in terms of hygiene, but I see halos.

I rotate shadowing different workers in the ward, and today it's the nurses; time to check the inventory of anesthetics. I turn a bottle of propofol over in my hands, a viscous cloudy-white paralytic that one doctor playfully calls "the milk of amnesia." I never shake off my sense of surprise when propofol produces blackout in patients; when they awaken, they are often unable to recall certain events that took place before the drug's administration.

Propofol shares some properties with fentanyl, another common drug used in the trauma ward's resuscitation area, emergency operating theater, and ICU. Both have the potential to induce unconsciousness and sometimes amnesia. Both are difficult to procure. India was and is one of the world's leading exporters of opiates, but anesthetics can be difficult to come by inside public facilities. The critical substances of sedation, pain relief, and induced forgetting have chemical trails that move out of South Asia, with little tracing back in (K. Sunder Rajan 2017).

Many actions in trauma care proceed according to the assessment of consciousness. To assess a person's level of consciousness, medical staff score patients based on neurological tests. A frequently used one is the Glasgow Coma Scale (GCS), which assigns points based on a patient's response to different stimuli.

A patient may be, for example, "E1V2M3"—a doctor will quickly assess that this patient is at serious risk for death because of the impaired neurological response. There is no eye movement (E1), barely comprehensible sounds (V2), and only intermittent flexion of limbs (M3). This is one way in which triage works: lower-GCS, higher-risk patients get priority for attention. But the GCS score must be assessed constantly. It is assessed before surgery, after surgery, and then at regular intervals. Asking for a name can be a way to check in on someone and to calculate a clinical metric. The meaning of any response, including any name uttered, may matter less than the fact that *something* is uttered, depending on who is scoring the response. Frequently, it is not the content of the response but rather the potential decrease in the total GCS score that worries doctors. This portends neurological damage. By contrast, a GCS score that increases over time may indicate recovery (Teasdale et al. 2014).[6]

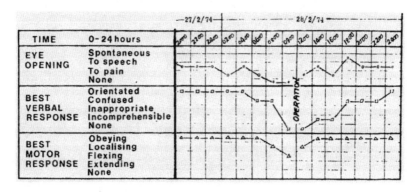

ORIGINAL GLASGOW COMA SCORE (TEASDALE AND JENNETT 1974)

TABLE 4.1 GLASGOW COMA SCALE

Eye Opening (E)

1	None
2	To pressure
3	To speech
4	Spontaneous

Verbal Response (V)

1	None
2	Sounds
3	Words
4	Confused
5	Orientated

Best Motor Response (M)

1	None
2	Extension
3	Abnormal flexion
4	Normal flexion (withdrawal)
5	Localising
6	Obeying commands

SOURCE: Original Glasgow Coma Score (Teasdale and Jennett 1974)

To obtain a GCS score for the severely injured, one must disturb the patient. To assess movement, one can observe at a distance. But to assess pain response, one must get close and stimulate the patient: a rub on the sternum or a shoulder pinch is usually recommended. The clinical rationale is that the intensity of the injuries that patients experience from traffic accidents renders them too comatose and thus too far from the waking world. Strong stimuli are needed to elicit a neurological response. What might be considered a disturbance is part of care in the ward, a gesture of moving someone toward living through attempted inquiry. A doctor provokes a patient in order to obtain crucial information: Is this person getting better or worse? What needs to be done, given the neurological status? What might they need to tell relatives?

Several of the senior surgeons explain that in the 1970s, during the initial years of Central's trauma services, they adapted Euro-American trauma scoring systems to the specificities of Central's trauma ward. For example, the Central Scale, as they called it, looked like this:

1—Fully conscious
2—Responds to verbal communication
2A—Slightly drowsy
2B—More drowsy
2C/2D—*Rowdy*
3—Responds only to stimuli
3A—Purposeful withdrawal from pain
3B—No purposeful withdrawal from pain; flexor movement
3C—Decerebrated
4—Doesn't respond
4A—No ventilator required
4B—Ventilator required

In the Central Scale, one can assess consciousness, a category of person based on movement (*rowdy* or not), and resource needs (ventilator required or not), all in one scale.

Regardless of the scales used, India faces epidemiological changes alongside the increases in trauma that are stretching the demands on neurosurgeons. The rise of cardiometabolic diseases makes strokes increasingly common, and this pulls neurosurgeons into such cases with increasing regularity. There are changes in the landscape of the political economy of medicine and health technology as well. Neurosurgery as a public hospital practice must contend with the potential profits that private hospital medicine can reap with the rise in neurosurgical need. The proliferation of CT scans and "full-body scans" via the private diagnostic industry increases demands from general practitioners and patients themselves for neurosurgical consults and possible actions on imaging.

In hospitals like Central, care proceeds in the context of these trends and also constitutes them in real time, in the slow stretches of time between the call for a neurosurgery referral and the actual arrival of a neurosurgeon in the trauma ward. For patients, these trends add up to several things at once. Neurosurgeons are scarce. They may be available to perform surgery, but follow-up is hard to mobilize. The subtleties of traumatic brain injuries—with and without surgery—can mark someone's life indelibly. After neurosurgery, and after discharge and the return home, these subtleties persist in the questions that someone asks of themselves and that others ask of them: Is this me, or is it the trauma?

The effort required to respond to inquiries can be exhausting, frustrating, and dreadful for patients. With another Unknown patient, a surgeon named Dr. R attempts to assess his GCS score. "Say your name!" she calls out to him. He murmurs a woman's name. "Fatima, Fatima," he says. She could, theoretically, end the assessment there and shift her attention to another patient, because he is responding to verbal inquiries, and she can successfully assess the verbal component of the GCS. Yet she lingers. "Who is Fatima?" she asks him. The man says one word in reply. But neither Dr. R nor the anesthetist, Dr. B, knows what that word means. Between the two of them, they speak Marathi, Hindi, English, Gujarati, Bengali, and a little Tamil, but they don't understand what he is saying.

They do not want to confuse the utterances of delirium for the utterances of determination, and so they reflect more on the word and decide that it is a kinship term. They know enough of what an utterance *might* be across Indian languages to intuit that the man is likely not saying "vegetable" or "dance." They decide that he answered the question "Who is Fatima?" with a proper answer, a term of relation, but they are unsure if it is mother, wife, sister, sister-in-law, daughter, niece, or someone else. They continue the trace. "What language do you speak?" Dr. R asks him, in Hindi. He doesn't reply. She repeats the question in Marathi, and he doesn't reply. She changes her approach and attempts to get a phone number, which across India may be spoken using English numbers.

"Number, number," Dr. R says in English.

"Zero." "Three." "Seven."

Dr. R writes these down and looks at him to continue.

"Zero." "Three." "Seven."

She tells him she already has those.

He repeats the numbers, pausing after each one. He gets frustrated and shakes his head.

"Where are you from?" she asks him, in Hindi.

"Manipur," he replies.

Dr. R turns to Dr. B, the anesthetist, who is writing notes at the desk. "Arrey! You're Bengali, right? Speak to him in Bengali." Bengali is not Manipuri, the language spoken by many residents of the state of Manipur. But maybe the patient knows Bengali owing to the geographic proximity between the northeastern Indian state of Manipur and its neighbor, West Bengal.

Dr. B comes over and tries some Bengali: "What is your name? Where are you from?"

The man doesn't answer and begins to cry.

"Does anyone speak Manipuri?" Dr. R asks loudly. She brings over the orderlies. No, they say, they don't know Manipuri. Dilip Mama and Raju Mama speak Hindi, Marathi, and several of the vast number of Marathi dialects spoken across Maharashtra. They understand Konkani and Kannada, too, but that's headed south, not northeast toward Manipur.

Dr. R holds the paper in her hand, a number moving toward a name: 037.

As I continue to receive tutorials on GCS scoring, I realize that I am confusing the means for the ends of personalization. It is true that collisions sunder people's identities from their bodies and that medicine attempts to suture the two again as it aims for stability. Although the doctors and I may share the same scores for the same patient—what is called *inter-rater reliability*—we may not share the purpose of the scores. The purpose of the GCS is to assess consciousness to understand the severity of trauma. As names emerge along the way, personalization may happen, but the ends are to move toward a different clinical possibility for a person. It takes me a while to absorb this, because I am an ethnographer, and so I presume that consciousness is the door to knowing who a person is and that being conscious is required to know someone. The doctors, though, presume that consciousness is the door to knowing if a person will live and that being conscious is someone's ticket to move out.

———

Someone calls my name; it is Arif, the constable. It is a winter afternoon, and I haven't seen him in months. He has been assigned to an Unknown patient accident case in the ICU. The nurse points him toward the correct bed, where the patient is restless but not speaking, eyes closed. The patient has had several surgeries, most recently a procedure by the neurosurgeons to address his fractured skull and brain injury. His arms reveal intricate tattoos: a cobra, a heart with an arrow running through it, a sun with many rays, and a mottled figure that prompts a debate among the nurses upon his admission. They believe it is either Shivaji, the seventeenth-century leader of the Maratha Empire and a key local political figure, or Hanuman, the Hindu deity. The arrow looks a lot like Shivaji's arrow. The nurses settle on Hanuman because the tattoo seems to have a trace of a monkey's tail, and they agree that this man is Hindu. It would be odd for a Christian or a Sikh to have a Hanuman tattoo, and they debate whether tattoos are permitted in Islam.

Clues that might shift a scene and move a patient often loop back onto categories of person, religion, caste, and geographic community. The man is in restraints to prevent self-extubation, and his muscles flex and bulge when he moves, so one doctor names him "Hero," a term used in daily slang to reference streetwise protagonists with adventures that often involve connections to the police and to the underworld.[7] Some nurses give him nicknames that reflect different names for Hanuman in Hinduism. Certain assertions—here, that this man is Hindu—may be reaffirmed even if a name is not apparent. Although nicknames can make an Unknown sort of known, no one can announce the nickname into the microphone. There will not be relatives outside to hear it, and if there were, they wouldn't recognize it.

Arif takes photos of the tattoos on his mobile phone and uploads them to a police WhatsApp group. Arif asks the resident in charge about the man's chances for survival. "Diminished" (kami hai), the resident replies. "Ventilator," the resident adds a moment later. The invocation of the machine means that the patient is in critical condition. Arif takes this in.

There is another Unknown patient next to the man with the tattoos, and Arif is supposed to identify him too. This Unknown patient is sleeping; he was in a railway accident last night. The doctors attempt to wake him. The man opens his eyes and speaks words but no discernible name. "Say your name!" (naam bolo!), a doctor commands, lightly tapping on his chest to begin the GCS assessment. The man does not respond. I am not sure what he might be seeing and thinking. But I cannot unlink the link I see: the doctor on one side of the bed, Arif on the other, and the patient in the middle.

Over the next few days, the GCS score of the man with the tattoos improves. On arrival, his GCS score was E1M1V1. This is dire. Two days later, it is E1M3VT. This is bad but going somewhere. In two days, his eye response does not change, but his motor skills improve. He shifts from no verbal response to a not-assessable verbal response (VT), because he is now intubated and on a mechanical ventilator. He has some downs before his ups: a patch of pneumonia and some trouble with his intercostal drains. Blood spurts out when the resident changes the drain tube's position, gushing with each breath the man takes, and it gets on the nurse's white uniform. "Chhee!" (yuck) she scolds the doctor, a tsk-tsk for his carelessness. She can't seem to get the blood out with alcohol; we share stain-removal tips.

I walk into the ward a few days later and see several doctors and nurses gathered around his bed. He is off the ventilator (although his tracheostomy remains), and this is a nudge toward the possibility of vital information. He is awake and talking, barely, but it's something. Now he offers his name on command. His GCS score has improved significantly. The name he utters turns out to be the same name tattooed on his arm. That is all he says. "Look!" a doctor says to him, pointing at me. "Someone from America has come. Talk to him!" He smiles and gives a tiny hand wave but remains silent.

Dr. J puts a sheet of paper in front of the man. It has a list of numbers, zero through nine, and they ask him to point to one digit at a time, to eventually constitute a mobile phone number. Slowly, he moves his finger. Dr. J waits until he sees a proper ten-digit number and sits down at the desk in resus. He phones the number and lets it ring, but no one answers.

Dr. J turns to proverbs to maneuver the situation around this apparent dead end. "If the Lord protects him, no one can kill him" (jaakho rakhe saiyaa, mar sake na koi).[8] The phone number is a clue that for now leads nowhere. But with God's protection, he thinks things might change. There might be consciousness, and with consciousness there might be information, something that gets the patient closer to a name, which gets him closer to kin, which gets him closer to release.

———

Lifelines of identification can merge, and they can conflict.

The casualty ward informs the trauma ward that an accident case is en route. I am shadowing the intern today, and I go with him down the hallway to casualty and see the police surrounding a stretcher. The medical officer in casualty has just declared the man in question dead, so the alert about a potential patient for the trauma ward is now irrelevant. The police are fishing through a thick pile of documents the man arrived with: a passport, train tickets, a job application, an electricity bill to be paid, and a CV (curriculum vitae). According to the CV, the man works in commercial plumbing. His CV describes him as having a "strong work ethic" and "demonstrated ability in identifying strategic opportunities." There is a photo on the passport, and other forms of identification, so his name and his face are known, yet there is no one yet to claim him.[9]

The constables want to see his phone contact list in order to find his relatives. The home screen on his phone can be unlocked only by drawing a pattern of lines, some sort of shape that unboxes the black box. It is a pattern lock. If the lock opened with a fingerprint, the police could presumably use his finger. One constable zigs and zags a couple of patterns with no success. Another patient's relative is waiting in the hallway, watching, and volunteers a suggestion. "You should just take the phone to my friend who can hack it and unlock it." The constable declines. He tries placing his own SIM card into the dead man's phone, but, again, no success.

Closing a case rarely works through straight lines, so there are shadow ways of personalization through approximation.[10] The constables shuffle through the stack of papers again and see a photo, and on the back is a phone number, which one dials on speakerphone. "Yes, I know him," the man who answers avers to the constables. "He is dead and is at the hospital," they say. "Please come get him." "No, no, I don't know him," the man on the phone responds suddenly. He calls them sisterfuckers and hangs up. They pull out their own phones, photograph the dead man's face and body, and depart.

Stories circulate in newspapers about cops who perform last rites for the unclaimed dead, because no one else will. But as they do the work of tracing, police can go from heroes to thieves in a moment's accusation. There are just as many stories among hospital workers about cops who are less charitable and take other things besides photographs, like jewelry and cash, before turning the bodies over for the postmortem.[11] I meet a constable in the ward who accompanies an accident case; the guard at the door passes around an envelope of sunflower seeds, and we all chew while the constable fills in her paperwork. The constable says she handled five hundred dead bodies last year at her assigned railway station, many of them Unknown persons. "I was felicitated for all this work. I got a special award." If she took a photo of each of them, just as Arif did, that's five hundred pictures on her phone. The guard asks her how she knows which last rites to perform if the name of the Unknown person stays unknown. Muslims are circumcised, and Hindus are not, she says. Catholics often have tattoos of crosses. You just have to figure it out, and she has a talent for identification.

There are overlapping official forces that situate the hospital space in between doctoring and policing. There is a police station (*chowki*) inside Central's casualty ward to coordinate the paperwork of registering any case that requires a First Information Report, which is the start of a police case. Private security guards or state commandos guard the hospital, while city police attach to specific cases and move in and out of the wards fit-fully. One day, in the ICU, a police officer in plain clothes, presumably un-dercover, comes in to photograph the face of an Unknown patient. Sister Nidhi won't allow it. Photos are not allowed unless the police officer can show her explicit proof of permission, she says. Otherwise, he is to leave the patient alone. This patient must recover through rest: this, before any-thing else, is the work at hand, her work. Photos come later. Sister Nidhi also does not like it when plainclothes police come to the ward. "Arrey! Why aren't you in your uniform?" she asks him. Official work must be marked by official signs.

The cop says he has a two-day break of vacation to his family's village, and he's about to leave. Can he just photograph the patient's face and leave? Absolutely not, Sister Nidhi says. The patient is not stable, and the cop must wait for stability like everyone else working here. "What do you want me to tell you? We have our professional duty," she says. The cop nods. He asks me how many gods I believe in. I say maybe one but also maybe none. He gestures to the Unknown patient he is not allowed to trace. "Where science ends, the extraordinary begins," he says (jaisa peh science khatam hota hai, vahan se asadh chalu hota hai). Maybe it doesn't matter that he can't take the photograph. Maybe the expert sciences have reached their limits, and tracing lies in the domain of the divine.

———

During one of our interviews, I ask Arif what he does if the trail runs cold, like in detective work. What he does is not really like that, he replies. "When you get a clue, it's easy to trace someone" (clue milta hai toh trace karna easy hai). There's a key difference: detecting is ultimately about shin-ing light on a pivotal truth; tracing is ultimately about moving relations into alignment.[12]

There is a responsibility (*farz*) attached to tracing. It's the job of the police, and the foundation of his ethics, because efforts at tracing "keep bad times and misfortune at bay" (bure waqt na aaye). The effort of tracing, the force of getting close to a case, may be more critical than any single finding. Arif thinks tracing forms a base of good action in the world that averts bad times (*bure waqt*). The case may not close, but the effort counts. "We work from our hearts for the accident cases. There are no benefits or rewards, just blessings and prayers" (Dil se kaam karte hai, accident cases ke liye. Na koi fayda ya bakshish, sirf dua aur punya).

Arif sends me a picture of himself on the city's first local train with doors that close, the AC (air-conditioned) train. He hopes it prevents more accidents. We continue to exchange pleasantries on WhatsApp. I send good wishes for festivals, and he sends pictures from his daughter's birthday party. I wonder about photos of Unknown patient faces on his phone that he might be scrolling through in order to send ones of cake and candles. If our paths cross at the hospital, we have tea in the waiting area. I recognize that our relationship is sustained by two commitments. One is from his side, and it is mandatory: his work requires that he come to the hospital. The other is from my side. My work does not require anything of the sort; it is chosen.

I also am choosing the terms on which I will have a relationship to him, always worked out in relation to the ward for both of us: the medicolegal as an ethnographic ethical pressure. I begin from commitments to patient confidentiality. I recognize that Arif has commitments too, and he often asserts them in a double move, putting himself in relation to processes of law by putting himself inside the ward.[13] Sometimes via text messages he asks me questions such as "Did you speak to my patient?" (Hamaara pesant baat karta hai kya?), but I never have, because the patients he's asking about are either comatose or just regaining consciousness. I ask myself if there are hypothetical situations in which I would say yes. All I know is what I have learned from a career in ethnography: sharing information about a single person's life lights up listeners in wildly unpredictable ways. I am not a detective. My obligation goes first to patient confidentiality. Holding *this* line has consequences. It means having uneven relations with others that I recognize echo colonial, extractive forms of querying and informing. To not accelerate the tracing of a patient means having a particular relationship with the tracer and the traced. Once spoken, words cannot be unsaid, so I decide I would say nothing to him.

Still, we chat when we see each other and do so in generic terms, across past cases rather than the present ones of patients in the ward. One afternoon

Arif uses hand motions to describe all the body parts he's seen cut off. He narrates his efforts to identify people who are intoxicated, drug addicted, and homeless, forensics both satisfied and subdued. There are twists and turns. A man steals the wallet of another man and then gets hit by the train. Arif finds the wallet and thinks he's moving a body closer to its name but learns he's actually bringing a body closer to the name of someone else. Unlike for the doctors, who calculate a GCS score based on the mere utterance of words, for Arif and police like him, the content of the utterance matters.

Sometimes there's not much to go on. Arif once brought a man to the hospital who had no wallet, no pictures, no papers, and no money on his body; the force of the accident must have scattered the traces. But the man had a tailored shirt. This is relatively normal for middle-class office workers in Mumbai. Local tailors sew Oxford shirts all the time, and I often watch them stitching from stalls on the roadside when I'm in traffic, which is when I watch things. Arif noticed that the tailor had sewn his business name inside the shirt collar and that the business was in Ahmedabad, Gujarat. Arif made some phone calls and eventually tracked down the tailor in Gujarat, and through the tailor's customer records, he traced the identity of the Unknown patient. All from the shirt.

He is good at shirt tracing, as I learn when I see him three years later at another railway station. His kids have grown by leaps and bounds, and he has received a promotion and a transfer to this larger station. I ask him again about Unknown cases, and he tells a roughly similar story of solving an Unknown patient case through a shirt. The details are slightly different from the story he told before but of a similar gist. Arif noticed that a man wore a tailor-made shirt. He looked up the name of the tailor and visited the tailor's shop along with a scrap of fabric from the Unknown man's shirt. The tailor looked in his record books and found an address from the bill. Arif went to the address; it was a garage/car repair shop, and the owner said that one of his employees had been missing for two weeks.

More often, though, he traces surfaces of bodies. Religion is the grounding category of inquiry. A red-thread bracelet on the hand likely means a Hindu, as does a *tikka* (mark) on the forehead. Prayer beads and beards mark Muslim men. Cross tattoos and crucifix necklaces mark Christians. For men, circumcision is the first sign of Hindu-Muslim difference, a mark that has a complex and violent history of identification in the subcontinent after Partition and more recently in Mumbai during riots in the 1990s and 2000s (Mehta 2006) and in Delhi in 2020 (Editors, *Economic and Political*

Weekly 2020). But this all assumes that someone has called in to a police station with a report of a missing person. Many of the Unknown patients, however, have no such claim on them. No one near to them has attested to their absence, or, frequently, authorities refuse to hear these appeals.

I begin to notice traces of clothes in the ward. There are different approaches to forensic description for Unknown patients. For those brought in dead, the police inventory what is on the body, like papers and mobile phones. For those still alive, nurses in the trauma ward must itemize every article of clothing, jewelry, and cash as the orderly strips the patient to get them out of street clothes and into a pair of hospital clothes and under a bedsheet (which marks the act of hospital admission). This is done for all patients, because valuables must be handed over to the relatives.

One day, a man comes in with the following:

> Black colour bag
> Orange colour cloth
> Bag lock chain
> Mirror
> Rs 10 Coin (1)
> Rs 5 Coin (1)
> Rs 10 note (1)
> Chappal pair
> Black Baniyan
> Rudraksh bracelet
> Wheel soap
> Comb

Sometimes details about intentions arise, like a patient who is recorded as having "Train ticket (Pune to Kalyan)."

These written details are one way that institutions achieve proximity to bodies and set forensics in motion.[14] The process entails depersonalization, yet at the same time, certain categories of persons and even individuality itself may be upheld or reinscribed. For instance, a person in an Oxford dress shirt with a commuter's black backpack is unlikely to be treated as homeless or, in the parlance of the ward, *beggar log* (a beggar), *nasha karnewalla* (a drug user), or *sidewalla* (someone who inhabits the side of the road). Clothes register class distinctions and also may paper over internal complexities such as alliances and antagonisms between pavement dwellers at a specific railway station.[15]

Some days I count things in the ward admission book: men versus women (usually 90 percent men, 10 percent women), different age brackets, and Unknown versus known (30 percent Unknown is common, sometimes more). I also look at names. Surnames can delineate ancestral home geographies and caste communities. It's rarely straightforward. A person can have an upper-caste surname but live in a slum area. They may live in a building and room with a specific address number, meaning that they may have more resources or pull than others in the same slum who do not have that structural constancy (V. Das 2020, 70). Urban poverty spatializes intricately. And then there is the stuff that comes with names, the stuff on bodies, the things in pockets and bags. Being undressed when you arrive at the ward as a patient is a requirement of admission, and it takes everything away that's necessary for the outside world, especially clothes and money. The nurses carefully write down all of these things in the admission book. It indemnifies the hospital against accusations of theft, and it records a person as they entered the ward that day at that time, not the person always. It's a trace.

Writing about detective fiction, literary critic David Trotter (2000, 21) suggests that as readers, "we await closure" of a case but never quite get it. This is because we wrongly look for the detective to solve things through epistemology. We wrongly assume that knowing and interpretation are the ways that mysteries resolve. Trotter calls this mistaken assumption a "hermeneutic attitude" (24) around the body at the center of a mystery, usually a corpse.[16] At the center of this mistaken attitude, the materiality of the victim's body is elided, in favor of a dematerialized, abstract form of knowledge. I would add two thoughts to this claim.

First, because trauma creates a medicolegal case, the body of the investigator matters too. As investigators working in the scene of the trauma, police can assert their positions relative to both clinical and legal processes. Recall how Arif must continue to visit the patient inside the trauma ward for a statement because of the patient's compromised consciousness. The hospital and the police station may appear to be disparate authoritative institutions, but the accident's embodied consequences tie both together. And within that tie, authorities may wish for patients' bodies to offer a canvas for interpretation. Second, bodies can also frustrate detection, even as they impel it.[17] And because they frustrate knowing, it is important to question assertions that a contextual science such as ethnography has unlimited potential to decode social unknowns.

Arif tells me that his experiences with tracing are not unique and that his fellow railway constables are always tracing Unknown patients. He wants me to visit him again at the railway police station and talk to his colleagues. When I arrive, he is wearing a pink Oxford shirt, crisp and clean. I wonder about its label, whether if Arif turned up somewhere, they could trace him from the shirt. He has to finish typing up casework on a laptop, so I chat with his supervising officer, named Jadav. We sit in a jail cell that has been converted into an office. It has a desk, a bench, and a cabinet of case files, and my eyes keep coming back to the iron bars on the door.

Other officers come in and out, and they dress and undress into and out of uniforms; this is a space of unquestioned masculinity. They pipe in at points of agreement or disagreement. Jadav says he is motivated to do his job because there is contentment if a life is saved ("jeev vachla tar sukhun"). When I ask him how tracing an Unknown accident patient works, he smiles and corrects me: *every* accident victim is an Unknown until they speak or until someone claims them. One may be rich or poor, a businessperson or a day laborer, a beggar or a drug addict, but in the event of an accident, one is always Unknown until proven otherwise. Even though one might have neighbors, amid the density of the city, that does not guarantee identification. Jadav invokes a broader sense of estrangement: people know each other only through WhatsApp, and WhatsApp has ended relationality ("WhatsApp se relations khatam"). The police reinstate missing relations. This is affirmed while certain relations *among* the constables, and *between* the constables and the institution of the police, remain unspoken. These relations include those forged through police violence against Muslims and specific caste communities in Maharashtra, and through the quotas of reservations for seats in the police force for many of those same communities.

Jadav recalls the death of a day laborer who had been in a railway accident owing to an overcrowded train. The man had cement stains on his hands and feet. Jadav checked construction sites in the area and eventually determined that the laborer was from the state of Orissa. He found the family, but they could not afford to travel to Mumbai to claim the body and cremate it. They asked him to cremate the body, and he did. This incident and others like it affect one deeply, Jadav said ("khub lagth").

I show Arif a page in my field notebook listing all the occasions we have encountered each other. That first case, Unknown Male 3, stayed with me because he said the words, "This is my patient."

"What made you say that?" I ask.

"We are the parents [*maa baap*] for these patients. We look after them [*hum unke dekhbaal karte hain*]."

He elaborates this sense of parental obligation by reflecting on the duty he feels toward his own mother. He grew up in rural Maharashtra, the son of cow herders, one of ten children. His father died before Arif achieved his childhood aspiration to become a constable, and so Arif as an elder son felt especially protective of his mother. Though he had enjoyed the rewards and pleasures of the hajj, true paradise (*jannat*) was the dirt beneath his mother's feet. He takes out his phone and plays a video of him washing his mother's feet in a home ritual. He washes her feet and then drinks the wash water. This is the degree of respect toward his mother that he holds, he says, and one should be so fortunate as to have relatives. He wants the Unknown patients to have this possibility for connection.

He encountered Unknown cases from his first day on the job. At his first post in the city's outskirts, there was no mortuary at the hospital nearest to the railway station where he worked. There was a case of an Unknown man killed by the train on his first day. Arif buried the body behind the hospital in a makeshift burial ground and frequently visited the grave to ensure the stray dogs nearby hadn't dug it up.

I ask Arif where all the photos of the bodies go, wondering about the ways the cops hold so many dead faces on their phones, little pocket mausoleums. Arif shows me an online database for missing persons. It is called Shodh, meaning "seek" or "research." The police upload photos. They fill in details on skin color, from "wheatish" to "sallow," and body size, from "thin" to "fat." As a name arises, they may fill that in. Otherwise, in the line for "Victim Name," the label is simply "Unknown." The hope is that there will be a claim on the body, that an inquiry will trace as-yet-Unknown patients, that the threat of the Unknown will turn into an opportunity to make the familiar familial, and that the city of the Unknown will tilt a bit more toward a city of the identified.

The police have taken Shodh from website to public notice. In early February 2015, a large banner appeared at the city's main railway station. It included some of the faces of those persons whose photographs had found their way into the Unknown persons database. There is little description, just a gallery of faces of the injured intended to provoke inquiry. It was partly effective. According to news reports, a woman passing by the banner identified her missing relative who had been in an accident a year earlier. The police decided to show only faces on the banner, because other body parts may not be present or may be mutilated. "Pictures of railway accident victims could be gory due to the nature of the injury sustained," a police official reported. "Only their facial close-up shots are put up on signboards," he said (quoted in Natu 2015). A face arrives at the train station, with the intent to provoke inquiry and to tie identification to reconnection.

After Arif shows me the picture, I go to that train station, but the banner is gone.

I look at the Shodh banner on my computer screen: a picture of people looking at pictures of people. The faces on the banner are foregrounded, but one can tell that the bodies are lying in a hospital bed. Many of the faces are those of people who had previously been at train stations. They are being looked at by people who are currently at the train station. The macabre lineup brings the atmosphere of the clinic closer to the atmosphere of the world outside it. The movement of injury from the train into the hospital and back to the train station creates a circuit problem of its own, a circulation of body images through the medicolegal fabric of the ward and the world. The municipal public hospital comes into a counterpoint relation with the train station because of tracing, and I find myself pulled into that counterpoint motion. At the train station, I can trace the hospital; at the hospital, I can trace the train.

————————

Unknown patients pose varied problems in the trauma ward, with different effects on the work of tracing done through an uneasy alliance between clinical and juridical actions and ideas. Call this a techno-aesthetic whereby the noir of the city meets the noir of the hospital, in fluorescent bulbs and flatlines. Call it a sociality of postcolonial detection and surveillance. Call it an example of the medicolegal, the category that governs all accident cases in India, with the compounding of these institutions assumed and both doctor and police officer put on the case.

Strangers and estrangement may occupy theories of urban modernism (Simmel 1964), but perhaps there is a different way to engage them here by accounting for the lifelines of identification. There are multiple Unknown patients next to each other in the ward and next to each other on the poster of missing persons displayed at train stations. They are a set of figures that differ from those of more generic strangers, and a set of bodies who must live in a relatively constant state of epistemological and forensic stutter (see Sehdev 2018). With uneven results, and without the presence of kin, tracing reveals how and when personhood and identity do and do not matter for healing. These lifelines of identification reveal the limits of medical and legal ideologies premised on individuality. They show what might be learned about the ends and means of both de- and repersonalization in medicine.

Traces of movement, as much as traces of knowing, connect naming to surviving across compromised forms of consciousness.

Acts of tracing outline how care proceeds as medicine and law reach for the stability of social belonging. A police officer receives a medal from the railways for handling five hundred Unknown persons. There is recognition of the Unknown injured person, even if their case is not closed. There are inquiries that register as something between curiosity and apathy. Many have a procedural sensibility that we might call *bureaucracy*, or "red tape," as Akhil Gupta (2012) has understood the term for its relation between state process and state violence. While the cold stare of bureaucratic reason is most certainly present in these scenes, it is not the only force at play. Intrigue can accompany neglect. Mystery and resolution do not balance each other out. Clues can be left alone or taken up but without fanfare. Tracing can lead nowhere; inquiries can remain unresolved. Like the mobile phone's home screen, there can be a pattern lock, a crypt of information that one cannot quite open up.

Yet there is still embodied traffic across the domains of medicine and law. There is the reading of faces and tattoos and the approximation of phone numbers. Techniques of tracing can align with prior and future ones: WhatsApp exchanges and photos of faces become part of the technoscientific landscape of identification and surveillance in India today.[18] The hospital bed can be both a site of medicine and a site of interrogation one might find in a police station (Mehta 2006). From cops tracing shirts to surgeons phoning wrong numbers, estimating sociality has a specific end in mind: to trace the person in order to find their family and move the patient out of the ward.

It matters who wants the tracing to happen, and for what ends. Lifelines of identification may have multiple rationales. If doctors determine a GCS score for an Unknown patient, that does not necessarily change the status of knowing their kin connections. If Arif figures out the name of an Unknown patient in the ward, the patient's brain injury does not automatically resolve. The revelation of a name might eventually lead to contact with and eventual care by kin, if they are able to come to the hospital, and might yield "better outcomes," in clinical parlance. But there are no guarantees. Some efforts at tracing revolve around persons rendered too socially remote, as in the initial case of Unknown Male 3. Others may be more selective, as doctors and cops choose whether or not to pursue a patient's unidentifiable social and familial relations. Efforts to move forward, through the predictions of the GCS score, meet efforts to move backward, through the retrodiction of forensics. They can intermittently overlay, and they can also obscure each other. Closing a case can take shape less as closing the door on something, in some sort of declarative way that things are settled, and more as approximating different kinds of closeness. These approximations both constitute and transform trauma's traffic.

There's another Unknown man who arrives at the casualty ward. He experienced a railway accident; no life signs are apparent, and the doctors want to declare him dead. The cop who brought him scrolls through the contact list on the man's mobile phone and searches papers in a plastic bag for some sort of identifying information. There is a television script. "Oh, he must be a writer or a director," a nurse observes. Or an actor, maybe? The script is for a show titled *Pehla Pyaar, Pehla Gam* (First love, first sorrow).

The economy of attention shifts, and the simultaneous depersonalization and repersonalization of this man intensifies. Come to think of it, the cop observes, some of the names in the man's phone contact list seem sort of familiar, like the names of TV actors. Definitely not A-listers, he and the nurse agree, more like minor celebrities. Still, the nurse thinks, this possible link should go into the police report, because it's a clue. She pages through the script; its text shifts from Hindi to English at the bottom of one page. It is a screenwriter's direction to transition a scene with some closure: "CUT."

For the living, one might think that unimpeded consciousness would be enough to solve a situation, but it is not.[19] For the dead, one might think that inquiries by the biopolitical state might be enough to solve a situation, but they are not. This is because moving and knowing are both at stake, and tracing can set the Unknown en route toward kin and toward the ward's exit. That doesn't give things an end point, nor does it settle the Unknown person in a clear relation to the mass public.[20] With all these hermeneutics of inquiry in between fixity and motion, it can be difficult to settle someone into the presumed stability of kin and social structures. The situation involves noir without solutions, reverberations after impact, and uneven confrontations between medicine and law. But amid such instabilities, maybe someone will do the proximity work of identification: follow the circuit, close the loop, trace the lines.

Seeing

THE LIFELINES OF SURGERY

DOCTOR HOLDING
A CT SCAN UP TO
THE LIGHT TO SEE
A BRAIN. DRAWING
BY AUTHOR.

"All you talked about was that hospital." That's what the nurses in the Duke Hospital neurosurgery ICU tell me. It confuses them at first, because I am in a hospital but describing another hospital. Who are these "ward boys" and "sisters" I conjure? It is recorded in my file that I am "not fully alert."

I am infused with steroids to manage postoperative brain swelling, and my not-full alertness seems focused on Central's trauma ward. The numb weight of my head in a compression bandage leads me to believe that my operation is over *and* I am alive. I trawl through memories, words, and questions about the operations I can see to move closer to the one operation I cannot: seeing as a lifeline, surgery as its traffic.

———

The difference in temporality between planned versus emergency surgery is palpable. There is more time to plot, to hand-wring, to imagine bad outcomes, and to hope. My situation first strikes me as planned, because I get to choose whether or not the surgery happens, whether to accept my diagnosis or ignore it. But I never expected a brain tumor. Polarities of accidental and purposeful don't fit.

About a year and a half into my trauma project in Mumbai, I am in Durham, North Carolina, and the migraines commence. I dismiss them as the consequence of too much screen time. The world tilts, and I walk into walls. My doctor orders an MRI, I go dutifully, and a day later she phones me. "You're probably not going to remember anything I tell you, but here's what the imaging suggests . . . ," and she's right, I don't remember what she says at all, because my brain is generating one question: How am I supposed to move into medicine if I'm not the observer of the movements?

My partner and I decide to marry, in the forest, under an old tree. I draft a will and do-not-resuscitate paperwork.

I turn to my guides in Mumbai for advice, and they cast familiar images onto the unthinkable. "Just think of your tumor as a tiny little *kabuli chana*," says my closest friend and mentor in the city, just a little dried chickpea, the kind we snack on with our tea. And then there is the question of my relationship to the neurosurgeon, a person I admire but also keep questioning to learn about the tumor in the middle of my brain and how he plans to get rid of it. My friend, a surgeon herself, tells me I risk edging into the zone of wanting to do his job.

"Do you talk to the pilot when you're in a plane?" she asks.

"No."

"Then just walk onto the plane, sit in your seat, buckle your belt, and let the pilot do the flying." I am allowed to feel the takeoff, cruise, and landing, but it's futile to grab the navigational controls.

NOVEMBER 2015

Dear friends and colleagues,

I'm writing to share some news. Following several severe headaches and episodes of dizziness, I have been diagnosed with a tumor that lies in the center of my brain. I will undergo neurosurgery at Duke Hospital. The tumor's pathology—what it is, precisely, and to what degree it is benign or malignant—cannot be determined until the surgery. But I'm beyond lucky to have an outstanding neurosurgeon.

The most common postsurgical challenge is fatigue. But by the time spring semester begins, I hope to be back on my feet and teaching.

Some of you may know that I am now spending my time in Mumbai inside a public hospital to study traffic accidents and trauma surgery. There I have closely observed neurosurgeries. The neurosurgeons often position me next to them, with the patient's brain inches from my eyes. Bollywood hits play on the radio while the team works for hours on end. I also spend time in the ICU with the patients afterward. My own situation is worlds apart in so many ways. Ever so slightly, I feel at home in the strange dominion of the brain and am optimistic about the surgery and recovery.

Most important: Your support of Gabe during this time means everything to me. He can update you on my condition; just let him know and he'll add you to a notice list.

Ethnography becomes a lifeline. I rev the engines of medical anthropology and treat each of my clinical encounters as fieldwork. I ask the staff at Duke Hospital I interact with for their opinions, because if there's one thing I have learned at Central, it's that everyone has expertise. There is the MRI tech who settles me into the scanning tube; he sees these things all the time, he says from the other side of the glass wall, as does his wife, who also works as an MRI tech. When the gadolinium contrast enters my bloodstream and I taste cold metal, he jokes through the headset over my ears to distract me from the machine's banging. There is the IV nurse who preps me for surgery; she commutes three hours from a horse farm every day. She tells me not to worry; my surgeon is the best. I see how one's reputation can infuse a place.

In Central's trauma ward, there is an orderly who loves to look at the CT brain plates, flopping the films toward the fluorescent light to make a claim. He studied up until the tenth grade and has worked in the ward for decades; he sees many CT plates and listens to the doctors discuss them. Once he shows me a brain imaging film for a train accident patient with subdural hematoma and points out a white globule: "Mota spot" (big spot), he declares. Big but not a deal breaker. He is confident that the surgeons can handle it, and I admire his optimism.

A few hours before my surgery, the anesthesia attending checks on me one last time before I'm shifted to the operating theater (OT). She examines the X in black marker drawn on my shaved scalp. I ask her if I can see the tumor. She brings up my latest MRI on the monitor and flips through the section planes, animating my brain. The tumor blinks, a *mota spot*, I think. She gives it a look and disagrees: "It doesn't look too mean."

Before the anesthesia hits, I look up and see the face of the surgical orderly. He has worked this job longer than I have been alive. We share stories, and this last exchange before I go under spotlights a Black health-care worker caring for a white professor. This is the ichor of American health care, a system that extracts racialized care labor to make select bodies stay alive.

It is blank after. I wake in the ICU with a sense-memory unstable like frost, something jostling that sounds of raised voices. I ask the nurses and learn that as I emerged from anesthesia after the operation concluded, I attempted to pull out my endotracheal tube connected to the ventilator. It's common;

I recall the bucking and pulling among patients in Central's trauma ward. It's not that my injury is their injury, that my calamity is their calamity, that our reactions are the same and therefore our situations are the same. It's more a problem of lifelines that the ventilator makes especially evident: medicine moves us because we need it to. Also, we do not like it.

In the neuro ICU, my IVs feel heavy, and will someone turn off that goddamn monitor alarm? I want sleep, Jell-O, and my family. On rounds, a resident ventures to narrate the situation as a puzzle that has been solved. "Professor Solomon is an anthropologist and experienced sudden vertigo and debilitating migraines." The MRI, the blood tests, the discovery of the tumor, the surgery for the tumor, keep moving.

I like seeing medical education happen at the bedside. So much of my own understanding of trauma medicine at Central happens on rounds. Early in my project, years before I am a patient, I shadow doctors in Duke Hospital's Emergency Department to get a comparative sense of the trauma care I was studying in Mumbai. On rounds, I occasionally encounter my former undergraduate students from my medical anthropology courses, who now are medical students and residents. This is a delight. We talk about what they try to read in their nonexistent spare time and how they see ward life in motion.

But now I am the observed, not the observer. I attempt to insert myself into some of this narration and add something useful (was it me or the mannitol speaking, and is that division even tenable?). I am interrupted and shushed by a medical student. I am not sure why; perhaps they do not want to hear me. It strikes me as an inoculation against curiosity. I am fumbling to control the situation as I see it, even though this traffic is not mine to direct.

When I return home, I am reminded of surgery's remnants. I am not yet used to the screws and plates in my skull, and the resection leaves my neck muscles weak. I have not learned to compensate. Potholes on the road cut like an electric knife. But once home, I can register kindnesses. I am a rather private person, but when family, friends, and colleagues provide gifts and food and encouragement, it shows me the lengths people will go to support my survival. There are still things I'm unsure about when I revisit this time; memory is odd, and medical crises arrange cascades of information and decisions (if one is so fortunate as to have access to care in the first place). However, I am absolutely certain that a craniotomy and tumor resection (with others) is a different surgery than a craniotomy and tumor resection (alone). I had the former, and it afforded care before, during, and after the hospital.

Years after the surgery, I feel as if this book is coming along swimmingly. I have not written about my surgery or, really, surgery at all. My husband reads a draft and says, "It feels like there's something unsaid." He asks if I am comfortable holding back my brain surgery from readers. I hem and haw and protest. Often, when scholarly texts about medicine carry a whiff of the researcher's "personal experience," there are suspicions about the relationship between having illness and narrating illness (see, e.g., Boyer 2019; Frank 2013; Jain 2013; Lorde 1980; Moodie 2018; and Sedgwick 2000). Personal accounts belong in memoir but not in research, this line of critique goes. I don't buy it, but it's in the air. All I know is that pathology can be a threshold for living and that life must progress across it. There is enough health in me to see the wounds in others, and then there is a wound in me. There is enough health without crisis in me to do fieldwork on health crises, and then I have a health crisis.

What is common to both frames is that I see surgery partially. So much between them is different.

I do not share a crash with the patients in Central's trauma ward. Our structural and economic affordances are worlds apart. We do share the fact that we were not expecting to be in a hospital, and then through different pathways we are in a hospital. Those are the variables, but here are the stakes: I do not want readers—and especially my students—to think that all we need is a wounded narrator to bridge *here* to *there*, *me* to *them*, field to home, North to South. I do not think that when the sick write their experiences, something universally therapeutic happens and the show's over. No patients at Central are likely to ever make it to Duke Hospital. This condition is part of the *global* in *global surgery* and seems paramount as a starting point if I want to see two hospitals together.

————————

It's not only me who thinks comparatively about surgery. The first time I meet with my neurosurgeon, I describe my research in Central's trauma ward. He bristles. "Your surgery will not be like that," he says. "Like what?" I ask. My neurosurgery is not trauma neurosurgery, he explains, something I know. It is a procedural comparison, technical and also temporal. But I believe I also detect something in his words intended to reassure me, a suggestion that I won't have the jackhammer version of a craniotomy, a suddenness with a jagged edge.

Yet every surgery contains violence. It slices, resects, and burns. It clarifies fields of vision through the addition of fluid and suction's subtraction.

It sutures and staples and plates. It is rarely fast. It is a medicine of endurance, keeping surgeons, nurses, and orderlies on their feet for hours, craned over the person-body on the table. It requires a deftness of hands and eyes that invests surgeons with a command over medical knowledge worked out through touch. Violence causes the wounds that trauma surgery treats, and the treatment itself is violence—a violence that heals, hopefully, and keeps someone alive. Nonetheless, surgery is an incursion, and one's life depends on this incursion *and* on the person making the procedure proceed. It's a leap of faith for everyone involved. Surgery for trauma conjoins multiple specialties (general surgery, anesthesiology, neurosurgery, and orthopedics) into an event-practice of that leap, and surgery conjoins patients to the state.[1]

Surgery is the apotheosis of a site where the biomedical is never in question. In Central's trauma ward, the emergency operating theater (called the EOT or simply OT) is, in many senses, medicine's ideal site. It is a space of comparatively well-resourced and coordinated clinical practices. Improvised forms of treatment of minor trauma abound in smaller casualty wards around the country, where drugs, gloves, and bandages may be in short supply. But surgery cannot proceed without the supplies it requires; it is, after all, a science of protocols. There are high- and low-tech versions if one compares surgery globally, but there are basic minimums, and surgery does not happen without them. Central's trauma OT is put together rapidly and efficiently for patients, with care, attention, and checklists. The surgical nurses at Central are known throughout the hospital as among the best around; the orderlies as the most trained and experienced. It's a site of volume too. A surgeon in Central's trauma ward is partnering with some trauma surgeons from Sweden on research. The Swedish surgeons visit Central's ward and marvel at all it does. The Indian surgeon asks them how many trauma surgeries they performed on road traffic accident patients in the past year, and (so the story goes) they struggle to name more than five. "We did five yesterday," he responds.

In essence, the journey to the hospital, admission, and management in the trauma ward may be full of movements both created and disallowed, but these lifelines are ultimately preparatory, getting someone ready for surgery if it's necessary. This means that the stillness of the body on the operating table is the result of a series of accumulated movements before the first incision. Surgery's stasis has preconditions, and stasis in surgery (hopefully) morphs into ambulation afterward. Surgery is a lifeline precisely because it can restore the motion of living in ways no other intervention can.

The patient on the table is anesthetized to forget many of surgery's details. In the rearview mirror, surgery is a weighty blind spot for patients, a feeling-knowing that something was there but we're not sure what. Surgeons see surgeries in the rearview mirror often through the rubric of mistakes. I regularly attend the monthly mortality meetings for Central's Surgery Department, where all surgical deaths from each month—including trauma cases—are presented and discussed.

Surgical residents, like all doctors, can make mistakes. Faculty are relentless on this front. Central's surgery faculty are compassionate teachers, but under no circumstances do they tolerate mistakes. There is no reassurance of "Well, that's understandable" if someone screws up. You get reprimanded because you—the junior doctor—should never do it again. Lives are on the line. The patients are already brittle. There are possibilities for internal sutures to loosen or incision sites to become infected, and this should never happen to anyone, but if it does, more surgery may be necessary to fix the problem (if it's identified). But trauma patients are usually in critical condition or just on the other side of it. They have or are recovering from low blood pressure or low oxygenation and are on several medications for varying forms of physiological support. They would not be entering a revision surgery as blank slates. Trauma surgery is unforgiving.

Both the nurses and the service staff see how the residents experience things close-up, because they form coordinated, sometimes trusting relationships with these young doctors. A new surgical resident's first time inserting an intercostal drain or performing a tracheotomy, or a new anesthesia resident's first time placing a central venous catheter, is a major learning moment because these procedures are important and common in the ward. To work carefully and cleanly, doctors need hands to help, usually from an orderly or nurse who moves sutures and tools and scopes and suctions in and out of the surgical field. But the nurses and orderlies must also be careful about reporting any mistakes they see. The senior nurses and orderlies have watched and assisted the same procedures for decades and know how to do them correctly, but they are not doctors and can always be reminded of that.

At the mortality meetings, talk of staple misfires (Japanese staplers are excellent but expensive) and suture quality (German sutures are reliable but back-ordered) imbues PowerPoint presentations by residents about surgeries that ended in death. The surgery faculty are unrelenting, interrogating the residents on all possible angles of the death and pushing hard on the question of individual responsibility. Surgeons know that no procedure, not a single one, is simple. So much can go wrong, and the best surgeons know how to get out, safely, when this happens. Surgery's lifelines can be just as much about the withdrawal as the entry and the passage. Yes, the car hit the patient in the abdomen with such force and angle and location that perhaps the death was not to be averted by even the most well-resourced surgical units and the most nuanced techniques . . . but did the resident *truly* do the best possible job?

The residents prepare for the grilling in the hallway outside of the Surgery Department's auditorium, and I sit with them, going over the case presentation details before they are summoned into the room. These moments are far more than intellectual and strategic. They are the moments during which trainees learn to trust each other, to be transparent about the comparative strengths and weaknesses of their skills, and to back each other up. This sociality will be stretched in the OT when they are operating on patients and when quick, critical decisions are necessary. The department's senior orderly comes by, and we are startled by what looks like blood running down his face. He smiles and untucks a red marker from his pocket, excited that the faculty have asked him to reprise the part of a patient hit by a truck for a trauma care training down the hall. It doesn't look real enough, so we draw more injury on his face.

———

When I return to Mumbai and to Central's trauma ward in the months after my surgery, people see that I am different. There are questions about the scar stretching from the base of my neck to the top of my skull. The doctors, nurses, and service staff inquire about the procedure's details. I tell them what I know, which isn't a lot, and they understand. Patients know how things feel, but they do not necessarily see how medicine happened, and there is a difference.

I often eat lunch with a neurosurgery resident. When he hears about my surgery, he tells me that he's been doing similar procedures lately. They're always risky, because "the brain is like cheese," he says, clumping some dal and rice in his tiffin with one hand and jiggling the other in the air. "You can only disturb it so much." It's more gelatinous than most people realize. I show him a photo of the last entry in my journal the night before I was wheeled into the OT: a cup of orange Jell-O I ate in the dark, unsure what would happen after. I think about this when I begin observing autopsies, watching bodies lose brains on the table, their heads supported by a wooden block to blunt the chiseling, the pathologists slicing the brain to see what lies inside. Observation mind, again.

––––––––––

Surgery's focus on the patient is always a relationship, meaning that surgery is not just a practice in general but a practice committed *to* someone (see Cohen 2013b). This commitment is a curious black hole, the center of so much of the trauma story, yet the person at its center never remembers it. It's a forgotten duration, and it's easy for those not on the table to overlook it. It demands of me a different sort of ethnographic method. Perhaps I do not first write about surgery as much as I do the other features of trauma ward life because I take comparatively fewer notes during the long hours of operations. My notes register a slower pace in the OT than they do in the resus and ICU areas of the trauma ward, and in retrospect this is an error. It's not a difference in tempo so much as it's a difference in duration. My instruments of observation are tuned to seeing the immanence of cases, to hearing things spoken and watching interactions forged among doctors, patients, and families that register as "emergency" and "social." In the context of a six-hour operation, my tools get tired.

Or maybe it's a difference of proximity between the aim and object of those tools. I stay at a safe and sterile remove from the surgical field. I see surgery but at a different distance than the surgeons, because to be proximate is to endanger the patient, so I keep back.

When an operation concludes, I accelerate, hurrying to the OT's anteroom to take notes in a tiny corner with a desk and a Ganesh altar and stickers of Sai Baba on the wall. A garland of marigolds hangs from the vestibule, marking the OT as a consecrated space. This is a working, social space too, and so while I try to reflect on the procedure I just saw, the nurses and orderlies assigned to the OT try to help me understand what I just saw in context. They tell me comparison stories. I lose track of the procedure I just saw as I try to track what they have seen before. There are stories of the strange things that were discovered inside bodies during abdominal surgeries, from jewelry to batteries. There are the neurosurgeries that were especially notable, like the one where a man experiences a truck accident, a metal rod impales his skull, the surgeons operate for an entire day to remove it, the man survives, and everyone takes selfies with him, the ward's own Phineas Gage (see Hallam 2008; Macmillan 2002; and Prentice 2013).

In my surgical observations, I sometimes stand with the anesthetists, and other times I stand by the surgeon to glimpse the surgical field around the brain, chest, or abdomen, close but not too close. The emergency OT is a respite from resus and the ICU for me; there are only five or six people in the room at a time. No relatives are allowed in. I change clothes and scrub in. It's chilly and has a distinct soundscape. The anesthesia machine whirs. The surgery professor guides the resident by voice even though the performance is all about visualized tactility: "That's good." "Tighten up here." "Not there." "You don't understand." "Ah, now you understand." The tape over the patient's eyes makes zippy sounds when the anesthetist pulls it up to check the sclera for vital signs.

Surgeons tend to play Bollywood tunes on the radio. One day there is a man injured in a railway accident with blunt abdominal trauma on the table. The song "Tera Raasta Main Chhodoon Na" (I won't let you go) plays. The song, whose title translates literally as "I'll never leave your path," gets everyone tapping their feet, which feels useful after standing for hours in sandals on a concrete floor. The song comes from the soundtrack to *Chennai Express*, a 2013 film starring Shah Rukh Khan that tells the story of a man orphaned after his parents are killed in a car accident, who later in life boards a train and falls in love as a result. The train never seems far away, nor does the commitment to stay the course on another's track.

There is somatic levity, like during an anastomosis when a surgeon attempts to locate an intestinal tear and discovers the patient's undigested dinner from the night before, and people share their favorite recipes for *gawar* (cluster beans). The person who is the patient is not exactly forgotten, but a different bodily plane grounds the discussion. Much of this is made possible by the anesthesia that silences patients into forgetting.[2] Did they joke about me or around me when I was on the table, my brain open to the air? Were news stories discussed, department politics, pop culture, favorite recipes? What moved while I didn't?

It's 10 p.m., and I'm in a coffee shop in North Carolina with my husband, both of us trying to write. My back faces the barista, who is playing punk tracks. He approaches me. *Did you have brain surgery?* He noticed the scar on the back of my head and neck. *Yes*, I tell him, *brain tumor . . . I dodged a bullet.* He turns around, parts his hair, and shows me the scar from his craniotomy. It was Christmas last year, and he was rushing home on his motorcycle. He doesn't remember the crash, just waking up in the hospital, but one thing he knows for sure is that "you're never the same person once the air hits your brain." How does surgery shift us into someone else?

Maybe the answer lies in seeing surgery as a transit. I remember meeting with my neurosurgeon the afternoon before my procedure. I ask if he will take pictures or maybe a video of the surgery. Can I see? I watched craniotomies in Central's trauma ward, I explain, and that doesn't grant me expertise, but I believe I'm prepared to see my brain. I'm scared, and I'm curious. I want to *see* the stasis and the maneuvers, to see medicine hold me as it moves me.

One thing I like about him is his straight talk: "No," he says. No qualifiers, no explanation. Just *no*.

Feeling the groundlessness of surgery's lifelines, I try to be an ethnographer so I won't have to be a patient. I wonder, What does he make of this attempt to jump from one moving train onto another, from being a body to seeing a body?

5 Breathing

THE LIFELINES OF VENTILATION

Anand writes in a small notebook that he keeps by his bed, because he is on a ventilator and cannot speak. He jots questions and answers to his relatives who visit, to the doctors, to the nurses, and, sometimes, to me. A month after his admission to the ICU, he writes, "I am ready bree. But chest is not respoonce. Tomorrow I am ready Bree." I double-check with him, back-translating from English to Hindi to Marathi—yes, *Bree* means *breathe*. He wants to breathe, he is ready to breathe, but his chest is the place of breath, and it is not responding. He is still on a mechanical ventilator and wants to breathe without it.

Weeks later he writes, "I do not need the machine" (Mujhe mashin ki zaroorat nahin). The doctors begin the process of weaning him from the ventilator, but he gets agitated, and they reconnect him.

Who is breathing, and who is being breathed?

Weeks pass, and he writes, "My body correct. Ready 15 days." "Yes," I tell Anand. "You'll be ready."

―――――――

In the trauma ICU, moving breath through a ventilator constitutes a lifeline because it allows breathers to move air better and, potentially, to live. It oxygenates breathing bodies whose physiologies are unstable. One of the many consequences of traumatic injury—especially chest trauma—is respiratory distress, and trauma patients frequently develop acute respiratory distress syndrome and pneumonia (Treggiari et al. 2004; Watkins et al. 2012). These connections between compromised breathing and physiological instability make breathing a focus of care for survival and also reveal its pluralities. Ventilators move air into lungs so that patients will eventually achieve respiratory homeostasis and breathe more alone. Still, even as the ventilator can be life-saving, it is also life-threatening, because of the damage that long-term ventilation can cause to bodies. Critical care medicine directs the traffic of breath, supporting it while also cultivating its independence. Ventilation's agencies, biopolitics, and bioethics emerge as both traumatic injury and trauma medicine pressure the breath.

The lifelines of ventilation must be carved out of a context of rationing. A baseline fact of Central's trauma ward is that there are not enough ventilators in its ICU to respond to the demands of the city's trauma cases. There are fourteen beds in the trauma ICU, and at the time of my research, there were often ten working ventilators, sometimes more, sometimes fewer, depending on what was under repair. The patients who come to Central are already inserted into economies of scarcity in other domains of life, which makes facing it again in moments of brittle vitality all the more injurious and all the more insulting.

In coming to Central, patients are subject to ventilation's moral circuits and economies. Doctors cannot accede to a family's wishes to withdraw life support. My research began in the aftermath of a transformation in the juridical landscape of India's euthanasia laws. In 2011, the Supreme Court of India issued a judgment that allowed for certain conditions of life-support withdrawal under the category of "passive euthanasia."[1] Many formal legal processes and debates over the technical definition of passive euthanasia and its relation to persistent vegetative state followed, and in 2018, the Supreme Court issued a judgment recognizing living wills and advanced medical directives (Bandewar et al. 2018). As Indian bioethicists point out, everyday clinical practices around the end of life often had informal procedural structures before the 2011 court judgment, but institutional oversight remained unevenly applied or altogether unclear (Gursahani 2011).

At Central, an administrative team regularly visits the ward to confer with doctors about current patients in the ICU who might be formally diagnosed with persistent vegetative state and brain death according to clearly defined institutional protocols. Yet even with transparent end-of-life protocols, it could be challenging to distribute the limited number of ventilators assigned to patients in critical condition but with vital signs that do not (yet) indicate brain death. Effectively, once placed on a ventilator, such patients must stay on until they are able to breathe on their own or until they achieve death while being made to breathe. Even if the family wishes for life support to be withdrawn, doctors could not do this. Put simply, doctors are not the arbiters of a ventilator's availability because they do not make the sovereign decisions over the machine's potential. Only a dead or recovering patient can make the machine available for another person. Ventilators circulate agency in this way and distend its individuation, and they may anchor people in dramas that can stretch with no clear climax points and variable velocities of change. At the nexus of independence and support, and of life and death, ventilation creates social, moral, and mortal quandaries of breathing through trauma. This does not happen in the fixed location of the machine's on-off switch and cannot be lodged in either the ventilator alone or the patient themselves. The power of ventilation lies in the volatility in between.

Specifically, ventilation's lifelines entail a movement quality I call *social breathing*. Breathing is social because people and machines move air both materially and immaterially in times of distress. Breathing *seems* deeply individuated, because it is mostly thought to be autonomic: chests heave, and nostrils flare, sometimes at will, often without thinking. Yet in contexts of respiratory distress, breath must move between people, and between people and machines. These movements illustrate the uneven distributions of care technologies (Pols 2012), the meaningful shifts in air, the ways breathing involves copresence, and the circulation of life at the edges of death.[2] Perhaps we do not normally see the social in breathing until the individual is struggling to survive. But airway interventions like mechanical ventilation are deeply social techniques, and they shape survival in the ICU.

Across three gestural case studies, I depict social breathing as a dynamic intensity of intensive care. First, there are the movements of resuscitation through the handheld positive-pressure masks known as *Ambu bags* that kin squeeze to supplement necessary oxygen. Second, when Ambu bagging falters, there are the moves of intubation that introduce mechanical ventilation into the picture and create the hopefully temporary and life-saving connections between humans and breathing machines. Third, there are the motions of weaning, of removing someone from a ventilator. Communicating the fine line between recovery and the end of life happens here, as compromised lungs reach their limits of vital gas exchange. Relatives of ventilated patients formulate the ethics of their kin, who cannot speak while on life support, sometimes speaking to them and sometimes speaking for them as wishes get worked out, in ways that may approximate breathing for them too.

Social breathing exemplifies what Julie Livingston calls "a social phenomenology" (2012, 145), the extension of seemingly individuated bodily forms into social relation. Livingston's case study is pain from cancer, and she reveals how "every effort is made to socialize" the isolation of pain in cancer patients, often through laughter. Livingston demonstrates that the inner pain of bodies is social because it proves to be distributed in complex ways, even though "the biomedical technologies and techniques of palliation are sparse and put to uneven and uncertain use" (150). Similar to pain yet also unique, social breathing demonstrates that features of living that seem to be self-regulated must also be understood as moving in relation.

Social breathing also reveals the uncertainties that imbue access to life-support technology. In her landmark study of intensive care and dying in hospitals, Sharon Kaufman (2005, 272) argues that life support is surrounded by "several kinds of indeterminacy," whereby the mechanical ventilator concretizes competing pressures of faith, individual determination, the potential heroism of medicine, and the hospital's institutional logics. For Kaufman, the ventilator is the grounds of "choice" and "decision" in American hospitals at the end of life. Kaufman both details and complicates "the problems of when, why, and how to withdraw ventilator support so that the patient 'can be allowed' to die" (57). In Central's trauma ward, by contrast, such decisions are not up for adjudication by families, because of both proximate and distant bioethical pressures. Indeterminacies shape and are shaped by the act of moving onto and off of the ventilator.

Kaufman demonstrates how the ventilator is a critical bioethical site because of the ways it destabilizes certainties about dying in American hospitals—hospitals where the ventilator's presence is never in question. Yet as in most Indian public hospitals, Central's trauma ward ICU cannot guarantee the availability of ventilation. How does ventilation operate as a lifeline in this context? I show how ventilation positions a person's relation to medicine at what can seem like a T-junction and in some cases may be a dead end. On one side is dependency, being fixed on a machine, a continuous relation to biotechnology when the body is in critical condition. On the other side is autonomy, wherein one gains control over one's own breathing: as Anand put it, when one does "not need the machine." This turn toward breathing autonomy is the benchmark for eventual discharge.

Breathing on the ventilator makes these two poles of dependency and autonomy difficult to disaggregate. As a result, ventilation materializes and mediates different tensions between stasis and motion. There is the stasis of being immobilized in a bed while a tube snaked down the throat actively enables the body's gas exchanges. There is the exit from that bed that is more likely when a patient can breathe on their own, without the ventilator.

There is the release from the pain that accompanies all of the suction involved in keeping breathing tubes secretion-free, and there is the release from life—that is, dying—that may happen too.

A different politics of life support emerges as a result, one that anchors more in relational traffic and less in the ventilator's on-off and dependent-autonomous binary poles. When life-support technologies must be rationed, forms of living that seem to be self-regulated must also be located between stasis and flow. Describing these dynamics has implications for a deeper understanding of life support in India and elsewhere. It also elucidates the politics of public medicine in terms that are not situated fully in dependency, welfare, Supreme Court debates, or infrastructural lack. Instead, I point to bodies struggling to breathe and to bodies struggling to breathe others. These lifeline efforts, I argue, compose life-support politics.

Although the ventilator is an ever-present form in the ICU, much of what I learned about social breathing comes from the man I call Anand, whose account begins this chapter and to whom I shall return. Anand's extensive time spent moving on and off the ventilator provoked several questions for me: How can life support be understood as movements of *both* attachment and detachment, of breathing *and* being breathed, rather than being staked on one or the other? How do the experiential textures of ventilation blur qualities of flow and stuckness in medicine, in the sociality of medicine, and in sociality itself? And, ultimately, what does it look like to be moved by the lifelines of ventilation and to breathe through the technics and ethics of intensive care?

———————

In clinical and everyday worlds in India, people may invoke problems of breathing as a chronic form of disease (*saans ki bimaari*) or as an episode, "an attack" (*saans ka attack*) (V. Das 2015). This is how one might reckon asthma (Braun 2014; Fortun et al. 2014; Kenner 2018; Trnka and Trundle 2017; Whitmarsh 2008). Compromises of breath are especially evident in cases of tuberculosis (McDowell 2014; Venkat 2021). In the trauma ICU, the ventilator sounds out vital uncertainties. The machine beeps alongside its neighbors, orchestral, as if the machines are talking to each other. A nurse can be telling a story, or a doctor can be delivering vital information to relatives, and then the ventilator interrupts through its own language: punctuated, rhythmic, syntactic. I wonder how the patients hear it in their often comatose states. They are living through the noise; they *are* the noise, breathing with machines whose sounds update their aliveness.

Before the ventilator arrives into the frame, there are other eventful forms of making breath that are just as intensive. Through global circulations of emergency resuscitation techniques, the ABCs (airway, breathing, and circulation) are standard protocols when a patient arrives at the trauma ward. When someone's breath reaches its limits, it interrupts the ward, and doctors must find ways to make breath available from elsewhere. Oxygen saturation (SpO$_2$) is critical to determining how fragile a trauma case is, as is systolic blood pressure. If the patient cannot breathe properly on their own, and their oxygen saturation and vital signs dip below acceptable limits, they will be Ambu-bagged with a mask placed over their mouth. The anesthetist usually does this work. Sometimes the relative accompanying the patient does the Ambu bagging, squeezing the bag attached to the mask rhythmically, circulating breath from hands to lungs.

Like most things in medicine, with Ambu bagging there are protocols, which assume a scenario populated by specific persons—in this case, the patient and doctor. Then there are the actualities, populated by other bodies: relatives who often are the ones who do Ambu bagging on arrival, as well as other patients who set the terms of availability of a ventilator. "Do it like this, 'one, two, three,'" an anesthetist instructs a father, squeezing the green bag connected to the mask on the mouth of his son, who has been in a motorcycle crash. I ask the anesthetist for her thoughts on "the kin ventilator" (*sagewalli ki venti*). "Actually," the doctor says, "it's better to have him Ambu-bagged because at least it's monitorable. You can depend on it more than the ventilator." She brings the father a stool to sit on. A researcher in the ward watches the father squeeze the bag and remarks that, given the ward's resources, enrolling the relatives as accomplices in resuscitation is problematic but necessary. "But it should be someone strong," she says, someone who has the wherewithal to not cry, to not get distracted by their own exhausted body, to give themselves over to squeezing for their family member without pause or thought.[3] Human pumps may be more reliable than the machines that are overdue for maintenance and repair, but these forced circulations cannot falter. Breath becomes social because it requires assistance and forms an obligation of copresence. In these moments that medicine recognizes as its own turning points, another person shifts a patient's breath from autonomy to dependency and makes breathing social with each squeeze of the bag.

The anesthetist will take over the Ambu bagging in moments, but she is often busy preparing for the next possible attempt to work with the airway: intubation. This is how and when the ventilator comes into the picture, and it is the moment when the body shifts from the condition of resuscitation to the condition of longer-term life support. "Once intubated, the ventilator becomes the CPU for patients," an anesthetist says, using a computational idiom to describe the shift of life's controls from analog to digital, and from being located within a person to being located outside them. Intubation is not the end of this process. In Central's ICU, the general practice is that the endotracheal tube is used for seven days but no longer. After that, surgeons will perform a tracheostomy. The decision to vent is a fork in the road, one that opens to branching possibilities of action and consequence.

I do not see the anesthetist intubate Anand, but I imagine it happens as it does with most patients: after administering a sedative, she stands behind Anand's head, her eyes on his throat and chest. She inserts the laryngoscope slowly into his throat, angling the scope's blunt blade to visualize his epiglottis. With her other hand, she guides in a fresh endotracheal tube, inching it down . . . mouth, pharynx, past the vocal cords, into the trachea. The light on the laryngoscope and her angle of entry ensure this pathway. She directs the tube down the trachea and not down the esophagus. Inflating the stomach with air would kill Anand, and she also wants to avoid collateral damage, like breaking his teeth with the metal laryngoscope. Once the tube is in, the orderly connects it to the ventilator hookup. Anand is on life support after a snaking tube and a breathing machine add to the disturbances that follow the event that brings him to the hospital.

When Anand arrives at the trauma ward, it is the first time I see a mass-casualty traffic accident involving a family. There were many, many motorcycle accidents where pairs of people would come in injured, but until Anand's case I had not seen a car crash bring the members of one extended household to the ward, including parents, children, aunts, and uncles. The nurses and orderlies put up fabric screens for privacy around some of the beds, blocking lines of sight. Anand's wife does not survive the crash. Anand's children and his siblings-in-law do not have immediately life-threatening injuries and are sent elsewhere in the hospital for treatment. This leaves Anand in the trauma ward, diagnosed with blunt abdominal trauma.

Anand remains on the ventilator for eighty days. During this time, and during several years after his discharge, we strike up a connection. I learn that he is an advertisement sign painter. He hand-paints the walls by train tracks, window shutters, and building exteriors with catchy slogans for Parle biscuits, Pepsi sodas, and Videocon gadgets. He finished sixth grade, and the painter job took him across the country for work. He picked up language skills in the process, learning how to write in English, Tamil, and Kannada in addition to his first-learned languages, Marathi and Hindi.

As he breathes in the ICU, the ICU inhales the city. It is impossible to bound air, to stop it at the ward's portals. Air's circulations constitute and threaten social breathing, and Anand is contained within a climate that is both controlled and compromised. One afternoon I walk into the resuscitation area. It's separated from the ICU by a swinging door. It's May, and it's scorching outside. Monsoon has not yet reached Mumbai. The air quality index in the city has measured in the zone of unhealthy for a while now, and only the rain will bring relief. The ICU has high-blast air-conditioning, but the resus area does not. Newly arrived patients often shiver and complain of being cold, a common symptom of shock, so it's warmer in here. It is not uncommon for staff to pop into the ICU just for a little AC.

Anil, the ward's head ventilator technician, points out some blacker spots in the ceiling corners: mold. The climate makes it difficult to dehumidify the room, especially with the doors opening and closing all the time. Intensive care demands the motions of medicine, but air flows as bodies move in and out of the room's doors. The design of the HVAC system makes sealing things off simply impossible. A decade back, they fumigated the ICU to treat the mold, shifting the patients elsewhere for safety, but even after the patients returned, one of them got sick from the lingering fumes and died.

The fantasies, failures, and successes of controlling air's circulation underlie the history of ventilators. Intensive care medicine's own disciplinary history may be tracked through the developments of seals and vacuums, from the iron lung to the tracheostomy (Baskett and Safar 2003; Lock 2002; Safar 1996; Tercier 2005; Timmermans 2010; Weil and Tang 2011). In India, ICUs began as coronary care units in Mumbai (one at a public hospital and one at a private hospital), and these units later developed a focus on critical care for respiratory distress (Yeolekar and Mehta 2008). Technological shifts influenced what would count as a modern ICU. As Margaret Lock (2002) details, the development of artificial respiration ("breathing machines") entailed different types of machines and, in turn, different types of bodily envelopment and force over time. First, there was the iron lung of the 1930s that encased the bodies affected by polio, which caused the lungs to expand by applying negative pressure on the chest. Later iterations of the iron lung appeared in the 1950s, and their descendants today are called *ventilators* and stand at the bedside, monitoring breathing as they intervene in it. A tube down the throat replaces the body in the machine. Positive pressure replaces negative pressure. The machine is inside the breather, rather than the other way around. But changing the kinetics of air is only part of the problem. As life-support technologies become normalized in wealthier settings (including in private hospitals in India, where they are much more available than in public hospitals like Central), ventilators materialize the inequality of medical ordinariness, and moving on and off the machine can set the terms of care's affordances (Kaufman 2015).

Ventilators are complex machines that require trained professionals to operate, and critical but relatively invisible labor is involved in making social breathing work through machines that require monitoring and repair. It can be tempting to focus solely on the machines. But this may elide the machine's maintainers, to use Andrew Russell and Lee Vinsel's (2018) term for technological agents whose upkeep work connects industrial histories to social stratification, such that certain occupations become essential for the thriving of other bodies.

In Central's trauma ward, there are multiple maintainers. An engineer from the company that manufactures the ventilators is often present, fixing machines that have stopped functioning. One afternoon I watch him open up the body of a machine that has a piece of surgical tape on its top, where someone has written "NOT WORKING" in large letters. It is a box of many colors and shapes: wires, circuit boards, modules, and tubes. The engineer, a young man named Vikram, works quietly, with intense focus, between the beds of two patients each on (working) ventilators. He attaches a plastic glove to the machine's inspiratory line, and it inflates and deflates like a deep-sea creature. Vikram's hands are immersed in the viscera of the circuit box. It always looked to me as though he was performing surgery on the machines.

On his break, we talk. The first time he was sent to the trauma ward to repair ventilators, he felt confused by the scenes of injury and fragility that each patient's case presented. "I thought, 'Where am I?'" he says. Conducting repairs *inside* the ward felt so removed from the work on machines that he did back at the company headquarters. He terms his hospital work *fieldwork*. Despite the disturbing feeling and sights of the trauma ward ICU, he feels that it is his duty as an engineer to fix the ventilators; after all, who else could do this? He proudly notes that he is "on call"—meaning that the doctors and nurses have his cell phone number and can call him to repair the machines at any time of the day or night. But even with Vikram around, Anil often expresses concerns about maintenance. Mumbai's municipal government provides ventilators, Anil explains, but it does not offer adequate financial support to maintain them. "A person is on the venti for a week, but the machine can't go seven days without rest, it needs rest too," he says. Machines need respite and repair, just as humans do.

Anil began working in the ward twenty-five years ago as a lab assistant and now is in charge of maintaining all the instruments, especially the ventilators. He knows and remembers all sorts of options for support, and he is constantly calibrating the machines in ways that today's young residents don't even know exist, because now most support options are preprogrammed. "We can only try," he says, to support life with the ventilators. "The rest is up to God." This is especially true in the tenuous context of too many cases and too few ventilators: "Being a government hospital," he continues, "we cannot refuse patients. We cannot tell a patient to go elsewhere. In that condition, what do we do? We keep on Ambu-ing. And we ask the relatives to Ambu-bag the patient, and as soon as the ventilator gets free, we will make it available. In this condition, we are managing. We always tell them, 'We don't have a ventilator, but we will try. In the meantime, you have to Ambu.' If you have money, go to a private hospital. If you don't, wait." Anil foregrounds the importance of relatives for breathing life in emergencies where air partially circulates through stuck structures. He elevates timing and temporality as primary structures of life support in public medicine: if one cannot pay, one must wait to breathe. The circulation of air and the circulation of patients through the disjunctures of the health-care sector cannot be separated here. Breathing on a ventilator makes one apparent and attached to the discontinuities of both city and state.

The ventilator can trick people into closure, and it can twist language. On this May day, the ceiling fans whisk paper around. Someone is always turning the fans on or off, fiddling with the switches to get the right level of cooling but without too much disturbance of files and papers, which would puff away the archives of clinical records. The fans blow down onto a man who lies on a gurney after being hit by the local train. The senior resident wants to declare the man dead: "He's gone [ho gaya], and I'm going to inform the family." There is some discussion about the trains being late today and what to order for lunch. A nurse mentions a teenage girl who died similarly last month. She was wearing headphones and didn't hear the train coming; these attempts to create microworlds of privacy and pleasure simply can't hold against the city's juggernauts.

The chief resident summons the man's relatives. The doctors tried everything they could, he says, but the man's heart kept stopping. "But are there any chances he'll recover?" the sister-in-law asks. No, the resident says, "He is no more" (abhi toh nahin). This is in the hallway; the resident leads them into the ward, and they see the ventilator, still attached to the man. His wife asks the same question: "But are there any chances?"

Such situations add to the ICU's bioethical textures. Relatives frequently ask this question (*koi chances hai?*), and the question is especially common during a patient's transition to ventilation. The machine can signify medicine's feats and frailties. Critical care medicine's intensities are often visual: kin *see* the machine, they realize things are serious, they wonder if it might offer hope, and they know doctors cannot guarantee certainty. In asking the question, relatives fold expectations of divine grace and medical efficacy into the prospect of seeing something different from what they're seeing. They also ask the question in response to what they hear from doctors. The scripts for doctors to deliver news that a patient is dying or dead usually entail meting out information slowly. It is not uncommon for a patient to be very close to death, or even determined to be dead, yet the relatives are not always told this clearly. Rather, the rhetoric is to ease them into things: "Call your people from the village [*gaon*]" to get things in order, they're told. A pause is built into a lot of the status updates. "We'll see" (dekhte hai), the doctors will say, speaking sideways but truthfully, because the ventilator *can* bring someone back from death's brink.

These scripts can stretch time. They may allow doctors a certain denial of death and an evasion of blame in case the patient dies. Complicating things further, every physician has a different style of communication, and there can be variability in take-home messages across different conversations with different doctors, as kin listen and read between the lines. Scripts for delivering bad news also sync with the suspended animation of the ventilator, an extended pause before doctors may blame themselves, wondering if they could have done better, something that relatives sometimes wonder too. That which is clinical, that which is moral, that which is professional, and that which is technological move unevenly through impossible moments.

The man's ventilator beeps, and the sister-in-law points to it: "What's that?" (yeh kya hai?), she asks of the sound. The resident replies, "It's the machine breathing." This strange link seems to sink in; perhaps while nothing makes sense, something surfaces as true: breathing but dead. Chest rising but dead. Machine pumping but dead. This is conjecture on my part, because I do not ever ask anything in these moments at the knife-edge of life and death that this ward both cares for and puts on display. "He was my only brother!" the sister-in-law exclaims. The two women stand by the man's body, hold hands, and pray intently. One asks again, "Are there any chances?" The resident says no, the doctors tried all they could do, they tried hard. He moves into the ICU, perhaps reaching for release from the responsibility of explaining to a family in shock why the very machine that breathes life only half works: it beeps and blinks and pushes air but does not fully register its living partner. It is connected, and part of the circuit, yet life is not circulating.

For me, this is an object lesson: social breathing is not necessarily a symptom of living. Moving through the lifelines of ventilation, one does not guarantee the other.

––––––––––––

In moments when they are not by the bedside, nurses catch up on paperwork and with each other. I catch up on notes and develop a habit of sniffing my own shirt while I write, which smells like nothing until I leave the hospital, when the rush of fresh air pushes the phenol deep into my sinuses. A staff nurse takes stock of the ICU's occupancy; all the beds have patients. She catches up on the file of a man she thinks is a *charsi*, a generic term for someone who takes or is addicted to drugs (from *charas*, "hash/cannabis"). She has a hunch from his clinical signs that he has smoked *brown sugar*, a synthetic form of heroin. The senior anesthesia resident scribbles out orders for handling substance withdrawal.

The issue of withdrawal cements the case of another patient in the ICU, an elderly man named Ojas, but the withdrawal at hand is the removal of the ventilator. The resident examines Ojas, looks at his ventilator settings, and consults with her attending. Offhand, she asks, "Can't I just reduce?" By "Can't I just reduce?" she means, "Can't I just reduce the oxygen?" Even after being moved onto the ventilator, Ojas's prognosis is very poor. His brother, Prashant, visits constantly and frequently explains to anyone who will listen that Ojas *wants* to die.

"Can't I just dial it down?" the resident asks the attending again. The attending replies quickly, "No, no." That is not allowed. That would be active euthanasia. Active euthanasia is not legal in India, he explains. It is tantamount to killing. And so it is not done. If Ojas's condition were more stable, they would slowly reduce the assistance that the ventilator provides. In that hypothetical situation, his own respiratory system would take over. His chest muscles would get the hang of things again, and he could breathe independently. But for now, the doctors believe that he is likely to code if weaned from the ventilator. He does not currently meet the hospital's clinical benchmarks for persistent vegetative state or brain death. Everyone must wait and watch.

Ojas is the victim of a hit-and-run. He was out for his daily walk and was hit by a motorcycle, which sped off without stopping. "He was lying in a pool of blood. Lots of people stood around, but they did nothing," Prashant says. Prashant is not hopeful about his brother's outcome. "His days are numbered. If the Lord wants to take him, let him take him in his whole form." Prashant has refused to sign the consent forms for the surgeries that the ward's doctors insist would, in a standard protocol of treatment, extend Ojas's life. "He was not a drinker; he did not eat nonveg; he is a pious man. Let him have a peaceful death." In the suspended pauses of ventilation, life stories get worked and reworked.

Some nurses in the ward are open to Prashant's assertion that his brother wants to die. Others are more hesitant. After all, one points out, Ojas cannot talk, because he is intubated and comatose. So how can one assess Prashant's assertions? Are they coming from a place of compassion? Or maybe some property or money from an inheritance is at stake? What else might move when the machine ceases moving? Ward staff often don't know, and many do not *want* to know. For now, the ventilator offers other information: his vital signs (degrading) and his neurological signs, like spontaneous movement or response to pain stimuli (unchanged and not promising).

One nurse says to the trauma resident, "Just turn the ventilator off" (venti off kar ke do). She does not say this out of not knowing, for she has worked here for years and knows the law and the policies. She isn't surprised to hear the doctor reply with assertions that no, this cannot be done. There are protocols. One cannot simply turn the ventilator *off*; it is the patient who makes that happen, not us. We are not God. She says it, I think, as a wishful but impossible end to the impasse at hand. In the ICU, a place where so much talk is about what *should* be done (orders, protocols, rounds), it can be tricky to hear the reverberations of the ethics of life support. One might hear in "venti off kar ke do" the relational intricacies of Hindi verbs. The utterance involves the imperative mood of the compound verb form *kar dena*, "to do it for him," with the *kar* stem meaning "do" and *dena* meaning "to give," signaling that the doing should be directed away from the subject for another's benefit. *Turn off the ventilator (for him).* I do not assume that the nurse thinks this a benevolent action. Nor am I sure who the *him* is: Ojas or Prashant. But amid the uncertainties, one sees how social breathing—even at its ends—can be pluralized. Ojas's desires might not be clear because his injuries and the ventilator both dampen speaking, but that doesn't mean he's not present, for himself and for others around him.

"He's going, today" (jaata hai, aaj), another nurse observes. Her predictions are nearly correct: Ojas dies a day and a half later. The day following his death, I round with the residents. The one whose shift is ending points to the empty bed Ojas had occupied. No words, just a gesture to the empty space and the powered-down ventilator. "Good, he had to go," the incoming-shift resident says. By this she means not that Ojas's death was good, because dying in this place is not a good death. But it is good that he is no longer breathing in *this* room. To linger on life support in the ICU is a form of pain that no one should endure; social breathing on a ventilator should not be endless. I also see how in the context of the limited ventilator economy, the "good" of "he had to go" can mean "he had to go so that someone else could have the ventilator." These utterances can audit the breathing room for available ventilators, inseparable from the push and pull of bioethics on patients, staff, and kin. One surgeon, reflecting on Ojas and his death, glances upward, directing us to the expanse of the divine realm that encompasses the world of the ICU. She points a finger up: "That's where he's going," she says, his move off the ventilator allowing traffic to move again.

Sometimes the scenes in the ICU cut close, and I leap across the ocean by reading American accounts of life support, such as Sharon Kaufman's powerful ethnography of intensive care in the United States, . . . *And a Time to Die* (2005). Kaufman argues that the notion of "choosing" to breathe, or "deciding" to breathe, can be overdetermined by the ever-presence of technology that is immediately available to put someone on life support. In the American hospital setting, the ventilator and all the discussion around it can crowd out the already-limited spaces for families to arrive at critical decisions about life support. Kaufman explains how so much focus lies on the machine itself, and specifically its on-off possibilities, even as both doctors and families desire space to think and feel through what it might mean to take part in ending a life or keeping it going.

I see this in Central's ICU too, but the picture is different. First, there is the difference in ventilator economies: there aren't enough machines, which is the opposite problem of the US case, where *too much* medicine—ventilators at the ready—shapes life-support ethics. This too-muchness is a historical artifact, of course, and it is a luxury. I present an in-progress version of this chapter to an audience at my university in February 2019. During the question-and-answer time, a senior physician in the audience lectures me with authoritative disdain. He says that everything I explained in the previous hour about Central's ICU makes no sense to him, because it could all be solved in one go by simply ordering more ventilators. Why don't they order more ventilators? This is utter failure, he says. Yet I believe the failure in fact lies in his constrained imagination, one unwilling to accede that ventilators may not actually be as available or therapeutic as they seem, which becomes tragically clear precisely twelve months later when the coronavirus pandemic unfurls (Solomon 2021).

Second, at Central, the semantics of *machine* (machine), *venti* (ventilator), and *saans* (breath) are not binaries but blends. One evening I see a resident fiddle with a patient's ventilator. She speaks directly to the man in the bed, "Open your chest and take a deep breath; you have to get off the machine!" (chhaati kholke saans lo; machine ko choḍna hai). The overlay of ventilator and individuated agency is what I hear, rather than a bioethics mapped squarely onto the machine's on-off switch. I hear a doctor imploring a patient to gather up enough agency to make social breathing less social, so that he might live.

Third, the economic structures of treatment in the public hospital setting shape social breathing. At Central and other municipal public hospitals like it, the ventilator is included in the two hundred rupee/day bed charge. By contrast, ventilator support in a private hospital in Mumbai can be upward of ten thousand rupees per day. At Central, the idea that the ventilator would be rejected is not close at hand for most families, and if a ventilator *is* rejected, it says as much about social class as it does about bioethics. This is because people craft textured ethical relations to biomedical technologies, and in life-or-death situations in the public hospital trauma ward ICU, those relations often involve an assumption that ventilators are around for a good reason. Their absence would be another sting of inequality and unavailability. Their presence holds out the promise of life and the aura of hope for what medicine might fix.

The claims Prashant makes on Ojas and the ventilator resonate with depictions of the ventilator in Indian popular culture at the nexus of health-care economies and familial ethics. The ventilator often crystallizes questions of what is good for a patient, what is good for a family, and what is good for a hospital. Hindi film dramas such as *Ventilator, Staying Alive*, and *Piku* each take up the problem of hospital intensive care. In the films, the setting of the private hospital makes the availability of the ventilator seem guaranteed. The fantasy dilemmas center not on the scarcity of the machine but on the family's relationship to the machine's on-off status. This skips over the primary dilemma that patients in Central's ICU face: there may be no available ventilator for dramatization. In the private settings, it seems, breath is not the only substance whose exhaustion is at stake. There is also the question of when families will run out of money to pay for the seemingly endless breath of long-term ventilation for their kin, money that turns dying into profit for the private health-care system.

This tussle over the sociality of social breathing is structural from multiple vantage points. The very availability and nonavailability of life-support technology is wrapped up in everyday structures of governance and resource affordance. When people are in the grip of a dire situation and intensive forms of medicine may promise a way out, they rightfully *expect* something to be done. I never witnessed someone refusing the ventilator because they thought it was a threat. Ojas's case was one instance where I saw a relative assert wishes about control over the ventilator, but his brother, Prashant, did not deny the doctors the chance to intubate Ojas in the first place. The act of ventilating can be medicine's delivery on a promise, however uncertain the outcomes may be.

The trouble often begins afterward, when the ventilator gets too close.

––––––

As the weeks pass, some doctors begin to question Anand's willingness to detach from the ventilator; he's becoming a little too relational in his breath. They say that Anand exhibits "ventilator dependence" and that he is "addicted" to supported breath. Dependency is dangerous, and in this framing, the ventilator is understood to be as damaging as it is necessary. Besides a breathing tube's own mechanical damages (to internal tissue), there are the downstream risks of infection and "addiction." A ventilated person may just become too accustomed to assistance. Here *addiction* is a word and a pragmatics that overlays patients who stay on the ventilator too long, with staff always mindful of the future possible patient who will soon enter the ward, needing an (unavailable) machine.

"Anand gets anxious when we try to wean," an anesthetist says. *Weaning* is a common term in critical care medicine, and it is employed in the ward's vernacular language as well: *usko wean kar do*, "wean her." It implies calibrating the ventilator's set levels of oxygenation, air volume, and pressure. There is the metaphor here of slowly withdrawing a substance, of taking away in order for a person to self-regulate. The idea of weaning on a ventilator is that a patient will be weaned from artificial, assisted ventilation in order to again breathe on their own.

Anand is anxious because his ability to be weaned is undercut by secondary infections. He develops pneumonia and then a multidrug-resistant staph infection (MRSA). Residents come by when they can to vacuum the secretions from his tracheostomy and pump them into a large bell jar on a cart that orderlies must empty. The jars contain breath's undesirable liquid obstacles. Suction is done because secretions can seed secondary infections; ventilator-assisted pneumonia is a common occurrence and a constant concern (another way that air becomes a problem for life: this time, "dirty air"). Anand's eyes squeeze tears during suction; it's terribly painful.

I lead qualitative methods workshops for the clinical research staff sometimes, and once we do an exercise where they choose a medical technology and free-write their associations. One chooses the ventilator and writes, "I have always visualized it as a robot digging its hand into a God-made human and gradually sucking the life out of that soul." I think about this image when I see the orderlies suck out microbial life from Anand's breathing tubes, life that left unchecked can be deadly. I'm reminded of it when I see how relatives get enrolled in the process. I watch a resident instruct a patient's wife how to loosen secretions in his lungs by pretending that she is eating dinner. She is to feign the hand position of scooping up a ball of rice, thumb pressed against forefingers, and then thump on her husband's chest. So much work goes into making the lifelines of ventilation more vital than lethal, given their potential to be both things at once.

All of this work unfolds around patients who, in varying states of delirium and alertness, may or may not absorb what is going on around them. One day during one of these suctions on his trach tube, Anand grabs me and motions to his head, repeatedly. His sight lines stretch up toward the ceiling's fluorescent lights when he is supine. When he is propped up, he faces away from the curtained window into the scenes of the ward. He cannot look elsewhere. He takes his hands, folds them together, and then slowly draws them apart: he's been in here for a long time. I begin reading about the phenomenon of ICU psychosis and wonder about Anand's unending immersion in fluorescent light, ventilator beeps, suctioning, and bodily carnage.[4] It seems difficult to disentangle his breathing from the injuries of others, and I wonder if one of the intensities of intensive care is the exposure to violence.[5]

This is a teaching hospital, and so everyone jumps to attention when the senior faculty member comes for clinical rounds. The anesthesia professor named Dr. T arrives and moves to Anand's bed. "He's going into acute respiratory distress," Dr. T says. He quizzes the residents on acute respiratory distress syndrome. He adjusts the volume and oxygen on Anand's ventilator. "Your aim is to maintain physiology," he tells his residents, "but also to reduce the metabolic cost of breathing by unloading the ventilatory muscles." He instructs the senior resident on duty to give Anand some fentanyl, to help with Anand's agitation and tachycardia. They want Anand calmer in order to wean him off the ventilator. The anesthetist attempts to adjust the ventilator, to drop the oxygen support, but Anand keeps pointing at his chest. No, it's not enough air, he seems to be signaling. Please don't dial it down. Anand has endured rounds like this every morning, where doctors collectively assess and decide what's next. Some patients remain quiet for it, but Anand is an active participant, communicating through gesture.

Medical professors always remind their residents to consider a strategy for weaning after a patient has been stabilized on mechanical ventilation: they must visualize the off-ramp even as they navigate the highway entrance. "Oxygen is injurious," Dr. T reminds his residents. It causes free radical damage. The very thing we think is a help needs to be carefully calibrated.[6] The ventilator is an ally who also damages you. And weaning is often nonlinear. Life support may be reduced, and the patient's breathing strengthens, only to falter again a few hours later, when the machine's support will be amplified again. "Ventilators are harmful to the patient," Dr. T tells them. Anand is listening.

The changeover from inspiration to expiration, called the *trigger*, is of critical importance to the intensivist. "Normal" or "spontaneous" breathing has a ratio of about 1:2 (one second of inhaling to two seconds of exhaling). The ventilator can change this ratio up to a point, but certain modes on the ventilator, if not monitored correctly, might move the breath too forcefully and distend the alveoli, which can cause cardiac arrest in patients already on the verge of shock. "Weaning is torture for anesthetists," a resident says, especially with trauma patients who may have rib fractures and intercostal drains for internal bleeding that make weaning harder to achieve. Weaning is a careful dance, a game of cat and mouse with the breath.[7]

Weaning is also a dance with willpower. After Dr. T departs from morning rounds, I ask one of the residents how the instructions to wean Anand off the ventilator might eventually play out. The resident, as a young doctor under the close watch of a faculty supervisor, affirms that he will obey the attending's instructions, of course, but honestly? He thinks that no amount of coaching or positive feedback will help Anand, because Anand is not helping himself and doesn't have the courage (*himmat*) to make weaning possible.

I understand that no one thinks Anand can handle the truth about his wife's death until he is more stable. But the conflicting demands of ventilation's lifelines seem impossible. He is supposed to breathe relationally while accepting the loss of a relation that no one will explain to him. He must also demonstrate the power to not breathe relationally, to detach his breath and body from the ventilator, even though his secondary infections suggest that he is getting sicker in part because the ventilator assists the movement of air's pathogens into his lungs. He should breathe on his own, even as this room overdetermines the relationality of social breathing. He is supposed to mobilize the power to stop the ventilator. But how can someone be expected to manage the traffic of things that are not only theirs to move?

———

After he has breathed with the ventilator for a month, a moral economy ties Anand to the ventilator in terms of willpower. He's having a so-so day, he writes to me in his notebook. A nurse asks how he is doing today, and he points his finger to the ceiling. She takes this (correctly) as a gesture to God's control over whether he will live or die. "No, no, it's not God's will," she scolds him—"Breathe, yourself!" (Devo nahin! Khud!). He nods. He makes the gesture of hand to mouth to signal eating, and I think he's saying he's hungry, but he corrects me by emphasizing the gesture's direction toward me: he wants to *feed* me, once he gets out.

An anesthetist pulls me aside. "Anand's body has been sedentary for weeks," he says. "It's giving up on him." Another anesthetist says that it's because he's tachycardic, and he's tachycardic because he's nervous and scared. The ventilator works as a proxy for willpower through its possible removal from the scene of instruction. If Anand really had the agency, the will, the drive, then the ventilator might not be necessary. In certain ways, the doctors fetishize the ventilator. Patients and families see and hear this clearly, but I don't assume they completely organize their fantasies of recovery/healing around it. People mainly just want to get out: to be "ready," as Anand put it, to be somewhere else. I think back to Anand's first note—"Chest is not respoonce. Tomorrow I am ready Bree." He expresses willpower and imagines a tomorrow, even with intense uncertainties at hand. The doctors imagine a tomorrow for him too. But this comprehensive tomorrow is one in which he is not on a ventilator and also does not have a wife. It is a tomorrow that cannot be revealed to him until he shoulders more of the burden of breathing. The ventilator becomes a gatekeeper of the ward's versions of truth and time and hope.

Still, truths can be incorrect. It has been months since Anand arrived in the ward, and during this time, the residents come and go, often on only monthly rotations. It's the nurses, the orderlies, and I who stay. This means that the nurses organize themselves around the duty of keeping a version of the truth. The nurses tell me that "the truth" is that Anand doesn't know his wife is dead, and no one will tell him lest he lose faith in living and breathing. Telling him the truth might undo all his progress. But surely he's asked, I say. Maybe so, they say. Still, it is too risky to say anything to him about his wife, they warn. I settle on one thing to keep saying to him: "Just take a good long breath" (acchha laamba sans le lo). It's as common an exchange between us as "Good morning" (nod) and "How are you feeling today?" (thumb up or down, or a flip between).

I see Anand's relatives outside the ward one afternoon. He's doing better and seems ready for transfer to a regular ward, out of the ICU. The relatives say that they have told Anand that his wife is at home and they want him to get better. He seems weaker (kamzor) lately. They're giving him breathing room to recover by not telling him the truth. Anand's family has faced multiple, unexpected losses in an instant. Their presence is already a lot, because it is not guaranteed, and when it does manifest, it is laborious and bears costs. There are decisions and actions that may appear to those *outside the family* as acts of omission but *within the family* may constitute a form of keeping someone alive. I believe this is also true, albeit differently, for the nurses and service staff. They often become proxy arbiters of a family's secrets, revelations, and aspirations to move someone so that they may live.

An anesthetist who grows very close to Anand tells me months after Anand's discharge that he, the doctor, thinks Anand, the patient, is a remarkably intelligent man. "Anand even knows all the venti settings," he says. After months of having all his relatives visit except his wife, Anand obviously could put the pieces together. Perhaps he didn't let on to his relatives that he knew the truth about his wife, but patients know plenty even when they can't speak. The anesthetist says that he saw the psychiatric reference notes in Anand's file, which suggest that Anand communicated to the psychiatrist that he indeed knew his wife had died in the accident. The note describes Anand's feelings of low mood, hopelessness, and worth-lessness, for which the psychiatrist prescribed an antidepressant.

Anand is a favorite patient for some of the doctors and nurses, and a thorn in the side for others, but everyone keeps exhorting him to breathe on his own. His family feels similarly. They tell me that they do not want him to grow depressed. He may be breathing, but breathing in *this room*, the ICU, is not the social breathing they want for him, nor is it the kind of breathing they think he wants. They want him moved out of the hospital. They want him to come home, a different site for the social. Everyone in the ICU agrees, and each tinkers with his breathing's obstructions in any way they know how.

Before he goes home, Anand is shifted to other parts of the hospital, a step-down from the trauma ICU. The extent of his chest issues means that he doesn't go directly to a general ward, as patients often do. Instead, he goes to the intermediate respiratory care unit, which has only three pa-tients, is spotlessly clean, and is nearly silent. He is not at ease when I visit. To preserve the peace, I write in his notebook.

"Are you OK?"

He points to his legs and scribbles. "No sitting no standing. Muscle power is weak." He is still on the ventilator.

A few weeks later, Anand returns to the trauma ward; the intermediate respiratory care unit wants the trauma anesthetists to complete his wean-ing. The ventilator by his bedside is turned off, although his tracheotomy tube remains in place. He smiles and swipes his hand in the air with the everyday gesture that means "I left it" (*chor diya*). He writes in his note-book, "I am leave it ventilator." He writes that he has been thinking about the number of days the doctors say he must stay in the general ward. He has calculated based on that number the precise day when he will go home. He wants us to have a pizza and Thums Up cola when that happens.

One of the surgery residents tells me that he's pleased to see Anand so happy and imagines him spinning around the general ward in his wheelchair, jovial, and basking in the sunshine outside. The nurses begin compiling the heaps of papers from his file at their desk in preparation for his discharge.

He receives a confirmation X-ray before leaving the ICU, and it shows that there is a patch of infection at the site of his intercostal drain incision. The anesthetist is upset. Anand was so close to getting out of here, and this damn patch showed up, and now it seems to be diminishing his lung capacity. There is no choice but to intubate him again and reattach the ventilator. He looks groggy and rests with one eye closed and one open.

But Anand heals. The patch disappears. He is extubated, the ventilator gets turned off, and the trach tube gets removed. He is transferred to the general ward, where there are nearly a hundred beds in contrast to the fourteen beds of the trauma ICU. The general ward has windows open to the outside, and relatives and doctors moving in and out. Relatives are a key care resource in these parts of the hospital. Patients receive multiple daily meals consisting of dal, sabzi, rice, and two slices of white bread, but relatives supplement that with food from home. Unlike in the trauma ward, where relatives are not allowed to bring solid food to patients because they are generally pre- and postoperative, here in the general ward, food is the star. Much of the day is organized around mealtimes. In between, relatives sit on the beds of patients and often on the ground, sometimes sleeping in the hallways outside the ward on flattened cardboard boxes and taking turns visiting and feeding. When I arrive in the general ward, Anand is surrounded by his siblings and in-laws. He is still not allowed to eat solid food, and he cannot talk, owing to the irritation sustained from months of a trach tube rubbing up against his vocal cords.[8] A nurse feeds him white nutritional formula through a nasogastric tube. He takes in some water, squeaks a tinny "Good morning," and brings out his notebook.

"Injury hevi time," he writes. He also writes that he is happy. I'm not sure if the heaviness is over, as he is still healing from all manner of trauma, and the scattered gravity of breathing—"hevi time"—draws me away from concluding on a note of triumph or suffering, of clear starts or finishes. What stays with me is Anand's sense of "hevi time": how the ventilator moves social breathing in ways beyond on or off.

After Anand's discharge, our connection falters. He returns to his home village, a day's travel away from the city, and spends months there recovering. I return to the United States, and there are gaps in between my own visits back to the hospital. We both change our phone numbers and cannot connect on WhatsApp.

Several years later, I am at Central and see one of the residents who closely attended to Anand. He tells me that Anand was just sending him WhatsApp good morning messages. Anand is in Mumbai, it turns out, and occasionally visits the hospital to say hello to the staff, nurses, and doctors whom he connected with during his stay in the ICU. I take this in. I wonder what it must be like to return to the scene of so much struggle, but it makes sense. Three months is a long time to be in a hospital, and intimacies can develop in unpredictable ways.

Anand and I reconnect, and he meets me in the trauma ward. He is joking with the orderlies when I walk in. We decide to sit outside in the sun, and he reminds me of his wish to have a pizza, and so we walk to Domino's and order a large extra-veggie pizza; he requests that I eat all of it despite my efforts to serve him slices. We are close to the hospital, just blocks away in fact, but far enough away that no one from the hospital is there (it's expensive, anyways). This means that no one familiar is there to overhear our conversations. We are just an odd arrangement of a middle-aged Indian man and a getting-there foreign man. I put myself in eating-contest mode, eating slice after slice, hoping he will follow, but he just takes tiny bites. We ask the college students sitting at the table next to us to take photos. And we talk.

I quote him directly here, at length. There was much air expended around him by observers, caregivers, and kin speaking over and around him, for him, to him, breathing story into him about his wishes and needs. He is a breather too.

"Do you remember the notebook?"

He does.

"I would ask the doctors to take me off the machine each time. I didn't want the ventilator, I wanted to live, I wanted to get my children educated, I wanted to talk to them, but I couldn't talk over the ventilator, I could only write. I think a lot about those eighty days; they were the most different time in my life.[9] I never felt that I would leave the hospital, alive or dead. I didn't know when I would leave. I wasn't ever sure whether I would or would not be taken off the ventilator, because of what I would see in front of me. So many bodies passed before me. Only three I saw clearly. Just three people were saved, everyone else who was on the ventilator was dead.[10] I can't believe that I got my life back a second time. Now, no one would recognize me, I was very weak. When I got discharged, I weighed only thirty-two kilos; when I was admitted, I had weighed eighty-four kilos."

"When you left the hospital, what was that like?"

"The first days I was very weak. I would eat milk and vegetables and walk around. I walked for at least three hours every day. I had to take food through the nose for three months. I still have problems in my stomach. My sides pinch a lot. I have the same problems with breathing. There is no problem when I walk slow or on a flat surface. But it's a problem when climbing stairs or running. I can't carry anything heavier than five kilos. I feel weak. Before the accident I was a painter; I would paint things on shutters and walls. But now I work in telemarketing."

The smell of the paint, he says, makes it hard for him to breathe.

Unprompted, he speaks of the unfinished feeling that came of never seeing his wife's body. He refers to her death as "missus off ho gaya," saying that she "went off"—a conventional way to say that someone has died and also the way a machine turns off.

Over the years, he wondered if she had simply left him and gone to her father's village as if they had an argument.[11]

"What was it like when you left the hospital?"

"My whole life I had never taken a tablet, never been admitted to a hospital, never fallen sick with cough or cold, and I always wondered about why there are so many patients in the hospital. But when I had my accident and I was admitted here, then I realized what a doctor does and what a doctor means. So now, whenever I see this hospital, I don't feel good about patients getting on the ventilator. If a person survives being on the ventilator, it is like a second birth.[12] Coming back alive from the ventilator is not a common thing. Very few return. In my three months in the hospital, I saw a minimum of 182 bodies. Some were on the ventilator for twenty-four hours, some for thirteen hours, eight hours, two hours, or even an hour, and then they died. Earlier I would just see a dead body as it was. Now, if I am at a funeral and I see a body, I feel like I have been lying down next to dead bodies here in the hospital. Next to me on the ventilator, dead: that took away my fear of dead bodies. It was difficult to see them go, and yet I was still here. I felt I would also go. I felt that if they died, I would also die. This was the fear I had at times. A person is given life by God only once, but I was declared dead three times."

I interrupt him. He was declared dead?

"You know that, no? Three times I was declared dead. Several times when I was on the ventilator, I pulled out the tube. Then I had to breathe from the top of my chest, and I couldn't. Then they had to put the Ambu bag on me to revive me. This happened three times. This is why in my village they would tell me that there is something special about you, because God brought you back from such a place. God saved me, and now I will not die. I know that nothing will happen to me. After all this has happened, how could I die? Now I come to the hospital without any fear in my heart. I look at patients, people coming in ambulances, people carried on stretchers. I feel that the person who is on a ventilator should get off of it as soon as possible, and he should be saved. I tell God not to give that poor person such a life, to get the person off the ventilator as soon as possible. Nobody should be like that. No patient should be on a ventilator."

———

I look at a ventilator in the trauma ICU pushed into the corner, labeled "NOT WORKING," as the technician makes it workable. One might read the label as a sign of infrastructural lack, but I see it more as a sign of the demand for the ventilator, its centrality, and its work as part of the relational circuits of social breathing. I also see it as a condition of how ethnography might understand the politics of life support, when it is the exception rather than the rule that technology is disconnected from the circuits of social breathing.

The ventilator keeps narrative afloat, for some, and the ventilator makes writing happen. Anand stayed for months, far longer than most, conditioning our connection and the possibility for these stories. He stayed, and he breathed through the morass of impossible positions and obligations, with the ventilator beeping all the while. He was moved by the ventilator, and then he moved it. It took both to make living possible.

In a world where breathing isn't necessarily a guarantee of living, even when supported by a technology whose job is to move breath, a closer focus on what Anand calls "hevi time" might reveal more about the terms of breathing's relational affordances. "Hevi time" puts several taken-for-granted binaries into question: the breather and the breathed, the individual and the social, agency and patiency, and the domains of life and not life. Often the grounding question about the ventilator's bioethics is, "Is this life?" This question, frequently based in the one-way movement of breath from the ventilator to the static body, is premised on arriving at a clean cut between autonomy and dependency, and between the machine's on and off settings. It is an important question that I do not think should be dismissed, as it is the grounds of judicial authority and bioethical policy in many places and a close-at-hand way of settling pivotal decisions. But it is not the *only* question to ask. It is equally important, I think, to ask, "What is it to be moved to life?" This question roots in the lifelines of ventilation, the complex obstructions and flows of social breathing through the traffic of trauma.

Bioethical debates about ventilators are usually configured around the question of the presumed desire to live. In Anand's case, although that expression of agency seemed apparent, the ventilator also brings to bear the issue of being heard and being spoken for.[13] I see this reflected in Anand's notebook, in which a person comes to inhabit language through the ventilator's multiple, competing demands. There may have been striving to move beyond the ward's moral economy of breathing that adaptively but forcefully supported him. Relationality and individuality could shift, and thus I do not assume his writing had been only dialogical. He may also have been writing for himself, chronicling time in the hospital with exquisite detail. Such chronicles could be records to remember, and they also could be the stuff of propulsion, settling and advancing the days and nights in a clinical context filled with unpredictable progressions and setbacks. All I know is that I breathed him, maybe he breathed me, and our traffic would continue after he was gone.

6 Dissecting

THE LIFELINES OF FORENSICS

After our pizza lunch, Anand sends me WhatsApp messages: *Hi, hello, good morning, good evening.* He calls in the evenings and asks what I've had for dinner. He texts in the mornings and asks what I've eaten for breakfast. He phones one night and asks me if I'll tell people in America about him, because he wants me to tell the full story of his hospital stay. I explain how I write research, I ask what he is comfortable with me sharing, he specifies this, and I say okay, I'll tell. "Even your mother?" he asks. "Of course," I say, and I do. He is in his natal village in rural Maharashtra visiting family. He has remarried, and his two daughters are still in Mumbai with their step-mother, Aparna, whom the children call "Aunty." His father gets on the phone, and we make small talk. Anand says he'll be back in a few days, and let's have dinner. He wants *parathas* and Aparna's are the best.

I don't hear from him for a week. I send text messages but get no reply and try to not overthink it. I arrive at the trauma ward, and the nurses tell me, "That patient you know arrived at the hospital last night. He is dead." They are talking about Anand. They frame it as sudden and bizarre, which it is. He had returned from the village to Mumbai and collapsed one evening soon afterward. The family rushed him to the hospital, but it was too late, and the news stretches down the hall from casualty to the trauma ward. In the time since his discharge years back, Anand had kept in touch with some of the staff and nurses in the trauma ward. He would stop by occasionally to offer treats, a thank-you for all the care during his time there, passing around biscuits a few steps away from people on gurneys who would never get the chance to blur being a patient and a discharged person. "We are all in shock," Sister Shubha tells me. "So sad, really sad," Dr. D says. The orderlies have transferred his body to the morgue for the postmortem, one in a chain of shifts following death.

Death may be a domain where one expects to find stillness, yet medicine's traffic continues after life dissipates. Even if the certainty of a forensic investigation is never achieved, the binds between movement and medicine still carry force after death. Throughout this book I have argued that trauma must be understood in terms of relational, differential traffic rather than in terms of the static singularity of injured subjects. In this chapter I focus on the postmortem investigation as a critical condensation of this claim. Movements toward, through, and out of the domain of dissection underwrite its lifeline. These differences in motion transform trauma by identifying, shifting, and stilling corpses and spark tensions among the living who care for them. Intermittent forms of stasis and motion—traffic, after death—exert force on the dead and on the living. The forces of forensics become both necessary and threatening, constituting a lifeline. Stillness is part of this lifeline, but it is not the only part. Kinesis and stasis are both involved. The biopolitics of death from trauma are as much matters of who and what moves the dead as they are matters of achieving stable facts of death.

Death from trauma transports persons into a new relation with government authority. According to law, all cases of death from traumatic injury must undergo a medicolegal postmortem—that is, a dissection performed by someone with a specialty in forensic medicine. The medicolegal postmortem, also called a *forensic postmortem*, is also required in cases of patients who die within twenty-four hours of arriving at the hospital and in the context of any death deemed "unnatural" by police, such as apparent suicide. These requirements are laid out in the Coroner's Act of 1871, the Maharashtra Anatomy Act of 1949, the updated Coroner's Act that repealed and revised the 1871 act in 1999 and established specific postmortem centers in the state, and the national Indian Code of Criminal Procedure (see Ahmad 2019 and Barnagarwala 2016). Anand had endured traumatic injury years before from a major automobile accident, and this was the circumstance of our first encounter in the trauma ward. He arrived dead at the hospital owing to an unknown cause. His body would take the route of a medicolegal postmortem, drawing the family into a waiting game as the morgue held his body.

After several years observing cases in the trauma ward, I follow the paths of patients out of the ward to understand how the traffic of trauma endures. I begin fieldwork in the morgue in the months before Anand's death, observing postmortems of trauma cases and the everyday work of Central Hospital's forensic medical team. In the context of Mumbai's high level of traffic injuries and their high levels of mortality, death is a common way out of the trauma ward.[1] I split my days and nights, toggling between the trauma ward and the morgue, watching injury change from something someone might die from, to something someone does die from, to something whose lethality merits forensic attention. Typical of the way multisited methods divide attention, this means I am not in the morgue the day of Anand's postmortem. I am grateful for this displacement.

I return to the trauma ward. "Maybe his wife is relieved," Sister Archana wonders. His second wife, Aparna, had been his primary caregiver during his years of recovery after the accident, and these efforts can be exhausting. Sister Archana knows how widows face the headwinds of discrimination. She wishes Aparna a moment of reprieve and the ability to move on.

My phone rings later that night; it is from Anand's number, and this is a jolt. It is Aparna calling. She read my text messages to Anand on his phone, and she wants me to know what is happening. She knows that he and I stayed in touch, off and on, over the years. She knows that he wanted me to write about his experiences. Because the postmortem has concluded, she will return to the hospital tomorrow to collect his body so the family can move him toward last rites and cremation. Can we meet and talk? I agree.

I immediately call the two people I turn to for advice, both senior surgeons and both writers and researchers. They have dedicated their careers to work in public hospitals in Mumbai much like Central. Facing the family after a patient's death is all too familiar to them. One says, "Your job is to listen, full stop. Don't talk too much." The other tells me to accept the messiness and to resist attempts to make sense of it. Don't lose the pieces of Anand's time in the hospital, she encourages me, but don't expect that his death will make the pieces of the story align. His wife and daughter want to move him out of the hospital, and right now the postmortem stands between them and that aim.

I have plotted a line connecting Anand's time in the trauma ward, his time on the ventilator, our connections outside the hospital, and now his death. She warns me that I cannot assume that this tracking of propulsion and pause will add up to some grand reveal. Lines of reason have limits; they cannot delineate the incongruities of dying. She tells me not to dissect this. "Sometimes you walk into a film and get absorbed for hours," she says. "Then you walk outside, and the sunlight hits your eyes, and you blink, and you lose the storyline. You try to piece it back together, but you can't."

Death's gravity pulls. When death occurs in the trauma ward, it sets into motion the changing of a person from a *patient* to a *body* (these are the

English-derived words incorporated into Marathi and Hindi). A *patient* needs treatment and clinical attention. A *body* needs to be sent to the morgue for dissection to investigate the cause of death. Forensics, the retrospective inquiry into the cause of death, is not possible without the movement of bodies from the hospital's wards, *bodies* that had been *patients*. The necessary process of preparing bodies for the postmortem is often a lightning rod in the trauma ward.

A trauma ward surgeon, Dr. U, is explaining to the relatives of a deceased patient that the postmortem must be done to determine their uncle's cause of death (he calls it a *jaanch vaanch*, meaning "investigation" or "examination"). The relatives express frustration at what seems like unnecessary meddling and the imposition of uncaring state power, especially after medicine so clearly failed to do its job. They press Dr. U on the question of why this is necessary. It's clear what caused the death—a truck hit their uncle—and what more could possibly need to be known? Dr. U doesn't disagree with this assessment, nor does he justify it by explaining the difference between mechanism of injury (the collision with the truck) and cause of death (the effects of that collision inside the body). He simply says that the postmortem is a government regulation, so what can one do? ("sarkari niyaam hai toh kya kar sakta hai?"). One can do very little. Many doctors in the trauma ward believe the postmortem to be invasive and unnecessarily torturous to families. In many ways, Unknown patients are easily accelerated toward the postmortem, because their kin are not present to question this move. Yet shrugs of mandate like Dr. U's can authorize the hospital's hold on the body, an investigatory grip of the state that whisks away the corpse and tugs on the living.

At Central, pathologists carry out a clinical postmortem, and the consent of relatives is mandatory. By contrast, a medicolegal case does not require the consent of relatives for the forensic postmortem, which is carried out by forensic pathologists. In the public hospital setting, the force of the state cannot be underscored enough here. According to hospital regulations, a body intended for forensic postmortem shifts from hospital custody to police custody when it shifts from the trauma ward to the morgue. The postmortem is conducted, and the cause of death is determined, and then (and only then) can custody shift back to the family, along with permission to cremate or bury. When a case is a medicolegal case, this traffic of custody introduces even more shifts into already-fragile situations. One moment, relatives are told that their family member is no longer alive, because the hospital's countermoves against traumatic injury have proven unsuccessful.

Then they are told that the body must shift out of the trauma ward to make room for the living patients who need treatment and that because all trauma cases are technically medicolegal cases, a medicolegal postmortem is compulsory, and the body must be shifted to the morgue. It's an enormity and a shuffle.

The postmortem moves the corpse into domains of unfamiliarity. Families understand fully that the body is being shifted to the morgue, but relatives cannot be present during the postmortem, and this challenge is amplified by the fact that unfamiliar doctors and orderlies are carrying out the procedure. It is challenging enough for relatives to interface with a constantly shifting cast of medical characters in the trauma ward, but those characters have faces. They are locatable agents of the state. Now the body must move out of that zone of vague familiarity into the hands of state agents they cannot see, know, or talk to. In death, the traffic of the corpse under the authority of forensic medicine is largely invisible to kin, and new concerns emerge as the public hospital absents the corpse, moving it out of sight but very much not out of mind. The dissection of the postmortem now inflects and obstructs the other potential movements a body will undergo outside of the hospital, in rites of cremation and burial, movements that are freighted with meaning in South Asia (Copeman 2006; V. Das 2006; Desjarlais 2016; Parry 1994; Parry and Bloch 1982; Pinto 2008a, 2008b). Last rites cannot be performed while a body is in the morgue. All this amplifies the deep, moving, and indeed traumatic stakes here: what it means to have a family member enter a hospital and not emerge alive.

Throughout, as the postmortem desites the body from the trauma ward to the morgue, it shifts the logics, temporalities, clinical spaces, practices, and socialities of medicine's interface with death. It may seem counterintuitive to argue that the postmortem creates a lifeline, because it has no life to save as its object. But the postmortem demands that medicine move a body before it is released toward cosmological horizons by the family. The postmortem's findings may or may not catalyze the ways a family grapples with a person's death—that is, the degree to which they may remember, regret, and move on. Like the other lifelines of trauma I have detailed throughout this book, forensic medicine enacts movements and holds. It produces and transforms traffic in the process. The stillness of the corpse might suggest otherwise, but one of my aims here is to assert that a corpse is not always so still and that mortal stasis might be detailed in terms of its differential activity. Trauma's high mortality and the widespread effects of this mortality beyond the loss of a single life cannot otherwise be adequately understood through frameworks that assume a corpse to be devoid of motion.

The assumed inertness of the corpse emerges from several different corners of scholarly accounts of death and forensics. Social scientific and humanistic treatments of the postmortem usually approach it in terms of the knowledge the procedure produces. An effect of this approach is a certain reification of forensics as epiphenomenal, rather than as one investigation that ties to prior bodily inquiries. It is certainly the case that the discovery of a cause of death is important, and I do not question this. After all, this is the principal task of forensic medicine. Yet, precisely *for whom*, *how*, and *through which routes* forensic knowledge becomes meaningful are selective variables (M'Charek 2018). Knowing about the cause of death may extend to families, but I do not assume that the postmortem's results represent the entirety of death's meanings in the context of an accidental death.

This is why I have chosen to study the domain of the postmortem examination in terms of how it moves as much as I assess it in terms of what it knows. There are ethnographic limits on assessing such disturbances, of course. I cannot speak for the dead person being shifted. This in fact is the point: movement in medicine is powerful because it creates ever-changing proxies. Because movement is relational, the living can be understood to be deeply if unequally affected by the postmortem's moving operations on the dead. Attention to this relational movement reveals differences that are at the heart of medicine even after death (Mol 2002, 46). Also, perhaps, it can create a space for mourning and reckoning devastating scenes "that neither presumes denunciation nor a commitment to commensurability as the dominant value" (Cohen 2017, 115).

Studies of postmortem knowledge and authority demonstrate that forensic knowledge produced about the dead can be as socially divisive as it is unifying or satisfying (Jentzen 2010; Nelson 2009; Smith 2017; Timmermans 2007; Wagner 2008). In her study of maternal mortality statistics in Malawi, Claire Wendland (2016) argues that one cannot understand the evidence of death without understanding the effects of that evidence. For Wendland, one site to understand the instabilities of knowing death is the site of death's aggregation into epidemiological and demographic expertise. Similarly, scholars point out that forensic evidence can sow doubt about the violence that created it, in contexts ranging from sexual violence (Baxi 2014; Mulla 2014) to police confessions elicited through detention and torture (Lokaneeta 2020). Building on these insights, I show

how differences in motion underwrite differences in truth production and how the power of subjectification in death extends beyond knowing.

I also hope to contribute to a rather limited ethnographic literature on the postmortem, whose paucity likely stems from constrained researcher access. This literature tends to be anchored by a rich study in the United States by sociologist Stefan Timmermans (2007). Timmermans argues that the postmortem is ultimately about the establishment of authoritative knowledge. However, while authority is a key question of forensics, I do not believe that it is the only question. Dissection is a practice done to the dead and a practice that matters to the living. Authoritative knowledge and authoritative movement connect: What is done to bodies in the morgue anchors people's orientations to forensics as much as what is known when the practice concludes.[2] The lifelines of dissection move a corpse from the trauma ward to the morgue, and knowing and moving continue their fraught relation, both for the dead and for the living.

The trauma ward is filling up with smoke; I panic and think there is a fire and we must escape or we will die, and how will we evacuate the patients? I sniff and realize the smoke is insecticide, part of a routine mosquito-management protocol designed to keep dengue and malaria under control on the hospital campus, to forestall death among the living. The smoke scatters the fluorescent light as Sister Priya, the charge nurse, attempts to summon the orderly, Sanjay Mama, calling across the hallway, "Sanjay! Sanjay, bodypack karetze" (Sanjay, do the bodypack). Sanjay Mama brings over a rolling white fabric screen and puts it around a recently deceased patient's bed to offer some respectful privacy to the body. A relative of the patient in the adjoining bed asks the doctor to shift her aunt to a different bed, farther away. The white cloth screen signals a corpse, and the relatives and other patients in the ward see and know this.[3]

The patient in question was involved in a railway accident last evening. The police took him first to a smaller, nearby hospital, where he received some injections, and then brought him to Central. He arrived in a state described as "semi-conscious, disoriented" and with blunt abdominal trauma. Dr. T, the attending surgeon, says that the patient repeatedly said, "Kishor," but that's just a first name and not enough to find his family, so the man has been labeled as an Unknown patient. He underwent surgery to find the source of the abdominal bleed, but the exploratory laparotomy could not find it. His neurological status slowly declined overnight.

Dr. T has waved his mobile phone light over the nonresponsive pupils and checked the vitals multiple times, confirming his call that this patient is dead and setting into motion the body's shift from the domain of trauma medicine to the domain of forensic medicine, a shift from the trauma ward to the morgue.

In the trauma ward, the body must be prepared for this transfer toward dissection, a process called *bodypacking*. The work of supervising the processing of the dead in the trauma ward falls to the nurses. It is, as a result, largely women's work.[4] Sister Priya writes "Unknown Hindu male" on the pink death tags that will get tied to the hands as the body is wrapped for transfer to the morgue for the postmortem, the trauma ward's note of farewell. This is work that she does not care for, but she understands it to be as necessary as it is challenging. Nothing can happen without the administrative details, she asserts: if there are no pink cards, the body cannot leave the ward. If there is no record of the death, the body cannot leave the ward. Dissection cannot occur until the trauma ward affirms the conclusion of its own efforts: that trauma medicine is done, so that forensic medicine can begin.

A junior nurse, Sister Deepti, joins Sanjay Mama for the Unknown Male's bodypack. They ask me to stand at the foot of the bed to steady things, and they stand on opposite sides of the body, rolling it back and forth on its sides to ensure they've addressed every part. They must absent all the technologies and procedures of treatment in order to absent the body from the ward. They are subtractors of medicine as much as they are the preparators of the corpse (see Ariès 2013; V. Das and Han 2015; Guha 1987; and Parry and Bloch 1982). They subtract mechanical ventilation: Sister Deepti tugs on the endotracheal tube that had been attached to the ventilator, and it springs free from the man's mouth. They subtract hemodynamic support: Sanjay Mama pulls on the intercostal drain tube in the side of the chest. Deft moves are required here. "They won't accept a bloody bedsheet," Sister Deepti says of the morgue. Out go the IVs and the catheters; off go the bandages, the gauze pads, the tape. Sanjay Mama covers the man's face and genitals with clean gauze. They cross his feet and his hands. The tags that Sister Priya wrote out—the pink tags that read "Unknown Hindu male" along with his age—get attached to his wrists, binding him. We maneuver the large plastic sheet that wraps him. Sister Deepti tucks it in at the head and feet, the *pack* in *bodypack*. Sanjay Mama covers him in a blanket. There is a stretch of silence to acknowledge the gravity of the moment. Sanjay Mama wheels him over to the side. The families attending to the patients nearby are watching.

The bodypack is a movement form that stands in necessary relation to prior movements of treatment. Just ten hours ago, when the Unknown patient arrived, Sister Priya and Sister Deepti worked to make him not die. They pushed fluids, turned over his body to clean and powder it, and monitored his every move. Now their work is removed so that the morgue may make a claim on death. There are things that cannot be removed: the lacerations and punctures of traumatic injury, the cuts and bruises and staples and sutures that surgery inflicts and inserts. Evidence of death is not simply a summing up of the things added, because things are moved out, the corpse made knowable through subtraction.

Sister Deepti grabs a small bottle of eucalyptus oil from the staff locker and shakes a few drops on the body, part of the trauma ward's efforts to counter the effects of heat on flesh. Sister Priya enters vital details into the Death Book and reconciles this information with a list of the man's belongings in the admission book. She writes down the list of his belongings that he had on arrival to the ward in tight script.

When the bodypack is complete, I join Sanjay Mama and two other orderlies to move the body to the morgue. The pathways on the hospital campus are brick, and the metal trolley rumbles loudly. People see the body, close their eyes, genuflect, and walk to the other side of the path. We roll along a reminder of mortality. We pass by the dormitory for the nurses, and the orderlies wave to some friends. I nod to the body as we move along, as they try to adjust it now and again to keep it from jostling around too much. I say, "This is serious work" and inquire about what touching the dead might mean in relation to their other duties. I ask about how this labor intersects with caste, since it entails touching and moving the dead, but the domain of medicine can cloud too-simple assessments of caste based on contact with corpses (Arnold 1993). Clinical labor can bend the ordering of caste. Sanjay Mama is usually patient with my comments and questions, but he corrects me, not so much refuting the work as *caste* work but upholding the fact that it feels to him like *work* above all else. This is not hard work, he says. What's hard is getting up at 6 a.m. to do it every day, especially when these deaths do not seem to ever decrease in frequency. He's fifty-eight and close to retirement, and he wants to sleep in. He pushes the trolley with one hand and steadies the body with the other.

We arrive at the morgue, which is next to one of the main hospital cafeterias. The trolley rolls over discarded ketchup packets, and the air confronts us with vaporized chai and hot oil. There is a small office on the ground floor where we check in with the administrative recordkeeper, and then we crowd into the small elevator with several other people. The trolley has to go in the center, and so everyone must circle it. The morgue is one floor up. The building houses an antiretroviral therapy clinic, the hospital's medical records office, and the department of physical therapy, whose rooms are filled with bouncy balls and mats for stretching.

As the elevator climbs, I think about the stories I have been told about the morgue. An orderly in the trauma ward had previously been posted there and calls it "hospital ka last-stop," the last stop in someone's hospital itinerary. He folds his hands against his ear and tilts his head to the side, the sign of eternal sleep, for emphasis. And then there is the trauma ward's security guard, Chottu, with whom my conversations usually center on the degree of busyness in the ward. There are so many deadly traffic accidents, he says one day, that the morgue needs a sign that reads "mortuary house-full," where "house-full" refers to the sign posted outside movie theaters when a film is popular and there are no seats left. The surgery residents in the trauma ward tell me that while they attempt to study in the medical school library across from the morgue, it's hard to focus because of the ambient cries of sorrow from relatives waiting below.

The elevator opens. I am never sure who knows about the morgue's location on the second floor, but when the smell of formalin rushes in, one can sense how people in a tiny elevator share a momentary consensus that they're in a situation together for a long minute. Breaths get held. We wheel the body past a large plaque displaying a caduceus paired with the scales of justice. We pass the break room where the orderlies take their meals and their naps. We pass the storage room for samples—the "viscera room"—with various organs locked in pickle jars. We stop by the freezer room, where the bodies are put in cold-storage lockers, and the morgue orderly, Sayyan Mama, opens the thick steel door, sending special-effect-like plumes of cold fog across the hallway into the dissection room.

This is familiar territory for the trauma ward orderlies. They deliver bodypacked bodies regularly, and some are friendly with the orderlies in the morgue. But they do not like coming here, and they leave as soon as possible. I choose to stay.

———

The doctors in the trauma ward tell me it's puzzling that someone who claims to be studying the social dimensions of trauma would try to do the same thing in the morgue. They understand my ethnographic project. To them, *social* means the life circumstances of a patient and an accident. It also refers to the ways patients, doctors, nurses, staff, and kin interact in relation to those circumstances. They know that trauma is social, because *social* is what living people have and do. How can you track *social* in a morgue?

I attempt to counter. There are complex relationships of the type they are talking about in the morgue, I say, but they're shaped differently. I use the word *political* as an alternative to *social* to signal how the postmortem creates relationships between bodies and state power. They hear me out but are not used to corroborating these claims in specific terms, because they are not allowed in the morgue unless the forensic team calls them in for further details on a case. I have gained a privilege of access that is not afforded to them. The morgue is an exclusive space in this regard, and while it is true that all trauma doctors will have seen a postmortem examination as part of their medical education and see dying daily, most know the postmortem principally by its rendering on paperwork during mortality meetings. The morgue is run by the Forensic Medicine Department, but unlike other departments in the hospital, it technically falls under police jurisdiction. It is like an island in the middle of the hospital campus. The team is small compared to that of the trauma ward, with only a few faculty member supervisors and four resident doctors, two orderlies, and no nurses. If relatives do appear, they are only allowed to stand by the check-in desk, where they cover their mouths and noses with handkerchiefs while they wait.

When I submit an application for formal permission to observe autopsies, my supervisor in the hospital says, "You'll have to get used to the smell." It seems both correct and semantically loaded, *smell* signaling ways of marking caste and colonialism and nonvegetarianism, of pinpointing strangers and threats to order. All I know is that I smell different after being in the morgue, different than in the trauma ward, heavier, a reminder that parks itself in my sinuses and remains after I return home, shower, change clothes, walk to a gym, get on a treadmill, and don't stop running. It is not just smell that makes the morgue a sensory space; there is sound too. The marble tables and the stone tiles that cover the floor and walls of the dissection room make cleanup easier when the orderlies hose everything down. They also create an echo chamber. The relatives waiting to claim bodies cannot see inside the postmortem room, but they can hear inside, the stone-on-bone thwack of hammer and chisel (see Kamil et al. 2016).[5]

On a breezy January morning, Sayyan Mama, the morgue's senior orderly, enters the morgue office and dries his hands with a handkerchief. He always offers candies from a little plastic bag in his pocket, and I develop an attachment to the peppermint ones; they make observing dissections easier. The cigarette vendor outside the hospital's gate sells hard candies from big jars for one rupee apiece, and I buy a handful each morning to trade flavors with Sayyan Mama, part gift exchange and part mint insurance. He tells me he is a "Central baby": he was born in this hospital.[6] He's worked here his entire adult life and previously worked as an orderly in the trauma ward, which means he has a detailed understanding of all the things that happen to bodies before they arrive here. But he likes it more here in the morgue, he says, because he has more responsibilities and he enjoys anatomy—it's a puzzle that never bores him.

Mornings are for breakfast ordered from the canteen, brought by the single delivery boy who seems semi-okay with bringing *idlis* to the morgue. Everyone eats before tackling paperwork, and Monday mornings entail catching up on weekend events. Sayyan Mama takes a glass jar from the top of the office refrigerator and sets it on the desk. A scorpion is floating in the fluid inside. He had caught it during a weekend nature walk near his home in the outer areas of the city, where he moved his family a while back after rents near the hospital became unbearable. He was born here in the center of the city and loved it as a young man but felt unnerved by the crowds and the expense as an adult. He wanted to live somewhere greener, more like his father's village in rural Maharashtra. After securing a government job in the hospital as an orderly, he saved money for decades and finally shifted his family to a home in the outer suburbs of the city. This past weekend on his nature walk, he lifted a rock and saw the scorpion waiting there. It fascinated him, he says; he's a nature lover. He caught the scorpion in a water bottle, brought it here to the morgue, and preserved it in formalin. It reminds him of home at work, his weekend in a jar. I ask if the preparatory paperwork is finished, if it's time for the day's first postmortem, because I need an escape hatch now. I am terrified of arachnids.

Dr. S, the senior resident, walks with me to the postmortem room. She runs her hand through her hair and checks for split ends, holding under her arm the clipboard with the sketch sheet for labeling the inventory of observations. Kumar Mama, the junior orderly, is waiting for us inside the postmortem room. He has already placed a body on each of the six green marble tables. The trauma case—the Unknown Hindu male I had seen in the trauma ward a few days earlier—is at the end of the room. We pass the body of a woman whose burns receive an extralong look from Dr. S later that day because of a generalized suspicion of dowry-related deaths in younger women.

"I'm tired today," she says.

Kumar Mama shows us the pink cards on the wrists, the cards that Sister Priya wrote out, and moves the body around, back to front and side to side, showing Dr. S the details: abrasions, incisions, the evidence of the trauma, and the evidence of the medicine and surgery to treat it. Dr. S begins her incisions and examinations and wonders out loud about the decisions of the trauma ward's surgeons. Was an exploratory laparotomy really necessary? The longer a body has been in the freezer room, the higher the pitch of the incisions, taut and zippery. Sternums of older bodies, calcified, crack louder than the softer young ones. Organs burp loose. I close my eyes to hear the postmortem.

———

The flesh of the corpse on the table isn't always the sole reference point for meaning or conversation in the morgue. A body is dissected, but so too is its presumed lifeworld. This plural force of dissection might suggest cold indifference to the dead. I choose instead to see it as a question of where and how the imagination will and won't spill out when death is ever-present (Khanna 2018; Seremetakis 1991).[7] I do not think that the workers in the morgue are immune to death or that they wear impermeable raincoats. I believe that one learns to move through the rain of corpses. The clinical imagination can be expansive, animating the dead's possible life while simultaneously working to surmise a probable cause of death.

The senior faculty member, Dr. N, walks into the room to check on Dr. S's dissection of the Unknown case. "I feel so tired," Dr. S tells him. "I don't even know why I came today. Maybe I should try meditation." There's just too much work, she says. It doesn't end. The cold-storage room has fifty chambers, and they are usually full, no matter how much effort toward emptying them the forensic team might make. The dissection proceeds, and she palpates the man's organs: heart, liver, stomach, lungs, feeling each for relative bogginess and solidity. Slices reveal interiors. Hearts concede white matter that evidences infarction. Lungs divulge tubercules. Trauma's shearing forces blood into spaces where it should not go.

As the examination unfolds, Sayyan Mama dissects another problem that he says is pressing: Kumar Mama's personhood. Kumar has only daughters and no sons. This is a real dilemma, Sayyan observes, for who will carry on Kumar's family's lineage (*vansh*)? Daughters marry out of the household, a lateral movement that renders them incapable of this important shift of descent. Only sons can provide the continuity required.

Kumar responds that he plans on having more kids; he's young and still has it in him. He is sure he can pass on his family name, plus his Honda motorbike, to a son. We are talking about personhood, the things that constitute kinship—"the peopling of life," as Sarah Pinto (2014) describes it. We are talking about who will receive Kumar's family name, the generational tectonics of kinship. We do it while looking down at a man whose name is still unknown, a man whose personhood is defined by the inability to identify him and his family, a man who will eventually be brought across the street to the municipal crematorium, where the Unknown Hindu dead go. *Vansh* grounds our inquiry into personhood, but it is not squarely about the personhood of the person who is dead in front of us.

In other cases, the morgue workers animate the imagined lives of the corpses on the table. Sayyan Mama is especially inclined to do this with Unknown cases. In a dissection of another Unknown patient run over by the local train, Sayyan speculates on the man's life. Unusually, the corpse is still in his clothes in the dissection room, unlike most bodies, which have all their clothes removed. It seems that the man on the table never made it to the trauma ward; he must have been dead on arrival at the hospital, which explains why the bodypack has not been done. The orderlies in the casualty ward must have skipped over stripping the man from his clothes, and Sayyan wonders if this is because the man is wearing several layers of shirts. Sayyan counts each shirt as he removes it, one after the other, each hiding various things in sewn-in pockets: a cigarette (*beedi*), a coin, and a phone charger (he pronounces it *kharab*, broken, and offers it to Dr. N). The man was likely homeless, he thinks, and believes that only someone with mental illness would wear so many shirts.

Kumar disagrees. The multiple shirts mark the sign of poverty, not mental illness: "This is what poor people [*gharib log*] have to do." They must change one layer of clothes for another, moving one up and one down. Though the matter of the corpse's poverty may seem settled on the table, the person the corpse is imagined to have been moved through poverty in life. To truly understand poverty, one should pay attention to its embodied movement effects. Kumar frequently reminds everyone in the dissection room that the bodies on the tables are the bodies of *gharib log*, poor people. He points to the marks of inequality across the skin surfaces: labor, hunger, illness. You don't need dissection to see it, he argues.

Kumar speaks about poverty from multiple positions. He earns a comparatively meager salary as the morgue's junior orderly, and at the same time, he is a government civil servant with a job and a home. He is also

North Indian, in contrast to the rest of the people in the morgue, who are Maharashtrian, and he asserts this difference often. Differences among the living may complicate the relationships between contact with the dead and the assertion of regionalized caste categories in this space. Local political dramas can get replayed in moments of touching dead bodies, spotlighting perceived differences between Maharashtrians and North Indians, between upper- and lower-caste Hindus, and between those living in the city and those living in its peripheries. Jokes and everyday philosophizing delineate differences between men and women, between Hindus and Muslims, between the police and the doctors ("Do not ever trust the police, they're rotten to the core," one of the forensic doctors tells me as they sign off on police paperwork that gives the police formal access to postmortem evidence). A bright line is understood to divide people who see what happens in a morgue and people who do not. The personhood of the living is constituted by their relation or nonrelation to death.

As Dr. S continues her dissection, Kumar Mama begins to sing:

Unknown si ho gayi zindagi
koi dekhta nahin
koi puchta nahin
koi sochta nahin

The Unknown's life has ended
No one sees anything
No one asks anything
No one thinks anything

I ask where the song comes from, and he says he just made it up. I say it explains it all: when "no one asks anything" and "no one thinks anything," the imagination halts when life does. Stasis of the imagination can be dangerous. Dr. S snorts and tells Kumar to focus and to help her peel back the dura from the brain. "Gross hematoma!" she declares, looking at the pooled pocket of blood. "I've found it!" She scribbles "HI" for "head injury" on the picture of the brain on the clipboard. This arrival at knowing concludes part of her work but not Kumar's. He begins stitching the abdomen closed with loopy baseball sutures.

What kind of medical gaze operates here, when regard for personhood happens alongside regard for damage to the body's underlying structures? Knowing constitutes the medical gaze, according to Michel Foucault's chapter "Open Up a Few Corpses" in *The Birth of the Clinic* (1975). For Foucault, death offers the opportunity of stasis, and this stasis creates the possibility to sharpen medicine's power/knowledge over the body. As pathologists engage in medical investigation on corpses, they confer value on disease through different forms of perception articulated between the atlas of anatomy and the corpse in front of them on the dissection table. This is how Foucault details the development of "the medical gaze": "The sight/touch/hearing trinity defines a perceptual configuration in which the inaccessible illness is tracked down by markers, gauged in depth, drawn to the surface, and projected virtually on the dispersed organs of the corpse" (164). The stillness of the corpse enables the dynamism of new forms of medical knowledge.

I am not convinced that this sense of the medical gaze holds. There are tectonics of movement conditioned by the historical and enduring colonial relationships to forensic knowledge production. There are also shifts in the object of attention. The staff in the morgue at Central might spend time working on still bodies, but the potential movements of those bodies shape the means and ends of their work.[8] It is less "the postmortem" that is at stake and more the quantity of postmortems that defines their days, which determines how much they can keep up with the influx of bodies. The high incidence of major trauma cases compounded with high mortality rates moves bodies into their workspace at a rate that challenges their ability to conduct dissections. The more I become used to the ways that the morgue gets used to corpses, the more I find myself questioning an overemphasis on the static corpse as a font of knowledge production, even as I understand its importance. An overfocus on the stilled corpse cannot fully reveal what it means to be moved by death.

"A corpse is an incongruous presence," writes anthropologist Robert Desjarlais (2016, 100) in the context of Tibetan Hyolmo Buddhist funerary rituals. He continues, "A corpse is mute. It is flat, unresponsive. . . . Yet it's through engagements with that emptiness that people grasp that a person has died" (100–101). This is due in part to the moral charge of the dead's materiality, a feature several scholars of South Asia term the *biomoral* to indicate the ties between bodily material and practices and South Asian moral worlds, especially in contexts of death (Alter 2000; Berger 2013; Copeman and Reddy 2012; Halliburton 2016; Marriott 1968; Parry 1985). Annemarie Mol suggests a different quality of the corpse's semio-material potential, focusing less on substance and more on practice, perhaps on the grounds between biomoral and biopolitical. Writing about a corpse about to undergo autopsy, she explains, "It is about to be dissected. But however mute, this corpse is active" (2002, 49). For Mol, muteness does not guarantee unresponsiveness in dissection. The possibility of knowing in the postmortem is something that distributes across both the dissectors and the dissected, and it does so through practice.

Years after my fieldwork in Central's morgue, I am in Amsterdam, where I seek out Rembrandt's paintings of autopsies. I find myself in front of *The Anatomy Lesson of Dr. Jan Deyman* (1656) and *The Anatomy Lesson of Dr. Frederik Ruysch* (1683). The grandeur of Dutch surgeons' guilds displays the pedagogical force of anatomy, spotlit amid dark hues. The explanatory panel next to the portraits notes, "Every year the guild was allowed to give a public anatomy lesson using the cadaver of an executed criminal. It was always well attended."

I regard the body on the table. *He looks so frozen*, I think, and I begin to question corpse tunnel vision.

A police constable arrives in the morgue office; he is assigned to the case of the Unknown person who yelled out "Kishor" before dying in the trauma ward. "He was found between the tracks," the constable says, and holds up his mobile phone to show photos. One is shot directly from above, another from the body's side, with the train tracks in the background. Other photos offer time-series accounts of *hamaals* moving the body from the tracks into the police van. It is nighttime, and the mobile phone's camera flash casts an amber luster. The next series of photos focuses on the arms. The body is one hundred feet from us in the postmortem room, but we investigate it on a small screen. He shows another railway accident photo; he has become used to it (*normal zhale*), like the doctors here in the morgue.

There is something in one of the photos of the body that stands out. Inside one arm is what the constable calls a "cartoon"; it is a tattoo of a cartoon character. With some Googling, the doctors relay the specific character to the cop. He politely agrees the image is a match and proceeds with the paperwork without including the detail, and the moment of potential recognition passes. The constable thinks that the "Kishor" Unknown patient will be identified, though. Not because of the tattoo but because this person was clearly not a trash collector, a beggar, or a pavement dweller. His clothes suggest he possibly comes from a good home and therefore might be identified. What he is wearing allows the presumption of a proper home with a family, a family that might be looking for a body wearing a certain color T-shirt, a metal bangle, or a particular gemstone ring. What the state records on admission is what the state will look for after death. It is the traffic of state recognition of the body's exterior signs, just as much as the findings of the postmortem dissection, that might condition the family's pull toward the morgue.

For those who have families waiting, the paperwork shuttles around, and eventually a relative can collect the deceased for last rites. The orderly will move the body from a refrigerated cubby in the cold-storage room onto a metal trolley, cover it with a sheet, and wheel it into the middle of the hallway to meet the relatives (who are almost always men). Down the elevators they will go, and after they sign more paperwork in the small office on the ground floor, the body is released back into the custody of the family.[9] But what if no one comes? What happens to Unknown bodies once they leave the dissection table, and what potentials for ordering life-worlds are possible when family cannot be present? Perhaps the morgue might be "hospital ka last-stop," as the one orderly had said, but still, the real last stop in life is cremation or burial, the thing that happens after the morgue in a setting where cremation and inhumation are pivotal thresholds between personhood and cosmology.

Kumar walks me to one end of the hallway, where there is a window with iron bars, and points his finger through them. From the second floor, I can see the smokestack. I also see why I never glimpsed the crematorium (*smashanbhoomi*) from the road: stately, thick trees guard it. Kumar says that the police take the Unknown bodies from the cold-storage room to this municipal crematorium across the street.

A visiting local clinical researcher in the trauma ward who has an interest in ethnography and is unaffiliated with the hospital offers to go with me to the crematorium. We cross the street, holding out our hands to ward off the cars speeding around the traffic circle. We pass pharmacies and diagnostic labs, and then quiet seeps in as the lane narrows, shady and protected. The crematorium's open gates face a Shiva temple. We approach an old building by the entrance and meet the facility supervisor, Ranveer. We apologize for the drop-in, explain my association with the hospital and the research project, and ask if or when it might be possible sometime to learn more about the cremation of the Unknown bodies sent from Central's morgue. He explains there are no rituals happening at the moment, and now is a good time. He invites us for tea, and seats us opposite a triptych portrait of Ambedkar, Shivaji, and Phule.

Ranveer has supervised this crematorium for many years, after working at a cemetery in the suburbs. He worked his way up through jobs in the municipal government, starting as a servant in the BMC (the Mumbai municipal government) headquarters and then moving onward and upward. His job at the crematorium offers what he always wanted: an office, a desk, and independence. It was his destiny to work with the dead, he says. He has no immediate family. He sleeps, eats, and bathes here. I inquire about matters of caste: Who works here? How does caste work here? He affirms that yes, the workers in this facility belong to similar caste groups, but caste shows itself less through identity claims and more through social interactions with the relatives of the dead, who comport themselves in specific ways relative to the crematorium's workers and who may or may not drink the crematorium's filtered tap water.

With Unknown patients, he says, last rites run quite smoothly. There is no one to protect or assert community and caste lines, no one to insist on particularities that might slow things down. "For those who have no one, they have the municipality and the police," he says (jinko koi nahin hain, unke BMC aur police hain), a care of the state that can accelerate departure from this realm and—sometimes—can repersonalize those depersonalized through trauma.

The attendant who supervises the furnaces explains how he controls the temperature and turns the bodies. As he demonstrates the buttons and knobs and points out the wood piles, he notes that he was just in Central Hospital this morning. His breathing bothers him, and now he regularly visits the outpatient department at the hospital for tablets. Another one of the attendants comes over to hear what is happening and says that he is on dialysis. He thinks the diabetes is starting to win. The ties to mortality and to the hospital stretch across bodies. They leave us, as a cremation is about to begin. Men enter the gates shouldering a body on a bier. A group of women bear offerings of cloth and apples. Funerary rituals critically order life (V. Das 1976; Doniger 2014).[10] I immediately walk in the other direction and exit—in no way do I wish to disturb this. I leave, and go home, unaware that during this visit to the crematorium, Anand's body is being dissected across the street.

I return to the morgue a few days later at lunchtime. The regularity of lunch break offers some small comforts. During lunch in between dissections, we spread newspaper on the table and pull out our tiffins, everyone dipping rotis into others' gravies, sharing food and thoughts on work and not-work. Unlike in the trauma ward, where Hindi often shores up differences between the Maharashtrian staff and doctors from elsewhere in India, Marathi rules in the morgue as most of the residents and staff are Maharashtrian, and their tiffins reflect it. I test out Maharashtrian recipes and then start bringing in other regional Indian dishes on request, preparing for shifts by cooking, packing, and bringing in foods from the North, East, and South ("What sort of people eat just rice and *sambhar* [vegetable stew]?" Dr. S would jab). I learn who likes more ginger in their sabzi, who likes more tamarind, and who likes more green chili.

Dr. D, one of the faculty supervisors, shares his *methi thepla* (fenugreek flatbread) and chutney. Dr. R streams the midday news on his mobile phone, propped up on the printer that spits out cause-of-death findings. Today it's corruption scandals and the suspicious-seeming death of Bollywood actress Sridevi. When the livestream news finishes, we watch WhatsApp videos, "news" of a sort, that update us on bodily horrors around the country: stabbings, car crashes, lynchings, things that the group finds gory (*raktaranjit*) and that offer points of comparison and contrast to the bodies they dissect down the hall. In the downtimes during the day shift, I read the pathology and forensic medicine textbooks scattered throughout the room, ones that teach by case studies, like John F. Kennedy's assassination and the execution of Buck Ruxton (Blundell and Wilson 1937; Ratna n.d.). In between, I watch the postmortems of people down the hall who never make it into textbooks and ruminate on factoids from the books so I have something to say at lunch. I discover a chapter about death from automatic firearms and ways to trace the damage left in the wake of a bullet's trajectory. "See this?" I point to the pictures as we chew. "This is America."

Lunch is also time to absorb the lighter side of things, when the resident pathologists mercilessly taunt each other. As in most branches of medicine, dark humor is integral. The morgue is an intensely different space from the trauma ward on several fronts. One aspect that strikes me the most is that there are no patients to potentially live or die. That was already decided. There is no laughing in the face of the threat of death; there is laughing with death all around.[11] The residents tell piercing jokes at each other's expense: about clinical competence, about married life, about single life, about dating life, about television-watching habits, about crushes on film stars, about local politics, about all the construction and traffic in the city, about Narendra Modi and Donald Trump, about sneaker brands and style trends, about caste, about climate change. A badminton match played outside the building settles the score in the evenings.

Lunch is also a space to voice backstories, like Dr. S's upbringing, her decision to enter medicine, and her decision to specialize in forensic medicine. She wanted to solve murders but has learned over time that forensics is "a dead branch" of medicine: dead bodies, dead things, no money. It's public hospital medicine. But it has predictable shifts and no emergency calls in the middle of the night. She likes her sleep.

Yet, because forensic medicine is a dead branch of medicine, she says, it presents a dilemma: What does it mean to work in a highly stigmatized branch of medicine? What does it mean to be a doctor in a specialty that is at once despised and essential to the workings of the state? The postmortem constitutes a lifeline, but its labor is fraught. Forensic medicine has one of the lowest score cutoffs for residency admission, giving it a reputation as a place for doctors who cannot achieve the marks to enter other specialties. Comparatively few women pursue it, owing to its associations with death that might inflect their moral reputation and marriage prospects. The facilities affirm a sense of neglect, and the orderlies—who are as much practitioners as the doctors—speak their frustrations in terms of the relationship between institutional neglect and labor. The green marble tables in the dissection room are stately and solid, but the drains in their centers clog easily. The ventilation needs improvement. New supplies of protective gear and instruments are intermittent. The seals on the door to the cold-storage room don't always stick. Many who work in the morgue feel invisible to the hospital, even though the law makes their work essential to the hospital, and there is no one else who can do it. There are expressions similar to some expressed by staff in the trauma ward: that such spaces can feel like a dumping ground (Mittal et al. 2007; Pandit 2016). To work in this space requires one to corral the dissections and the stigmatization of the dissections, to bound the work so that it does not overtake one's life.

Yet these boundaries remain tenuous. At lunch another day, we watch WhatsApp montage videos that string together motorcycle crashes. Dr. S remarks that there's no need to have your head smashed open in a motorcycle crash when you could just come to the morgue, where they will pry open your skull. "You can just come here," she says, "where we give you *moksha*!" Liberation, *moksha*, is the release of the soul and among some Hindus is linked to the explosion of the skull during cremation. Dr. R says all of this talk is disturbing; it reminds him of a dream he had where he rode his motorcycle and crashed. He wishes to share the dream and writes it down after speaking it aloud.

In the dream Dr. R was in a motorcycle accident. This precipitated a release of his soul from his body, which gave him the ability to see his own dead body. He saw his body on the road, and then the dream shifted scenes, and he saw his body in the morgue's cold-storage room where corpses are kept before the postmortem. He watched as his colleagues took his body from the storage room to the postmortem room and put it on one of the six green marble tables. They moved his body through the dissection protocol. Later, I imagine the paper document that the doctors would complete on the clipboard as Kumar Mama stitched him closed.

EXTERNAL EXAMINATION—MALE, HINDU

Condition of the clothes—Body wrapped in plain white sheet

Special marks on the skin—Not applicable

Condition of the body—Well-built, cold

Rigor mortis—Generalized, well-marked

Extent and sign of decomposition—Postmortem lividity present, no signs of decomposition

Features—Natural, eyes closed, teeth intact, tongue inside mouth, no oozing from ears or nostrils

Condition of skin—Dry, pale

Position of limbs—Straight

The dream continued: Dr. R watched his friends examine his body but grew restless as the dissection proceeded. He wanted his soul to be liberated, to be released from the continued cycles of birth, suffering, and death that his earthly body had experienced, for however many incarnations. But the intrusions of the postmortem, its cutting and hammering and sampling, prevented his soul from entering the body so that it could move toward proper release.

"I asked them to let me back into my body," he remembers. "But suddenly they cut open my head and opened my cranium and took out my brain. I kept asking them to let me back into my body, but they wouldn't listen, and they opened my abdomen and my stomach." This was too much to bear, all these movements that prevented the one essential movement at stake for his transition to reincarnation. His soul left the morgue, flying away from the hospital, out of Mumbai, away from the city to his home village in rural Maharashtra. There he encountered the village deity (*kuldevta*), Mahakali, who "gave him more power." Mahakali told him, "You are alive!"

In this proclamation from the deity, he realized that he may have been dead, but death was not what he imagined. In death, he could still move. Mahakali's power enabled this and allowed his soul to express freedom through motion: he roamed the mountains and returned to her whenever he needed more power, "when my power was becoming low." And in the dream's conclusion, he returned to the scene of the accident. "I saw my motorcycle totally damaged, and blood was spread all over the motorcycle and the soil." At this moment of confronting the crash scene, he awoke.

In Dr. R's dream, he cannot stop the autopsy from moving, even though he is deeply familiar with the people opening up his body. He wants it to stop, but the imperative of forensics gives dissection velocity, and it must continue. Other movements ensue, like the movements of his soul, the free roaming made possible by his encounter with Mahakali. This culminates in his roaming back to the frozen diorama of the crash. There is the dissection of his body and his own dissection of the situation, from the vantage point of an external observer, a body that is simultaneously on and off of the dissection table. The trauma, the reckoning of the trauma, and the fleshy trajectories of the trauma mix.

I do not believe he is necessarily saying that his dream offers a clear-cut interpretive lens. I want to listen less for what the dream knows and more for what the dream moves. There may be no great revelation of the cause of death and no final insight gleaned from the postmortem. But there is movement against any attempts to bound the living from the dead, and the postmortem from life. This struck me the most about the dream and conditioned my way of understanding the morgue in the time that followed. Even amid familiars, the postmortem's traffic must continue. There is no stopping the demand for movement, as the pressure of the law still bears out on bodies, after death, into other realms.

Throughout this chapter I have decentered the corpse as a static form and focused on the lifelines of forensics through different vectors of dissection. The lifelines of forensics transform the meanings and values of trauma through a traffic of corpses, as death generates transformative movements. The answer to the question of *why* a death is caused lies in part in differences in movement and highlights how traffic inflects the political and scientific claims of forensics. Anthropologists Charles Briggs and Clara Mantini-Briggs (2016) make the powerful observation in their work on the deaths of children from rabies in Venezuela that what is truly at stake is the absence or presence of a response to parents' questions as to *why* their children died. The movement practices of the postmortem are one powerful site to think about the texture of the why. Authoritative knowledge matters in forensics. How it matters has much to do with the movement of corpses. This knowledge does not always scale up, effect change, or spark discovery, and yet corpses still must move. From bodypacking in the trauma ward, to transfer across the hospital campus, to movements onto, through, and off of the dissection table, the lifelines of forensics bind movement to medicine, after death. There are limits to what an unmoving corpse can offer as the portal to both description and explanation in this context.

For the hospital and those in its wake, the most proximate challenge is the need to move the dead. For families who do not want the postmortem or its insights, the postmortem's movement is a vexed pause on closure. For families who *do* want it—and many indeed do—the movements of the postmortem may seem too slow given the overload the morgue faces. Absenting the dead body has different implications for different waiting parties: the postmortem is a bottleneck, and it is a black box. Grappling with death from trauma requires understanding how, in both cases, things keep moving.

I leave the morgue to meet with Aparna and her daughter in the canteen. I walk down the dark stairwell and appreciate why ghost stories abound here. The pathology residents say that ghost stories are stupid, but they also can't figure out why the elevator seems to act on its own at night, moving between random floors even when no one is around. Perhaps there are afterlives of movement that exceed the body.

Over lunch, Aparna and her daughter talk, and I listen. They revisit the car crash, Anand's months in the trauma ward, his ups and downs, and, most of all, his complex relationships to the ventilator. As they reintegrated Anand into life at home after discharge, his daughters improved at school. I know that a hospital stay reveals just one version of a person, not necessarily the definitive one. The version of Anand that we seem to share at the table is a survivor and a puzzle, a person who after months of stuttered movement in the trauma ward somehow managed to exit the hospital, alive. And then years later he suddenly collapsed. "It was right in front of my eyes," Aparna says. It makes no sense. "What is the medical reason for this?" the daughter asks me. How can someone avert a bad death, survive trauma, and then just drop? How can you move through medicine successfully and then die?

I say I don't know.

I don't know the reason Anand died, and I don't know what the post-mortem did say about it. I do know what it can be like to lose a father and to witness how medicine fails to prevent that loss. I do not know what it is like to lose a loved one and then face the forces of their postmortem. This doubled unknowing seems paramount. Ultimately, I do not know how it feels to have a postmortem detour the traffic between the hospital and the grave. There are a few things I think I know but do not ask about to confirm; there is enough forensics going on. Given the months of Anand's stay in the trauma ward, his family must have seen other patients die in the beds around him. They now confront death again and may be obligated toward two tasks: "building a world that the living can inhabit with their loss and building a world in which the dead can find a home" (V. Das 2006, 58).

"You must be busy and have somewhere to go now," Aparna suggests. They ask where the morgue is located, and I point. We leave our chai and veg sandwiches on the table.

I leave the canteen and stand in a sunny field that the hospital's intramural sports teams use as a cricket pitch. There has been talk lately of plans to build a tower here. The hospital is in the middle of the city, and expansion must happen inward. There are hopes that the new building will expand patient care but also concerns that the departments slated to move into the tower will be the "superspecialty" medical disciplines, not trauma care or forensics. I blink. A game is on, and radiology is beating orthopedics.

7 Recovering

THE LIFELINES OF DISCHARGE

At the hospital gate by the trauma ward's exit, a sign reads "Outside" in Marathi, Hindi, and English (*baaher/baahar/outside*). Sometimes I picture the patients inside the trauma ward sitting up, gathering their things, and walking out, finished, *bas*, enough, we're done. They'd march out of the ICU past the servant room and breeze past the chalkboard listing patients, injuries, bed numbers, and doctors in charge. Chottu, the guard, would pull the door open, underneath the stone lintel with TRAUMA SERVICE etched in deep. They'd hang a left, arrive outside, and face the sun. What would the hospital be moving back into the city? Trauma's closure? Trauma's treatment outcomes? Trauma's bodies? And what of the fact that when patients leave the ward, they return to the city that wounded them? All this recursivity frustrates straight lines. What is the outside of trauma, and can one ever exit its traffic?

———

"I didn't need all the money," Neeraj says (mujhe poore paisa nahin chahiye). I am sitting with my research assistant, Gyan, in Neeraj's living room to learn about life after discharge from the trauma ward. Gyan and I meet at Central and then head together to Neeraj's neighborhood in eastern Mumbai. The journey reveals the chain of mobilities involved in leaving the hospital to return home: a bus, then a rickshaw, then a walk on foot to his neighborhood, called Fertilizer Colony because of the petrochemical factories nearby; it consists of mostly one-level homes divided into neat lanes with a common drainage line. The highway divides it from the "new" locality emerging opposite; cranes piece together apartment towers for low-income families who qualify for slum-relocation schemes.

Neeraj and his friend, Sai, appear on a motorbike, and we trail them on foot to the home. In the living room, *Doraemon* is on the TV for the kids, and Neeraj gets avuncular, lowering the volume on the cartoon so the kids can watch and we can talk. "The driver just drove away; maybe he was drunk . . . he saw what happened and then left." Neeraj didn't need the truck driver to pay all of his treatment costs, but something would have been a gesture of goodwill.

Sai agrees. He was there when a dump truck hit Neeraj's motorbike and sped off. "If we had caught the driver, we would have made him pay . . . if not all of it, at least half of it." The driver would have landed in jail if they had pursued a formal legal case.

"Even the driver knew that it was his fault [*uska galti tha*]," Neeraj asserts.

Despite this, they didn't pursue him. Instead, the friends focused on getting Neeraj to the hospital. Now discharged from the hospital, he stays at home and hopes he can return to his job as a private diagnostic laboratory assistant, transporting blood samples around the city on his motorbike.

Neeraj's family spent 40,000 rupees (around US$540), which included the ambulance rides and the hospital expenses. Sai thought about selling his mobile phone and motorbike to help the family pay for the treatment. Some of the costs were covered under the state government's free treatment plan for low-income families, the Jeevandayee Scheme. The rest they were responsible for, out of pocket. Recovery is partly about recovering from the financial shock of injury; a gesture of compensation from the truck driver might have helped.

In the meantime, Neeraj thinks about the driver.

———————

After the accident, there are the movements to and through the hospital, and after discharge, a case still has the potential for momentum and stuckness. What sorts of traffic emerge as a result? Changing forces of movement—the kinetics of recovery—accrue outside the hospital as a case takes on different tempos and rhythms of feeling and comprehension. Changing qualities of language, action, ethics, and bodily ability fold people back into the rhythms of life during a particular time-space—discharge—when medicine ostensibly has taken a step back. Discharge is a lifeline because it effectively charges the potential to survive injury with different kinetic forms. A case may change in terms of its structural potentials, felt qualities, visibilities, and resonances of connection and conflict among kin and neighbors. Recovery is a domain of uncertain motion.

As previous chapters have discussed, trauma's medicolegal features underscore the involvement of police in trauma cases, the identification of Unknown patients, and the forensic inquiries of the postmortem. During the time-space of recovery, trauma's medicolegal aspects may intensify and shift. There can be the slowing and freezing of claims, as formal institutions such as lawyers and courts may catalyze or arrest a settlement.[1] Recovery's kinetics may change with the acceleration of accusations among estranged neighbors. Forces may remain constant, at rest, and may attenuate if a case is dropped or hits a limit. There may be a letting go of the frustrations of never being able to face the injury's perpetrator (especially in hit-and-run cases such as Neeraj's). There may be negotiated settlements through confrontation with the agents of blame. There may be refusals to forgive the agents of the injury, and a commitment to expose wrongdoing (see V. Das 1995). "Traffic" and "accident" may relate through counterpoint and exchange outside of formal clinical spaces.

I highlight the kinetics of recovery to reflect on two scholarly conversations. The first conversation comes from disability studies, which offers insight into living with a differently abled body-mind. This diverse scholarship demonstrates that disability can be understood as generative of social meaning even as it marks bodily change and reveals the instabilities between disability's medical and social models (Addlakha 2018; Clare 2017; Crosby 2017; V. Das and Addlakha 2001; Friedner 2015, 2022; Hartblay 2020; Kafer 2013; Kohrman 2005; Livingston 2005; Ralph 2014; Rouse 2009; Schalk 2013; Shuttleworth and Kasnitz 2004; Staples 2014; Wool 2015). The second conversation concerns medicolegal claim making, such as Kaushik Sunder Rajan's (2017) research on the links between constitutional law and biomedicine in India, and João Biehl and Adriana Petryna's research (Biehl 2013; Biehl and Petryna 2011) on the process of "judicialization" in Brazil, which details how Brazilians sue the government to access affordable drugs. This conversation examines how pursuits of compensation in health take form as a politics of justice (Berlant 2005; Brown 1993; V. Das 1995; Ewald 1993; Fortun 2001; James 2010a, 2010b; Morrison 2020; Nelson 2015; Geeta Patel 2007; Petryna 2002; Poole 2004).

These conversations and the case study of trauma's recovery offer a generative site to address what philosopher Georges Canguilhem (1991) terms "the question of the normal" (see also Elden 2019). Reflecting on Canguilhem's work, Stuart Elden notes that for Canguilhem, normality is fundamentally mutable and "adapted to context" (2019, 16). While discharge may seem at first glance the conclusion to pathology, it often begins new or shifted normalities in life projects. Assessing these kinetics as lifelines can reveal how the traffic of trauma continues to operate, how the hospital continues to exert influence even though bodies are not located in its spatial bounds, and how social forms outside the hospital come to bear upon trauma's trajectories. The problem of "moving on" underscores how recovery and disability become a part of life.

Discharge, or "going home," begins in the trauma ward as bodies learn to bear weight again, experience traction and balance, and, frequently, reconcile themselves to the pain of the injury and the pain of the surgery to fix the injury, pain that does not end when the discharge papers are signed. In the hospital's eyes, when patients walk and talk and improve in metrics of blood pressure and neurological scores, they are no longer critical. Soon they will not need the trauma ward anymore, at least not as inpatients (some may need outpatient follow-up). Each manifestation of recovery reveals aspects of accommodating traumatic injury into one's life, aspects that often get deferred until after discharge. The traffic of trauma continues to shape lives through what medicine calls *sequelae*—the consequences of injury—after the hospital considers its work done. Sequelae must be understood, then, in terms of unequal movements.

While the chapter focuses on what this traffic means for patients, it is important to note that injury's sequelae matter for providers too. Clinical and service staff often desire to see what happens to patients after discharge. The trauma ward's surgeons may see discharged patients in outpatient department hours but not always. The nurses and service staff rarely get the opportunity to see patients after discharge even though often that is precisely what they want. They want to know outcomes, they want to know how the person and the family are doing, and they want to see something different from the scenes of uncertainty that their labor must otherwise focus on. They know sequelae may be disabling; there is no assumption that what lies on the other side of the trauma ward will be easy. But their limited opportunities to see outcomes and to see movements toward recovery can weigh heavily. Being in medias res all the time can make endurance for the work hard-won.

For patients, differences in recovery may point out how trauma comes to matter differently in the home than it does in the hospital. A case often entails settlements broader than the bodily and financial damages that a family has incurred through one person's injury. The Hindi term *mamla*, meaning "matter," "concern," or "affair," is important here. Because of the medicolegal dimensions of traumatic injury, when the loanword *case* is used in Hindi and Marathi in the context of an injury, it generally refers to the hospital case or the police case. *Mamla* includes these features but also encompasses a wider kinetics of the injury event and aftermath. I highlight this term not only because of its ubiquity in conversation but also because its usage shows how the qualities of a case move into the fabric of everyday life. Discharge can set the terms of a case's continuities rather than merely its conclusion. The field of actions that discharge sets into motion—its lifelines—becomes the stuff of recovery across clinical, domestic, and legal domains and in terms of both motion and stillness.[2]

As my fieldwork progresses, it develops its own kinetics: wake up, drink South Indian coffee, commute to the trauma ward, write notes about the commute, watch the ward, have lunch with doctors, watch the ward, drink tea with nurses, watch the ward, drink tea with service staff, watch the ward, eat dinner with doctors, watch the ward, head home in traffic, shower, run, shower, cook, take notes, sleep. Sometimes I invert the rhythm for an evening or overnight shift. If I can't sleep, I fuss in the kitchen and pickle stray vegetables.

In my dreams I see accidents that have not happened. Two people on a motorcycle zoom by my taxi without helmets, and I imagine a surgeon picking out gravel from their abrasions under fluorescent light. From the windows of the moving train, I watch people crossing the tracks and seamlessly picture them in the ICU under blankets and full of tubes. I sometimes dream about my own body appearing in the trauma ward after some drastic event like my taxi colliding with a truck. I look up, supine, from a clanky metal gurney and see the faces of the nurses and doctors and staff I normally encounter standing. I feel I'm in good hands.

These fantasies of the hospital as a totalizing site of care and cure suggest to me that I have failed to grapple with patients as people outside the hospital. I am blind to survival even though I know better. It's complacency with the idea that things start with admission and end with discharge. It's fieldwork whose boundaries are dictated by the institution, a complicity enabled by focusing on the hospital. Social science research might call this *site saturation*, and I do not like it. Something is missing. The damage of the event is there, and the hospital is there, but what of the time and place after the hospital? The hospital cannot reveal this.

Epidemiologists at Central who are studying the trauma ward's outcomes tell me that they wish to better understand postdischarge outcomes. They aim to create a trauma registry in India, and to do so they must assess key metrics like thirty-day mortality from traumatic injury. A patient may spend the first ten days following an accident in Central's trauma ward and then be discharged and return home. But the epidemiology team needs to know if that person is alive twenty days later. They design a study based on phone calls to discharged patients to assess this variable, but they also want to move beyond the binary of alive/dead. They want to understand what public health research calls *quality of life* after discharge (see Michaels et al. 2000).

In particular, the epidemiologists are interested in whether global clinical metrics like postinjury functionality screening might adequately capture the "Indian" dimensions of life after injury. Perhaps, they wonder, ethnographic interviews can address this issue. For instance, how much (if at all) do global norms for assessing disability and functionality rely on individualistic frames? Do the functionality instruments that measure the ability to perform basic activities like eating and using the toilet account for the complex ways that families are often closely interwoven in the recovering person's life? Is there something missing in standardized metrics? Can global health rubrics really do justice to trauma's local specifications? Together, we develop and receive permission for a small, qualitative pilot study to describe the life circumstances of people who were discharged from Central's trauma ward.

I proceed with caution. Any research that emanates from the hospital, like other authoritative institutions, may register as part of that institution's aims for knowledge production. What my ethnography describes about recovery in the home, and what it concludes about discharge, always carries the potential to be wrapped up in prior relations to the insult of injury and to the treatment of that insult in the hospital. The ethnographer may also become enrolled in someone's quest for justice, and their presence may catalyze a case's juridical qualities. In reflecting on the psychiatric case of Pierre Riviére, Michel Foucault (1982, 235) describes that when clinical and legal languages meet, they create a "coding system" that organizes facts and sets them up for interpretation, rather than a reconstruction of an event's history. Like it or not, ethnography is part of this system.

Patient kin and hospital staff circle the hospital campus on their breaks, perusing the offerings: cigarettes and newspapers, noodles and sugarcane juice, omelets and coconut water, spoons and plates to bring back to the wards to eat home-cooked food. Walking west leads to a historically Maharashtrian neighborhood, quiet and lined with trees. Heading east leads to a historically Jain neighborhood, with a temple on the corner that stands watch over drugstores and outpatient offices. North leads to Dharavi, a neighborhood of neighborhoods with layered linguistic, geographic, occupational, and caste communities. Women from a caste community of potters arrange clay bowls by the road, and European tourists shuffle around them on slum tours. Schoolkids mill about, construction workers saw through metal rods, and hawkers fry *bhajias*. String encircles banyan trees; women have completed the Vat Purnima puja recently, fasting and winding thread amid prayers that their husbands should live well. The neighborhood turns Tamil speaking, and dry goods shops sell *murukku* (twisted rice and dal snacks) and banana chips.

It is mostly unfamiliar space to me, but I see familiars. On the way to visit a discharged patient, I run into Prakash, the afternoon-shift orderly in the mortuary. He lives in Dharavi and walks to work, as many of the hospital workers do. On a similar walk, my neck tickles, and I dismiss it as the wind. But the tickle persists, and I spin around; the trauma ward orderlies have trailed me from the hospital this whole time, tickling and then disappearing into the crowd when I glance back, a tease. We giggle in the middle of the street. The cars don't care and honk their horns, and the orderlies head home. The hospital always feels close.

At Yellama's house, her grandson guides us from the main road to the home, a one-room structure with an upstairs loft. Images of Hanuman and family photos decorate the walls. Her immediate family—husband, sister, son, daughter-in-law, and husband's sister—sit around her. I learn over time that visits like this will almost always be in full view of the family. Just as the event of the accident often unfolds in full view of the public, the interview of the home visit is open for the full view of kin. There are no doors here that disallow the presence of relatives, like in the hospital. The tables turn on gatekeeping. I'm not in the hospital, but I'm by people's beds again.

I also represent the hospital. Gyan has phoned every person we visit, explaining the purpose of the visit and asking for permission multiple times, setting and reconfirming appointments. He has explained that if the patient wishes to see a doctor with questions about care, that will be arranged, but that is not what our visit is for. Nevertheless, we carry the institutional association, and so the hospital anchors our position in these visits, even if I wish it to be otherwise. I can move out of the hospital, but it moves with me.

Yellama begins with the accident itself. "My husband had gone to his village," Yellama says of the day of her accident. "I thought I'd complete my work; the rest of the family had gone to the village. I thought I'd work until nighttime. My neighbor came along with me." She caters small social gatherings and had chapatis to deliver, and her younger neighbor helps. A few blocks from Yellama's home, they tried crossing the road where there was a concrete divider between the lanes. There was a gap that made it possible for the two women to cross, rather than walking a half kilometer to the next intersection with a traffic signal. "She is a bit thin, and I'm a bit heavy. So I had to turn sideways. A lorry came all of a sudden, hitting me. It hit me on one side. It went over me. My skin came off, bruised. They had to take some skin from my inner leg and replace it. The whole leg became swollen. They had to squeeze out the fluid from all the swelling. The leg became black there." She hikes up her housedress, and we see her thighs, abraded and patchy, and her swollen ankle. "It still can't be lifted."

Yellama is matter-of-fact about these things, ticking off facts from her place on the bed, as Gyan and I sit on canisters of rice, her family surrounding us. She is demonstrative. She takes several bottles off the shelf: Horlicks, a multivitamin, a stool softener. She is assiduous about doing everything the doctors have suggested.

Yellama has a neighbor who works at Central Hospital as a nurse. Moments after the truck hit her and sped off, the young woman she was walking with phoned this nurse, who told them to bring Yellama in a taxi to the hospital immediately. The accident happened only half a kilometer from the hospital, so it was a quick ride. "Since I have diabetes, the doctors told me that if it had taken more time, it would have been bad," she says. "My bones were not hit. They made me unconscious using an injection." The hospital experience was fine, she thinks, but the road remains treacherous: "Make good roads," she advises us. "You know the traffic signal next to the hospital? There is no signal on that side nor on this side. I was standing by the side of the road, I was not there to die. My neighbor crossed over; that is why I tried to cross, but [the truck] came all of a sudden. I couldn't go ahead or come back."

Yellama is one of the first discharged patients that Gyan and I meet, and she introduces a tension that carries through the remainder of our home visits: the tension between fate and fault. Perhaps God scripted her injury, she says, making it a matter of fate (*takdeer*), but it was certainly also a matter of fault (*galti*).[3] "My plight was lodged in my fate" (apna takdeer mein apna takleef rehta hai), Yellama tells us. But she cannot discount the troubling regularity of hit-and-runs in the city, events that stretch far beyond the more lurid and high-profile cases that most poor residents in Mumbai know well.[4] She experienced a hit-and-run too and knows she will never catch the driver of the truck who ran into her. Fate did not script this. However, she does not wish to linger on insisting on fault; it is a waste of time to worry about such things. "I don't keep anything in my heart" (kuch nahin mann mein nahin rakhte).

When Gyan and I revisit this moment and this expression, we struggle to account for the fact that Yellama is the only woman we are ultimately able to visit, likely because of her older age. Gyan and I are both men, and even when we bring another, younger female researcher into the process of the home visits, we find that often the families of injured young women are hesitant about our visits. There are few women on our list of discharged patients, but still we see the muting of women and their bodies in the trauma registry, and we worry about replicating this in the home visits and our publications based on the home visits. We are also cautious about the potential for Yellama to shoulder the ways that gender gets factored into differences in recovery as research data aggregate. Yes, part of what really matters to her is fate, but we must be careful about suggesting that she is a faithful older woman whose figuration seems cut-and-dried. We do not know Yellama, just as we do not truly know any of the people we visit. We refuse to foreclose the possibilities for her contentment and relief that go along with the pain and stress of the accident and the injury. We see how asking people about their experience in the hospital as a way to understand recovery may paper over the relief of being out of the hospital, and how revisiting trauma in the speech of a home-visit interview puts constraints on what might be hearable as a response. We know only the situation of encountering patients, and so we commit to narrating the situation of settlement, particularly because our sample is small and may not merit generalization in clinical outcomes research. We convince the researchers in the hospital to change the sampling method when they scale up our pilot study into something larger: female patients must be oversampled to potentially address the silences around them.

Yellama tells us that she can circle the neighborhood on foot now, with some assistance, but mostly she remains at home. She would like to work again but is not sure that is possible. The family renovated the bathroom inside the home to accommodate her needs for different ways of squatting and bearing weight on her legs. There are many threads of conversation about banalities, important banalities, the things public health researchers might call *functionality*. Things like: Can someone return to work? Do daily chores? Wash themselves or clothe themselves? Algorithms and statistical regressions can compute the visit into metrics of quality of life, but Gyan and I do not do this. We hear what it takes to return to a new or reconfigured normal, and note it down.

Yellama's son takes us from the home to the main lane of the neighborhood and explains that the *mamla* of the hit-and-run, its mattering, its potential for settlement, demands that the family confront a calculus. The family didn't have the money or time to attempt to make a case against an unknown driver, and so they declined to deal with the police or the court. They do not know who drove the truck that hit Yellama, so there is no one specific to blame and no one specific to lodge a case against. The case's kinetics is partly determined by *not* making a case. The family galvanizes around support for her and cannot support a legal case because this is not a realistic option. Aspirations for compensation can become a nonstarter, as efforts to secure normality and justice draw out.

Small lanes lead to Kurla Station, and the morning crowd of commuters fills the lanes before filling the trains. Gyan and I take a rickshaw from the station to Sunil's neighborhood. "Ask the *chaiwallah* to tell you the location of the one who was in the accident," his family tells us over the phone. The *chaiwallah* points us to Sunil's lane, and we see his family standing outside their home, the wrought iron by the door interwoven with plants and vines. We climb the metal stairs to the loft, wondering how someone with any sort of orthopedic injury might navigate them. We settle into a tidy room with a cloth mat on the floor set up for the interview. Sunil is sitting in the corner for the interview and says little. He is in his early twenties. His mother shows us the hospital file, and it contains only X-rays. The rest of the papers have gone to the insurance company, and this is notable. All of the home visits we conduct involve poor families living in slum housing, including Sunil's. But this family is the only one we visit that had bought a formal insurance plan and used it to pursue an insurance settlement. His mother thinks the settlement is underway. Perhaps because someone from the insurance office took the original papers, that lends credence to their promise to process the case, but for now, the outcome has not been communicated to the family.

There is another notable feature of this encounter. The three members of Sunil's immediate family—his mother, father, and brother—tell us they prefer to tell the story, rather than asking Sunil to do it.

It wasn't unusual for a family to speak in place of the injured person. We had interviewed another family with a son close to Sunil's age, and in that instance, too, the family largely spoke on his behalf. But this setup does formalize the matter of a family speaking *for* the person, the patient, the one-body injured party. It can involve speaking around them, absenting them. These are multiauthored illness narratives, and they can rely on desirable, neutral, and uncomfortable silences. We are visitors and do not set the terms of encounter, its frames of personhood, nor its narrative proxies.

Sunil's father and brother recount the event. Sunil had been walking in the neighborhood and was suddenly knocked down by a young man on a motorbike who zoomed by. Bystanders immediately nabbed the driver of the bike. The father asserts that this was an act of intervention in a scene of wrongdoing against a familiar person, not a stranger: "The local public knows Sunil."

When Sunil's brother arrived at the scene, he took Sunil to the police station in Kurla. Sunil was bleeding and vomiting and had passed out. "He was unconscious, completely unconscious." He notes that the police at the station were concerned about the possibility of a brain injury and explained that Sunil should go to the hospital. But Sunil's brother insisted on remaining at the police station until a case was registered. The police registered a First Information Report to make the case official, and they charged the motorcycle driver under a statute for causing grievous injury (Indian Penal Code Section 338).

Satisfied that the legal necessities had been completed, Sunil's brother hired a taxi to take Sunil to a casualty ward at a nearby small public hospital. Doctors there performed CT scans, which took some time, he says. The doctors recommended that Sunil be transferred to the trauma ward at Central as hematomas of the brain were a specialist matter and there was no neurosurgeon at this smaller hospital. "They said he might have a blockage [*jam*] of blood in his brain, and they didn't have the facility [to treat him]. He had begun to vomit more." The family hired a taxi to take Sunil to Central.

The brother continues: "The doctors [at Central] said that if the brain jam comes out through medications [and not surgery], it's your luck." They got lucky. Although Sunil did have a brain hemorrhage, he ultimately did not require neurosurgery. The doctors at Central were able to manage it medically; it was small enough to resolve on its own, they asserted. Sunil stayed in the ICU for over a week and then was sent home. There were some challenges associated with ensuring that he had the correct nutrition (a glucose solution for five days and no solid food), but otherwise the family managed. The case shares many of the features of recovery stories I hear from other families: a close call, a struggle, the multiple and at times competing messages that come with trying to get a clear sense of what will happen when someone has brain trauma. What stands out in Sunil's case, however, is his brother's insistence on taking him to the police station as the first stop, rather than the hospital. There is effort to produce a legal case before the formalities of a medical case ensue. We ask why.

"Nobody told us to do it that way," Sunil's brother replies. "We took him [to the police station] ourselves. In my mind, I was afraid that boy [the motorcycle driver] would run away, and if something were to happen, who would be responsible? After all, he's my brother, right? How could I have let the driver go?" Responsibility entailed correct forms of documentation and evidentiary production, ensuring that proper legal mechanisms for redress would be in place. To settle responsibility in the legal record required that the lifeline of Sunil's treatment begin at the police station, which effectively renders Sunil first as belonging to the legal category of victim before he belongs to the medical category of patient.

Sunil's father adds, "The thing is, the *bike-wallah* [driver] was a Muslim."

Gyan glances my way. We both know that we are in a neighborhood that was immersed in violence during the city's 1993 riots, events described as "communal" fractures between Hindus and Muslims. We have discussed how relations among households constitute a "locality," a neighborhood geography of caste, class, religion, and social history. Before visiting any locality in Mumbai, we talk about the complex relationships between communal violence's exceptionality and its banality that can imprint a neighborhood (Appadurai 2000b; V. Das 2006; Ghassem-Fachandi 2012; Hansen 2002; Mehta 2006; V. Rao 2007a). We talk about what these relationships might look like in the context of present-day Hindu nationalism as it differentially imbues the political energies of the locality, city, state, region, and nation. To what degree are these differences figuring into the situation we find ourselves in, as the family narrates Sunil's case?

The brother fills in details:

As soon as I took Sunil to the police station, the police inspector said that they'd keep the bike driver there. He said we should take Sunil to the hospital and start his treatment and then bring the police the report. They would tell us what to do or what not to do. They came to the hospital later when his treatment started, at night. We thought Sunil was all right, that it was an accident, there would be a bit of treatment, and the doctors would send him home, no tension at all. But he spent all of Diwali in the hospital. There are rules and laws in place, sir, but things will be okay only if these policemen perform their duty. But these cops let everything go for ten to fifteen rupees [bribe].

It is not simply that Sunil, a Hindu, is hit by a Muslim. There are police in the frame, and one cannot guarantee that one's wishes for order and enforcement of law will happen without the family's effort. The brother believes the police feared that Sunil's head injuries might be serious, and only because of this did they actually file their reports. No one is to be trusted, including the police.

Sunil's father asserts that in the face of police inaction and corruption that may let the guilty party slip away, fate (*takdeer*) is irrelevant. "There's nothing like fate here; this is fault. If it was fate, then a bike could hit you even when you're at home. If one has to die, one can die in a hospital or die at home. Why does one die on the road? Because of accidents. There's no destiny here. It is human fault [*yeh naseeb ka kuch nahin, yeh galti hai*]." In contrast to Yellama, with her appeals to fate, Sunil's father emphasizes fault as a mode of recounting injury.

Sunil's mother has been relatively quiet as the father and brother detail the case. She notes that not everything went smoothly at the hospital: she felt that there was too much wait time, and she had to flag down nurses to take care of Sunil in moments when the pain was unmanageable for him. As her husband makes recourse to fault, she reminds everyone in the room, "We still have to remember God at some point." Maybe God is not clearly the cause of the accident, she says, but God still lies somewhere, somehow in the everyday ways of asking for things to be better after an unforeseen event. She explains that the family had just returned from a visit to their *pujari* (priest) in Nashik and are followers of a *baba* (spiritual leader). She points out his picture on the small altar in the room. "He is a powerful healer."

"People with a lot of money come to him; his job is to build success. Real estate developers come to him," the brother adds.

But even with belief, one needs evidence, he says. The family put blame into motion by confronting the police with Sunil's injury as evidence. Now, as they reflect on it, other forms of evidence join the wound. Sunil's father notes that the biker did not wear a helmet, did not have a proper license to drive the bike, and had two pillion riders instead of the permitted one pillion rider. "The biker's parents had come to the hospital, because their son was in the police station and they were a bit afraid that something might happen to Sunil." The fate of Sunil and the fate of the biker get tied together in this retelling of the story. One young man is in the hospital; another is in the police station.

"The biker's parents tried to get their son out of the police station, but Sunil was in the ICU, and that's why the police wouldn't release him," Sunil's brother says.

Sunil's father narrates the encounters with the biker's family at the hospital and later after Sunil came home:

> The kid who hit him, he's a Muslim. [The biker's] father came to us and said, "My child made a mistake, so whatever amount you spend on medicines, I will give you in cash." I said, "First let Sunil get better, then we will make the settlement in the police station." After Sunil's discharge, the father came to our home to give us money. He said, "Whatever your expenses were, I will pay you back." So we said we lost 15,000 rupees, and we are letting go of the losses incurred to our business. "We are only telling you the money we spent on medicines," we said. If we had added the business losses, it would have gone beyond 100,000 rupees.

The biker's father agreed to the 15,000-rupee settlement. But a few days later, he returned to Sunil's home and informed the family that his relative had counseled him to wait for the court to make a decision on fault and compensation. Sunil's father was furious that the man would renege on his offer to pay for Sunil's medical costs. "Some relative of his goaded him into doing this" (usko koi relative ne uksaya).

Sunil's father responded by demanding 50,000 rupees (around US$700) instead of 15,000, through a formal legal case in court. "He could have just agreed to the first offer, but he had to act shrewd [chalak]."

I am curious about the stretch of movements over time narrated here as the mamla, from the crisis of the accident to the crisis of negotiation identified as a site of settlement. I do not assume that this particular mamla fully encompasses how two families may live in the same locality. I want to leave open the possibilities that prior forces in a neighborhood's history may influence a case's kinetics and that a case may shift proximal relations, and I do not assume that a case precisely tracks relations of living in proximity. How recovery is lived in place is a question to be asked of specific households, not something assumed from the start. In this case, Sunil's family and the biker's family did not know each other well, the brother explains. Their proximity is mainly geographic and not interactional. The brother explains that the biker's family lives close by. But the two families do not often interact.

These back-and-forth moves between neighbors can set the context of medicolegal matters, as traffic and accident come into new relations through transactions and negotiations. Traffic figures less as the accident's cause and more as the accident's consequence. The specificity of the neighborhood matters as well. Anthropologist Deepak Mehta writes of a moment when he interviews the son of a sick man who gave evidence to the Srikrishna Commission, the inquiry into the Bombay bomb blasts and riots of 1992–93. The son tells Mehta that when police visited the home to question the sick father, the son "didn't know whether this house was a *thana* [police station] or a hospital." Mehta argues that understanding violence requires understanding how it traverses and transforms social spaces, including home spaces otherwise presumed to be hermetically sealed, such that the "house becomes a hospital and/or police station" (2006, 221).

In this light, the language of causality may not be fitting for explaining the texture of the encounter between Sunil's parents and the biker's parents. That is, it may not be accurate to assert that communal tensions *cause* the rift. It may be more accurate to note how recovery's kinetics can be wrapped up in a neighborhood's dynamic traffic of trust and suspicion, a traffic that changes when a traumatic injury of a young son gets introduced into its dynamics. A case can shift and freeze common sense about a household's social position in a locality, a locality in which police will look the other way, perpetrators escape, and neighbors respond to domestic quandaries with self-interest and schemes. Recall how Sunil's brother directed us to the home in the first place: "Ask the *chaiwallah* to tell you the location of the one who was in the accident." I am struck by this condition of possibility for our visit: the *chaiwallah* who watches the neighborhood and who may be a household ally. Lifelines of discharge can become microhistorical flows created by those who keep recovery moving, from tea sellers to insurance adjusters.

Social rifts can deepen when suspicions are confirmed, such as the idea that Sunil's trauma stems not only from the collision but from the shrewdness of a neighbor and the community they represent. However, I am not willing to write out settlement or forgiveness as a possibility because, again, the home visit is a snapshot and not the album. What holds true across these possibilities is that the injured, their families, and a neighborhood get caught up in recovery's kinetics.

In Irfan's neighborhood, flags fly next to a mosque. We meet Irfan by the mosque, per his instructions over the phone. Vegetable sellers surround us; school has let out, and the kids are over the moon about it, their weighty Dora the Explorer backpacks bouncing. As in many of these encounters, I'm unsure precisely who I am looking for. In the trauma ward, the category of patient refers to a person in a bed, so the elision is easy—too easy. In the home visits, I know a person was a patient, but I do not always know what they look like, so the elision isn't smooth, which is a relief.

A man in his fifties with a walker waves to us. Limping a bit, he leads me and Gyan down a shaded, cool route into the cluster of storefronts and homes that open onto this narrow passage. I think about the route home, the first time someone returns from the hospital, and what it might mean to encounter it again, this time helped by others. The home's main room centers around a bed raised on brick stacks and a gorgeous, intricate wood armoire with a television. Gold-framed Quranic scriptures decorate the walls. An older man lies on the bed; we are told he is Irfan's brother. During the interview Irfan's nieces and nephews move in and out of the room, sometimes filling in details, buttressing his memory.

The narrative is kaleidoscopic. Irfan does not center the event of the accident on his map of recovery. Instead, the hospital is the epicenter of the problem.

"The hospital's people screwed my family" (mujhe family ko hospital-walu ne chutiya banaya hai), Irfan says. "I went to Central Hospital, and they did everything wrong, see for yourself. This is the kind of drilling [in my leg] you guys from Central Hospital did." He stands up and walks over, loosens his pants a bit, and asks us to put our hands on his hip to feel the bumps of metal under his skin.

Gyan and I reemphasize that we are not doctors from the hospital, knowing that we certainly look like doctors from the hospital. We repeat the purpose of the study. Irfan says he understands, and perhaps he should phone his friend, a doctor in the neighborhood, to interpret the clinical details for us. But he does not and continues.

Irfan fell out of a moving train near Dombivili Station. He was adjusting his eyeglasses, and they slipped, and as he tried to catch them, he slipped and fell out of the open doors of the train and into a small lake the train was passing by.

The colors faded, and I fell down, and I tried to catch my glasses and fell out of the train. I fell into water. That's why I survived. I came out [of the water] with the help of a wooden pole. There was water for nearly five hundred meters. I was conscious for an hour. Two policemen arrived. I was feeling giddy, so they brought a stretcher. They told me they could not get hold of an ambulance. I got on the stretcher, and then I lost my senses. I regained consciousness after two days. Later, I could only recognize my nephew. The whole neighborhood had come [to the hospital], and I didn't recognize anyone. At home, my wife, one of my daughters, and everyone else said that I should be prescribed medicines for this.

"The colors faded" suggests, perhaps, that he fainted from hypotension or dizziness (*chakar*), a wash of instability I recognize after a decade studying diabetes (Solomon 2016). Irfan remembers that policemen picked him up, put him on a stretcher, and took him to a nearby government hospital. The doctors there said that Irfan needed to be transferred to Central Hospital given the severity of his injuries and especially the complex fracture in his hip. That hospital had registered Irfan as an Unknown patient, without identification, but someone found his daughter-in-law's phone number in a small pocket diary in his shirt. The police phoned her to say that a man with her phone number had fallen from the train.

His daughter-in-law was shocked when she received the call. "It is only when the police called," she says, "that we came to know what happened and that there was no place for him [at the smaller hospital]. They said that they will bring him [to Central] in an ambulance, and then they would call us once they reach here. That's when we asked how much will it cost, and that's when they said the price."

The police told her that because no government ambulance was available, a private ambulance would need to be arranged to transport Irfan from the small hospital to Central, and that it would cost three thousand rupees. "There was not a lot of hope of him surviving," she adds.

Irfan and his family explain that the time at Central was anything but healing. He had superficial head injuries, but the injury to the hip required orthopedic surgery. Once he became stable in the trauma ward, orthopedic surgeons worked on the hip, and he was transferred postoperatively to the orthopedic ward. But there he encountered hospital staff who demanded bribes for care. "After two days," he says, "I started troubling my family to take me home and treat me from home. They placed a rod in my leg. That cost 8,500 rupees. They charged a hundred rupees for the bed. And they charged me for passing urine and charged me money for defecation."

We are startled by this. A charge for urination and defecation?

"Yes," he repeats. "I have a video clip, I will show you. As you enter the [orthopedic] ward, the helpers would charge us a hundred rupees." His relative has the video on her mobile phone, and the family is keeping it as evidence to release to a reporter.

Fed up with the situation, Irfan took a discharge against medical advice after two days, and the family admitted him to a private hospital closer to home. There, he says, the treatment was excellent ("A to Z treatment," he calls it). That private hospital had to fix the mistakes he claimed Central made. The first involved treatment of his head wound. "They bandaged it. They said, 'Uncle, you have an infection there.' The doctor said that it was going to be infested with worms. It was cheaper to work on it before the worms set in. They did a good job on that. You wouldn't even know that it was injured. That place was first-class."

At Central Hospital, the orthopedic surgeons put rods in his hip joint to address the fracture. The problem, he tells us, is that the rods were inserted incorrectly. "My hip is still not right," he says. "I cannot squat in the bathroom. We had to convert our toilet into a Western-style commode. The bigger problem was what those rods were doing to me. It feels like something is stuck there. Like after you drop your sandals and then when you put them back on, you still feel sand stuck in between them. After eight days, the doctors asked me to try sitting. I did sit. But it was as if my leg was immersed in water."

He moves his leg around to show us the ways it does not move properly. "I need another operation. In a few months, they will take these rods out and put in new rods, because they [the doctors at Central] placed the rods incorrectly." Irfan worked at a company that manufactured building materials. He sees a direct link between the rebar metal rods (*salli*) he knows from construction work and the rods placed in his legs. "I have worked in construction, inserting metal rods. The rods they put in the roads, those are manufactured by my company. I used to work on those rods. When a rod is inserted in the right way, you can feel it." He stands up and asks us to feel his hip again.

Now his days are spent talking to his brother, who is recovering from a recent heart attack. "He tells me about his medical condition, and I tell him about mine, and it goes on like that." But they are also days inflected by pain, nonstop pain, he says. He takes out a packet of pills. I make out the drug name and see they are benzodiazepines. He calls them "pain medicines" (*dard ki goli*). He says he got them from the neighborhood chemist. "It is good that I take the pain medicines on time. I take ten of these every day." If he takes fewer than ten, he says, he would be in pain. And he would not sleep. "It costs a hundred rupees for these pain medications. It is with the help of these pills that I am sitting here," he says. Yet he feels confused at times. Sometimes he wakes up in bed with his wife next to him and wonders who this strange woman is. He is stuck between the pills and the botched surgery, both forms of medicine that should in theory lead toward some sort of resolution but instead lead to confusion. Later that evening, after I get home, I phone a physician friend and check on the drug and the dosage. She says it's a miracle he's not a zombie.

His body is gaining momentum in its recovered capacities, but the inertia of his case seems constant, stuck in legal limbo:

> What happened was wrong. I have a full file prepared. I have even spoken to a lawyer who told me to ask my family doctor to prepare the case file for me. Then the lawyer tells me that I will lose the case. He said if I have the money, to carry on preparing the file for five to six months, and then in the seventh month he will call me. He said this in 2016. It is 2017 now, and the case is still not on, what do you say to this? He told me that it will take 2,000 rupees, and it will be finalized in five to six months. No lawyer would ever say that he will lose. He said that it will take time. When we talk, he says that I should take a doctor with me too. Those doctors [at Central] have to be exposed. I will call the media, I will go to the police station.

Irfan repeats that his desire is to "expose" Central Hospital through the media.[5] He says he knows that we are connected to the trauma ward and that the trauma ward at Central was not the problem. It was the orthopedic ward where he says the mistreatment happened. He encourages us to go "undercover" in the orthopedic ward. "If you go quietly, see what happens there. If no one recognizes you, then you will be able to see what happens. You will come to know what happens there . . . a person can die there." And then there is the paperwork, the winding trails of a case's materiality. He shows us the stack of hospital papers. We see an application on hospital letterhead for a 10,000-rupee reduction in total costs for poor patients. But his family did not submit it. We do not ask why, but we work with him to retroactively claim the coverage.

Irfan's wife enters the room as we shuffle through papers. She was horrified by the experience at the hospital. "That place was like a mental asylum [*toh aisi jaga dala tha pagal khane ki tara*]. There was little hope of him surviving, but after the operation we thought it would be a better place. But it was a place where there were people without hands and no one to look after them. Some had no hands, some were missing parts of their head, some were without noses, some had cut legs. And the bathroom was overflowing with sewage, such a place they put him in."

Irfan raises the financial dimension of the mistreatment. "If everything went well there, it would have been all right. We don't have money, so I had to borrow money on interest [*byaaz*] from here and there. Suppose I borrow money from you, wouldn't you agree that you would want it back? Right or wrong? How long would you bear with me to get your money? That's the point. There's no money. In poverty, it takes money borrowed with interest to get a person treated." Irfan says it cost more than 100,000 rupees total in terms of the expenses at all three hospitals—the small one the police took him to first, then Central, and then the private one. He still must settle his debts with a neighborhood moneylender from whom he borrowed cash to pay for all the costs.

He asks how borrowing money works in America. I say that being in debt for medical treatment is very common where I come from and that no one anywhere should have to endure such an insult. "But they can't hide anything there," he insists of the United States. There is no way that such poor treatment would go unnoticed.

This conviction about exposing the hospital takes shape in conversation with each of the many mentions of "mistake," or *galat*, that he recounts. The rods are put in incorrectly. There are mistakes in his medical file. At several points in the interview, he says of the whole affair, "It's really a mistake" (sahi yeh galat hai). He is living on with injury but also living on with an embodied mistake, one he can feel every time he tries to walk. He repeats a claim that we heard in our visit to Sunil's home: it is human error (*galat*), not fate (*takdeer*), that is operating here, Irfan says. But the agents and circumstances are different from those in Sunil's account. Here the humans who err are the hospital staff who should be healing the injury, not a reckless motorcycle driver who causes the injury. The fault, *galti*, lies squarely in the domain of medicine. While law might be leveraged against medicine, Irfan does not trust the legal system. So his best shot, he thinks, is to achieve compensation through the circulation of public media.

Compensation for traffic accidents involves a complex of institutional mandates, sites of adjudication, and formal processes. The Motor Vehicles Act of 1988, which at the time of my research was undergoing updating (and which was amended in 2019), governs certain features of compensation; the Workmen's Compensation Act does as well (Kannan 2014, 267). People injured on the railways may be granted compensation, with the amounts specified on a body-part basis in the railway regulations. Those are the policies, but the processes are also multifaceted. A series of pathways to claims and to compensation developed in the wake of the Consumer Protection Act, charging individuals with the responsibility to lodge claims while also offering pathways to circumvent overloaded juridical bureaucracies. There are Motor Vehicles Claims Tribunals empowered by the Motor Vehicles Act to have authority similar to a civil court. The Railways Tribunals empowered by the central government's Railway Claims Tribunal (Procedure) Rules of 1989 have the authority to litigate claims of loss of livelihood owing to injury. Many of these processes rely on certification by doctors as to the nature and extent of disability. That Irfan sought discharge from the hospital against medical advice complicated this matter further.

It is unclear from our conversation which legal apparatus the lawyer he hired is interacting with. Indeed, it seems quite clear to Irfan that the lawyer has not even decided to take up the case at all. Irfan's aim is the acceleration of a case whose visibility and reception have grown static. His lawyer has not moved the case. The state's apparatus for compensation is not moving the case, if they have even been presented with it, which seems doubtful. Consequently, there seems to be only one way to speed matters up: recourse via public accusation by circulating what for him and the family counts as evidence—the video clip. There is fault in medicine, but just as punitive is the stasis of the case, a potential for movement that the institutions of law and medicine do not take up. It is here that he must intervene.

He asks us what his next steps should be. He thinks the hospital will be as bureaucratic and obstructive as the legal system, and the possibilities for redress must lie elsewhere. "I have told you the truth of what happened, so what should I do? In my mind, I think I should collect all the proof and that wrong report the hospital made, and tell people how the hospital took money from us. Then the hospital would get into trouble for making wrong reports."[6] This is why he must expose the hospital. He often sees such exposés on TV. "You see many hospitals getting into scandals on TV; so many exposures are being shown" (Hospital kitna lafda chal raha hai dekh rahe hain aap TV par bhi. Kitni exposure ho rahi hain). They're regular fare, and so it can't be too hard to make such a case.

He is correct about the hospital. I tell the senior faculty surgeons in the trauma ward that there is a former patient who experienced serious mistreatment. I get understanding nods and am told that this is completely out of their hands because it didn't happen in their department, their domain, but they will share the information, and maybe the concerned authority in orthopedics might take it up. Returning to the hospital to potentially right a wrong feels like missing a target. Early in our conversation, Irfan tells us that the whole affair was a "near miss" (bal bal bach gaya). Usually, this term is used as an expression for avoiding a terrible encounter. Irfan narrates the miss as doubled. There is the kind of near miss from something lethal that saves you. His fall from the train is a near miss because he did not die. Yet he also describes his case's kinetics as a near miss because the case evades the push of the very forces that might have delivered a desired outcome. He misses the possibility to have a legal case proceed. He misses the possibility to have a corrective surgery that might remediate the mistake that he claims the doctors at Central made. I feel a near miss too, the feeling of inability to draw attention to a discharged case; my own position in the complex hospital ecology does not lie in the department that needs to listen. Recovery—and the ethnographic encounter coincident with it—emerges as a set of potential moves, as Irfan crafts a forensic report of his past with the hospital and a plan for future exposure, both designed from home.

In the trauma ward, "the home" of patients was something that the ward was at pains to selectively filter. After discharge and after the return home, the trails flow in different directions. The home may be the place to reveal dimensions of the injury that were not speakable in the hospital. It may be the place to piece the time in the hospital together. And it may be a place to piece oneself and the family together. The fuller extent of the injury may reveal itself and become sedimented as disability, through materializations of toilets and stairs.

But not all of my "visits" with discharged patients are in homes; there is one exception, Prakash. Prakash insists that we talk at the hospital. Before we first contact him on the phone, we reach his brother by phone, because the number listed on Prakash's hospital record is his brother's. Gyan asks for Prakash's phone number. We should have no trouble reaching him, his brother replies. "He's just lying at home [*ghari padle asthi*]." It's a slightly askew phrasing, more akin to *He's just lying around the house* than simply saying *He's at home*.

Prakash tells Gyan that he prefers to meet at the hospital because he has a follow-up appointment in the occupational therapy ward. We know from the record that his hand was amputated following a railway injury, but little more.

Prakash phones us when he is in the occupational therapy department. Gyan and I go to meet him there, in the same building as the morgue; Gyan holds his breath as the elevator rises past the morgue. In the occupational therapy department, the main area is open and busy. Physiotherapists encourage patients to stretch over large therapy balls and hold their hands as slow steps mark progress. There are patients learning to walk again, to pull again, to push again, and to bear their own weight again. It is a place to recover habituated ways of balanced action and to craft new ones. Prakash waits for us by the elevator. We cannot find a quiet spot to talk amid the activity of the room, so we decide to sit outside on the steps of a building undergoing renovation. I put my handkerchief down for Prakash, and Gyan rips out paper from his notebook so our butts don't turn white from the concrete dust.

Prakash worked as a loan officer at a bank, doing collections work, and he is unmarried. He lives with his sister and his elderly mother, for whom he shared care-work responsibilities with his married brother, who lives not too far away. The conversation floats around these demographic details of age, work, community, and family but soon skirts the railway accident.

Prakash says that it was not an accident. "I am not going to lie. Honestly, I was trying to commit suicide."

We pause. Suicides, both attempted and realized, appear often in the trauma ward. But their legal, social, and intimate edges do not usually line up with a first-person account of intent. Nor do I ever ask about such matters. As part of Gyan's training, we discuss Jocelyn Chua's ethnography on suicide in South India, particularly her emphasis on refraining from asking, "What happened?" at the start of an interview. For Chua, listening rather than direct inquiry is a commitment to "take seriously the power of uncertainty itself to transform reality and relations between people" (2014, 24).[7] Gyan and I follow this approach. We both know that once in the trauma ward, any person who has attempted suicide will be surrounded by people from the regimes of both medicine and law asking *kya hua?* (what happened?)—sometimes tenderly, sometimes not. Each time the question is asked, a case's kinetics may shift and move recovery in unexpected ways.

Does Prakash wish to stop this conversation? He can stop at any time, we explain before beginning the interview, and we repeat this again now.

No, he says. He wants to tell us this story.

He had been without a job. And his mother, in her mid-eighties, was not well. She would wake up in the morning "and just blabber things." She was depressed. She spoke in ways he couldn't understand. She would see things that were not actually there. So he would not leave her by herself. He was committed to watching her as much as possible. At the same time, he was trying to get a job. He added up the expenses that his household incurred: it was him, his mother, and his unmarried sister living together. Their apartment building had recently been renovated, and so the housing-society maintenance fees had increased.

He remembers going to the train station:

> I was on the train platform. It was raining heavily, and it was muddy all around my feet. I saw a train coming. At the same instant that I fell, the train stopped. I was between the two railway tracks. And when I fell, I didn't realize anything, and there was darkness before my eyes [*jab main ghira, tabi mujhe kuch maloom nahin pada . . . aisa mera aank ke saamne andera aa gaya*]. And my hand was over the railway track. I was trying to lift it off, but the wheels went over it. Someone pulled me out [from the tracks]. They are building a new platform, since the number of train carriages has increased. There are stones and rocks on the tracks. The whole hand was gone.

Much after that was hazy. He didn't know that his hand had been amputated until much later, in the hospital. He does not remember the details of the arrival at the hospital. "But they did something to my hand. And they were using a knife. I thought my hand would be all right."

At night, he had phantom sensations, feeling as if his hand was still there ("aisa lagne ka, ki haath hai mera"). He watched the other patients: "The ward was for accident cases. Someone fell off a bike, someone fell off a train. There was a man who fell off the train, and both his legs had to be amputated. Someone had pushed him out of the train between Diva and Kalwa Stations. He was a Christian. There was another man who was a Patil [a Gujarati]. Both have been discharged now."

We ask how his family encountered the situation.

"My mother and sister didn't come to the hospital," he says. "Because on the day I was in the accident . . . I mean, the day I went to commit suicide [*jis din mera accident hua tha . . . ya . . . jis din main suicide karne gaya tha*], my mother was admitted to a different hospital. She went to my elder brother's place after her discharge. She didn't know that this has happened. But my neighbors in my building came to visit."

When he returned home after nearly two weeks in the hospital, his mother was still staying with his brother, and his sister was staying elsewhere. But the family felt that his mother couldn't stay at his brother's indefinitely. "So one day we had to tell her that such and such happened. And then my mother saw me. I also started feeling, 'What have I done?' I came to understand later. At the time, when I was doing it, I didn't think a lot. I felt that I really didn't want to be alive anymore. But I don't know."

Prakash rolls up his shirt sleeve. There are two rubber bands wrapped around his inner arm. These are for incense sticks, so he can still perform *aarti* (offering light to deities). He shows us the scars from the stitches on his shoulder.

> Everyone in the family was saying, "What have you done?" And they also said, "What has happened has happened." My mother and my sister help me scrub places on my neck where I can't reach when I take a bath. As for cost, I don't know the total, because my brother has not shared that with me. He did everything. Medicines here are free, but sometimes there are medicines that have to be purchased from outside the hospital. I haven't told my brother about the medicines they prescribe for physiotherapy. So much has happened. I have given him so much trouble. When people visit our home, they ask, "What have you gone and done to yourself?"

When injury is self-inflicted, the terms of fate, forgiveness, and adjudication shift.

He hopes the physiotherapy might address some of the problems he has with daily activities. He loves to cook. But now he feels that stirring a pot on the stove with one hand might cause it to topple. He tried tying rags on the amputated arm and fixing a spoon and tongs there, but it wasn't as steady as he wished.

The orthopedic team he still visits for follow-up recently told him that he has healed enough to receive a prosthetic hand. "This duplicate hand is going to be heavy," he says. "And so the muscle has to grow strong, so I have to lift bags of onions and potatoes [to prepare]. I am trying to get a desk job. But my hand is gone, so I can't count bills. I am trying to get a job at the document verification section of the bank. Even now, I don't sit idle at home. I keep writing something or other with my left hand."

Prakash takes out a diary from his bag. It was a gift from his nieces for the Gudi Padwa holiday a few years back. It has inspirational quotes printed on the pages. He opens the first page and reads out loud, methodically, in English: "Let the words have power to absorb the energy that lies in you. . . . As the pages of this book unfold, add new chapters to your life." He shows us the pages where he wrote with his right hand and the pages where he now writes with his left hand. He thumbs through other blank pages, so we can read the English text he has copied from the journal's inspirational quotes, using them as practice for writing with his left hand.

> *Death will never respect anyone, it will never care for anything. It is an infinite cycle that will come in life.*
> *Worry less, dance more, love often, be happy, think positively, exercise daily, eat healthy, work hard, stay strong!*

"One shouldn't just sit at home, just keep on writing," he says (ghar pe baitne ka nahin, likte hi rehne ka).

We walk to the snack kiosk by the trauma ward waiting area. There is room to sit on a bench in between people sleeping. We sip lemonade. Prakash slumps a bit. He says that the prosthetic limb camp is not for another few months. What if he waits all this time and they cannot make something fit for him? The hospital, now taking shape as the space of physiotherapy, seems to be deferring his case, making it ever more inert. Kinetic changes are not guaranteed. What will he do about his hand?

Gyan tries to keep the tone upbeat. Prakash says he likes the inspirational quotes, so Gyan offers some of his own, and invokes *rangoli*, the ritual form of placing colored powder in patterns:

> I believe each of our lives has a purpose. It is like *rangoli* designs. In a *rangoli* the green or pink color doesn't know what its role is. All it feels is that it is lying there. But when someone from outside sees the *rangoli*, they see the whole design. They can see that if the green wasn't there, then the

whole design wouldn't make sense. Same with the pink. I feel we cannot go up and see the whole design. We just lie there in the *rangoli*. We may be just a dot, but from above, the dot is important. Just remember that whatever may be the problem in life, just remember that we have a purpose, every life has a purpose.

We walk back with him to the physiotherapy department and say good-bye. He phones us later, to say that it was break time in the physiotherapy department, and he was heading home. It is simply a call to catch up, to update, to keep the present moving.

———

Recovery's kinetics imprint the return home from the trauma ward, through a shift in time and space that can feel like a change in seasons. The wind blows differently, textures of life adjust, and the home's physical environments morph to accommodate changed embodiments. As injury is taken up in neighborhoods and in homes, retrospection can sketch perpe-trators and heroes into particular sequences of events. The hospital itself may anchor the event of injury as people reflect on their experiences in the trauma ward, for better and for worse. The injury and the treatment of the injury may move in sync as the rearview mirror reflects matters of blame, responsibility, solidarity, fate, justice, and forgiveness. Closure is hard-won in this context, as people inhabit the space of the *mamla* of the accident and as trauma morphs within the domestic domain through re-configured relations between traffic and accident.

It is one thing to conclude from the accounts discussed here that re-covery is a body's movement in the continuous present; this is partly true. But framed as a lifeline through traffic, recovery also points to potentials for additional shifts. When the researchers at the hospital ask what I am learning about functionality and disability from the home visits, I say that these matters are inextricable from matters of compensation and justice. I say that we cannot assume that the terms of recovery are the same for everyone who leaves the trauma ward and that accounts of the same recov-ery differ depending on who is and is not speaking. Sometimes the healing of a wound seems to constitute recovery. Yellama's accounting of her case seems to suggest this, at least in her account. Her son's account, however, suggests that there is a stream of action and desire on the part of the family as she heals: they wish to make a case against the driver of the truck but cannot. There is no evidence. There is no case to build.

For Prakash, focused on finding new work and exploring the possibility of a prosthetic hand, recovery seems like picking up the pieces and finding ways to relate to family and neighbors who introduce questions of "What have you done to yourself?" into daily interactions. In that questioning, everyday gestures such as cooking, cleaning, working, and writing inflect recovering. We also note that Prakash's injury, which is to his hand, sets him apart in terms of mobility potential when compared to people for whom it might be far more difficult to travel to the hospital for physiotherapy. The pressures of his family also merit mention. Each time Prakash said, "One shouldn't just sit at home," I heard the echo of his elder brother on the phone: "He's just lying there." Prakash is actively pursuing not sitting at home, but venturing out of the home for now entails returning to the hospital for physiotherapy.

This return to the hospital, in words if not in space, characterizes many of the home visits. Discharge might register as a momentous occasion for both the hospital and a patient in a given case. But is this line of recovery really a vector, one-way? Our visits suggest that things are more roundabout and that the lifelines of recovery bend toward the clinic both willingly and unwillingly. The space and time of discharge open up connections between comprehension and compensation. Patients often take up questions of blame and specify blame in terms of distinctions between fate (*takdeer*) and fault (*galti*). If the medicolegal is a domain that characterizes life in the hospital, so too must it be understood as a domain that does not necessarily guarantee justice. Discharge is less punctuation and more continuation.

This recursion of the injury, this looping of a case, comes to mark the traffic of trauma after discharge. One can make a claim for compensation, but the path through formal and informal channels of justice is long and unpredictable. Perhaps it makes more sense to strike a deal between the two parties, as in Sunil's family's attempt to control the terms of settlement, before the biker's father decided to pursue a court case. Perhaps it makes more sense to attempt a media exposure, as Irfan's family debates when the discussions with the lawyer lead nowhere. When a patient is discharged home, trauma's recovery mutates through stasis in motion.

Epilogue

THE TRAFFIC OF MEDICINE

The siren roars as the ambulance speeds by. There has been little traffic on the roads since lockdown began in March 2020. I live blocks away from a skilled nursing facility and from Duke University Hospital, and the sirens have been constant. We do not yet fully know how the coronavirus works, but we know its sounds. These sirens warble, the Doppler effect unencumbered by traffic's snare.

I glance at a small bottle of hand sanitizer I bought at a chemist's shop in Mumbai after queueing for supplies. In March I returned to the United States from Mumbai a day before Prime Minister Narendra Modi mandated that 1.2 billion people observe stay-at-home orders. The immobilization of some bodies was deemed necessary to deter the virus's progression. In the days before the order, I needed to meet with my coinvestigators at Central Hospital but refused to go into the trauma ward and its ICU. I had been on an international flight weeks prior. Biopolitical poles scale up and down: mobility is a privilege and a threat; air's circulation affirms life but can be lethal. I did not understand the complexities of possible asymptomatic transmission of the coronavirus at that time, but I did not want or need that information. In a context of privileged not-knowing, I would not risk the possibility of further threatening the breathing of those in the trauma ward and of intruding on the fraught but crucial circuits of social breathing keeping people alive.

Ventilators remained in critical supply in India. The government's ban on all flights in March 2020 made importing essential parts for these complex machines difficult (Rajagopal 2020). Broader-scale circulations of capital, bodies, and panic materialized: the massive shifts of migrant laborers across the country, the groups of men barricading neighborhoods against "outsiders" in the name of quarantine, the empowerment of the police to use violent force against anyone suspected of breaching curfew, the shifting of labor structures for women from within the home, and the takeover of private-sector health-care facilities by state and local governments to confront the demands for care.

In mid-May 2020, ventilators moved through the jet streams of the earth's atmosphere. The United States donated and sent two hundred ventilators to India, a "gift" from President Donald Trump to Prime Minister Narendra Modi to combat what Trump called "the invisible enemy" of the virus. The gift raised questions of a potential quid pro quo because this gift occurred one month after India lifted its ban on the export of hydroxychloroquine and sent supplies of the drug to the United States (N. Basu 2020). The drug was not seen as an effective treatment for COVID-19 by clinicians, but it was by Trump, and so the medicine moved. Sometimes lifelines work through evidence; sometimes they work by decree.

Available beds in Mumbai's public hospitals for COVID-19 patients grew limited by the end of May 2020, and the municipality attempted to garnish beds from private facilities. This was an event, but it would become a wave, a repeated ebb and flow in the year that followed. Early concerns about ventilator availability shifted to concerns about the availability of oxygen support, as hospital protocols shifted to oxygenate patients as early as possible. Unknown patients' bodies—those who die from complications of COVID-19 alone, because they live at a distance from kin or because their kin also have died from coronavirus complications—crowded Mumbai's cemeteries (Khan 2021). Mumbai's roads emptied, as did the local trains, which would later be open to vaccinated people. People saw the sky again, as traffic's hazy exhausts dispersed. Central's trauma ward still operated but at much lower capacity. There were several high-speed road accidents on the now-empty highways and roads, but few railway accident injuries to care for. Some of the staff were transferred to other spaces in the hospital to provide care for COVID-19 patients. One calamity shifted the traffic of expertise away from another. Things settled. Another wave of cases a year later, in April 2021, drew oxygen and ICU bed supplies perilously low. Doubts emerged around official counts for all infection-related deaths, and health-care workers and relatives became proxy recordkeepers of the dead (C. Ratna 2020; C. Ratna 2021). The labor of ICU staff, morgue attendants, and crematorium workers made headlines. How bodies might move—to a hospital, onto oxygen and ventilators, into death, and homeward—were problems charged with the nation's survival.

The pandemic continues to expose the enduring dilemmas of movement in global medicine and public health. Ambulances may take hours to respond. Emergency rooms fill up, triaging scarce resources. Health-care workers labor beyond their limits and with compensation structures that may not recognize overtime, extraordinary and enduring work, and the widespread attrition of staff that moves responsibilities around in unsustainable ways. There remains hope around the life-saving potential of coronavirus vaccines and treatments but frustrations that they are not moving through mass-distribution channels quickly enough, especially in relation to viral variants. Visits by relatives of COVID-positive patients in ICUs remain restricted. Often patients die alone, particularly those whose families cannot be located. Ventilator and airway supplies stretch thin. The morgues may fill to capacity.

As life gets lived through the mobile modalities of the pandemic, the critical movements of lifelines—and the traffic of medicine—come into stark relief.

The coronavirus pandemic dramatizes the core argument of this book: that surviving threats to health entails a cascade of uneven movements. I began this epilogue with a view from the pandemic with some hesitation, knowing that while the coronavirus deserves detailed ethnographic attention, other enduring health challenges—such as injury—may lose important visibility. Furthermore, I was not present at Central beyond March 2020. Still, what I witnessed in the trauma ward in the time before the pandemic echoes through the transformations wrought by COVID-19. That is to say, this book has argued that traffic's double edges of vitality and lethality constitute medicine itself.

Through lifelines, traumatic injury and trauma medicine entail unequal movements that are embodied, emplaced, and biopolitical. Lifelines constitute and transform the traffic of trauma and reveal alternatives to thinking trauma and its care only in terms of either stillness or speed. Through unevenly distributed gestural practices, lifelines may confer improvement, and they may spark unintended effects. Their motions are also signs, signs that mark how injurious events like traumatic injury can generate life even as they exhaust life, and how medicine moves and gets moved by social and political realities. Each of the book's chapters has traced lifelines of trauma medicine through practices of carrying, shifting, visiting, tracing, breathing, seeing, dissecting, and recovering. Throughout, differences in embodied movements demonstrate how injury is relational, temporal, and spatial. The crisis of the public hospital in India and elsewhere is a crisis of movement, often situated between—but rarely settled at—poles of absolute stuckness and totalizing flow. The politics of medicine and public health, then, is a politics of differences in movement. These differences are matters to be described rather than assumed.

The claims outlined at the book's beginning—that lifelines are embodied, infrastructural, and narrative—prompt questions about the broader resonance of this book's findings. The first concerns the ways that wounds form a site for theorizing sociality. What might it mean to account for dilemmas of health from within their scenes of movement? How might wound culture be understood as a condition of contemporary life? To address these questions requires grappling with the qualities that expand and constrict the movements of wounds, and locating trauma in motion.

Second, it is crucial to question how trauma's spaces of treatment operate as sociopolitical spaces in ways beyond formal location. While trauma may be thought to be frozen inside the body, it can be better understood as a moving milieu. This is a claim on the kinetics of health-care access and delivery. To understand how public hospitals shoulder the burden of a health crisis requires closer attention to the unequal conditions of movement that enable a crisis to enter, pass through, and leave the clinic. Many of the cases in this book are cases of imminent death that were first brought to private facilities first, only to be shifted to hospitals like Central because patients cannot afford private-sector treatment costs. These delays are deadly. They mark out the cityness of the city hospital, insofar as the inequalities of urban space are not static; they actively shape mobilities and the vital conditions movements might create. Delays—stutters in movement—are also a signal: the lifelines of public medicine cannot be thought apart from their relations to privatized landscapes of care. Clinical motion, then, is motion in differential relation to capital and access.

Finally, there is the question of narrative. Matters of voice, the availability of story, the experience of being spoken to and for, and multiple and sometimes competing forms of inquiry—especially among medicine and law—inflect the ethnographic scenes of these pages. Movement structures the relationship between crisis and narrative, and between calamity and ethnography. These relations require close attention to when stories widen or constrict, how illness narratives get pluralized, and how narration may work by proxy. They also require accounting for the ethnographer's uncertain proximities to these scenes, whether in words, sketches, or other modes of ethnographic attention.

Ultimately, the potentials of lifelines lie in their qualities of differential movement. Local repertoires of movement gain vital value through medicine's moves. Lifelines constitute persons as patients in terms of punctuation, convergence, rhythm, and tempo. The specific forms of lifelines vary, from translocation to adjustments in place, and they may be different in terms of intensity and pace. Across gestural forms, movements are foundational to the flux of life under threat. Neither the thing called "the wound" nor the thing called "surviving" stays perfectly still or at a set speed. Differences in movement are trauma's conditions of possibility and charge trauma with embodied, moving qualities after an accident has seemingly ended on the road or on the train. This traffic, a continuity of differences, connects somatic subjects to power through the medicalization of movement. This dynamic certainly extends beyond my case study of trauma to other crises of health. The power of medicine is the power of traffic: a power of moving and being moved.

———

Walter Benjamin wrote of the physiognomy of the city, an idea he coined to connect the objects and events of urban exhilaration and trauma (Buck-Morss 1991). Benjamin used the term to refer to the works of Edgar Allan Poe, in a diagnostic of urban noir where dead and anonymous bodies are a regular feature of city life. There is much to say about the colonial politics of such framings. There is also much to say about the dimensions of movement that make death apparent in Poe's writing, as in "The Masque of the Red Death" in which each of the revelers drop "in the despairing posture of his fall" (Poe 2010). For Poe, death does not simply happen; it moves. It moves through people, arresting them, felling them. As in the case of Raghu, whose fall from the train began this book, movement concretizes death; bodies drop.

Poe's account of the fictitious Red Death written in 1842 resonates with the all-too-real march of the coronavirus pandemic. One might conclude that mass mortality ends with stillness and that stories must end with the final shudder of the fall. But in keeping with the ethos of this book, I would like to conclude with the ongoingness of traffic's uneven motions. To do so is to imagine the potential for life to transition in ways other than the full stop.

Before I left Mumbai in March 2020, I spoke on the phone with the physician, artist, and poet Gieve Patel. We had hoped to meet in person, but it seemed risky, so phone it was. Patel spent a career working in public hospitals much like Central and turned toward reflections in painting and in poetry to process their scenes of impossibility. With pen and paper, I had begun drawing my ethnography in order to reckon with my ethnography; Patel inspired my interest in connecting words and images.

I asked him about a particular poem of his that moved me, entitled "Public Hospital":

How soon I've acquired it all!
It would seem an age of hesitant gestures
Awaited only this sententious month.
Autocratic poise comes natural now:
Voice sharp, glance impatient,
A busy man's look of harried preoccupation—
Not embarrassed to appear so.
My fingers deft to maneuver bodies,
Pull down clothing, strip the soul.
Give sorrow ear up to a point,
Then snub it shut.
Separate essential from suspect tales.
Weed out malingerers, accept
With patronage a steady stream
Of the underfed, pack flesh in them,
Then pack them away.

Almost,
I tell myself,
I embrace the people:
Revel in variety of eye, color, cheek, bone;
Unwelcome guest, I may visit bodies,
Touch close, cure, throw overboard
Necessities of distance, plunge,
Splice, violate,

With needle, knife, and tongue,
Wreck all my bonds in them.

At end of day,
From under the flagpole,
Watch the city streaming
By the side of my hands. (Gieve Patel 1976, 15)

Patel explained that his everyday encounters in the hospital shaped the poem, which narrates the shifting momentum of bodies. Being present with wounded bodies is kinetic: plunge, splice, violate, pack away, embrace. Medicine cascades us, tenuously, through lifelines: "Watch the city streaming / By the side of my hands."

NOTES

Introduction

1   On volatile movements, see Grosz (1994).

2   Marian Aguiar (2011) describes the train in India in terms of the affective relations among speed, life, and death. For instance, the train forms the still backdrop to the carnage of the 2008 terror attacks on Chhatrapati Shivaji Terminus and also sits still as it frames the fast-paced dancing for the closing montage of *Slumdog Millionaire*.

3   Like many of my Indian colleagues who talk to people about the Mumbai local trains, I frequently face a simple question: Why don't the doors close? Common answers include: because no institution will pay for it or because doors that can close safely while still maintaining the trains' roughly thirty-second stay at a given station are expensive and too new a technology. Air-conditioned trains with closed doors have begun to run in recent years on the Western Line. For a comprehensive history of the Mumbai rail system, see Aklekar (2014).

4   Importantly, *injury* also has a legal definition: under Section 44 of the Indian Penal Code, "the word 'injury' denotes any harm whatever illegally caused to any person, in body, mind, reputation or property." Available at https://www.indiacode.nic.in /handle/123456789/2263?sam_handle=123456789/1362.

5   The picture of mortality from road accidents comes primarily from burden-of-disease reports, which have been the linchpin of advocacy for the uptake of transport injuries as a legitimate and growing public health concern. Figures from a nationally representative survey in India based in verbal autopsy data estimated a death rate of 20.7 deaths per 100,000 people for men, and 5.7 per 100,000 for women (Hsiao et al. 2013). The global incidence of these injuries is either static or decreasing in most geographic regions, except, notably, South Asia and Africa, where they are in fact rising (India State-Level Disease Burden Initiative Road Injury Collaborators 2020). Injury prevention is an established field of public health, and roads have been in its sights for quite some time. But, increasingly, surgery has become a key domain for making sense of and sounding the alarm around road traffic injuries. This coincides with the rise of "global surgery," the christening and renaming of the enterprises of surgical outreach teams and Lancet Commissions that circulate conferences, camps set up to perform operations, white papers in journals, and on-site training visits. Here, the matter of road traffic injuries—which are technically classified as trauma—may fall under the umbrella of other types of surgical interventions, such as obstetric procedures or

neurosurgery. Questions of cost-effectiveness and feasibility, such as "Is surgery for the rich, or can surgery be done safely worldwide?" guide ways of researching injury. These different assemblies of expertise, commitment, ethics, and resources structure how the world might understand the deaths of 200,000 Indians from road traffic accidents in 2015. And like many aggregates, this number hides the specifics that matter, such as the location of deaths: 36 percent on the spot at the crash site, 11 percent during prehospital transport, and 53 percent at the hospital—with little known about postdischarge mortality and morbidity. See Gururaj (2005) and N. Roy (2017) for in-depth analyses of mortality statistics. Also see V. Patel et al. (2011); and I. Roberts, Mohan, and Abbasi (2002). On global injury burdens, see Meara et al. (2015).

6 See Mohanan (2013) for a study of the "shock" of accidents on household economies in India; Manoj Mohanan delineates how in the face of serious injury of a person in the household, families are able to smooth out spending in many domains, but debt remains an important and common way to do so. Also see Krishna (2011). A study from North India estimates the prevalence of catastrophic expenditure resulting from injuries (primarily road traffic injuries) at 22.2 percent of participants sampled for the study; catastrophic health expenditure refers to expenditure on health care above 30% of consumption spending; see Prinja et al. (2019).

7 On "the interval" as a critical space-time form, see Fisch (2018).

8 See Sundaram (2009) on how discourses of urban degradation move from decrying the failures of infrastructures to proposing neoliberal solutions.

9 My thanks to Nikhil Anand for this provocation.

10 Lewis Mumford's *Technics and Civilization* (2010) proposes technics as a rubric for understanding the relationship between technology's affordances and its damages to human life. Mumford recounts different ways that medicine itself has a technics. From antiseptics like carbolic acid that derive from coal to the light bulbs in X-rays, medicine itself works through intimacies with technological shifts, intimacies that Jennifer Terry (2017) frames as "attachments" in her case study of contemporary biomedicine's entanglements with war-making technology. My use of *traffic* gestures to these attachments between medicine and violence but makes a particular claim about the centrality of movement and mobility to such attachments. On writing violence, see Nelson (2009).

Theorists of the accident in cultural theory often fetishize the agent of wounding itself as the accident's primary source (Figlio 1983), and gesture to problems of compensation as an accident's core consequence (Figlio 1982). Many appeal to Paul Virilio's argument that technology embeds its own disaster, what Virilio (2007) terms "the original accident," such that the shipwreck lies in the invention of the ship. This is a suggestive framing, but it is too static for my needs. It is premised on looking backward, not forward to the problem of living on with trauma. This is why I can only take technology-focused structural claims so far: they make it difficult to remain open to surprises in the moving after-ness of injury, in forms that may not replicate what seemed preordained. See Fisch (2018); Jain (2006); and Siegel (2014).

11 These might be understood as "shifting poetic forms" of the road (Stewart 2014), such that infrastructures reveal their aesthetics. This builds on, but also differs from,

urban theory that takes generalized movement as its central assumption (Thrift 2008). For Penny Harvey and Hannah Knox (2015), incidents of harm on roads create "ambivalences" and open up questions about the difference between reckoning infrastructure through its prior relations of neglect, on one hand, and its futures of risk management, on the other. But because I am immersed in the trauma ward where the present moment of an accident is still unfolding, my approach is necessarily different.

12 On health care in colonial Bombay, see Ramanna (2002, 2012). That Central Hospital is a postindependence institution means that both oral and written histories of its work bear different kinds of attention to British colonial power than the histories of other large hospitals in Mumbai that opened before independence.

13 A set of complementary ideas to wound culture are those of "signature injury" and "woundscapes," as detailed in Terry (2009).

14 The figure of the flaneur cannot hold as an exemplar for southern somatic urbanisms if one follows Sundaram's claim that the bodies in the cities of the Global South are in a foundational relationship to traffic accidents; the flaneur is already embodied in relation to the environment. What I suggest here is that the environment is in relation to the body, such that to walk is to be exposed to planned infrastructural violence even as it is to enjoy the city and to move for life. One must move to live, but doing so comes with a significant chance of injury, which sparks movements anew. The flaneur, discussed at length in Walter Benjamin's commentary on Charles Baudelaire, also inhabits much of the critical theory of "everyday life." This occurs, notably, in the work of Michel de Certeau, whose essay "Walking in the City" has the flaneur guide the reader through political possibilities and constrictions (de Certeau 2011). De Certeau elaborates themes of habitability, exile, and visibility in speaking and walking, deeming the latter to be poetic. Walking is one form of what de Certeau calls a "tactic," a practice integral to everyday life. In urban space, such a life is based on what we might describe in shorthand as the shock of the urban in Benjamin (W. Benjamin 1968; Buck-Morss 1992) and Georg Simmel (1903). Yet Lauren Berlant resists certain ingrained ways of thinking the urban and shock, by asserting that such "everyday life theory no longer describes how most people live" (2011, 8). Here Berlant aims to depart from a model of life based on the "cognitive overload in the urban everyday" (9). One challenge is to read this insight alongside, through, and sometimes against assertions of body/city reverberations; as Simmel notes, "Man does not end with the limits of his body or the area comprising his immediate activity. Rather is the range of the person constituted by the sum of effects emanating from him temporally and spatially. In the same way, a city consists of its total effects which extend beyond its immediate confines" (1964, 419). For a different genealogy of shock's epistemic force and location in war, see Geroulanos and Meyers (2018).

15 Michel Foucault adapted the term *milieu* from Georges Canguilhem to address "the space in which a series of uncertain elements unfold" (Foucault 2009, 20). For Canguilhem (1991), *milieu* refers to the contextual environment of an organism. For Canguilhem, notions of normality and pathology are relative and may vary according to

what gets counted as "the environment." In Foucault's rendering, a milieu is "what is needed to account for action at a distance of one body on another" and "the medium of an action and the element in which it circulates" (2009, 20–21). I draw on facets of both definitions to clarify trauma as medium, action, and object of relational relocation, fixation, runaround, and feedback loop. See Annemarie Mol's (2002, 122–23) reading of Canguilhem, particularly on the matter of norms, and Veena Das's (2015) approach to norms.

16 On tracing, see Napolitano (2015). As I explored in my previous work on metabolism and metabolic illness (Solomon 2016), bodies and environments may not respect hard-and-fast inside/outside bounds. I make a similar claim here: traffic and trauma operate as connected modes of embodiment through unsteady and uneven passages and set the terms of how the world gets inside bodies and how bodies exist within the world.

17 Berlant's engagement with shifts and adjustments in action is meant to assess particular qualities of everyday sociality rather than specific internal states of a body (as Lefebvre does). Disturbances allow Berlant to analyze social and political tectonic historic changes—such as the attrition of the social support net in the United States—as they manifest in interpersonal encounters that may not scale up to "an event" as such.

18 The history of ambulances in India is mostly traced as the history of the St. John Ambulance service. For a contemporary ethnography on ambulance services in the United States, see Jusionyte (2018).

19 Stories "find cracks in the order of things, then wedge themselves into the cracks and shape them with the resonance of other stories" (Lepselter 2016, 55).

20 Lauren Berlant and Diane Nelson taught me this, a painful gift. I miss you.

Chapter One: Carrying

1 On gesture, see Birdwhistell (1952) and Manning (2016).

2 The paper cited here was published as a state-level EMS service began in Maharashtra. The authors anticipate the rollout of the service and find its potential a relatively "moot point" because of the high cost of funding the system. Instead, the authors recommend "reinforcing the existing system of informal providers of taxi drivers and police and with training, funding quick transport with taxes on roads and automobile fuels, and regulating the private ambulance providers, [which] may prove to be more cost-effective in a culture where sharing and helping others is not just desirable, but is necessary for overall economic survival" (N. Roy et al. 2010, 150). The speedy response desired is the transgression of traffic. This would ensure that the injured do not die en route, a phenomenon that occurs enough to merit news attention, although the more likely (and, in some ways, more complex) doom scenario is that an injured person's vitals become so muted while in transit to the hospital that, upon arrival, the systemic damage is too extensive to remedy fully. Much of the choreography of ambulances in India both derives from and continues to relate to pregnancy, labor, and delivery.

3   One might understand this as "the interval," the space-time analytic Michael Fisch (2018) develops in his ethnography of Tokyo's subway system. For Fisch, the interval denotes the time in between trains arriving at a station. The critical interval in play in my own work is the time between event and care, which makes intervals necessarily somatic.

4   Appadurai's use of "mobile civil forms" refers to grassroots and transnational nongovernmental organizations and research action networks; he is not specifically referring to mobility in its most literal sense. But his gesture to the mutually influential movements of thought, capital, and politics is helpful to think through in terms of the mortal situations where localization and fixity *within* mobile forms are at stake.

5   Local political parties in Mumbai invest in ambulances too, perhaps most visibly in the Shiv Sena ambulance fleet (Katzenstein, Mehta, and Thakkar 1997). Jim Masselos suggests that Shiv Sena ambulances asserted a "locality presence" similar to party branch offices (*shakhas*), "as if its members were protected by a larger and caring entity" (2007, 181). A connected explanatory framework is premised on the intersection of death, grief, and iconicity. This explanation, which circulated among some physicians in my field sites, is based on the idea that Shiv Sena scion Bal Thackeray supported the ambulance service in order to commemorate the 1995 death of his wife, Meena, from cardiac arrest and the 1996 death of his son Bindumadhav from a road accident. Here the ambulance's aid to Mumbaikars emerges from the gendered tragedies of a political dynasty. Thus, even before an ambulance attends to a call, it is invested with a deep historical, material, and semiotic charge, a charge that both reflects and transforms how infrastructural transitions mark the politics of inequality.

6   Data on the specific locations of accidents are often not widely available; instead, aggregate figures provide the basis for trend analysis in Mumbai and elsewhere (Mohan, Tiwari, and Mukherjee 2016).

7   Ieva Jusionyte (2018) employs a different approach, one in which the anthropologist trains as an EMT. This methodological pathway was not possible for me. The 108 ambulances in Mumbai and Maharashtra are not always staffed by EMTs as such; they are often staffed by doctors, including doctors of AYUSH medicine—Ayurveda and Unani medicine (BAMS/BUMS graduates; BAMS is Bachelor of Ayurveda Medicine and Surgery; BUMS is Bachelor of Unani Medicine and Surgery). This is part of a broader effort by the state to employ nonallopathic physicians through government schemes. Some organizations recognize these doctors as EMTs once they have been trained in prehospital care protocols, especially by public-private partnership training organizations that train in basic life support, cardiac emergencies, pregnancy, and trauma at the EMT Basic, Intermediate, and Paramedic levels. There is a slippage among *EMT*, *paramedic*, and *doctor* here. Some EMTs may have nursing or pharmacy educational backgrounds and are thought to be assets to emergency response because of their formal clinical training. Also, the landscape of provision is multilayered: in Mumbai the 108 ambulance is free and does pickup calls for emergencies; by contrast, the 1298 service handles interfacility transfers (e.g., between nursing homes and hospitals), and this service is not free.

8 My sincere thanks to Dr. Barry Saunders for thinking this through with me.

9 The history of emergency telephone numbers like 108 in Mumbai is a history of signals and, furthermore, a history closely linked to the railways. See D. Kumar (1997) for an explanation of the history of the telegraph in India in the mid-1800s and the links between the telegraph and the railways.

10 There is a contrast here between *public* and *janta*: the former refers to the figure of the crowd; the latter is more a figure of the population.

11 Maybe it is the shared feature of logistics that offers the possibility for jokes about ambulances: the challenge of how to get from the site of injury to the site of treatment before someone dies. Logistics become the idealized form of resolving the tensions between death and mobility, as several ethnographies of medicine's movements explain. In his study of Doctors without Borders (Médecins sans frontières), anthropologist Peter Redfield (2013) writes about emergency vehicles such as ambulances and supply trucks as part of the "vital mobility" of the organization's efforts. Redfield describes one moment during a relief mission in Uganda when a medical relief supply truck experienced a flat tire: "The hole deflated not just a tire, but also the larger medical mission invested in the vehicle; when brought to a standstill we were simply another group of people on a rural road with a lot to carry," he writes (71). In one moment, a truck is just a truck, and the demands of conveyance come into stark relief.

12 In Indian historiography, ambulances appear as signs of different social forms. They articulate British presence, particularly in the World War II era, which is when emergency medicine solidly crossed over from the military front lines to civilian contexts. Mumbai has its own vernacular history of ambulances, beginning with the national St. John ambulance in the nineteenth and early twentieth centuries, later taken up by the Bombay Parsi Panchayat. They articulate gender as well; as historian Mridula Ramanna (2008) notes, women physicians were "intermediaries" who sometimes served as doctors in the Red Cross ambulances of the early twentieth century in colonial Bombay.

13 At the time of my research, an NGO called SaveLife grew increasingly influential across India. Its primary aim was to reform a set of laws that prohibited the involvement of bystanders in accident events and more generally to change public awareness about the consequences of intervening. It successfully lobbied India's lower parliamentary house (the Lok Sabha) to change the national Motor Vehicles Act to include text on the importance of Good Samaritans. This work also resulted in the creation of a Good Samaritan Act. For a list of ongoing policy documents related to the Good Samaritan Act, see Ministry of Road Transport and Highways, "Good Samaritan," n.d., accessed January 13, 2022, https://morth.nic.in/good-samaritan. Much of this debate centers on changing the practice of the *Panchnama*—the police record of statements by witnesses, or *panchas*.

14 There are different terms for the person who carries luggage at India's train stations. A formal Marathi term is *bharvahak*, "carrier" or "loader," and there is also the Urdu-derived term *mazoor*, "worker," but these are used less often. When I would ask for terms other than *hamaal*, some people offered *coolie*. *Coolie* may be used conversationally in

everyday speech but also has derogatory force (Bahadur 2013; Bear 2007). In clinical settings, *hamaal* is far more common. Local-language news accounts often reference "accident *hamaals*" in stories about railway injuries, suggesting their commonplace relation to train-related injuries. Formally, *hamaals* are assigned to class D in the Indian Railways employment structure, which also includes cleaners (*safaiwalas*).

15 This can align the work of the *hamaal* in some senses with the body work of *aghoris*, Hindu ascetics who attend to the charnel grounds. See Parry (1994) and Barrett (2008). As Jonathan Parry and Maurice Bloch note, "Having reached beyond carnality, [*aghoris*] bombastically declare themselves impervious to the most polluting substances and actions" (1982, 37).

16 These announcements were recorded in the early 1990s by a woman selected for her "soft" voice. See Chaubey (2013).

17 Luc Boltanski (1999) delineates categories of persons who are Good Samaritans, in both the biblical story and the philosophy that Hannah Arendt derives from it. For Boltanski, this adds up to the politics of pity and the politics of charity.

18 See Srivastava (2013) on the figure of the informant in detective work and Jain (2006) on the figure of the bystander in American injury law.

19 "Uska smell jo hai uska vo jaata nahin hai gaadi se, toh usse dusre patient ke liye bhi, acche patient ke liye bhi buraai hai, aur hume bhi gaaḍi me bethne ke liye buraai hai."

20 "Woh dash ho gaya, phir main ne dekha hi nahin toh mai us samay dekne bhi nahin gaya, itna darr gaya tha main uss time par. Uske baad phir aise hi, jaise habit ho jati hai aur main toh yeh hai ki main sikh gaya line peh ki jiska samay ata hai woh hi jata hai. Jiska time ho gaya ussi ka accident aisa hota hai."

21 On habits of movement, see Grosz (2013).

Chapter Two: Shifting

1 *Shift*, a noun imported from English into Hindi and Marathi, also can refer to a duration of assigned work, as in an evening shift or a morning shift. Shifts are what everyone in the ward must do, patients and providers both.

2 A midsized secondary hospital like Maitri operates with an annual budget of 554 million rupees (US$8.34 million). A more specialized tertiary public hospital like Central, by contrast, can operate with an annual budget of nearly 3 billion rupees (US$45.2 million). The BMC's (Brihanmumbai Mahanagar Palika, abbreviated in English as BMC for the municipal government's former name of the Bombay Municipal Corporation) coffers are quite full, as journalists regularly point out, but the money is just not dispensed to those who need it. However, the municipal budget for health care for 2018–19 was US$540 million (3,637 crore of rupees), which is a marked increase, owing in no small part to advocacy efforts and scandals about the state of disrepair of facilities at all levels. My designation of levels of trauma centers stems from the ways that Indian trauma surgeons frame the hospital system, which is based on the designations of the American College of Surgeons. This is one way

in which trauma care at specialty centers in India has been influenced by ATLS (advanced trauma life support) trainings.

3   On the ways that science and medicine become the spaces and contexts for state claim making, see Cohen (1999) and Visvanathan (1987).

4   Take, for example, the case of a day laborer who arrived at a municipal hospital casualty ward with fever and body aches. He knew from earlier lab tests that he had low platelet counts; the casualty medical officer advised his admission to the hospital for treatment. But then the decision got reversed. Another doctor informed him he would have to go home, with some medicines to take on his own. The man went to the media to complain, and a local newspaper carried the story. "As I couldn't afford a private hospital, I opted for a BMC-run hospital. . . . Just because we are poor, don't we have the right to live? How can the hospital be so irresponsible? I am the breadwinner of my family, so I can't afford to die," he said (Chakraborty 2017).

5   These were the costs of care at Maitri during my fieldwork: paper for casualty exam, 10 rupees; X-ray, 30 rupees; sonography, 100 rupees; and CT, 1,200 rupees.

6   Another approach to triage concerns thresholds (Petryna 2002, 120). Adriana Petryna details how policymakers make decisions based on specific markers, something that is resonant for my case study as well. In her study of nuclear disaster, it is dose. In my study of traumatic injury, it is often systolic blood pressure.

7   There are also technical names for the positions. For instance, dresser is *vran upcharak*, but I never heard this used in speech; instead, the English-derived terms are used.

8   Rudolf Mrázek writes of concentration camps, "The enclosure that worked as a membrane was not merely a technological device—a device of the future at least. The membrane had become organic. It grew into the camp people's bodies" (2015, 10). The Mumbai casualty ward, too, is like a living membrane that stays with people through their sensory and bureaucratic apperceptions, which are inseparable.

9   This metaphor echoes the research of anthropologist Lorna Rhodes, who conducted ethnography in a US urban emergency psychiatric ward, which staff and patients also depict as a funnel. These appeals to movement lead Rhodes to conclude that hospital staff and those they treat "experienced their relationships to [clinical] disposition as a movement among individually negotiated options" (1991, 41).

10 I have translated *taklif* as *affliction*; "What's troubling you?" might be more apt. However, *taklif* is a capacious phenomenological and cosmological rubric, as Veena Das (2015) demonstrates, and I believe *affliction* better captures the gravity of the matter even in the punctuated space of the casualty queue.

11 On the power formations in play as medicine itself shifts to diagnostic inquiry in the clinical encounter, see Foucault (1975). For a response to Michel Foucault's notion of the technology of the self in the space of the clinic, see V. Das (2003).

12 The doctors speak primarily in Marathi, given that this is a Mumbai municipality hospital where Marathi use is both the norm and mandate, but they and the nurses use Hindi frequently too.

13 Often the pharmacist/chemist in a neighborhood dispensary winds up being the source of both pharmaceutical supply and pharmaceutical knowledge. See Peterson

(2014) and K. Sunder Rajan (2017). On the history of the fraught relationship between biomedicine and "other" traditions of medicine in South Asia, see Mukharji (2011) and Pinto (2008b).

14 See Mukharji (2016, 63) on medicine in India rendered as a form of consumption, which makes it an ideal place to study class positions historically.

15 On the politics of public medicine as a sociopolitical good, see Brotherton (2012).

16 The MLC cases share some properties with the other legal cases that appear in the casualty ward: police custody cases. The Code of Criminal Procedure (Sections 53 and 54) gives police officers the power to subject arrested persons to medical examination in order to produce evidence, and it gives arrested persons the right to demand a medical examination for purposes of disproving the grounds of the arrest. In the casualty ward, most staff understand the custody exam procedure to be a safeguard against police violence once someone is held in jail, for if the exam shows no injuries but injuries happen while in police custody, there is a record of evidence that the arrested person can appeal to.

17 It is true that this request asks that the most severe punishment be levied. But the context is one where, often, all that people want at base is to ensure that the police take the case seriously. Everyone knows that the probability of the case going anywhere is low. So sometimes appeals to severity in utterance are more than anything else an appeal that the case be recognized in the first place. It can take extreme language to get the state to budge, or to feel as if you might come closer to accomplishing that.

18 Restraint in clinical settings in India is undergoing reflection and potentially revision, particularly in light of the Mental Healthcare Act, 2017. See Raveesh and Lepping (2019).

19 One exception is for patients with evidence of a head injury; the anesthetist may want them propped up to manage intracranial pressure, but this presumes that the person can be put on an adjustable trolley, which may not be available.

20 A related term one hears is *badmaash*, "of bad livelihood." See Singha (2015, 242).

21 She thought Aamir Khan's character in *Rangeela* was a quintessential rowdy. Others thought that Gabbar Singh in the film *Sholay* was a rowdier rowdy. And, they reminded me, there was *Rowdy Rathore*.

22 For Thomas Blom Hansen, the hooligan is key to understanding the microgeographic landscape of relations between Mumbai's mostly Hindu police force and Muslim inhabitants of the city. *Hooligan* can turn into *Muslim* quickly, a semantic shift that hypervisibilizes Muslims through police profiling and everyday rumor (Hansen 2001, 245).

23 One of the challenges in estimating survival advantage is thinking through comparisons in trauma registries, with the US National Trauma Data Bank often serving as the comparison point for studies elsewhere. Epidemiologists and biostatisticians working on creating an Indian national trauma registry suggest that strong predictive models for survival can emerge when aggregate data from India are used. See Gerdin et al. (2016).

Chapter Three: Visiting

1 The ward has specific gendered labor structures, from the feminization of nursing work and the work of sweepers (all of whom are female, except for one male nurse) to the masculinization of the work of orderlies and ward boys. Doctors, nurses, and staff tend to refer to the kin of the injured person through collective nouns: as *relatives*, *sagewale* (kin, relatives), or *saathwale* (those who accompany someone). See chapter 2.

2 See Kannan (2014) for detailed analysis of the specific judgments, legal precedents, and dilemmas that constitute the grounds of medical negligence and compensation in India.

3 Household economies appear in other ways as well. At the moment of either discharge to the general ward (if the patient is stable) or death (if the patient did not make it out of the trauma ward), the nurse is responsible for informing family members of the total charges for the hospital stay. She does not collect the money (there is a separate cashier in another part of the hospital), but nonetheless she announces the bill. These situations can be the grounds for producing what gets counted as class and caste markers; in other words, differences between people in the ward sometimes break down as differences between patients' family members and everyone else.

4 On the expansive ways that "bad" families inflect life in India, especially through the rubric of *seva* (selfless service), see Cohen (2000).

5 This is in contrast to the pervasive sense of a loss of home that Anne Allison (2013, 78), drawing on Gaston Bachelard, analyzes as a fragile existentialism for Japanese under regimes of precarity.

Chapter Four: Tracing

1 Throughout this chapter and others, I capitalize *Unknown* as a reminder that it is a category of person in the hospital. I considered giving the unidentified patients pseudonyms and extending to them the same form of identification in the ethnography as I have granted the nameable persons in this book. However, I wish to insist on their status as Unknowns to capture their unique situations and to continually assess if, when, and how those situations register with the hospital. It strikes me as a counterproductive act of hubris to assume that the ethnographer who assigns a name resolves the situation. Instead, my approach is to insist on the Unknown, in order to query when and how medicine moves in response and to build a politics of recognition from there.

2 On the power of documentation, see McKay (2017).

3 Road accidents fall under the jurisdiction of the Mumbai Police. By contrast, railway accidents compel the involvement of railway authorities. In Mumbai railway policing is enacted by two connected agencies: the Government Railway Police (GRP) and the Railway Protection Force (RPF). The RPF is charged with protecting railway property ("watch and ward"). The GRP, by contrast, is a law-and-order police force. Accidents on railways fall under the jurisdiction of the GRP. While these two forces of railway policing—the RPF and the GRP—are organizationally separate, both have

histories inflected by railway accidents, as Laura Bear describes in her account of the 1854 Indian Railway Act. A series of accidents in 1850 on the East Indian Railways prompted the colonial government to institute norms of policing, but the objects of the policing were Indians themselves, specifically "the inadequacies of the Indian and potentially wayward European/Eurasian railway worker" (Bear 2007, 69). In essence, while contemporary railway accidents—the ones I describe in this book—tend to cleave into the parties of the victim, the constable in charge, and potentially the accused, earlier iterations of accidents on the railways distilled different questions of blame, labor, and willingness to carry out colonial authorities' mandates.

4 In the trauma ward, two terms are commonly used for Unknown patients. The first is *anoḷakhi*, "unrecognized," which appears more in written form—this is the term that police often use in official inquiries, whether it be an open police case for a missing person or a death inquest. The second is the English word *unknown*, which is coupled conversationally with Hindi or Marathi, e.g., *Unknown patient ala*, meaning "an Unknown patient has come." The English certainly marks the imprint of colonial administration. Other terms may be used in daily speech in the city for unfamiliar persons; in Marathi these might include *aprichit*, meaning "unfamiliar," or *adnyaat*, meaning "nameless." But in the ward, *Unknown*, lexically, always seemed to have "patient" as its object of description: *Unknown (patient)*. Furthermore, the injury category is always tied to the name: *Unknown Male (Railway Traffic Accident)*. Names may not be known, but accident types are, because these are knowledge forms the ward generates and assigns.

5 Nancy Rose Hunt (2015) draws on the work of Georges Canguilhem, and specifically how Canguilhem turned to Bachelard to understand how imagination can be inexhaustible and therefore defy physiology—a "function without an organ," as Canguilhem put it (1991, 145). One might put these insights into conversations about the ways brain injury can destabilize extant ways of knowing trauma, as cases such as that of Phineas Gage exemplify.

6 The GCS has its issues, but it is relatively simple to teach and to use. Retrospective commentaries on the scale's decades of clinical use note that as a general index it is relatively reliable, meaning that the sum total of the three scores is useful for diagnosis and prediction. Utility and reliability may be harder to achieve within the subdivided indices of eye activity, motor function, and verbal response. Consequently, some physicians urge caution in making clinical decisions based on an E, M, or V score alone. The GCS is "reductionist yet standardized," so you lose precision but you gain a quick form of understanding. In trauma, quick understanding is vital (Laureys, Bodart, and Gosseries 2014).

Notably, the GCS is not the only scale that clinicians use for assessing consciousness. In Central's ward, it is the most common. Other scales used by doctors at Central include the AVPU scoring system, which measures "Alert / Verbal / Pain / Unresponsive," and also the Level of Consciousness scale. Many senior surgeons who had been working in the ward before the systematic introduction of the GCS still use the Level of Consciousness scale in their heads, even while they train their own residents in the GCS and write GCS scores in medical records.

7 The reference spans a variety of genres, from the cinematic (e.g., the 1983 film *Hero*) to the technological, especially the Honda Hero brand of motorbikes.

8 This aphorism also refers to a song title in the 1973 film *Suraj Aur Chanda*.

9 A claim can refer to identification, in terms of tying state demands for knowing its population to individual bodies, as in the mass biometric program of Aadhaar (Cohen 2017). A claim also can be a question of recognition, of seeing the other as a familiar (Cohen 2001; Taylor 2008).

10 See Geschiere (2003) on "the dark side of kinship."

11 On the history of police surveillance in India, see Singha (2015); for an ethnographic account, see Jauregui (2016).

12 Terminology matters here. It is important to me that Arif upholds *trace karna*, "to trace," as the basis of his work. *Jasus*, "detective" in Hindi, can also mean "spy." This can be the work of formal state espionage or more everyday kinds of inquisitive meddling (*jasusigiri*), like a powerful elder (e.g., a parent, landlord, or relative) rifling through one's things to ferret out potential proof of misdoing (e.g., cigarettes, nonvegetarian food).

13 Hindi allows for the majestic plural. Arif's statement "hamaara usko maa baap hai" can be read as either "I am his parent" or "We are his parents," and "hamaara pe-shant" as either "my patient" or "our patient." The choice of *I* or *we* in the first instance is the difference between him and the police, and in the second instance the difference between him alone and the inclusion of me in the picture. Place—and emplacement—are critically important too. Arif emplaces himself interior to the case by being interior to the hospital. A different way of saying this is that he can make a claim on "my patient," a possessive claim, only by entering the ward. The proximity between law and medicine here is worked out through the intimacies a police constable can achieve by entering and spending time in hospital space. The hospital becomes the site where the law, via tracing, can be enacted interiorly.

14 Political scientist Jinee Lokaneeta (2020) has argued that the forensic techniques of the Indian police reflect a "structural contingency" of state power, at the nexus of policing's pastoral and repressive functions. Forensic techniques reveal moments of the everydayness of policing, and contexts to understand how police officers generate a sense of pragmatism and purpose. Lokaneeta considers these in the context of the avowed objectivity of truth-making techniques, from narcoanalysis to forensic psychology. Taken together, these forms reveal "the state's flawed attempt at an art of government based on a rational regime" (18), particularly in the contemporary context of Indian police reforms. On forensics in South Asia and elsewhere, see Burney (2000); Burney and Hamlin (2019); Carroll (2002); Mitra (2020); Mulla (2014); Rosen (1953); Saunders (2010); Sengoopta (2004); Sharafi (2019, 2020); and Siegel (2014). Reading bodies for signs is also a long-standing tradition in anthropology (Bateson and Mead 1942), a tradition inseparable from forms of colonial power.

15 On the complex social worlds forged at railway stations, see Steinberg (2019).

16 On the epistemology of detective fiction, see Ginzburg and Davin (1980). The cross-hatched frameworks of detection and modernity have particular resonance in postcolonial South Asia. On the origin and development of detective fiction in India and

the figure of the *jasus*, rendered as detective and as spy in the making of India through information, see Bayly (1996) and Orsini (2004). Also see Creekmur (2014); Gopalan (2013); Khair (2008); and Mukherjee (2003).

17 See De León (2015) on the ways that grief and closure can and cannot align in the context of finding missing bodies. On the question of responsibility after death, see Allison (2017) and V. Das (2006).

18 Faces collate in everyday political campaign photos, from parties small to large, and from events magnificent to banal. Earlier passersby in the nineteenth and twentieth centuries would see the lineup of faces also as a police lineup, such that the historical resonance among colonial forensic technologies, crime sheets, mug shots, and police inquiry is there too. There is resonance here with the history of collating faces in medicine, one that Barry Saunders (2010, 154) traces back to the "rogue galleries" of British police investigation and to the work of Francis Galton. There is also the specificity of the face as the provocation of detective work. See, for example, Doyle (2008) and Moretti (2005). On the forensic politics of the face, see M'Charek (2018).

19 For Ravi Sundaram, the fear and anxiety of urban noir entails "moving between the body of the crowd, traffic, neighbourhoods, and also in the material traffic of images and objects. It is the ability to move rapidly between unequal social groups, spaces and media that gives the contemporary experience of urban fear an edgy, neurological feeling" (2009, 31). Edginess is just one of many affects that scholars of Indian cinema name as characteristic of the genre of film noir in South Asia. For Ranjani Mazumdar, for instance, film noir in India evokes a perceptual breakdown, as filmmakers create atmospheres of paralysis, desperation, and vigilante action in cities (2011; also see Mazumdar 2008). Mazumdar's analysis of the film *Dombivli Fast* exemplifies this imaginative form. Also see Prakash (2010b).

20 Often the endgame of closing a crime case is an effort to address the deformation of the civil, and the collapse between inner and outer worlds. See Cohen (2009).

Seeing

1 See Cohen (2013a) on the red light outside the surgery OT as the sign of sovereignty in India. On the training of young surgeons, see Bosk (2003).

2 Histories of anesthesia are inextricable from histories of gender and race. See Buck-Morss (1992); Duden (1998); and Owens (2017).

Chapter Five: Breathing

1 The most cited and debated case anchoring euthanasia debates in India is the case of Aruna Shanbaug. While space does not permit a full analysis of this case, it is worth noting that Shanbaug's case was not one of ventilation; it was one of a feeding tube. Her case also began when she was raped by an orderly at the hospital where she

worked as a nurse; the circumstances of sexual assault that underpinned her persistent vegetative state were often ironed out in media reports. Such absences constituted a relationship between gender and life support. They allowed her body and the care that nurses devoted to it to bridge court cases surrounding quandaries about mechanical ventilators for patients who are ill and injured. The elision of sexual violence, in this case, allows bioethics to become thinkable. See Gursahani (2011) and Nair (2016).

2   On breath as a capacity for survival in the face of state violence, see Sharpe (2016) on "aspiration" and Crawley (2016) on breath as a critical aesthetic of Pentecostalism.

3   On the distribution of clinical labor among families in India, see Van Hollen (2003).

4   Clinical researchers refer to the delirium experienced by patients in the ICU by several different names. But as Brian McGuire and colleagues point out, "the supposition that there are features intrinsic to the ICU environment that can cause a psychiatric syndrome has rarely been critically discussed" (2000, 909). They question the overlay of space and compromised consciousness. They argue that instead of "ICU psychosis" or "ICU syndrome," what is really at stake here is *delirium*, and that its location in the ICU is important but only part of the story.

5   Kaufman (2000) elaborates how a persistent vegetative state creates the quandary of distinguishing between feeling pain and not feeling pain. On the tenuous boundaries between dying and the law, see Buchbinder (2018a, 2018b, 2019).

6   Anesthetists carefully monitor arterial blood gas reports and coordinate those figures with specific levels of inspired oxygen (FiO_2). *Ventilation* is a generic term for specific modes of the ventilator: the anesthetist can set it to produce continuous positive airway pressure, positive end expiratory pressure, or several other effects.

7   I am sometimes asked if I ever saw doctors take someone off a ventilator without a weaning stage in cases that did not meet brain death or persistent vegetative state standards. The answer is unequivocally no. See Kaufman (2015) on the ways that US hospitals can produce seemingly infinite options in the face of persistent vegetative states and Tercier (2005, 226) on the "slow code."

8   While this moment of speaking again was certainly momentous for Anand, I also took it as a broader sign of recovery in a place where the prevalence of injuries means that many people will be experiencing something similar. In this way, breath-as-voice makes the space of history, as Rudolf Mrázek notes: "Voices and noises . . . produce a *historical* space" (2010, 243).

9   "Woh zindagi ka sabse mera alag time tha."

10   "Mera saamne se kitna body gaya only three people see clear. Sirf three people bach ke gaya, baki sab jo bhi ventilator pe the, they were dead."

11   "Usko jo body hai mene dekha nahin toh mujhe abhi bhi feel hai ki woh kahi aur chala gaya hai, usko jaga ho gaya hai aur who mujhe chodke chali gayi hai, her father's house."

12   "Ventilator pe koi bhi patient jaata hai toh mujhe achcha nahin lagta hai, ventilator is second time birth. Ventilator pe jaane ke baad mein woh aadmi agar bach gaya toh uska dobara janam hai." There is much to think with here in terms of the invocation of the second birth, a form of social mattering to caste Hindus.

13 As Veena Das explains, sometimes the problem with narrative isn't a failure of the narrative of the self; instead, it is "how words are not found meaningful by others" (2015, 104).

Chapter Six: Dissecting

1 The four technical categories of exit are discharge, step-down, discharge against medical advice, and death.

2 Timmermans's argument rests on a study undertaken in a coroner's office, likely owing to the structure of forensic pathology in the United States, where such offices exist outside of hospitals. In India, by contrast, a postmortem is conducted *within* the hospital campus in many settings. It may be the same hospital where the patient died, or if no coroner's unit exists at that hospital, the body will be transferred to a larger hospital with a forensic medical team, a transfer for which the family must arrange and pay. Even before a postmortem begins, then, there may have been pivotal shifts. Further, Timmermans's analysis focuses on the science of the postmortem itself; that is his aim, and he attends to it well. Yet this tight focus cannot grapple with the ways that the deceased and their family may have *already* experienced investigations, tests, and inquiries while the person was alive and undergoing treatment.

3 The white sheet as the sign of death has deep semiotic resonance in India. For a haunting example from Hindi literature, see Premchand's *Kafan* ("The Shroud") (2004). The white sheet/shroud is a regular feature of railway police offices as well. Each station in Mumbai is supposed to have at least one white sheet on hand in order to give a respectful cover to the dead killed on the train tracks.

4 On the relations between gender and death, see Allison (2017); Danforth (1982); V. Das (2006); Panourgia (1994); and Seremetakis (1991).

5 I did not speak to relatives of the deceased as I felt it could introduce disrespect and confusion in a setting already overdetermined by state power over bodies. Instead, I observed the daily work of the morgue from the perspective of the two classes of workers: forensic doctors and orderlies. I interviewed both about their education and work experiences. My work was supervised by faculty in the department at all times and overseen by the department's head. Given that these are medicolegal cases wherein the determined cause of death can have vast consequences for surviving family members, at no point did I note identifying information on specific cases during an observation shift. This ensured not only that identifying information would stay out of my research materials but also that my research materials remained decoupled from the legal dimensions of the cases.

6 For a resonant case at Charity Hospital in New Orleans, see Lovell (2011).

7 C. Nadia Seremetakis notes that exhumers "endow the dead with time" or "separate the dead from time" (1991, 229). I am pointing here to the ways that the forensics team separates the dead not so much from time but instead moves the dead *through* time. This is how they stretch death's temporalities.

8   Fabien Provost (2017) argues that the "completeness" demanded by medicolegal autopsy in India is "more a required condition for the admissibility of medico-legal evidence in courts than a well-defined medical idea" (24). I am sympathetic to the effort to question "complete" autopsies, but in the interest of moving beyond questions of knowing, I foreground questions about the broader economy of a corpse's movements.

9   Some families hire a private ambulance to do the transport work here, at great expense. Others contact undertakers directly because they have vans that double as transport for the living and the dead. The transport of the dead can also differentiate along lines of religion, because community religious organizations may have a vehicle for this purpose. The state-run 108 ambulance service I detail in chapter 1 has explicit rules against transporting corpses.

10 See Derrida (2010) on differences between burial and cremation as they undergird matters of psychic trauma.

11 Contrast this with Julie Livingston's (2012) account of death in the hospital in Botswana.

Chapter Seven: Recovering

1   What counts as the court and what the court does can be two different matters: one is formal, and the other is experiential. Veena Das (1995, 148) elaborates different visions of a court in India: it can be a public space, or it can be a risk regulator, wherein guilt is made irrelevant.

2   Notably, Canguilhem (1991, 95–97, 119–21) discusses trauma to the leg in making this point.

3   One might understand *galti* and *takdeer* as problems of theodicy. On judicial forms in India, see S. Basu (2015); V. Das (1995, 2019); Lemons (2019); Sehdev (2018); K. Sunder Rajan (2017); and R. Sunder Rajan (2003).

4   The most notable case is that of film star Salman Khan.

5   He uses the English-inflected Hindi term *expose karna*—to expose. See Mazzarella (2006) on the mediation of scandal in Indian public media.

6   "Toh abhi batao aap ko bata diya sachi baatein abhi kya karna chahiye yeh batao. Mere dimaag mein vahi aaya sabhi proof ikatta karte hain yahan aur joh hospital ki galat report saat hazaar ki galat report hai paisa deta hai, galat report banayega phasega voh."

7   See Stevenson (2014) on "mournful listening."

REFERENCES

Adams, Vincanne. 2002. "Randomized Controlled Crime." *Social Studies of Science* 32 (5–6): 659–90.

Addlakha, Renu. 2018. "The Sociology of Disability." In *Critical Themes in Indian Sociology*, edited by Sanjay Srivastava, Yasmeen Arif, and Janaki Abraham, 313–29. New Delhi: Sage.

Agamben, Giorgio. 1999. *Remnants of Auschwitz: The Witness and the Archive*. Translated by Daniel Heller-Roazen. New York: Zone.

Aguiar, Marian. 2011. *Tracking Modernity: India's Railway and the Culture of Mobility*. Minneapolis: University of Minnesota Press.

Ahmad, Shaikh. 2019. *Medical Ethics and Legislations for Doctors, Part 3*. New Delhi: Educreation Publishing.

Aklekar, Rajendra B. 2014. *Halt Station India: The Dramatic Tale of the Nation's First Rail Lines*. New Delhi: Rupa.

Allison, Anne. 2013. *Precarious Japan*. Durham, NC: Duke University Press.

Allison, Anne. 2017. "Greeting the Dead: Managing Solitary Existence in Japan." *Social Text* 35 (1): 17–35.

Alter, Joseph S. 2000. *Gandhi's Body: Sex, Diet, and the Politics of Nationalism*. Philadelphia: University of Pennsylvania Press.

Amrith, Sunil. 2006. *Decolonizing International Health: India and Southeast Asia, 1930–65*. London: Palgrave Macmillan.

Amrith, Sunil. 2007. "Political Culture of Health in India: A Historical Perspective." *Economic and Political Weekly* 42 (2): 114–21.

Amrute, Sareeta. 2015. "Moving Rape: Trafficking in the Violence of Postliberalization." *Public Culture* 27 (2): 331–59.

Anand, Nikhil. 2017. *Hydraulic City: Water and the Infrastructures of Citizenship in Mumbai*. Durham, NC: Duke University Press.

Anjaria, Jonathan Shapiro, and Colin McFarlane, eds. 2011. *Urban Navigations: Politics, Space and the City in South Asia*. London: Routledge.

Ansari, Shahid. 2018. "No Solid Mechanism to Lift Injured Passengers and Dead Bodies at Mumbai Stations." *News Asia Leaks*, May 28, 2018. https://www.newsasialeaks .com/no-solid-mechanism-to-lift-injured-passengers-and-dead-bodies-at-mumbai -stations/.

Appadurai, Arjun. 2000a. "Grassroots Globalization and the Research Imagination." *Public Culture* 12 (1): 1–19.

Appadurai, Arjun. 2000b. "Spectral Housing and Urban Cleansing: Notes on Millennial Mumbai." *Public Culture* 12 (3): 627–51.

Ariès, Philippe. 2013. *The Hour of Our Death*. New York: Vintage.

Arnold, David. 1993. *Colonizing the Body: State Medicine and Epidemic Disease in Nineteenth-Century India*. Berkeley: University of California Press.

Arnold, David. 2004. "Race, Place and Bodily Difference in Early Nineteenth-Century India." *Historical Research* 77 (196): 254–73.

Bachelard, Gaston. 1971. *The Poetics of Reverie: Childhood, Language, and the Cosmos*. Translated by Daniel Russell. Boston: Beacon.

Bahadur, Gaiutra. 2013. *Coolie Woman: The Odyssey of Indenture*. Chicago: University of Chicago Press.

Bandewar, Sunita V. S., Leni Chaudhuri, Lubna Duggal, and Sanjay Nagral. 2018. "The Supreme Court of India on Euthanasia: Too Little, Too Late." *Indian Journal of Medical Ethics*, n.s., 3 (2): 91–94.

Banerjee, Dwaipayan. 2020. *Enduring Cancer: Life, Death, and Diagnosis in Delhi*. Durham, NC: Duke University Press.

Barker, Judith C. 1993. "On the Road to Health? Road Traffic Accidents in Pacific Societies: The Case of Niue Island, Western Polynesia." *American Journal of Human Biology* 5 (1): 61–73.

Barker, Judith C. 1999. "Road Warriors: Driving Behaviors on a Polynesian Island." In *Anthropology in Public Health: Bridging Differences in Culture and Society*, edited by Robert Hahn, 211–34. New York: Oxford University Press.

Barnagarwala, Tabassum. 2016. "Mumbai's Deadly Mortuaries: Acute Lack of Forensic Experts, Medical Staff at Post-mortem Centres." *Indian Express*, June 30, 2016. https://indianexpress.com/article/cities/mumbai/mumbais-deadly-mortuaries -acute-lack-of-forensic-experts-medical-staff-at-post-mortem-centres-2884457/.

Barrett, Ron. 2008. *Aghor Medicine: Pollution, Death, and Healing in Northern India*. Berkeley: University of California Press.

Baru, Rama. 2003. "Privatisation of Health Services: A South Asian Perspective." *Economic and Political Weekly* 38 (42): 4433–37.

Baru, Rama. 2017. "Casualisation of the Health Workforce and Erosion of Trust in Public Hospitals." 3rd International Conference on Public Policy, panel T17A P11, session 3, June 28–30, 2017, Singapore.

Baskett, Peter, and Peter Safar. 2003. "The Resuscitation Greats: Nancy Caroline—from Mobile Intensive Care to Hospice." *Resuscitation* 57 (2): 119–22.

Basu, Nayanima. 2020. "US Not Giving Ventilators to India in Exchange for HCQ, It's about Partnership: Top Official." *Print*, May 19, 2020. https://theprint.in /diplomacy/us-not-giving-ventilators-to-india-in-exchange-for-hcq-its-about -partnership-top-official/425028/.

Basu, Srimati. 2015. *The Trouble with Marriage: Feminists Confront Law and Violence in India*. Berkeley: University of California Press.

Bateson, Gregory, and Margaret Mead. 1942. *Balinese Character: A Photographic Analysis*. New York: New York Academy of Sciences.

Baviskar, Amita. 2003. "Between Violence and Desire: Space, Power, and Identity in the Making of Metropolitan Delhi." *International Social Science Journal* 55 (175): 89–98.

Baxi, Pratiksha. 2014. *Public Secrets of Law: Rape Trials in India*. New Delhi: Oxford University Press.

Bayly, C. A. 1996. *Empire and Information: Intelligence Gathering and Social Communication in India, 1780–1870*. Cambridge: Cambridge University Press.

Bear, Laura. 2007. *Lines of the Nation: Indian Railway Workers, Bureaucracy, and the Intimate Historical Self*. New York: Columbia University Press.

Becker, Gay. 2007. "The Uninsured and the Politics of Containment in U.S. Health Care." *Medical Anthropology* 26 (4): 299–321.

Bedi, Tarini. 2016. "Taxi Drivers, Infrastructures, and Urban Change in Globalizing Mumbai." *City and Society* 28 (3): 387–410.

Bedi, Tarini. 2018. "Urban Histories of Place and Labour: The Chillia Taximen of Bombay/Mumbai." *Modern Asian Studies* 52 (5): 1604–38.

Benjamin, Solomon, and R. Bhuvaneswari. 2001. "Democracy, Inclusive Governance and Poverty in Bangalore." Working Paper, no. 26, International Development Department, University of Birmingham Institute of Development Studies.

Benjamin, Walter. 1968. *Illuminations*. New York: Schocken Books.

Berg, Marc, and Annemarie Mol, eds. 1998. *Differences in Medicine: Unraveling Practices, Techniques, and Bodies*. Durham, NC: Duke University Press.

Berger, Rachel. 2013. "From the Biomoral to the Biopolitical: Ayurveda's Political Histories." *South Asian History and Culture* 4 (1): 48–64.

Berlant, Lauren. 2005. "The Subject of True Feeling: Pain, Privacy and Politics." In *Cultural Pluralism, Identity Politics, and the Law*, edited by Austin Sarat and Thomas R. Kearns, 52–66. Ann Arbor: University of Michigan Press.

Berlant, Lauren. 2011. *Cruel Optimism*. Durham, NC: Duke University Press.

Berlant, Lauren. 2016. "The Commons: Infrastructures for Troubling Times." *Environment and Planning D: Society and Space* 34 (3): 393–419.

Berlant, Lauren. 2022. *On the Inconvenience of Other People*. Durham, NC: Duke University Press.

Berlant, Lauren, and Kathleen Stewart. 2018. *The Hundreds*. Durham, NC: Duke University Press.

Bhalla, Kavi, Nidhi Khurana, Dipan Bose, Kumari Vinodhani Navaratne, Geetam Tiwari, and Dinesh Mohan. 2016. "Official Government Statistics of Road Traffic Deaths in India Under-represent Pedestrians and Motorised Two Wheeler Riders." *Injury Prevention* 23 (1): 1–7.

Bhalla, Kavi, Veena Sriram, Radhika Arora, Richa Ahuja, Mathew Varghese, Girish Agrawal, Geetam Tiwari, and Dinesh Mohan. 2019. "The Care and Transport of Trauma Victims by Layperson Emergency Medical Systems: A Qualitative Study in Delhi, India." *BMJ Global Health* 4 (6): 1–12.

Bhandarkar, Prashant, Priti Patil, Kapil Dev Soni, Gerard M. O'Reilly, Satish Dharap, Joseph Mathew, Naveen Sharma, Bhakti Sarang, Anita Gadgil, Nobhojit Roy, and Australia-India Trauma System Collaboration. 2021. "An Analysis of 30-Day In-Hospital Trauma

Mortality in Four Urban University Hospitals Using the Australia India Trauma Registry." *World Journal of Surgery* 45 (2): 380–89.

Biehl, João. 2007. *Will to Live: AIDS Therapies and the Politics of Survival*. Princeton, NJ: Princeton University Press.

Biehl, João. 2013. "The Judicialization of Biopolitics: Claiming the Right to Pharmaceuticals in Brazilian Courts." *American Ethnologist* 40 (3): 419–36.

Biehl, João, and Adriana Petryna. 2011. "Bodies of Rights and Therapeutic Markets." *Social Research: An International Quarterly* 78 (2): 359–86.

Biehl, João, and Adriana Petryna. 2013. *When People Come First: Critical Studies in Global Health*. Princeton, NJ: Princeton University Press.

Birdwhistell, Ray L. 1952. *Introduction to Kinesics: An Annotation System for Analysis of Body Motion and Gesture*. Washington, DC: Department of State, Foreign Service Institute.

Blundell, Robert Henderson, and George Haswell Wilson. 1937. *Trial of Buck Ruxton*. London: W. Hodge.

Boltanski, Luc. 1999. *Distant Suffering: Morality, Media and Politics*. Cambridge: Cambridge University Press.

Bosk, Charles L. 2003. *Forgive and Remember: Managing Medical Failure*. Chicago: University of Chicago Press.

Bourdieu, Pierre. 2000. *Pascalian Meditations*. Stanford, CA: Stanford University Press.

Boyer, Anne. 2019. *The Undying: Pain, Vulnerability, Mortality, Medicine, Art, Time, Dreams, Data, Exhaustion, Cancer, and Care*. New York: Farrar, Straus and Giroux.

Braun, Lundy. 2014. *Breathing Race into the Machine: The Surprising Career of the Spirometer from Plantation to Genetics*. Minneapolis: University of Minnesota Press.

Bridges, Khiara. 2011. *Reproducing Race: An Ethnography of Pregnancy as a Site of Racialization*. Berkeley: University of California Press.

Briggs, Charles L., and Clara Mantini-Briggs. 2016. *Tell Me Why My Children Died: Rabies, Indigenous Knowledge, and Communicative Justice*. Durham, NC: Duke University Press.

Brotherton, P. Sean. 2012. *Revolutionary Medicine: Health and the Body in Post-Soviet Cuba*. Durham, NC: Duke University Press.

Brown, Wendy. 1993. "Wounded Attachments." *Political Theory* 21 (3): 390–410.

Brunson, Jan. 2014. "'Scooty Girls': Mobility and Intimacy at the Margins of Kathmandu." *Ethnos* 79 (5): 610–29.

Buchbinder, Mara. 2018a. "Access to Aid-in-Dying in the United States: Shifting the Debate from Rights to Justice." *American Journal of Public Health* 108 (6): 754–59.

Buchbinder, Mara. 2018b. "Choreographing Death: A Social Phenomenology of Medical Aid-in-Dying in the United States." *Medical Anthropology Quarterly* 32 (4): 481–97.

Buchbinder, Mara. 2019. "The Power of Suggestion." *Medicine Anthropology Theory* 6 (1): 5–29.

Buck-Morss, Susan. 1991. *The Dialectics of Seeing: Walter Benjamin and the Arcades Project*. Cambridge, MA: MIT Press.

Buck-Morss, Susan. 1992. "Aesthetics and Anaesthetics: Walter Benjamin's Artwork Essay Reconsidered." *October* 62:3–41.

Burney, Ian. 2000. *Bodies of Evidence: Medicine and the Politics of the English Inquest, 1830–1926*. Baltimore: Johns Hopkins University Press.

Burney, Ian, and Christopher Hamlin. 2019. *Global Forensic Cultures: Making Fact and Justice in the Modern Era*. Baltimore: Johns Hopkins University Press.

Canetti, Elias. 1962. *Crowds and Power*. New York: Viking.

Canguilhem, Georges. 1991. *The Normal and the Pathological*. Translated by Carolyn R. Fawcett. New York: Zone.

Carroll, Patrick. 2002. "Medical Police and the History of Public Health." *Medical History* 46 (4): 461–94.

Caruth, Cathy. 2016. *Unclaimed Experience: Trauma, Narrative, and History*. Baltimore: Johns Hopkins University Press.

Causey, Andrew. 2017. *Drawn to See: Using Line Drawing as an Ethnographic Method*. Toronto: University of Toronto Press.

Chakraborty, Gautam, Arun B. Nair, and Riya Dhawan. 2009. "Study of Emergency Response Service—EMRI Model." National Health Systems Research Centre Report. New Delhi: Ministry of Health and Family Welfare.

Chakraborty, Rupsa. 2017. "Mumbai: Shatabdi Hospital Refuses to Admit Patient with Low Platelet Count." *Mid-day*, December 22. https://www.mid-day.com/mumbai/mumbai-news/article/mumbai-shatabdi-hospital-refuses-to-admit-patient-with-low-platelet-count-18845181.

Chaubey, Vedika. 2013. "The Face behind the Voice You Hear in Local Trains Every Day." *Mid-Day*, March 8, 2013. https://www.mid-day.com/news/india-news/article/The-face-behind-the-voice-you-hear-in-local-trains-every-day-203352.

Chu, Julie Y. 2016. "Boxed In: Human Cargo and the Technics of Comfort." *International Journal of Politics, Culture, and Society* 29 (4): 403–21.

Chua, Jocelyn Lim. 2014. *In Pursuit of the Good Life: Aspiration and Suicide in Globalizing South India*. Berkeley: University of California Press.

Clare, Eli. 2017. *Brilliant Imperfection: Grappling with Cure*. Durham, NC: Duke University Press.

Cohen, Lawrence. 1999. "Where It Hurts: Indian Material for an Ethics of Organ Transplantation." *Daedalus* 128 (4): 135–65.

Cohen, Lawrence. 2000. *No Aging in India: Alzheimer's, the Bad Family, and Other Modern Things*. Berkeley: University of California Press.

Cohen, Lawrence. 2001. "The Other Kidney: Biopolitics beyond Recognition." *Body and Society* 7 (2–3): 9–29.

Cohen, Lawrence. 2007. "Song for Pushkin." *Daedalus* 136 (2): 103–15.

Cohen, Lawrence. 2009. "Lucknow Noir." In *Homophobias*, edited by David Murray, 162–84. Durham, NC: Duke University Press.

Cohen, Lawrence. 2011. "Migrant Supplementarity: Remaking Biological Relatedness in Chinese Military and Indian Five-Star Hospitals." *Body and Society* 17 (2–3): 31–54.

Cohen, Lawrence. 2013a. "Foreign Operations: Reflections on Clinical Mobility in Indian Film and Beyond." In *Critical Mobilities*, edited by Ola Soderstrom, Didier

Ruedin, Shalini Randeria, Gianni D'Amato, and Francesco Panese, 213–32. London: Routledge.

Cohen, Lawrence. 2013b. "Given Over to Demand: Excorporation as Commitment." *Contemporary South Asia* 21 (3): 318–32.

Cohen, Lawrence. 2017. "Duplicate." *South Asia: Journal of South Asian Studies* 40 (2): 301–4.

Coleman, Leo. 2017. *A Moral Technology: Electrification as Political Ritual in New Delhi.* Ithaca, NY: Cornell University Press.

Conrad, Peter. 2007. *The Medicalization of Society: On the Transformation of Human Conditions into Treatable Disorders.* Baltimore: Johns Hopkins University Press.

Cooter, Roger. 2003. "Of War and Epidemics: Unnatural Couplings, Problematic Conceptions." *Social History of Medicine* 16 (2): 283–302.

Cooter, Roger, and Bill Luckin, eds. 1997. *Accidents in History: Injuries, Fatalities and Social Relations.* Amsterdam: Brill Rodopi.

Copeman, Jacob. 2006. "Cadaver Donation as Ascetic Practice in India." *Social Analysis: The International Journal of Anthropology* 50 (1): 103–26.

Copeman, Jacob, and Deepa S. Reddy. 2012. "The Didactic Death: Publicity, Instruction and Body Donation." *HAU: Journal of Ethnographic Theory* 2 (2): 59–83.

Crawley, Ashon T. 2016. *Blackpentecostal Breath: The Aesthetics of Possibility.* New York: Fordham University Press.

Creekmur, Corey K. 2014. "Indian Film Noir." In *International Noir,* edited by Homer B. Pettey and R. Barton Palmer, 182–92. Edinburgh: Edinburgh University Press.

Crosby, Christina. 2017. *A Body, Undone: Living On after Great Pain.* New York: New York University Press.

Crowley-Matoka, Megan. 2016. *Domesticating Organ Transplant: Familial Sacrifice and National Aspiration in Mexico.* Durham, NC: Duke University Press.

Czerwiec, MK. 2017. *Taking Turns: Stories from HIV/AIDS Care Unit 371.* University Park: Pennsylvania State University Press.

Danforth, Loring M. 1982. *The Death Rituals of Rural Greece.* Princeton, NJ: Princeton University Press.

Das, Jishnu, and Jeffrey S. Hammer. 2004. *Strained Mercy: The Quality of Medical Care in Delhi.* Washington, DC: World Bank.

Das, Veena. 1976. "The Uses of Liminality: Society and Cosmos in Hinduism." *Contributions to Indian Sociology* 10 (2): 245–63.

Das, Veena. 1995. *Critical Events: An Anthropological Perspective on Contemporary India.* New Delhi: Oxford University Press.

Das, Veena. 2003. "Technologies of Self: Poverty and Health in an Urban Setting." *SARAI Reader* 3:95–102.

Das, Veena. 2006. *Life and Words: Violence and the Descent into the Ordinary.* Berkeley: University of California Press.

Das, Veena. 2015. *Affliction: Health, Disease, Poverty.* New York: Fordham University Press.

Das, Veena. 2019. "A Child Disappears: Law in the Courts, Law in the Interstices of Everyday Life." *Contributions to Indian Sociology* 53 (1): 97–132.

Das, Veena. 2020. *Textures of the Ordinary: Doing Anthropology after Wittgenstein*. New York: Fordham University Press.

Das, Veena, and Renu Addlakha. 2001. "Disability and Domestic Citizenship: Voice, Gender, and the Making of the Subject." *Public Culture* 13 (3): 511–31.

Das, Veena, and Jacob Copeman. 2015. "On Names in South Asia: Iteration, (Im)Propriety and Dissimulation." *South Asia Multidisciplinary Academic Journal (SAMAJ)* 12. https://journals.openedition.org/samaj/4063.

Das, Veena, and Clara Han, eds. 2015. *Living and Dying in the Contemporary World*. Berkeley: University of California Press.

Davis, Dána-Ain. 2019. *Reproductive Injustice: Racism, Pregnancy, and Premature Birth*. New York: New York University Press.

De Boeck, Filip, and Sammy Baloji. 2016. *Suturing the City: Living Together in Congo's Urban Worlds*. London: Autograph ABP.

de Certeau, Michel. 2011. *The Practice of Everyday Life*. Translated by Steven Rendall. Berkeley: University of California Press.

De León, Jason. 2015. *The Land of Open Graves: Living and Dying on the Migrant Trail*. Oakland: University of California Press.

Deomampo, Daisy. 2016. *Transnational Reproduction: Race, Kinship, and Commercial Surrogacy in India*. New York: New York University Press.

Derrida, Jacques. 2010. *The Beast and the Sovereign, Volume 1*. Translated by Geoffrey Bennington. Chicago: University of Chicago Press.

Desjarlais, Robert. 1997. *Shelter Blues: Sanity and Selfhood among the Homeless*. Philadelphia: University of Pennsylvania Press.

Desjarlais, Robert. 2016. *Subject to Death: Life and Loss in a Buddhist World*. Chicago: University of Chicago Press.

Dewachi, Omar. 2015. "When Wounds Travel." *Medicine Anthropology Theory* 2 (3): 61–82.

Dewachi, Omar. 2017. *Ungovernable Life: Mandatory Medicine and Statecraft in Iraq*. Stanford, CA: Stanford University Press.

Dhareshwar, Vivek, and Radhika Srivatsan. 1996. "'Rowdy-Sheeters': An Essay on Subalternity and Politics." In *Subaltern Studies* 9, edited by Shahid Amin and Dipesh Chakrabarty, 201–31. New Delhi: Oxford University Press.

Dickey, Sara. 2000. "Permeable Homes: Domestic Service, Household Space, and the Vulnerability of Class Boundaries in Urban India." *American Ethnologist* 27 (2): 462–89.

Doniger, Wendy. 2014. *On Hinduism*. New York: Oxford University Press.

Dossal, Mariam. 1997. *Imperial Designs and Indian Realities*. New York: Oxford University Press.

Doyle, Arthur Conan. 2008. *The Adventure of the Cardboard Box*. Project Gutenberg. Accessed January 17, 2022. https://www.gutenberg.org/files/2344/2344-h/2344-h.htm.

Duden, Barbara. 1998. *The Woman beneath the Skin: A Doctor's Patients in Eighteenth-Century Germany*. Cambridge, MA: Harvard University Press.

Edensor, Tim. 2013. "Rhythm and Arrhythmia." In *The Routledge Handbook of Mobilities*, edited by Peter Adey, David Bissell, Kevin Hannam, Peter Merriman, and Mimi Sheller, 163–71. New York: Routledge.

Editors, *Economic and Political Weekly*. 2020. "Politics of Communal Violence in Delhi." *Economic and Political Weekly* 55 (9). https://link.gale.com/apps/doc/A616194593/AONE?u=duke_perkins&sid=summon&xid=32eed98d.

Edwards, Martin. 2009. "Triage." *Lancet* 373 (9674): 1515.

Elden, Stuart. 2019. *Canguilhem*. New York: John Wiley.

Elyachar, Julia. 2011. "The Political Economy of Movement and Gesture in Cairo." *Journal of the Royal Anthropological Institute* 17 (1): 82–99.

Evans, Steve. 2008. "Mumbai Trains: 8 Million Passengers a Day." Flickr. https://flickr.com/photos/babasteve/2644313615/in/photolist-52ENj4-cX5ShG-8fUkGH-e4SFbS-CDJJQ-wRrHW4-PV4uDQ-8hzbqZ-2gjMmHN-XDkR27-qq8SWh-bZpUz-BZ7GBN-70i1Gj-65V9zx-2cDXhgD-nedBUu-2gqfvhU-7mTNvp-2mani7J-DQg N9X-ptC5c-JxiV5k-2jXBRT2-jtWixY-dKURRU-9dFUGM-2ghjL62-7yLpq6-7DGpTZ-dGRhco-BSMrvq-9bXsDt-5diDiz-HD4N7x-c9k4RJ-8VnQGq-vZpH5-aCoKCg-7MZyKp-bd343x-2aj7Dp3-2ipzt8z-2iGBZ6X-aCrzNh-2gQQj5G-cRm Sq-9yPMnH-65qfhN-4gpQuU.

Ewald, François. 1993. "Two Infinities of Risk." In *The Politics of Everyday Fear*, edited by Brian Massumi, 221–28. Minneapolis: University of Minnesota Press.

Farmer, Paul. 2004. "An Anthropology of Structural Violence." *Current Anthropology* 45 (3): 305–25.

Fassin, Didier, and Richard Rechtman. 2009. *The Empire of Trauma: An Inquiry into the Condition of Victimhood*. Princeton, NJ: Princeton University Press.

Figlio, Karl. 1982. "How Does Illness Mediate Social Relations? Workmen's Compensation and Medico-Legal Practices, 1890–1940." In *The Problem of Medical Knowledge: Examining the Social Construction of Medicine*, edited by Peter Wright and Andrew Treacher, 174–224. Edinburgh: Edinburgh University Press.

Figlio, Karl. 1983. "What Is an Accident?" In *The Social History of Occupational Health*, edited by Paul Weindling, 180–206. London: Croom Helm.

Finkelstein, Maura. 2019. *The Archive of Loss: Lively Ruination in Mill Land Mumbai*. Durham, NC: Duke University Press.

Fisch, Michael. 2018. *An Anthropology of the Machine: Tokyo's Commuter Train Network*. Chicago: University of Chicago Press.

Fortun, Kim. 2001. *Advocacy after Bhopal: Environmentalism, Disaster, New Global Orders*. Chicago: University of Chicago Press.

Fortun, Kim. 2012. "Ethnography in Late Industrialism." *Cultural Anthropology* 27 (3): 446–64.

Fortun, Kim, Mike Fortun, Erik Bigras, Tahereh Saheb, Brandon Costelloe-Kuehn, Jerome Crowder, Daniel Price, and Alison Kenner. 2014. "Experimental Ethnography Online: The Asthma Files." *Cultural Studies* 28 (4): 632–42.

Foucault, Michel. 1975. *The Birth of the Clinic: An Archaeology of Medical Perception*. Translated by A. M. Sheridan Smith. New York: Vintage.

Foucault, Michel, ed. 1982. *I, Pierre Rivière, Having Slaughtered My Mother, My Sister, and My Brother . . . : A Case of Parricide in the 19th Century*. Translated by Frank Jellinek. Lincoln: University of Nebraska Press.

Foucault, Michel. 2009. *Security, Territory, Population: Lectures at the Collège de France, 1977–78*. Translated by Graham Burchell. New York: Picador.

Frank, Arthur W. 2013. *The Wounded Storyteller: Body, Illness, and Ethics*. Chicago: University of Chicago Press.

Friedner, Michele Ilana. 2015. *Valuing Deaf Worlds in Urban India*. New Brunswick, NJ: Rutgers University Press.

Friedner, Michele. 2022. *Sensory Futures: Deafness and Cochlear Implant Infrastructures in India*. Minneapolis: University of Minnesota Press.

Fruzzetti, Lina. 1982. *The Gift of a Virgin: Women, Marriage, and Ritual in a Bengali Society*. New Brunswick, NJ: Rutgers University Press.

Gandhi, Ajay. 2013. "Standing Still and Cutting in Line: The Culture of the Queue in India." *South Asia Multidisciplinary Academic Journal (SAMAJ)*. https://journals.openedition.org/samaj/3519.

Ganti, Tejaswini. 2012. *Producing Bollywood: Inside the Contemporary Hindi Film Industry*. Durham, NC: Duke University Press.

Gerdin, Martin, Nobhojit Roy, Monty Khajanchi, Vineet Kumar, Satish Dharap, Li Felländer-Tsai, Max Petzold, Sanjeev Bhoi, Makhan Lal Saha, and Johan von Schreeb. 2014. "Predicting Early Mortality in Adult Trauma Patients Admitted to Three Public University Hospitals in Urban India: A Prospective Multicentre Cohort Study." *PloS One* 9 (9): e105606.

Gerdin, Martin, Nobhojit Roy, Monty Khajanchi, Vineet Kumar, Li Felländer-Tsai, Max Petzold, Göran Tomson, and Johan von Schreeb. 2016. "Validation of a Novel Prediction Model for Early Mortality in Adult Trauma Patients in Three Public University Hospitals in Urban India." *BMC Emergency Medicine* 16 (15): 1–12.

Geroulanos, Stefanos, and Todd Meyers. 2018. *The Human Body in the Age of Catastrophe: Brittleness, Integration, Science, and the Great War*. Chicago: University of Chicago Press.

Geschiere, Peter. 2003. "Witchcraft as the Dark Side of Kinship: Dilemmas of Social Security in New Contexts." *Etnofoor* 16 (1): 43–61.

Ghassem-Fachandi, Parvis. 2012. *Pogrom in Gujarat: Hindu Nationalism and Anti-Muslim Violence in India*. Princeton, NJ: Princeton University Press.

Ghoshal, Rakhi. 2015. "Bade Logon Ki Tarah: Pregnant and Poor in the City." *Inter-Asia Cultural Studies* 16 (2): 160–73.

Gidwani, Vinay K. 2008. *Capital, Interrupted: Agrarian Development and the Politics of Work in India*. Minneapolis: University of Minnesota Press.

Ginzburg, Carlo, and Anna Davin. 1980. "Morelli, Freud and Sherlock Holmes: Clues and Scientific Method." *History Workshop*, no. 9: 5–36.

Gladman, Renee. 2010. *Event Factory*. St. Louis, MO: Dorothy, a Publishing Project.

Gladman, Renee. 2016. *Calamities*. Seattle: Wave Books.

Gladman, Renee. 2017. *Prose Architectures*. Seattle: Wave Books.

Gold, Ann Grodzins. 2017. *Shiptown: Between Rural and Urban North India*. Philadelphia: University of Pennsylvania Press.

Gopalan, Lalitha. 2013. "Bombay Noir." In *A Companion to Film Noir*, edited by Andrew Spicer and Helen Hanson, 496–511. Chichester, UK: Wiley Blackwell.

Gore, Radhika. 2019. "The Power of Popular Opinion in Everyday Primary Care Provision in Urban India." *Global Public Health* 14 (4): 528–41.

Goswami, Manu. 2004. *Producing India: From Colonial Economy to National Space*. Chicago: University of Chicago Press.

Grosz, Elizabeth A. 1994. *Volatile Bodies: Toward a Corporeal Feminism*. Bloomington: Indiana University Press.

Grosz, Elizabeth A. 2013. "Habit Today: Ravaisson, Bergson, Deleuze and Us." *Body and Society* 19 (2–3): 217–39.

Guha, Ranajit. 1987. "Chandra's Death." In *Subaltern Studies 5*, edited by Ranajit Guha, 135–65. New Delhi: Oxford University Press.

Gupta, Akhil. 2012. *Red Tape: Bureaucracy, Structural Violence, and Poverty in India*. Durham, NC: Duke University Press.

Gupta, Saksham, Monty Khajanchi, Vineet Kumar, Nakul P. Raykar, Blake C. Alkire, Nobhojit Roy, and Kee B. Park. 2019. "Third Delay in Traumatic Brain Injury: Time to Management as a Predictor of Mortality." *Journal of Neurosurgery* 132 (1): 289–95.

Gursahani, Roop. 2011. "Life and Death after Aruna Shanbaug." *Indian Journal of Medical Ethics* 8 (2): 68–69.

Guru, Gopal, and Sundar Sarukkai. 2019. *Experience, Caste, and the Everyday Social*. New Delhi: Oxford University Press.

Gururaj, G. 2005. "Injuries in India: A National Perspective." In *Background Papers: Burden of Disease in India*, 325–47. New Delhi: National Commission on Macroeconomics and Health, Ministry of Health and Family Welfare, Government of India.

Hage, Ghassan. 2009. *Waiting*. Melbourne: Melbourne University Publishing.

Hallam, Elizabeth. 2008. *The Anatomy Museum: Death and the Body Displayed*. London: Reaktion.

Halliburton, Murphy. 2016. *Mudpacks and Prozac: Experiencing Ayurvedic, Biomedical, and Religious Healing*. New York: Routledge.

Hamdy, Sherine, and Coleman Nye. 2017. *Lissa: A Story about Medical Promise, Friendship, and Revolution*. Toronto: University of Toronto Press.

Hansen, Thomas Blom. 2001. "Governance and State Mythologies in Mumbai." In *States of Imagination: Ethnographic Explorations of the Postcolonial State*, edited by Thomas Blom Hansen and Finn Stepputat, 221–54. Durham, NC: Duke University Press.

Hansen, Thomas Blom. 2002. *Wages of Violence: Naming and Identity in Postcolonial Bombay*. Princeton, NJ: Princeton University Press.

Hansen, Thomas Blom, and Oskar Verkaaik. 2009. "Urban Charisma: On Everyday Mythologies in the City." *Critique of Anthropology* 29 (1): 5–26.

Hartblay, Cassandra. 2020. "Disability Expertise." *Current Anthropology* 61 (S21): S26–S36.

Harvey, Penny, and Hannah Knox. 2015. *Roads: An Anthropology of Infrastructure and Expertise*. Ithaca, NY: Cornell University Press.

Healey, Madelaine. 2013. *Indian Sisters: A History of Nursing and the State, 1907–2007*. London: Routledge.

Hodges, Sarah. 2005. "'Looting' the Lock Hospital in Colonial Madras during the Famine Years of the 1870s." *Social History of Medicine* 18 (3): 379–98.

Hodges, Sarah. 2018. "Plastic History: Caste and the Government of Things in Modern India." In *South Asian Governmentalities: Michel Foucault and the Question of Postcolonial Orderings*, edited by Stephen Legg and Deana Heath, 176–97. Cambridge: Cambridge University Press.

Hsiao, Marvin, Ajai Malhotra, J. S. Thakur, Jay Sheth, Avery Nathens, Neeraj Dhingra, Prabhat Jha, and the Million Death Study Collaborators. 2013. "Road Traffic Injury Mortality and Its Mechanisms in India: Nationally Representative Mortality Survey of 1.1 Million Homes." *BMJ Open* 3 (8): e00261.

Hull, Matthew S. 2012. *Government of Paper: The Materiality of Bureaucracy in Urban Pakistan*. Berkeley: University of California Press.

Hunt, Nancy Rose. 2015. *A Nervous State: Violence, Remedies, and Reverie in Colonial Congo*. Durham, NC: Duke University Press.

Hurd, John, and Ian J. Kerr. 2012. *India's Railway History: A Research Handbook*. Leiden: Brill.

Illich, Ivan. 1976. *Medical Nemesis: The Expropriation of Health*. New York: Pantheon.

Indian Express. 2014. "Dial 108, One of 161 Ambulances Promises to Reach You in 20 Mins." March 2, 2014. https://indianexpress.com/article/cities/mumbai/dial-108-one-of-161-ambulances-promises-to-reach-you-in-20-mins/.

India State-Level Disease Burden Initiative Road Injury Collaborators. 2020. "Mortality Due to Road Injuries in the States of India: The Global Burden of Disease Study 1990–2017." *Lancet Public Health* 5 (2): E86–E98.

Jain, S. Lochlann. 2006. *Injury: The Politics of Product Design and Safety Law in the United States*. Princeton, NJ: Princeton University Press.

Jain, S. Lochlann. 2013. *Malignant: How Cancer Becomes Us*. Berkeley: University of California Press.

Jain, Lochlann. 2019. *Things That Art: A Graphic Menagerie of Enchanting Curiosity*. Toronto: University of Toronto Press.

James, Erica Caple. 2010a. *Democratic Insecurities: Violence, Trauma, and Intervention in Haiti*. Berkeley: University of California Press.

James, Erica Caple. 2010b. "Ruptures, Rights, and Repair: The Political Economy of Trauma in Haiti." *Social Science and Medicine* 70 (1): 106–13.

Jauregui, Beatrice. 2016. *Provisional Authority: Police, Order, and Security in India*. Chicago: University of Chicago Press.

Jeffrey, Craig. 2010. *Timepass: Youth, Class, and the Politics of Waiting in India*. Stanford, CA: Stanford University Press.

Jentzen, Jeffrey M. 2010. *Death Investigation in America*. Cambridge, MA: Harvard University Press.

Jusionyte, Ieva. 2018. *Threshold: Emergency Responders on the US-Mexico Border*. Berkeley: University of California Press.

Kafer, Alison. 2013. *Feminist, Queer, Crip*. Bloomington: Indiana University Press.

Kamil, Sabeeh, Saumya Rajput, Minu Sunil, Aditi Chaurasia, and Arneet Arora. 2016. "Methods to Open the Skull at Autopsy: An Analysis." *Journal of Indian Academy of Forensic Medicine* 38 (3): 334–37.

Kannan, K. 2014. *Medicine and Law*. New Delhi: Oxford University Press.

Katzenstein, Mary, Uday Singh Mehta, and Usha Thakkar. 1997. "The Rebirth of Shiv Sena: The Symbiosis of Discursive and Organizational Power." *Journal of Asian Studies* 56 (2): 371–90.

Kaufman, Sharon R. 2000. "In the Shadow of 'Death with Dignity': Medicine and Cultural Quandaries of the Vegetative State." *American Anthropologist* 102 (1): 69–83.

Kaufman, Sharon R. 2005. *. . . . And a Time to Die: How American Hospitals Shape the End of Life*. New York: Scribner.

Kaufman, Sharon R. 2015. *Ordinary Medicine: Extraordinary Treatments, Longer Lives, and Where to Draw the Line*. Durham, NC: Duke University Press.

Kenner, Alison. 2018. *Breathtaking: Asthma Care in a Time of Climate Change*. Minneapolis: University of Minnesota Press.

Kerr, Ian J. 2003. "Representation and Representations of the Railways of Colonial and Post-colonial South Asia." *Modern Asian Studies* 37 (2): 287–326.

Khair, Tabish. 2008. "Indian Pulp Fiction in English: A Preliminary Overview from Dutt to Dé." *Journal of Commonwealth Literature* 43 (3): 59–74.

Khajanchi, Monty Uttam, Vineet Kumar, Ludvig Wärnberg Gerdin, Kapil Dev Soni, Makhan Lal Saha, Nobhojit Roy, and Martin Gerdin Wärnberg. 2019. "Prevalence of a Definitive Airway in Patients with Severe Traumatic Brain Injury Received at Four Urban Public University Hospitals in India: A Cohort Study." *Injury Prevention* 25 (5): 428–32.

Khan, Arman. 2021. "Cemetery Workers Struggle to Keep Up with Mumbai's COVID-19 Deaths." *Caravan*, July 31, 2021.

Khanna, Ranjana. 2018. "Speculation; or, Living in the Face of the Intolerable." *Journal of Middle East Women's Studies* 14 (1): 109–15.

Kohrman, Matthew. 2005. *Bodies of Difference: Experiences of Disability and Institutional Advocacy in the Making of Modern China*. Berkeley: University of California Press.

Krishna, Anirudh. 2011. *One Illness Away: Why People Become Poor and How They Escape Poverty*. New York: Oxford University Press.

Kulkarni, Vivek. 1997. "'Badla': The Mumbai Derivative." *Economic and Political Weekly* 32 (42): 2747–49, 2751.

Kumar, Deepak. 1997. *Science and the Raj: A Study of British India*. New Delhi: Oxford University Press.

Kumar, Vineet, Pritam Suryawanshi, Satish B. Dharap, and Nobhojit Roy. 2012. "The Great Indian Invisible Railroad Disaster." *Prehospital and Disaster Medicine* 27 (2): 216.

Kumar, Vineet, Pritam Suryawanshi, Satish B. Dharap, and Nobhojit Roy. 2013. "Ready, Steady, Go or Just Go? The Question of Stabilization before Transport for Trauma Victims." *Injury* 44 (11): 1654–55.

Lamont, Mark. 2012. "Accidents Have No Cure! Road Death as Industrial Catastrophe in Eastern Africa." *African Studies* 71 (2): 174–94.

Laureys, Steven, Olivier Bodart, and Olivia Gosseries. 2014. "The Glasgow Coma Scale: Time for Critical Reappraisal?" *Lancet Neurology* 13 (8): 755–57.

Lee, Doreen. 2015. "Absolute Traffic: Infrastructural Aptitude in Urban Indonesia." *International Journal of Urban and Regional Research* 39 (2): 234–50.

Lefebvre, Henri. 2004. *Rhythmanalysis: Space, Time, and Everyday Life*. London: Continuum.

Lemons, Katherine. 2019. *Divorcing Traditions: Islamic Marriage Law and the Making of Indian Secularism*. Ithaca, NY: Cornell University Press.

Lepselter, Susan Claudia. 2016. *The Resonance of Unseen Things: Poetics, Power, Captivity, and UFOs in the American Uncanny*. Ann Arbor: University of Michigan Press.

Leys, Ruth. 2010. *Trauma: A Genealogy*. Chicago: University of Chicago Press.

Livingston, Julie. 2005. *Debility and the Moral Imagination in Botswana*. Bloomington: Indiana University Press.

Livingston, Julie. 2012. *Improvising Medicine: An African Oncology Ward in an Emerging Cancer Epidemic*. Durham, NC: Duke University Press.

Lock, Margaret. 2002. *Twice Dead: Organ Transplants and the Reinvention of Death*. Berkeley: University of California Press.

Lokaneeta, Jinee. 2020. *The Truth Machines: Policing, Violence, and Scientific Interrogations in India*. Ann Arbor: University of Michigan Press.

Lorde, Audre. 1980. *The Cancer Journals*. New York: Penguin.

Lovell, Anne M. 2011. "Debating Life after Disaster: Charity Hospital Babies and Bioscientific Futures in Post-Katrina New Orleans." *Medical Anthropology Quarterly* 25 (2): 254–77.

Low, Setha M. 2000. *On the Plaza: The Politics of Public Space and Culture*. Austin: University of Texas Press.

MacLeish, Kenneth T. 2013. *Making War at Fort Hood: Life and Uncertainty in a Military Community*. Princeton, NJ: Princeton University Press.

Macmillan, Malcolm. 2002. *An Odd Kind of Fame: Stories of Phineas Gage*. Cambridge, MA: MIT Press.

Manning, Erin. 2016. *The Minor Gesture*. Durham, NC: Duke University Press.

Marriott, McKim. 1968. "Caste Ranking and Food Transactions: A Matrix Analysis." In *Structure and Change in Indian Society*, edited by Milton Singer and Bernard Cohn, 133–71. New York: Wenner-Gren Foundation for Anthropological Research.

Masselos, Jim. 1982. "Jobs and Jobbery: The Sweeper in Bombay under the Raj." *Indian Economic and Social History Review* 19 (2): 101–39.

Masselos, Jim. 2007. "Formal and Informal Structures of Power in Mumbai." In *The Making of Global City Regions: Johannesburg, Mumbai/Bombay, São Paulo and Shanghai*, edited by Klaus Segbers, 168–85. Baltimore: Johns Hopkins University Press.

Mazumdar, Ranjani. 2008. "Spectacle and Death in the City of Bombay Cinema." In *The Spaces of the Modern City: Imaginaries, Politics, and Everyday Life*, edited by Gyan Prakash, 401–32. Princeton, NJ: Princeton University Press.

Mazumdar, Ranjani. 2011. "Friction, Collision, and the Grotesque: The Dystopic Fragments of Bombay Cinema." In *Noir Urbanisms: Dystopic Images of the Modern City*, edited by Gyan Prakash, 150–86. Princeton, NJ: Princeton University Press.

Mazzarella, William. 2003. *Shoveling Smoke: Advertising and Globalization in Contemporary India*. Durham, NC: Duke University Press.

Mazzarella, William. 2006. "Internet X-Ray: E-Governance, Transparency, and the Politics of Immediation in India." *Public Culture* 18 (3): 473–505.

Mazzarella, William. 2010. "The Myth of the Multitude, or, Who's Afraid of the Crowd." *Critical Inquiry* 36 (4): 697–727.

Mazzarella, William. 2017. *The Mana of Mass Society*. Chicago: University of Chicago Press.

McDowell, Andrew. 2014. "Troubling Breath: Tuberculosis, Care and Subjectivity at the Margins of Rajasthan." PhD diss., Harvard University.

McGuire, Brian E., Christopher J. Basten, Christopher J. Ryan, and John Gallagher. 2000. "Intensive Care Unit Syndrome: A Dangerous Misnomer." *Archives of Internal Medicine* 160 (7): 906–9.

M'Charek, Amade. 2018. "Dead Bodies at the Border: Distributed Evidence and Emerging Forensic Infrastructure for Identification." In *Bodies as Evidence: Security, Knowledge, and Power*, edited by Mark Maguire, Ursula Rao, and Nils Zurawski, 89–109. Durham, NC: Duke University Press.

McKay, Ramah. 2017. *Medicine in the Meantime: The Work of Care in Mozambique*. Durham, NC: Duke University Press.

Meara, John G., Andrew J. M. Leather, Lars Hagander, Blake C. Alkire, Nivaldo Alonso, Emmanuel A. Ameh, Stephen W. Bickler, Lesong Conteh, Anna J. Dare, and Justine Davies. 2015. "Global Surgery 2030: Evidence and Solutions for Achieving Health, Welfare, and Economic Development." *Lancet* 386 (9993): 569–624.

Mehta, Deepak. 2006. "Collective Violence, Public Spaces, and the Unmaking of Men." *Men and Masculinities* 9 (2): 204–25.

Melly, Caroline. 2017. *Bottleneck: Moving, Building, and Belonging in an African City*. Chicago: University of Chicago Press.

Messinger, Seth D. 2010. "Getting Past the Accident." *Medical Anthropology Quarterly* 24 (3): 281–303.

Michaels, Andrew J., Claire E. Michaels, Joshua S. Smith, Christina H. Moon, Christopher Peterson, and William B. Long. 2000. "Outcome from Injury: General Health, Work Status, and Satisfaction 12 Months after Trauma." *Journal of Trauma and Acute Care Surgery* 48 (5): 841–50.

Mitra, Durba. 2020. *Indian Sex Life: Sexuality and the Colonial Origins of Modern Social Thought*. Princeton, NJ: Princeton University Press.

Mittal, Shilekh, Mukesh Yadav, Harnam Singh, Gaurav Sharma, and Rahul Chawla. 2007. "Current Scenario of Forensic Medicine in India." *Journal of Indian Academy of Forensic Medicine* 29 (2): 59–60.

Mohan, Dinesh, Geetam Tiwari, and Sudipto Mukherjee. 2016. "Urban Traffic Safety Assessment: A Case Study of Six Indian Cities." *IATSS Research* 39 (2): 95–101.

Mohanan, Manoj. 2013. "Causal Effects of Health Shocks on Consumption and Debt: Quasi-Experimental Evidence from Bus Accident Injuries." *Review of Economics and Statistics* 95 (2): 673–81.

Mol, Annemarie. 2002. *The Body Multiple: Ontology in Medical Practice*. Durham, NC: Duke University Press.

Moodie, Megan. 2018. "Birthright." *Chicago Quarterly Review* 26:149–54.

Moretti, Franco. 2005. *Signs Taken for Wonders: On the Sociology of Literary Forms*. London: Verso.

Morrison, Toni. 2020. *The Source of Self-Regard: Selected Essays, Speeches, and Meditations*. New York: Vintage.

Moskop, John C., and Kenneth V. Iserson. 2007. "Triage in Medicine, Part II: Underlying Values and Principles." *Annals of Emergency Medicine* 49 (3): 282–87.

Moskop, John C., David P. Sklar, Joel M. Geiderman, Raquel M. Schears, and Kelly J. Bookman. 2009. "Emergency Department Crowding, Part 1—Concept, Causes, and Moral Consequences." *Annals of Emergency Medicine* 53 (5): 605–11.

Mrázek, Rudolf. 2010. *A Certain Age: Colonial Jakarta through the Memories of Its Intellectuals*. Durham, NC: Duke University Press.

Mrázek, Rudolf. 2015. "Thick Whisper and Thin Victory: Concentration Camps' Contribution to Modern Acoustics." *Social Text* 33 (1): 1–25.

Mukharji, Projit Bihari. 2011. *Nationalizing the Body: The Medical Market, Print and Daktari Medicine*. London: Anthem.

Mukharji, Projit Bihari. 2016. *Doctoring Traditions: Ayurveda, Small Technologies, and Braided Sciences*. Chicago: University of Chicago Press.

Mukherjee, Upamanyu Pablo. 2003. *Crime and Empire: The Colony in Nineteenth-Century Fictions of Crime*. Oxford: Oxford University Press.

Mulla, Sameena. 2014. *The Violence of Care: Rape Victims, Forensic Nurses, and Sexual Assault Victims*. New York: New York University Press.

Mumford, Lewis. 2010. *Technics and Civilization*. Chicago: University of Chicago Press.

Nair, Sreelekha. 2016. "Aruna Shanbaug and Workplace Safety for Women: The Real Issue Sidestepped." *Indian Journal of Medical Ethics* 1 (1): 47–52.

Nambisan, Kavery. 2020. "Aspatre/Haspatal." In *Keywords for India: A Conceptual Lexicon for the 21st Century*, edited by Rukmini Bhaya Nair and Peter Ronald deSouza, 122–23. London: Bloomsbury.

Napolitano, Valentina. 2015. "Anthropology and Traces." *Anthropological Theory* 15 (1): 46–67.

Naraindas, Harish. 2006. "Of Spineless Babies and Folic Acid: Evidence and Efficacy in Biomedicine and Ayurvedic Medicine." *Social Science and Medicine* 62 (11): 2658–69.

Narayan, Kirin. 1992. *Storytellers, Saints and Scoundrels: Folk Narrative in Hindu Religious Teaching*. Philadelphia: Univeristy of Pennsylvania Press.

Natu, Nitasha. 2015. "GRP Initiative of Putting Pictures of Accident Victims at Stations Bears Fruit." *Times of India*, February 20, 2015. http://timesofindia.indiatimes.com /India/GRP-initiative-of-putting-pictures-of-accident-victims-at-stations-bears -fruit/articleshow/46316318.cms.

Nelson, Diane M. 2009. *Reckoning: The Ends of War in Guatemala*. Durham, NC: Duke University Press.

Nelson, Diane M. 2015. *Who Counts? The Mathematics of Death and Life after Genocide*. Durham, NC: Duke University Press.

Nguyen, Vinh-Kim. 2010. *The Republic of Therapy: Triage and Sovereignty in West Africa's Time of AIDS*. Durham, NC: Duke University Press.

Nunley, Michael. 1998. "The Involvement of Families in Indian Psychiatry." *Culture, Medicine and Psychiatry* 22 (3): 317–53.

O'Meara, M., K. Porter, and I. Greaves. 2007. "Triage." *Trauma* 9 (2): 111–18.

Orsini, Francesca. 2004. "Detective Novels: A Commercial Genre in Nineteenth-Century North India." In *India's Literary History: Essays on the Nineteenth Century*, edited by Stuart Blackburn and Vasudha Dalmia, 435–82. Bangalore: Permanent Black.

Owens, Deirdre Cooper. 2017. *Medical Bondage: Race, Gender, and the Origins of American Gynecology*. Athens: University of Georgia Press.

Paik, Shailaja. 2014. *Dalit Women's Education in Modern India: Double Discrimination*. London: Routledge.

Pandian, Anand. 2009. *Crooked Stalks: Cultivating Virtue in South India*. Durham, NC: Duke University Press.

Pandit, Sadguru. 2016. "Forensic Medicine Loses Its Lustre for Maharashtra Doctors." *Hindustan Times*, August 18, 2016.

Pandolfo, Stefania. 2018. *Knot of the Soul: Madness, Psychoanalysis, Islam*. Chicago: University of Chicago Press.

Panourgia, Neni. 1994. "Essay Review: Objects at Birth, Subjects at Death." *Journal of Modern Greek Studies* 12 (2): 261–69.

Parry, Jonathan. 1985. "Death and Digestion: The Symbolism of Food and Eating in North Indian Mortuary Rites." *Man* 20 (4): 612–30.

Parry, Jonathan. 1994. *Death in Banaras*. Cambridge: Cambridge University Press.

Parry, Jonathan, and Maurice Bloch. 1982. *Death and the Regeneration of Life*. Cambridge: Cambridge University Press.

Patel, Geeta. 2007. "Imagining Risk, Care, and Security: Insurance and Fantasy." *Anthropological Theory* 7 (1): 99–118.

Patel, Gieve. 1976. *How Do You Withstand, Body*. Bombay: Clearing House.

Patel, Sujata, and A. Thorner. 1995. *Bombay: Metaphor for Modern India*. Delhi: Oxford University Press.

Patel, Vikram, Somnath Chatterji, Dan Chisholm, Shah Ebrahim, Gururaj Gopalakrishna, Colin Mathers, Viswanathan Mohan, Dorairaj Prabhakaran, Ravilla D. Ravindran, and K. Srinath Reddy. 2011. "Chronic Diseases and Injuries in India." *Lancet* 377 (9763): 413–28.

Perrow, Charles. 2011. *Normal Accidents: Living with High Risk Technologies*. Princeton, NJ: Princeton University Press.

Peterson, Kristin. 2014. *Speculative Markets: Drug Circuits and Derivative Life in Nigeria*. Durham, NC: Duke University Press.

Petryna, Adriana. 2002. *Life Exposed: Biological Citizens after Chernobyl*. Princeton, NJ: Princeton University Press.

Phadke, Shilpa. 2007. "Dangerous Liaisons—Women and Men: Risk and Reputation in Mumbai." *Economic and Political Weekly* 42 (17): 1510–18.

Phadke, Shilpa, Sameera Khan, and Shilpa Ranade. 2011. *Why Loiter? Women and Risk on Mumbai Streets*. New Delhi: Penguin Books India.

Pinto, Sarah. 2008a. "Consuming Grief: Infant Death in the Postcolonial Time of Intervention." In *Postcolonial Disorders*, edited by Mary-Jo DelVecchio Good, Sandra Teresa Hyde, Sarah Pinto, and Byron Good, 359–77. Berkeley: University of California Press.

Pinto, Sarah. 2008b. *Where There Is No Midwife: Birth and Loss in Rural India*. New York: Berghahn Books.

Pinto, Sarah. 2013. "Movement in Time: Choreographies of Confinement in an Inpatient Ward." In *Senses and Citizenships: Embodying Political Life*, edited by Susanna Trnka, Christine Dureau, and Julie Park, 79–98. New York: Routledge.

Pinto, Sarah. 2014. *Daughters of Parvati: Women and Madness in Contemporary India*. Philadelphia: University of Pennsylvania Press.

Pinto, Sarah. 2015. "The Tools of Your Chants and Spells: Stories of Madwomen and Indian Practical Healing." *Medical Anthropology* 35 (3): 263–77.

Poe, Edgar Allan. (1854) 2010. "The Masque of the Red Death." Project Gutenberg, https://www.gutenberg.org/files/1064/1064-h/1064-h.htm.

Pols, Jeannette. 2012. *Care at a Distance: On the Closeness of Technology*. Amsterdam: Amsterdam University Press.

Poole, Deborah. 2004. "Between Threat and Guarantee: Justice and Community in the Margins of the Peruvian State." In *Anthropology in the Margins of the State*, edited by Veena Das and Deborah Poole, 35–66. Santa Fe, NM: School of American Research Press.

Povinelli, Elizabeth A. 2021. *The Inheritance*. Durham, NC: Duke University Press.

Prakash, Gyan. 2010a. *Mumbai Fables*. Princeton, NJ: Princeton University Press.

Prakash, Gyan. 2010b. *Noir Urbanisms: Dystopic Images of the Modern City*. Princeton, NJ: Princeton University Press.

Prasad, Ritika. 2016. *Tracks of Change: Railways and Everyday Life in Colonial India*. Cambridge: Cambridge University Press.

Premchand. 2004. "The Shroud (Kafan)." Translated by Frances W. Pritchett. Accessed January 17, 2022. http://www.columbia.edu/itc/mealac/pritchett/00urdu/kafan/translation_kafan.html.

Prentice, Rachel. 2013. *Bodies in Formation: An Ethnography of Anatomy and Surgery Education*. Durham, NC: Duke University Press.

Prinja, Shankar, Jagnoor Jagnoor, Deepshikha Sharma, Sameer Aggarwal, Swati Katoch, P. V. M. Lakshmi, and Rebecca Ivers. 2019. "Out-of-Pocket Expenditure and Catastrophic Health Expenditure for Hospitalization due to Injuries in Public Sector Hospitals in North India." *PloS One* 14 (11): e0224721.

Provost, Fabien. 2017. "Bodily Signs and Case History in Indian Morgues: What Makes a Medico-Legal Autopsy Complete." *Human Remains and Violence: An Interdisciplinary Journal* 3 (2): 22–37.

PTI. 2017. "Maharashtra Government to Totally Fund Phone-an-Ambulance Service." *Economic Times*, October 19, 2017. https://health.economictimes.indiatimes.com /news/industry/maharashtra-government-to-totally-fund-phone-an-ambulance -service/61137691.

Qadeer, Imrana. 2000. "Health Care Systems in Transition III: India, Part I. The Indian Experience." *Journal of Public Health Medicine* 22 (1): 25–32.

Qadeer, Imrana. 2013. "Universal Health Care: The Trojan Horse of Neoliberal Policies." *Social Change* 43 (2): 149–64.

Raheja, Gloria Goodwin, and Ann Grodzins God. 1994. *Listen to the Heron's Words: Reimagining Gender and Kinship in North India*. Berkeley: University of California Press.

Rajagopal, Divya. 2020. "Aviation Ban May Cause Shortage of Ventilators in India." *Economic Times*, March 20, 2020. https://economictimes.indiatimes.com/industry /healthcare/biotech/healthcare/aviation-ban-may-cause-shortage-of-ventilators-in -india/articleshow/74726896.cms.

Rajasulochana, Subramania Raju, and Daya Shankar Maurya. 2018. "108 in Crisis: Complacency and Compromise Undermine Emergency Services' Potential." *Economic and Political Weekly* 53 (25): 1–10.

Ralph, Laurence. 2014. *Renegade Dreams: Living through Injury in Gangland Chicago*. Chicago: University of Chicago Press.

Ralph, Laurence. 2020. *The Torture Letters: Reckoning with Police Violence*. Chicago: University of Chicago Press.

Ramanna, Mridula. 2002. *Western Medicine and Public Health in Colonial Bombay, 1845–1895*. Delhi: Orient Blackswan.

Ramanna, Mridula. 2008. "Women Physicians as Vital Intermediaries in Colonial Bombay." *Economic and Political Weekly* 43 (12/13): 71–78.

Ramanna, Mridula. 2012. *Health Care in Bombay Presidency, 1896–1930*. Delhi: Primus Books.

Ramberg, Lucinda. 2014. *Given to the Goddess: South Asian Devadasis and the Sexuality of Religion*. Durham, NC: Duke University Press.

Ramphele, Mamphela. 1993. *A Bed Called Home: Life in the Migrant Labour Hostels of Cape Town*. Athens: Ohio University Press.

Rana, Chahat. 2020. "In 2020, Health Workers Counted Their COVID-19 Casualties Because the Government Did Not." *Caravan*, December 30, 2020. https:// caravanmagazine.in/health/health-workers-counted-their-covid19-casualties -because-the-government-did-not.

Rana, Chahat. 2021. "Citizens Collect Data as Government Obscures Oxygen Shortage Deaths Based on Technicalities." *Caravan*, August 6, 2021. https://caravanmagazine

.in/health/citizens-collect-data-as-government-obscures-oxygen-shortage-deaths
-based-on-technicalities.

Rao, Anupama. 2020. "The Work of Analogy: On Isabel Wilkerson's 'Caste: The Origins of Our Discontents.'" *Los Angeles Review of Books*, September 1, 2020.

Rao, Vyjayanthi. 2007a. "How to Read a Bomb: Scenes from Bombay's Black Friday." *Public Culture* 19 (3): 567–92.

Rao, Vyjayanthi. 2007b. "Proximate Distances: The Phenomenology of Density in Mumbai." *Built Environment* 33 (2): 227–48.

Rapp, Rayna. 2004. *Testing Women, Testing the Fetus*. New York: Routledge.

Ratna, Kalpish. n.d. "East of Kailash." Unpublished manuscript.

Raveesh, Bevinahalli Nanjegowda, and Peter Lepping. 2019. "Restraint Guidelines for Mental Health Services in India." *Indian Journal of Psychiatry* 61 (s4): s698–s705.

Redfield, Peter. 2013. *Life in Crisis: The Ethical Journey of Doctors without Borders*. Berkeley: University of California Press.

Rhodes, Lorna A. 1991. *Emptying Beds: The Work of an Emergency Psychiatric Unit*. Berkeley: University of California Press.

Roberts, Elizabeth F. S. 2012. *God's Laboratory: Assisted Reproduction in the Andes*. Berkeley: University of California Press.

Roberts, Ian, Dinesh Mohan, and Kamran Abbasi. 2002. "War on the Roads: The Public Health Community Must Intervene." Editorial. *British Medical Journal* 324 (7346): 1107–9.

Rosen, George. 1953. "Cameralism and the Concept of Medical Police." *Bulletin of the History of Medicine* 27 (1): 21–42.

Rouse, Carolyn. 2009. *Uncertain Suffering: Racial Health Care Disparities and Sickle Cell Disease*. Berkeley: University of California Press.

Roy, Ananya. 2009. "Civic Governmentality: The Politics of Inclusion in Beirut and Mumbai." *Antipode* 41 (1): 159–79.

Roy, Nobhojit. 2017. "Towards Improved Trauma Care Outcomes in India: Studies of Rates, Trends and Causes of Mortality in Urban Indian University Hospitals." PhD diss., Karolinska Institutet, Sweden, 2017.

Roy, Nobhojit, Martin Gerdin, Samarendra Ghosh, Amit Gupta, Vineet Kumar, Monty Khajanchi, Eric B. Schneider, Russell Gruen, Göran Tomson, and Johan von Schreeb. 2016. "30-Day In-Hospital Trauma Mortality in Four Urban University Hospitals Using an Indian Trauma Registry." *World Journal of Surgery* 40 (6): 1299–307.

Roy, Nobhojit, Vikas Kapil, Italo Subbarao, and Isaac Ashkenazi. 2011. "Mass Casualty Response in the 2008 Mumbai Terrorist Attacks." *Disaster Medicine and Public Health Preparedness* 5 (4): 273–79.

Roy, Nobhojit, V. Murlidhar, Ritam Chowdhury, Sandeep B. Patil, Priyanka A. Supe, Poonam D. Vaishnav, and Arvind Vatkar. 2010. "Where There Are No Emergency Medical Services—Prehospital Care for the Injured in Mumbai, India." *Prehospital and Disaster Medicine* 25 (2): 145–51.

Russell, Andrew, and Lee Vinsel. 2018. "After Innovation, Turn to Maintenance." *Technology and Culture* 59 (1): 1–25.

Sadana, Rashmi. 2010. "On the Delhi Metro: An Ethnographic View." *Economic and Political Weekly* 45 (46): 77–83.

Sadana, Rashmi. 2018. "At the 'Love Commandos': Narratives of Mobility among Inter-caste Couples in a Delhi Safe House." *Anthropology and Humanism* 43 (1): 39–57.

Safar, Peter. 1996. "On the History of Modern Resuscitation." *Critical Care Medicine* 24 (2): 3s–11s.

Saunders, Barry F. 2010. *CT Suite: The Work of Diagnosis in the Age of Noninvasive Cutting.* Durham, NC: Duke University Press.

Schalk, Sami. 2013. "Coming to Claim Crip: Disidentification with/in Disability Studies." *Disability Studies Quarterly* 33 (2). https://dsq-sds.org/article/view/3705/3240.

Scheper-Hughes, Nancy, and Margaret M. Lock. 1987. "The Mindful Body: A Prolegomenon to Future Work in Medical Anthropology." *Medical Anthropology Quarterly*, n.s., 1 (1): 6–41.

Schlich, Thomas. 2006. "Trauma Surgery and Traffic Policy in Germany in the 1930s: A Case Study in the Coevolution of Modern Surgery and Society." *Bulletin of the History of Medicine* 80 (1): 73–94.

Sedgwick, Eve Kosofsky. 2000. *A Dialogue on Love.* Boston: Beacon.

Sehdev, Megha Sharma. 2018. "Interim Artifacts of Law: Interruption and Absorption in Indian Domestic Violence Cases." PhD diss., Johns Hopkins University.

Sengoopta, Chandak. 2004. *Imprint of the Raj: How Fingerprinting Was Born in Colonial India.* New York: Pan Macmillan.

Sennett, Richard. 1994. *Flesh and Stone: The Body and the City in Western Civilization.* New York: W. W. Norton.

Seremetakis, C. Nadia. 1991. *The Last Word: Women, Death, and Divination in Inner Mani.* Chicago: University of Chicago Press.

Shaikh, Juned. 2014. "Imaging Caste: Photography, the Housing Question and the Making of Sociology in Colonial Bombay, 1900–1939." *South Asia: Journal of South Asian Studies* 37 (3): 491–514.

Sharafi, Mitra. 2019. "The Imperial Serologist and Punitive Self-Harm: Bloodstains and Legal Pluralism in British India." In *Global Forensic Cultures*, edited by Ian Burney and Christopher Hamlin, 60–85. Baltimore: Johns Hopkins University Press.

Sharafi, Mitra. 2021. "Abortion in South Asia, 1860–1947: A Medico-Legal History." *Modern Asian Studies* 55 (2): 371–428.

Sharp, Lesley. 2006. *Strange Harvest: Organ Transplants, Denatured Bodies, and the Transformed Self.* Berkeley: University of California Press.

Sharpe, Christina. 2016. *In the Wake: On Blackness and Being.* Durham, NC: Duke University Press.

Sheller, Mimi. 2004. "Mobile Publics: Beyond the Network Perspective." *Environment and Planning D: Society and Space* 22 (1): 39–52.

Shem, Samuel. 2010. *The House of God.* New York: Penguin.

Shuttleworth, Russell P., and Devva Kasnitz. 2004. "Stigma, Community, Ethnography: Joan Ablon's Contribution to the Anthropology of Impairment-Disability." *Medical Anthropology Quarterly* 18 (2): 139–61.

Siegel, Greg. 2014. *Forensic Media: Reconstructing Accidents in Accelerated Modernity.* Durham, NC: Duke University Press.

Simmel, Georg. 1903. *The Metropolis and Mental Life.* Translated by Kurt H. Wolff. Chicago: University of Chicago Press.

Simmel, Georg. 1964. *The Sociology of Georg Simmel.* Translated by Kurt H. Wolff. New York: Simon and Schuster.

Singha, Radhika. 2015. "Punished by Surveillance: Policing 'Dangerousness' in Colonial India, 1872–1918." *Modern Asian Studies* 49 (2): 241–69.

Sivaramakrishnan, Kavita. 2019. "An Irritable State: The Contingent Politics of Science and Suffering in Anti-cancer Campaigns in South India (1940–1960)." *BioSocieties* 14 (4): 529–52.

Smith, Lindsay. 2017. "The Missing, the Martyred and the Disappeared: Global Networks, Technical Intensification and the End of Human Rights Genetics." *Social Studies of Science* 47 (3): 398–416.

Solomon, Harris. 2015. "Unreliable Eating: Patterns of Food Adulteration in Urban India." *BioSocieties* 10 (2): 177–93.

Solomon, Harris. 2016. *Metabolic Living: Food, Fat, and the Absorption of Illness in India.* Durham, NC: Duke University Press.

Solomon, Harris. 2021. "Living on Borrowed Breath: Respiratory Distress, Social Breathing, and the Vital Movement of Ventilators." *Medical Anthropology Quarterly* 35 (1): 102–19.

Sriram, Veena, Rama Baru, and Sara Bennett. 2018. "Regulating Recognition and Training for New Medical Specialties in India: The Case of Emergency Medicine." *Health Policy Plan* 33 (7): 840–52.

Sriram, Veena, Gopalkrishna Gururaj, and Adnan A. Hyder. 2017. "Public–Private Implementation of Integrated Emergency Response Services: Case Study of GVK Emergency Management and Research Institute in Karnataka, India." *Surgery* 162 (6): s63–s76.

Sriram, Veena, Adnan A. Hyder, and Sara Bennett. 2018. "The Making of a New Medical Specialty: A Policy Analysis of the Development of Emergency Medicine in India." *International Journal of Health Policy and Management* 7 (11): 993–1006.

Srivastava, Sanjay. 2013. "Thrilling Affects: Sexuality, Masculinity, the City and 'Indian Traditions' in the Contemporary Hindi 'Detective' Novel." *Interventions* 15 (4): 567–85.

Staples, James. 2014. *Leprosy and a Life in South India: Journeys of a Tamil Brahmin.* Lanham, MD: Lexington Books.

Steinberg, Jonah. 2013. "The Social Life of Death on Delhi's Streets: Unclaimed Souls, Pollutive Bodies, Dead Kin and the Kinless Dead." *Ethnos* 80 (2): 248–71.

Steinberg, Jonah. 2019. *A Garland of Bones: Child Runaways in India.* New Haven, CT: Yale University Press.

Stevenson, Lisa. 2014. *Life beside Itself: Imagining Care in the Canadian Arctic.* Berkeley: University of California Press.

Stewart, Kathleen. 2014. "Road Registers." *Cultural Geographies* 21 (4): 549–63.

Stonington, Scott. 2020. *The Spirit Ambulance: Choreographing the End of Life in Thailand*. Berkeley: University of California Press.

Street, Alice. 2014. *Biomedicine in an Unstable Place: Infrastructure and Personhood in a Papua New Guinean Hospital*. Durham, NC: Duke University Press.

Subramanian, Ajantha. 2019. *The Caste of Merit: Engineering Education in India*. Cambridge, MA: Harvard University Press.

Sundaram, Ravi. 2009. *Pirate Modernity: Delhi's Media Urbanism*. London: Routledge.

Sunder Rajan, Kaushik. 2006. *Biocapital: The Constitution of Postgenomic Life*. Durham, NC: Duke University Press.

Sunder Rajan, Kaushik. 2017. *Pharmocracy: Value, Politics, and Knowledge in Global Biomedicine*. Durham, NC: Duke University Press.

Sunder Rajan, Rajeswari. 2003. *The Scandal of the State: Women, Law, and Citizenship in Postcolonial India*. Durham, NC: Duke University Press.

Tambiah, Stanley Jeyaraja. 1996. *Leveling Crowds: Ethnonationalist Conflicts and Collective Violence in South Asia*. Berkeley: University of California Press.

Taussig, Michael T. 1980. "Reification and the Consciousness of the Patient." *Social Science and Medicine: Part B: Medical Anthropology* 14 (1): 3–13.

Taussig, Michael T. 2011. *I Swear I Saw This: Drawings in Fieldwork Notebooks, Mainly My Own*. Chicago: University of Chicago Press.

Taylor, Janelle S. 2008. "On Recognition, Caring, and Dementia." *Medical Anthropology Quarterly* 22 (4): 313–35.

Teasdale, Graham, and Bryan Jennett. 1974. "Assessment of Coma and Impaired Consciousness: A Practical Scale." *Lancet* 304 (7872): 81–84.

Teasdale, Graham, Andrew Maas, Fiona Lecky, Geoffrey Manley, Nino Stocchetti, and Gordon Murray. 2014. "The Glasgow Coma Scale at 40 Years: Standing the Test of Time." *Lancet Neurology* 13 (8): 844–54.

Teltumbde, Anand. 2020. *Dalits: Past, Present, Future*. London: Routledge.

Tercier, John Anthony. 2005. *The Contemporary Deathbed: The Ultimate Rush*. New York: Palgrave Macmillan.

Terry, Jennifer. 2009. "Significant Injury: War, Medicine, and Empire in Claudia's Case." *Women's Studies Quarterly* 37 (1/2): 200–225.

Terry, Jennifer. 2017. *Attachments to War: Biomedical Logics and Violence in Twenty-First-Century America*. Durham, NC: Duke University Press.

Thiranagama, Sharika. 2012. "'A Railway to the Moon': The Post-histories of a Sri Lankan Railway Line." *Modern Asian Studies* 46 (1): 221–48.

Thiranagama, Sharika. 2019. "Rural Civilities: Caste, Gender and Public Life in Kerala." *South Asia* 42 (2): 310–27.

Thomas, George, Sandhya Srinivasan, and Amar Jesani. 2006. "Reservations and Medical Education." *Indian Journal of Medical Ethics* 3 (3): 82–84.

Thrift, Nigel. 2004. "Driving in the City." *Theory, Culture and Society* 21 (4–5): 41–59.

Thrift, Nigel. 2008. "Pass It On: Towards a Political Economy of Propensity." *Emotion, Space and Society* 1 (2): 83–96.

Ticktin, Miriam I. 2011. *Casualties of Care: Immigration and the Politics of Humanitarianism in France*. Berkeley: University of California Press.

Timmermans, Stefan. 2007. *Postmortem: How Medical Examiners Explain Suspicious Deaths*. Chicago: University of Chicago Press.

Timmermans, Stefan. 2010. *Sudden Death and the Myth of CPR*. Philadelphia: Temple University Press.

Treggiari, Miriam M., Leonard D. Hudson, Diane P. Martin, Noel S. Weiss, Ellen Caldwell, and Gordon Rubenfeld. 2004. "Effect of Acute Lung Injury and Acute Respiratory Distress Syndrome on Outcome in Critically Ill Trauma Patients." *Critical Care Medicine* 32 (2): 327–31.

Trnka, Susanna, and Catherine Trundle. 2017. *Competing Responsibilities: The Ethics and Politics of Contemporary Life*. Durham, NC: Duke University Press.

Trotter, David. 2000. "Fascination and Nausea: Finding Out the Hard-Boiled Way." In *The Art of Detective Fiction*, edited by Warren Chernaik, Martin Swales, and Robert Vilain, 21–35. New York: Springer.

Van der Geest, Sjaak, and Kaja Finkler. 2004. "Hospital Ethnography: Introduction." *Social Science and Medicine* 59 (10): 1995–2001.

Van Hollen, Cecilia. 2003. *Birth on the Threshold: Childbirth and Modernity in South India*. Berkeley: University of California Press.

Varma, Rashmi. 2004. "Provincializing the Global City: From Bombay to Mumbai." *Social Text* 22 (4): 65–89.

Varma, Saiba. 2016. "Love in the Time of Occupation: Reveries, Longing, and Intoxication in Kashmir." *American Ethnologist* 43 (1): 50–62.

Varma, Saiba. 2020. *The Occupied Clinic: Militarism and Care in Kashmir*. Durham, NC: Duke University Press.

Veetil, Deepa Kizhakke, Jyoti Kamble, Debojit Basak, and Nobhojit Roy. 2016. "Direct versus Transferred Severely Injured: Different Context, Similar Findings." *Injury* 47 (2): 510.

Venkat, Bharat Jayram. 2021. *At the Limits of Cure*. Durham, NC: Duke University Press.

Virilio, Paul. 2007. *The Original Accident*. Translated by Julie Rose. London: Polity.

Visvanathan, Shiv. 1987. "From the Annals of the Laboratory State." *Alternatives: Global, Local, Political* 12 (1): 37–59.

Wagner, Sarah. 2008. *To Know Where He Lies: DNA Technology and the Search for Srebrenica's Missing*. Berkeley: University of California Press.

Watkins, Timothy R., Avery B. Nathens, Colin R. Cooke, Bruce M. Psaty, Ronald V. Maier, Joseph Cuschieri, and Gordon D. Rubenfeld. 2012. "Acute Respiratory Distress Syndrome after Trauma: Development and Validation of a Predictive Model." *Critical Care Medicine* 40 (8): 2295–303.

Weil, Max, and Wanchun Tang. 2011. "From Intensive Care to Critical Care Medicine: A Historical Perspective." *American Journal of Respiratory and Critical Care Medicine* 183 (11): 1451–53.

Weizman, Eyal. 2017. *Forensic Architecture: Violence at the Threshold of Detectability*. New York: Zone.

Wendland, Claire. 2016. "Estimating Death: A Close Reading of Maternal Mortality Metrics in Malawi." In *Metrics: What Counts in Global Health*, edited by Vincanne Adams, 57–81. Durham, NC: Duke University Press.

Whitmarsh, Ian. 2008. *Biomedical Ambiguity: Race, Asthma, and the Contested Meaning of Genetic Research in the Caribbean*. Ithaca, NY: Cornell University Press.

Wiler, Jennifer L., Christopher Gentle, James M. Halfpenny, Alan Heins, Abhi Mehrotra, Michael G. Mikhail, and Diana Fite. 2010. "Optimizing Emergency Department Front-End Operations." *Annals of Emergency Medicine* 55 (2): 142–60.

Wolshon, Brian, and Anurag Pande. 2016. *Traffic Engineering Handbook*. Hoboken, NJ: John Wiley.

Wool, Zoë H. 2015. *After War: The Weight of Life at Walter Reed*. Durham, NC: Duke University Press.

Wool, Zoë H., and Seth D. Messinger. 2012. "Labors of Love: The Transformation of Care in the Non-medical Attendant Program at Walter Reed Army Medical Center." *Medical Anthropology Quarterly* 26 (1): 26–48.

World Health Organization. 2014. "Injuries and Violence: The Facts 2014." Accessed January 17, 2022. https://apps.who.int/iris/handle/10665/149798.

Yeolekar, M. E., and S. Mehta. 2008. "ICU Care in India—Status and Challenges." *Journal of the Association of Physicians of India* 56:221–22.

Zaman, Shahaduz. 2004. "Poverty and Violence, Frustration and Inventiveness: Hospital Ward Life in Bangladesh." *Social Science and Medicine* 59 (10): 2025–36.

Zaman, Shahaduz. 2005. *Broken Limbs, Broken Lives: Ethnography of a Hospital Ward in Bangladesh*. Amsterdam: Het Spinhuis.

Zaman, Shahaduz. 2013. "Silent Saviours: Family Members in a Bangladeshi Hospital." *Anthropology and Medicine* 20 (3): 278–87.

Zink, Brian J. 2006. *Anyone, Anything, Anytime: A History of Emergency Medicine*. St. Louis: Mosby/Elsevier Health Sciences.

Zink, Brian J. 2011. "The Biology of Emergency Medicine: What Have 30 Years Meant for Rosen's Original Concepts?" *Academic Emergency Medicine* 18 (3): 301–4.

Zola, Irving. 1972. "Medicine as an Institution of Social Control." *Sociological Review* 20 (4): 487–504.

INDEX

body, 3–4, 21, 84, 240n16; and caste status, 95–96; and the city, 14–15, 233, 239n14; and death, 177–84, 188–93, 233, 196–99; dependencies, 30, 85, 89; identifying, 109–113, 121, 126–32; and injury, 39–43, 45–46, 49, 72–74, 95–96, 109; and movement, 4–8, 12, 16–18, 22, 39, 49, 55, 56–60, 67–69, 71–72, 232; and recovery, 202–5, 227; of the researcher, 35, 136–39, 145; social dimensions of, 74–76, 150–51; and ventilation, 148–49, 153–56. *See also* embodiment; dissection; injury

bodypack, 181–83

Boltanski, Luc, 243n17

Bombay Municipal Corporation. *See* Brihanmumbai Mahanagar Palika (BMC)

brain, 80, 136–38, 140, 143–44, 145–46; and death, 89, 95, 149–50, 159–60, 250n7; and identity, 110–13, 121–22, 133–34; and traumatic injury, 54, 64, 75–76, 120, 211–12, 247n5. *See also* Glasgow Coma Scale (GCS); neurosurgery

breath and breathing: and autonomy, 151–52, 161–62, 167–68, 250n8; and death, 157–59; as event, 152–53; sociality of, 150, 153, 155–63, 166, 168–69, 172–73; and survival, 250n2. *See also* ventilation

Briggs, Charles, 25, 198

Brihanmumbai Mahanagar Palika (BMC), 243n2

bureaucracy, 13, 24, 50, 133, 221–22

BVG India Ltd., 33

Canguilhem, Georges, 203–4, 239n15, 247n5

capital, 13, 229–30, 232, 241n4

care, 3–7, 23–26; and breathing, 148–52, 155–56; and family, 80–86, 89–90, 105–6, 169; inequality of, 65, 77, 115–16, 138, 149; informal, 31; labor of, 82, 84–86, 250n3; prehospital, 30–35, 38–39, 50–51; posthospital, 205–6; and shifting, 57–60; and social belonging, 133; and tracing, 110–13, 115–16, 133; as violence, 164–65. *See also* access; family and kinship

carrying: and caste status, 42–43; costs of, 32–33; infrastructure and urban mobility, 30–32, 51–52, 242n11; moral qualities of, 45–47. *See also* ambulance services; *hamaal*; 108 service

case, 204–5, 210, 221, 227; and closure, 124, 126, 129, 133–34; kinetics of, 202–3, 214–15, 219, 221–22; legal versus medical, 211–14; medicolegal (MLC), 67–71, 110, 129, 132, 176, 178–79, 203, 215, 245nn16–17, 251n5; singularity of, 78. *See also* accident; event and eventedness; *mamla*

caste, 42–43, 45–46, 64, 93–95, 97–100, 115–16, 183, 185, 193, 212, 207, 246, 250

casualty, 66–67

casualty medical officer (CMO), 60–71

Central Hospital: annual budget, 243n2; attacks on doctors, 86–87; and colonialism, 81–82, 239n12; and COVID-19 pandemic, 230–31; and economies of scarcity, 49–50, 149, 151, 155–57, 162–63; postdischarge outcomes, 206; protocols, 119, 153–54, 178–79; and surgery, 141–43; and traffic accidents, 13–14, 37, 39; and trauma, 8–9, 20–21, 23, 119–20; and triage, 55–58. *See also* hospital; Maitri Hospital

chot (Hindi). *See* injury

Chua, Jocelyn, 69, 223–24

city and cityness. *See* urban and urbanism

claim, 248n9

class, 10–11, 40, 45–47, 64, 93–94, 127–28, 162, 245n14, 246n3, 251n5. *See also* rowdy

clinical mobility, 51. *See also* Cohen, Lawrence

CMO. *See* casualty medical officer

Code of Criminal Procedure, 245n16

Cohen, Lawrence, 18–19, 51, 11, 144, 244n3, 246n4, 248n9, 249n20

colonialism, 6–7, 13–14, 74, 81–82, 85, 126, 233, 239n12, 242n12, 246n3, 247n4, 248n14, 249n18; and postcolonial India, 6–7, 14, 92–94, 109, 132, 248n16. *See also* rowdy

communication, 80–81, 85, 87–88, 90–91, 94, 158, 244n12

compensation, 221

complaints, 69

event and eventedness, 24–25, 62, 84, 99–100, 204–5; 240n17, 241n3. *See also* accident; disturbances; encounter; injury; *mamla*

everyday and everydayness, 11–12, 18, 49, 62–63, 81, 83–84, 100, 204–5, 234–35, 239n14, 240n17. *See also* Berlant, Lauren; crisis; domesticity

family and kinship: and burden of postmortem, 178–80; and care labor, 86, 101, 105, 169, 250n3; and clinic, 85; and communication, 90–91, 211; as disruptive force, 89–90, 116, 246n4; and movement, 83–84; and personhood, 187–88; and social mattering, 110; as threat, 116; and ventilation, 150, 153. *See also* domesticity; home

fieldwork, 22–23, 56–57, 138, 156–57, 176–77, 205. *See also* ethnography; observation; seeing

Fisch, Michael, 241n3

flaneur, 239n14

flow, 14–16, 55–56, 58–60, 72, 77, 152, 231–32. *See also* kinetics; movement; shifting; stasis; temporality; traffic

forensic architecture, 70

forensics, 176–77; and authority of the state, 178–79, 185; and face, 249n18; as lifeline, 179–81, 197–98; and medical gaze, 189–90; and movement of bodies, 177–78; and policing, 248n14; and postmortem, 176, 178–81, 189–91, 198, 251n2; and production of knowledge, 180–81, 189–91, 198; scholarly accounts of, 180–81; stigmatization of, 195. *See* death; dissection

Foucault, Michel, 90, 189–90, 206, 239n15, 244n11

functionality, 209–10

Galton, Francis, 249n18

Gandhi, Ajay, 60

GCS. *See* Glasgow Coma Scale

gender, 9, 75, 88, 93–94, 99, 104; and death, 251n4; and labor, 246n1; in research, 209; and women physicians, 242n12. *See also* family and kinship; masculinity; rowdy; visitation

gesture, 240n1

Ghoshal, Rakhi, 115

Glasgow Coma Scale (GCS), 113, 117–23, 133, 247n6

glitch, 77. *See also* triage

global, 9, 13, 30–31, 43, 59, 140, 206, 237n5

Global South, 4, 9, 239n14

golden hour, 36

Good Samaritans, 242n13, 243n17

governmentality, 62

Government Railway Police (GRP), 246n3

GRP. *See* Government Railway Police

Gupta, Akhil, 62, 69, 133

Guru, Gopal, 100

hadsa (Hindi). *See* accident

Hage, Ghassan, 62

hamaal (railway porter), 40–46, 242n14, 243n15, 245n22. *See also* carrying

Hansen, Thomas Blom, 245n22

Harvey, Penny, 238n11

health: casualization and corporatization of, 20, 34, 40, 86–87; costs of, 10, 163, 203, 238n6, 248n2; global, 4, 59, 206, 230–31; inequalities in, 138, 163; and injury, 9, 237n5, 238n6; public, 20, 34, 50–52, 77, 232, 237n5; and technology, 119–20; and traffic, 30–32, 38. *See also* access; ambulance services; hospital

health utopia, 51. *See also* Cohen, Lawrence

Hinduism and Hindus, 89, 97, 102, 115, 121–22, 124–25, 127–28, 182, 186, 243n15, 250n12; and cremation, 187–89, 195–196; nationalism and anti-Muslim violence, 212–13, 245n22

hit-and-run, 160, 203, 209–10

HIV. *See* human immunodeficiency virus

Hodges, Sarah, 14, 99

home (site), 81–85, 105–6. *See also* discharge; domesticity; family and kinship; recovery

homelessness, 16–17

hooligan (figure), 245n22

hospital (site), 13–14; and caste, 97–99; cityness of, 14, 82, 232; colonial history of, 14; differences in, 56–58; and disturbances,

89–90; and event of injury, 227; everydayness of, 234–35; government, 64; and home,
81–85, 105; institutionality of, 21; levels of
hospital systems, 243n2; movement and mobility of, 51–52, 87; neighborhood, 61–64;
and policing, 124–25; public, 49–51, 74–75,
89, 115–16; as totalizing site of care and cure,
205; as transitional, 21
House of God, The (Shem), 82
human immunodeficiency virus (HIV), 59
Hunt, Nancy Rose, 247n5

identification, 109–111, 120–21, 246n1, 247n4,
248n9; as approximation, 124–25; and
healing, 132–33; as lifeline, 110, 113, 123–24,
132–34; and names, 114–16, 122; and privacy,
116; and repersonalization, 111–12. *See also*
tracing
Illich, Ivan, 111
immobility. *See* mobility
India: assessing disability and functionality,
206; boundaries of the household, 85; and
colonialism, 13; and COVID-19 pandemic,
229–30; and detective fiction, 248n16; distribution of clinical labor, 250n3; economic
liberalization in the 1990s, 11; euthanasia
laws, 149, 159–60, 249n1; forensics in
policing, 248n14; as global exporter of
opiates, 116–17; and Good Samaritans,
242n13; grounds of medical negligence and
compensation, 246n2; health-care costs,
10, 238n6; and health technology, 119–20;
history of ambulance services, 240n18,
240n2, 241n5, 242n12; history of ICUs in,
155; link between constitutional law and
biomedicine, 203; medicine as a form of
consumption, 245n14; medicolegal requirements of postmortems, 176; and movement
of medicine, 19; postcolonial governmentality in, 14; and public health, 51; and public
hospitals, 115, 231–32; and railway system,
13, 237n2, 242n9; and restraints in clinical
settings, 145nn18–19; and suicide, 223–24;
traffic accidents in, 4, 9, 237n5; 2008 terror
attacks, 237n2; urban public cultures of

mobility, 31; and ventilation, 163; wound
culture of, 14–15. *See also* Mumbai
Indian Code of Criminal Procedure, 176
Indian Penal Code, 237n4
Indian Railway Act of 1854, 246n3
inequality, 93–95; and caste, 100; and
embodiment, 188; and health services, 21,
64, 156, 162; and infrastructure, 10, 12, 241;
and injury outcomes, 10; urban conditions
of, 232
infrastructure, 238n11; and injury, 5, 7; and lifelines, 12–13; and modernization projects, 11;
and relationality, 51; structural conditions
of, 12. *See also* railway system; traffic
injury, 4–6, 9, 17; defining, 237n4; narrativiz-
ing, 24–26; relational kinetics of, 5; sociality
of, 18; and triage, 77–78; and urban environment, 7–8, 14. *See also* accident; trauma;
wounds
institutionality, 21
intensive care, 3, 54–55, 71–72, 138–39, 144–45,
165, 250n4; bioethics of, 158, 160–61;
economy of, 161–63, 229–31; history of
in India, 155–56; as a lifeline, 148–52; and
reverie, 113–14
interrater reliability, 121
interval, 238n7, 241n3
Islam and Muslims, 89, 97, 103–4, 122, 124–25,
127–28, 130, 188–89, 212–14, 245n22
iteration, repetition, 95

Jain, Lochlann, 17, 31–32
janta ("population"), 242n10. *See also* public
Jevandayee Scheme, 202
judicialization, 203
Jusionyte, Ieva, 241n7

Kaufman, Sharon, 20, 85, 151, 161–62
kinetics, 5–8, 12, 32, 56, 58, 75, 81, 105, 155–56,
202–5, 214–16, 227, 232, 235. *See also* care;
mamla; movement; trauma
kinetic subjectivity, 31–32
kinless dead, 110
kinship. *See* family and kinship
Knox, Hannah, 238n11

labor: and care, 85–86; and caste, 42–43, 61, 97–98, 100, 115–16, 183; casualization of, 20, 40; clinical, 23, 65–67, 82, 93–94; and families, 81–83, 86, 89, 105–6, 115, 250n3; and gender, 94, 246n1; and inequality, 93–94; momentum of, 114–15; racialized, 138. *See also* care; family and kinship; gender

language: and grammar, 248n13; and use, 248n12

Lefebvre, Henri, 17–18

lifelines, 5–7, 232–33; and carrying, 30, 35; and deathlines, 7, 30; and discharge and recovery, 202–3, 215, 227–28; and forensic postmortem, 176, 179–80, 195, 197–98; and home, 81–83, 105–6; and identification, 109–110, 112–13, 132–33; and infrastructure, 6, 12–13; and method, 22–26; and movement, 7, 233; and relationality, 17–18; and shifting, 56, 74, 77; and surgery, 141, 143; and trauma, 9–10, 231–32; and ventilation, 149–52. *See also* carrying; discharge; forensics; home; identification; shifting; surgery; ventiliation

life support, 151–54; ethics of, 159–62; and gender, 249n1; politics and economics of, 162–63, 172. *See also* ventilation

Livingston, Julie, 62, 150–51, 252n11

Lock, Margaret, 85, 155

logistics, 242n11

Lokaneeta, Jinee, 248n14

Maharashtra Anatomy Act of 1949, 176

Maitri Hospital, 54, 56–58, 60–67; annual budget, 243n2; costs of care, 244n5. *See also* hospital; shifting

mamla ("matter," "concern," or "affair"), 204–5, 210, 214–15, 227. *See also* case; event and eventedness; kinetics

Manning, Erin, 18

Mantini-Briggs, Clara, 198

masculinity, 74–75, 88–89, 95, 130–31, 246n1. *See also* gender; rowdy

"Masque of the Red Death, The" (Poe), 233

Masselos, Jim, 241n5

mattering, 4–6, 46, 67–69, 110, 132–33, 204–5, 210, 250n12

Maurya, Daya, 33–34

Mazumdar, Ranjani, 249n19

medical anthropology. *See* anthropology

medical humanities, 81–82

medicine: as consumption, 245n14; and domesticity, 85; emergency forms of, 77–78; and family, 116; and law, 110–12; and medical gaze, 189–90; and movement, 5, 7, 22; and power, 244n11; as practice, 21–22; and public health, 20–21; and social control, 111; as sociopolitical good, 245n15; and state, 244n3; success and failures of, 56–57; technics of, 238n10; and technological agents, 156; and urbanism, 7–8

medicolegal case (MLC). *See under* case

Mehta, Deepak, 215

membrane, 244n8

Mental Healthcare Act of 2017, 245n18

milieu, 239n15

MLC (medicolegal case). *See under* case

mobile civil forms, 32. *See also* Appadurai, Arjun

mobile publics, 32. *See also* Sheller, Mimi

mobility, 4, 26, 30–32, 40, 51–52, 59, 72, 86, 201, 228–29, 232, 238n10, 241n4, 242n11; and caste, 46, 99; gendering of, 74–75, 99. *See also* clinical mobility; movement; traffic

modernity and modernization, 11, 13, 132–33, 248n16

Modi, Narendra, 229

Mohanan, Manoj, 238n6

Mol, Annemarie, 21–22, 190–91, 239n15

mortality: and meetings, 142–143, 185; and statistical data, 80, 176, 206, 237–238. *See also* death

Motor Vehicles Act of 1988, 221, 242n13

movement, 4–8, 15–19, 20, 31–32, 59, 237n1, 241n4, 244n9; and caste status, 42–43, 45–46; and casualization of care labor, 40; during COVID-19 pandemic, 229–31; crisis of, 231–32; after death, 176–77, 179–80, 189–90, 233; frameworks of, 16; immobility and restraint, 72–73, 96–96; and infrastructure, 30–32, 51; intimacies of, 16–17; and kinship, 83–84; politics and inequalities of, 6, 12, 18–19, 20, 58, 233; and relationality, 17–18, 45, 72; in trauma care, 5–6, 8, 56–60; and urban public, 14, 37–38, 41, 50–52; and waiting, 59–60. *See* mobility; traffic

Mrázek, Rudolf, 244n8, 250n8

Mulla, Sameena, 9, 69

Mumbai, 4, 127–28, 155, 212, 239n12, 244n12, 245n22; ambulance services in, 34, 36, 241n5, 241n7, 242n9; and caste, 98; and COVID-19 pandemic, 230; infrastructural modernization, 11, 13; and public medicine, 20–21, 50, 162, 243n2; train system, 6–7, 30, 237n3, 242n9, 246n3, 251n3; and traffic, 10, 31; and traumatic injury, 10–11, 176–77, 241n6. *See also* India

Mumford, Lewis, 238n10

Muslims. *See* Islam and Muslims

Nambisan, Kavery, 81

Names and naming, 61, 86, 108, 114–116, 122, 129, 244n7, 246n1, 247n4

narration and narrative, 57, 140, 232; limits of, 82–83, 251n13; multiauthored, 211. *See also* ethnography

National Rural Health Mission, 33

neoliberalism, 34

neurosurgery, 58, 116, 119–20

Nguyen, Vinh-Kim, 59

noir, 233, 249n19

normality, 203–4, 239n15

Nunley, Michael, 85

nurses and nursing, 92–93

observation, 23–24, 102–3, 144, 251n5. *See also* ethnography; fieldwork; seeing; surgery

108 service, 32–34, 37, 43, 49–50, 241n7, 242n9, 252n9. *See also* ambulance services

ordinary. *See* everyday and everydayness

Osler, William, 82

Paik, Shailaja, 98–99

pain, 63, 73–74, 119, 164, 250n5; and management, 22, 73, 104, 117, 204, 219; and endotracheal suction, 152; and stimulus, 119, 160

Parry, Jonathan, 243n15

Patel, Gieve, 233–35

patienthood, 82–83, 111, 177–78

personhood, 82–83, 109, 111, 132–33, 187–88, 189–90

Petryna, Adriana, 203, 244n5

Pinto, Sarah, 20, 188

Poe, Edgar Allan, 233

policing, 109, 124–25, 246n3, 248n14

postcolonialism. *See under* colonialism

postmortem. *See under* forensics

post-traumatic stress disorder (PTSD), 20

praxiography, 21–22

Provost, Fabien, 252n8

PTSD. *See* post-traumatic stress disorder

public, 37–39, 41, 44, 50, 74–75, 242n9. *See also* crowds; rowdy

"Public Hospital" (Patel), 234–35

quality of life, 206

queues, 60–67

race, 249n2

Railway Claims Tribunal (Procedure) Rules of 1989, 221

Railway Protection Force (RPF), 246n3

railway system, 237nn2–3; and accidents, 47–49, 246n3; doors of, 237n3; history of, 13; and luggage carriers, 242n14; politics of, 6–7. *See also* hamaal

Rajasulochana, Subramania, 33–34

Ramanna, Mridula, 242n12

Ramberg, Lucinda, 99

Rao, Anupama, 98

recovery: kinetics of, 215–16, 227; medicolegal aspects of, 203–5; and movement, 202–4, 221, 227–28; and narration, 211, 216. *See also* discharge; home

Redfield, Peter, 242n11

relationality, 5–7, 17–18, 32, 90–91, 105–6; and breathing, 150–51, 173; and infrastructure, 18, 51; and movement, 17–18, 45; as social capital, 65; and trauma, 9, 16; and urban mobility, 51; and visitation, 89. *See also* social and sociality

religion, 21, 43, 114, 122, 127–28, 179, 192,
    252n9. *See also* Hinduism and Hindus;
    Islam and Muslims
Rembrandt, 191
repetition. *See* iteration
responsibility, 142–43, 212, 249n17
restraints, 72–73, 245nn18–19
resuscitation, emergency, 35, 38–39, 150, 153
reverie, 114
Rhodes, Lorna, 244n9
Rhythmanalysis (Lefebvre), 17–18
risk, 5, 10, 28–29, 40, 49, 62
rowdy (figure), 74–76, 119, 245nn20–21.
    See also agitation
RPF. *See* Railway Protection Force
Russell, Andrew, 156

Sadana, Rashmi, 51
Sarukkai, Sundar, 100
Satyam Technologies Inc., 33
Saunders, Barry, 249n18
SaveLife (NGO), 242n12
second delay, 31
security, 86–87, 88
seeing, 136, 144, 146. *See also* ethnography;
    observation; surgery
sequelae, 204
Seremetakis, C. Nadia, 251n7
service staff, 96–98, 100
Shanbaug, Aruna, 249n1
Sheller, Mimi, 32
Shem, Samuel, 82
Shetty, Suresh, 36
shift, 243n1
shifting, 54–57; and bodies, 67–68, 73–74; and
    communication, 71; costs of, 57–58; and infor-
    mation, 67–68; and narration, 57; of persons
    into patients, 75–76; and queues, 60–61; and
    relationality, 78; risks of, 57–58; standards for,
    59; and stasis, 76–77; and transfers, 77; and
    trauma, 55–56. *See also* triage
Shiv Sena ambulances, 241n5
shock, 31, 57, 72, 155; and urban life, 239n14
Shodh (online database for missing persons),
    131–32

Simmel, Georg, 239n14
site saturation, 205
Slumdog Millionaire (dir. Boyle), 237n2
social and sociality, 81–82; and breathing,
    150–51; and caste, 98–100; everyday,
    240n17; and injury, 18, 215–16, 232; locating,
    18; theorizing, 14; and tracing, 133. *See also*
    relationality
social breathing. *See under* breath and breath-
    ing; social and sociality
social phenomenology, 150–51
space, 81–82
Specialist Ambulance Service Ltd., 33
Srikrishna Commission, 215
Srivatsan, Radhika, 74
stability, 58
stasis, 15, 41, 56–57, 59–60, 76–77, 141, 151–52,
    176, 189–90. *See also* flow; kinetics; move-
    ment; traffic
Steinberg, Jonah, 110
Stewart, Kathleen, 18
Stonington, Scott, 20
strangers. *See* estrangement
street (space), 8, 14, 25, 30, 38, 83, 122
Subaltern Studies Collective, 74
subjectivity and subjectification, 110–13,
    180–81
Subramanian, Ajantha, 98
suicide, 44, 104–5, 116, 176, 223–24
Sundaram, Ravi, 14–15, 249n19
Sunder Rajan, Kaushik, 34, 203
surgery, 20–21, 23, 116, 140–46, 237n5, 249n1.
    See also seeing
survival, 5–7, 30–31, 84, 112–13, 148–50,
    245n23, 250n2

Technics and Civilization (Mumford), 238n10
Teltumbde, Anand, 98
temporality, 16–18, 19–20, 24–25, 87, 99–100,
    136, 144, 157, 204–6, 214–15, 227–28,
    240n17, 241n3; and movement, 14–15, 16, 19,
    55–56, 71–72, 76–78, 231–32; and prehos-
    pital care, 30–31, 50–51; and postmortem,
    179–80; and visitation, 82–85. *See also* event
    and eventedness; *mamla*

waiting, 56, 58–59, 62, 77. *See also* queues; shifting

waste, medical, 99

Weizman, Eyal, 70

Wendland, Claire, 180

"When I Hid My Caste" (Bagul), 98

willpower, 166–67

witnessing, 37–38

Workmen's Compensation Act, 221

wound culture, 15, 239n13. *See also* Sundaram, Ravi

wounds, 63, 232, 238n10

Zaman, Shahaduz, 82

Zola, Irving, 111